WALTON'S *LIVES*

Conformist Commemorations and the Rise of Biography

WALTON'S
LIVES

Conformist Commemorations
and the Rise of Biography

JESSICA MARTIN

OXFORD

UNIVERSITY PRESS

OXFORD

UNIVERSITY PRESS

Great Clarendon Street, Oxford OX2 6DP

Oxford University Press is a department of the University of Oxford.
It furthers the University's objective of excellence in research, scholarship,
and education by publishing worldwide in

Oxford New York

Athens Auckland Bangkok Bogotá Buenos Aires Cape Town
Chennai Dar es Salaam Delhi Florence Hong Kong Istanbul Karachi
Kolkata Kuala Lumpur Madrid Melbourne Mexico City Mumbai Nairobi
Paris São Paulo Shanghai Singapore Taipei Tokyo Toronto Warsaw

with associated companies in Berlin Ibadan

Oxford is a registered trade mark of Oxford University Press
in the UK and certain other countries

Published in the United States
by Oxford University Press Inc., New York

British Library Cataloguing in Publication Data

Data available

Library of Congress Cataloguing in Publication Data

Data applied for

ISBN 0-19-827015-1

1 3 5 7 9 10 8 6 4 2

Typeset by Graphicraft Limited, Hong Kong
Printed in Great Britain
on acid-free paper by
T.J. International, Padstow, Cornwall

For Francis

and

in memory of
Jeremy Maule

CONTENTS

Introduction   *ix*
List of Illustrations   *xiv*
Note on Terminology   *xv*
Note on Texts and Orthography   *xvii*
Acknowledgements   *xviii*
Abbreviations   *xx*

PART I: WALTON'S CONTEXT

1. Commemorative Strategies   3
2. Reading Plutarch, Writing Lives   32

   Plutarch as 'schoolemaister'   34
   Plutarchan Virtue and the Constant Mind   41
   Portraying Virtue   52
   Collection, Comparison, and Parallel   60

3. Godly Prototypes   66

   Texts   66
   Bodies   102
   Death   129
   'Life, Truly Writ'   152

PART II: WALTON'S *LIVES*

4. Walton's *Lives* of Donne and Herbert   167

   The *Life of Dr. John Donne*   168
   The *Life of Mr. George Herbert*   203

5. Walton's *Lives* of Hooker and Sanderson   227

   Introduction   227
   The *Life of Mr. Richard Hooker*   228
   The *Life of Dr. Robert Sanderson*   272

6. Walton's Legacy   300

Bibliography   316
Index   339

INTRODUCTION

This is a book about one aspect of the rise of biography as a distinct genre, as it was mediated and influenced by four of the five *Lives* written by Izaak Walton between 1640 and 1678. Its argument is the simple one that Walton's practice was crucial in shaping modern expectations of what a biography should contain. His work is latent in our views of how a biography should be organized, how seriously it should treat evidence (textual and oral); in how 'literary' an enterprise it should be conceived to be, how seriously it should regard narrative coherence; and most of all in our settled expectation of an intimate relationship between author, reader, and subject.

Obviously, Walton is not the only source for some of these expectations; but his contribution to them is very great. Much work has been done, for instance, on the historiographical prehistory of biography, and in this field Walton's influence is less clear, except in so far as he is an inheritor of Plutarch. I do not propose to retrace that ground. Nor do I wish to add more to the debate (if it is a debate) on Walton's factual reliability: that task was effectively completed in the late 1950s by the scholar David Novarr. The problem with the exercise, itself honourable, is that it judges Walton by the evolved standards of a genre which did not yet exist (which seems hardly fair) and which, in any case, are vexed to the present day.

I felt, instead, that it would be most helpful to investigate the conventions, and intentions, of the genre out of which Walton wrote: the exemplary biographical preface. (Only the *Life of Herbert* did not first appear as such a preface). The first half of this book studies these conventions. In its second half I look in some detail at the ways in which Walton developed, and in the end transformed, his generic material into something new. I have taken exemplary intention, itself the dominant principle governing Walton's practice, as my main focus throughout the whole, and have attempted to show how the different traditions Walton possessed fed into the new biographical form his *Lives* represent.

The exemplary inheritance of the biographical preface is mixed. Partly it derives from the celebratory conventions of classical funeral oratory, partly via Plutarch's parallel *Lives*, themselves conceived to provide virtuous matter for the reader's imitation, and most importantly via the homiletic traditions built into the funeral sermon as it was redefined after the Reformation. Looking at all Walton's *Lives*, it became clear that not only was this last his dominant influence, but that because four of his five *Lives* commemorate conformist ministers, clergy commemorations must form his most direct models. These are narratives which embody a principle best summed up in the commonplace 'Our Minister lives Sermons': that is, that clergy lives must also be represented homiletically. Many sixteenth-, and even more seventeenth-century Lives of this class began as funeral sermons: that is, as performed, verbal exhortations to virtue containing a section structured as chronological narrative, and not as simple precept.

Walton's writing-life of 1640 to 1678, not perhaps wholly coincidentally, sees the flowering of biographical narrative as a *textual* form, as distinct from one that transcribed (or reduced) a verbal performance in adapting the words of a sermon. On the whole, it is fair to say both that Walton wrote immeasurably better biographical prefaces than his contemporaries did, and that the form he chose had a longevity the funeral sermon could not have. I do not just mean that sermons went out of fashion whereas biographies became very popular. I also mean that sermons belonged at least as much in the pulpit as in print. While their textual forms were meant to recall, even in some sense to pre-serve, the unique hour in which they were acted, it was a com-monplace that the transfer was, all the same, from living voice to dead shadow. Oratory doesn't keep. Biography, on the other hand, offered a vitality quite explicitly textual, its structures breathing with images which interleaved bodies with books, voices with paragraphs, actions with narrations. As these new structures partly developed from the common images of religious oratory, so par-ticular qualities of Walton's combined with the conventions of the biographical preface to produce something different again, something to which the modern biography—or even, perhaps, its cousin the novel—is heavily indebted.

The unique feature (aside from his great talents) which moved Walton's development from the exemplary narrative to the particularized and intimate 'real' biography was, I argue, that he was a layman. He could not preach sermons: upon what grounds, therefore, could he exhort to virtue? Because he was not in orders, he had to find an authority to speak which relied neither on aristocratic standing nor on priestly function. This problem he solved in two ways. First, he presented himself as humble medium for the words and acts of an authoritative subject, and he followed his preference implicitly in his very extensive use of his subjects' own writings. His *Lives* could be called attempts at a kind of posthumous autobiography, with narrator as mediator. Secondly, he stressed his own personal knowledge of his subject where (as with the *Lives* of Donne and Sanderson) he could. Where he could not, he showed a high regard for the oral testimony of relations and friends, particularly if he could claim a personal acquaintance with them too. He on occasion privileged oral testimony over written records available to him. As a result, personal affection became a fundamental justification for his narrative efforts much more than in works by authors less handicapped by their status. These techniques, growing out of the particularity of Walton's position, added up to a new form of chronological narrative: where the author was mediating, artfully, the re-creation of the history of a life.

This all maps such a different line of exemplary inheritance from the one which animates Walton's commemoration of Sir Henry Wotton, that I have made the more-or-less arbitrary decision to omit that *Life*. Wotton was a politician and a courtier; and while I certainly think that Walton was concerned to present an exemplary Wotton, I also felt a different book was needed to accommodate the much more secular models Walton was (reluctantly) forced to use in that case. This book is already long enough. In the same spirit of arbitrary demarcation I take 1546 (the date at which the first eyewitness account of the death of Luther appeared in print) as a starting-point for the book, and 1688 as its approximate end-date.

In the second part I have departed from a chronological assessment, looking at the *Lives* of Donne and Herbert together in Chapter 4, and the *Lives* of Hooker and Sanderson in Chapter 5. This is because the two former *Lives* were not commissioned, but written according to the promptings of Walton's affection, whereas the *Lives* of Hooker and Sanderson were both more or less commissioned by prominent figures within the Restoration Church, and were written at least in part with a view to justifying it. There are, therefore, two different kinds of intentions operating, and it seemed better, for clarity's sake, to group them according to intention rather than hold grimly to the order they were written in.

Outside his own century, Walton's single most significant influence for the development of literary biography was upon James Boswell. Boswell came across Walton through Johnson, who admired chiefly the *Lives* and had projected overseeing a new edition of them, using Boswell as researcher and writing a Life of Walton himself. His plan never came to anything, although it was discussed at a tea-party with Dr Horne of Magdalene College, Oxford, and the plans for the edition recorded by Boswell in the *Life of Johnson*.

Boswell follows his account of the visit to Dr Horne with the famous report of Johnson's opinions on biography. 'It is rarely well executed', Boswell has his Johnson say of it: 'They only who live with a man can write his life, with any genuine exactness and discrimination; and few people who have lived with a man know what to remark about him.'[1] Few subjects can so fortuitously have commended their commemorators; and the remark mainly reflects, of course, upon Boswell's own text and practice. But Johnson's words emerge from a discussion of Walton, whose own opinions on the importance of author–subject intimacy he reiterates. Walton did not claim so much: for 'living with a man' he would agree to substitute acquaintance, and failing that, mutual acquaintances. But here, all the same, seems to lie a germ not only of the Boswellian stress on intimacy but of the fundamental problem this posed for an emergent genre. Authorizing the text in these terms made, of course, claims for its weight based firmly on direct witness, and only secondarily on skill, discrimination, or exemplary intention. Yet—as Boswell's Johnson stresses here —the most unimpeachable witness would not necessarily know what, or how much to say; or indeed how to say what he had to say well.

As so often in the *Life of Johnson*, Boswell uses the pronouncements he records to meditate on his own shortcomings. Did he or didn't he 'know what to remark' about Johnson? Walton may

[1] *Boswell's Life of Johnson*, ed. George Birkbeck Hill, revised L. F. Powell, 6 vols. (Oxford, 1934–50), ii. 446.

have made it possible for Boswell to sanction his own direct writing, speaking presence in his subject's narrative, but intimacy alone gave Boswell no clue about when, or how—or where—to stop. Equally typically, Boswell's own uncomfortable sense of generic bagginess becomes here a matter of record in a monumentally inclusive undertaking.[2]

Walton had taken exemplarity as a basic selection principle; indeed as an ethic. Because of his own peculiar authorial position, however, he had had to stress author–subject intimacy, making holes for his own and his subjects' particularized presence in the box of exemplary types he had inherited. Boswell inherited the box, but in developing the possibilities of intimacy inherent not only in Walton's practice but also in the new interest in *-iana* (as in 'Waltoniana') then burgeoning in France, he was left with a formal dilemma, of practice and of intention.[3]

Once particularity became an overriding principle, the biographer could no longer decide simply to inform, or improve, his *readers'* life practice, because the stress on the unique nature of every life made it difficult simply to recommend imitation. In more than one sense, this principle was effectively replaced by *recreation*. Consequently, as the holes enlarged for particularity left the exemplary shell torn and empty, the resurrected textual body of the subject, which had replaced the seventeenth century's speaking skeleton, emerged into a limitless space. Able to say anything, but without any pressing reason to say one thing rather than another (except that it had been said by a unique and remarkable someone who had once lived), biographer and subject were landed with a remit both vague and impossibly large. The 'table talk' element in other aspects of the memoir form gave some precedence to recorded conversation; the emergent novel (another form with a huge debt owed on its own account to early biography) made its own contribution.[4]

But that is another story.

---

[2] I owe a critical debt here to Ms Caron Freeborn, whose work for her University of Cambridge doctoral thesis on generic constraints on Boswell's *Life of Johnson* has influenced my discussion of Boswell's practice.

[3] See Ian Hamilton, *Keepers of the Flame: Literary Estates and the Rise of Biography* (London, 1992), 63–4.

[4] See Donald A. Stauffer, *The Art of Biography in Eighteenth Century England* (Princeton, 1941), 66–7, for a seminal discussion of the shared generic roots of biography and the novel.

LIST OF ILLUSTRATIONS

1.1. Exegesis and commemoration: from John Buckeridge, 'A
Sermon Preached at the Funeral of Lancelot [Andrewes]',
and John Whitefoote, Ἰσραὴλ Ἀγχιθανής, Deaths Alarum,
or the Presage of Approaching Death . . .   23
3.1. Engraved title-page of Thomas Fuller, Abel Redevivus
(London, 1651)   96
5.1. Title-pages of Hooker, Works (1662 and 1676)   233
5.2. Engraved title-page of Hooker, Works (1666)   234
5.3. Marshall engraved title-page of Fuller's Holy State (1641)   266
5.4. Marshall engraved title-page of Quarles's Shepheards
Oracles (1644)   267
5.5. Frontispiece of John Barnard, . . . The True Life . . . of
. . . Peter Heylyn (1683)   296

NOTE ON TERMINOLOGY

In choosing to look at literature on 'conformists', I inherit, of course, an inherent methodological problem about how to define conformity which I have not felt it appropriate (or even possible) to tackle head-on here. It is exacerbated by the changing (not to say conflicting) contemporary interpretations of it which surface through the 150 years I have chosen to look at, and by the extent to which every interested party slants his narrative to claim conformity for his own position. As far as this goes, the most I felt I could do was to try to indicate what kind of 'conformity' I am dealing with in any given narrative (including Walton's) within the main text. In one sense I have tumbled from frying-pan to fire because, after some anxious experimentation, I found the highly problematized terms 'Anglican' and 'Puritan' to be the most workmanlike broad modifiers of conformist churchmanship. This book does not, on the whole, deal with separatists; and the terms, which I recognize to be both anachronistic and imprecise, are for these very reasons safely outside the fluctuating vocabulary and bewildering variety of different oppositions taken up within the Church of England between the Reformation and the Glorious Revolution. While within the discourse of modern historians 'Anglican' and 'Puritan' rightly indicate challengeable positions, in early modern terms they signify almost nothing that can be historicized or debated by contemporaries. I use them only to indicate a (spacious) place to stand concerning ceremonies, episcopacy, and the duties of subject to monarch. They are not used to suggest anything at all with regard to the faith–works debate, which (within the English Church, at any rate) had been won by faith more or less throughout the period I discuss, and within which the rows about Arminianism must be seen as—admittedly acrimonious—disagreements only over what sort of predestinarian one was.

There is one final major decision I must explain. I have chosen to apply the adjective 'godly' to every life performed to figure an exemplary piety, in order to indicate my own sense that in the area of exemplary narrative there is an unexpected consensus about *behaviour* (though not about the politics behaviour is often supposed to justify). In this I have followed the diction of *all* my source material (i.e. 'Anglican' as well as 'Puritan'), where 'godliness' is a term fought over by both, the power of which lies in its very claim to be comprehensive. Undeniably that power is eventually undermined: the exclusive groups of 'the godly' of the 1620s and 1630s are more socially than morally identifiable. But since in contemporary terms no one would have used 'godly' as (really) a socio-historical identifier devoid of moral content, and since in an exemplary genre this would be peculiarly pointless, I do not do it here.

NOTE ON TEXTS AND ORTHOGRAPHY

I have confined virtually all the primary research to material printed—and therefore more available to the middle-class reader —within the sixteenth and seventeenth centuries. The only manu-script works I use are the two Lives of Bishop William Bedell, which did not reach print until the nineteenth century, and the formal Conversations recorded at Little Gidding, which have remained in manuscript until the twentieth. I have justified including these works as part of Walton's context by using them to illustrate common techniques which would clearly be familiar to contemporary life-writers, including Walton himself. I also use some manuscript notes of Walton's and of Daniel Featley's, and refer to one manuscript entry of Matthew Parker. In quoting, I have retained inversions of 'u' and 'v', and the use of 'i' for 'j', but contractions have been silently expanded. Orthography is given as it is printed. Dates are cited as they are printed on the title-page. References are given in Modern Humanities Research Association (MHRA) format, although I have occasionally had to modify citations to accommodate (for instance) very long titles, or books where several otherwise separate works have been bound together.

ACKNOWLEDGEMENTS

My grateful thanks go here to the Librarians and staff of a number of Cambridge libraries: the University Library, especially the Rare Books Room; the English Faculty Library; the Wren Library at Trinity College; the Parker and Butler Libraries at Corpus Christi and especially to Mrs C. P. Hall, Library Archivist; St Johns College Library; the Sancroft Library at Emmanuel, Selwyn College Library; Lucy Cavendish College Library; and the Founders' Library at the Fitzwilliam Museum. I am also indebted to the Librarians and staff of the British Library, and to Miss Suzanne Eward of Salisbury Cathedral Library, who allowed me to see several of Walton's books held there. My thanks go to Cambridge University Library also for allowing the reproduction of a number of illustrations from printed books for which it holds the copyright, and to the Master and Fellows of Trinity College for permission to reproduce illustrations held in the Wren Library.

My grateful thanks go also to the President and Fellows of Lucy Cavendish College, and to the Sutasoma Trust, for gifts of time, space, money, and encouragement in the form of a Junior Research Fellowship between 1994 and 1998, and then for a Research stipend for the academic year 1998–9.

What is good in this book has grown out of the kindness and generosity of many individuals: its weaknesses are all mine. I owe a great debt of thanks to Patrick Collinson, whose comments upon the text were extraordinarily useful, and whose encouragement I value almost more. I am also deeply grateful to the following for reading and commenting on chapters, or papers which grew out of (or into) chapters, or for other kinds of textual help: Dominic Baker Smith, Eric Carlson, Ian Donaldson, Stewart Eames, Kenneth Fincham, Peter Fisher, Caron Freeborn, Tom Freeman, Mary Garrison, Sean Hughes, Arnold Hunt, Richard Luckett, Diarmaid MacCulloch, Peter McCullough, Judith Maltby, Bernice Martin, David Martin, Kenneth Parker, Alison Shell, Francis Spufford, Margaret Spufford, Nicholas Tyacke,

Jason Yiannikou, and the anonymous readers for Oxford University Press.

My immeasurable debt is to Jeremy Maule, who gave, as always, with an open hand.

Finally, thanks to Stella for putting up with Walton for so much of her life.

ABBREVIATIONS

Barwick, *Sermon*

John Barwick, Ἱερονίκες *or the Fight, Victory and Triumph of St. Paul. Accommodated to the Right Reverend Father in God, Thomas* [Morton] *Late Lord Bishop of Duresme, in a Sermon Preached at his Funeral . . . on Michaelmas Day, 1659. Together, with a Life of the said Bishop* (London, 1660).

Barwick, *Life*

John Barwick, *A Summarie Account of the Holy Life and Happy Death of the Right Reverend Father in God, Thomas* [Morton], *Late Lord Bishop of Duresme. Added as a Supplement to the Sermon Preached at his Funerall . . .* (London, 1660).

Beza, *Icones*

Theodore Beza, *Icones. Les Vrais Portraits des Hommes Illustrées en Pieté et Doctrine . . . Traduicts du Latin*, trans. Simon Goulard, 2nd edn. (Geneva, 1581).

Clarke, *Marrow*

Samuel Clarke, *The Marrow of Ecclesiastical History, Divided into Two Parts: the First, Containing the Life of our Blessed Lord and Saviour Jesus Christ, with the Lives of the Ancient Fathers, School-Men, First Reformers and Modern Divines, The Second, Containing the Lives of Christian Emperors, Kings, and Sovereign Princes . . . Together with the most Lively Effigies of the most Eminent of them Cut in Copper*, 3rd edn. (London, 1675).

Clarke, *Lives*

Samuel Clarke, *The Lives of Thirty Two English Divines*, in *A General Martyrologie, Containing a Collection of all the Greatest Persecutions, from the Creation unto our Present Times . . .*, 3rd edn. (London, 1677), 2nd pagination.

DNB

Dictionary of National Biography, ed. Leslie Stephen and Sidney Lee, 83 vols. (London, 1883–1900).

Dryden

'The Life of Plutarch', in *The Works of John Dryden*, ed. N. T. Swedenborg, Jr., 20 vols. (Berkeley, 1958–74), xvii. 226–88.

Erasmus, *Works*   *The Collected Works of Erasmus*, 66 vols. (Toronto, 1974–).

Foxe, *Actes and Monuments* (1563)   John Foxe, *Actes and Monuments of these Latter and Perillous Dayes, Touching Matters of the Church, wherein are Comprehended and Described the Great Persecutions and Horrible Troubles . . . from the Yeare of our Lorde One Thousand, unto the Tyme now Present* (London, 1563).

Actes and Monuments (1570)   John Foxe, *Actes and Monuments of these Latter and Perillous Dayes . . .* (London, 1570), 2 vols.

Gauden, *Hooker*   *Richard Hooker . . . An Account of his Holy Life and Happy Death*, in *The Works of Richard Hooker* (London, 1662).

Hutchinson   *The Works of George Herbert*, ed. F. E. Hutchinson (Oxford, 1941).

Novarr   David Novarr, *The Making of Walton's* Lives (Ithaca, NY, 1958).

OED   *Oxford English Dictionary*, prepared by A. Simpson and E. S. C. Weiner, 2nd edn., 20 vols. (Oxford, 1989).

Plutarch, *Lives*   Plutarch, *The Lives of the Noble Grecians and Romans, Englished by Sir T. North anno 1579*, ed. W. E. Henley, 'The Tudor Translations' VII–XII, 6 vols. (London, 1895–6).

STC   *A Short-Title Catalogue of Books Printed in England, Scotland and Ireland, and of English Books Printed Abroad, 1475–1640*, first compiled by A. E. Pollard and G. R. Redgrave; 2nd edn., revised and enlarged, begun by W. A. Jackson and F. S. Ferguson, completed by K. F. Pantzer (London, 1986–91).

Walton, *Lives*   Izaak Walton, *The Lives of John Donne, Sir Henry Wotton, Richard Hooker, George Herbert and Robert Sanderson*, ed. George Saintsbury (Oxford, 1927).

Wing   *Short-Title Catalogue of Books Printed in England, Scotland, Ireland, Wales, and British America, and of English Books Printed in Other Countries, 1641–1700*, compiled by Donald Wing; 2nd edn. revised and enlarged (New York, 1982–98).

I have laid together a few sticks for the Funeral-fire, dry Bones which can make but a Sceleton, till some other hand lay on the Flesh and Sinews, and cause them to live, and move.

(Abraham Hill, *An Account of the Life of Dr. Isaac Barrow*, 1683)

PART I

Walton's Context

I

Commemorative Strategies

John Donne remarks in a sermon, 'You would scarce thank a man for an extemporall Elegy, or Epigram, or Panegyrique in your praise, if it cost the Poet, or the Orator no paines'.[1] Donne invites a congregation to assess their own worth primarily through an estimate of the 'paines' of their commemorators: to measure self-worth via a textual value. This is a joke, of course, but a revealing one. Though his form of address, in putting the 'Elegy' first, colloquially anticipates his listeners' deaths, the form of the question tells us clearly that the value of commemorative forms is their value for the living. He is, therefore, as much asking whether celebratory method can be assigned moral value by and for living readers.

He pursues the point in a letter addressed to George Gerrard which defends the *Anniversaries*. They are poems addressed to a dead subject. What are the principles governing the 'paines' Donne took?

But for the . . . imputation of having said too much, my defence is, that my purpose was to say as well as I could: for since I never saw the Gentlewoman, I cannot be understood to have bound my self to have spoken just truths, but I would not be thought to have gone about to praise her . . . except I took such a person, as might be capable of all that I could say. If any of those Ladies think that Mistris *Drewry* was not so, let that Lady make her self fit for all those praises in the book, and they shall be hers.[2]

In other words, his intentions are both exemplary and literary: 'to say as well as I could.' Donne justifies taking Elizabeth Drury as an ideal subject because he had never met her, which precluded 'just truths', and because in any case he had chosen her since she

[1] John Donne, *LXXX Sermons* (London, 1640), 130.
[2] John Donne, *Letters to Severall Persons of Honour* (London, 1651), 238–9.

'might'—a significant conditional—really bear such a treatment anyway. Besides, he argues quickly, the question of what the dead Elizabeth had been like was irrelevant. She of all women could not benefit from reading the *Anniversaries*. Only a living woman could take the point of the poems and make herself their true and truthful subject by imitating the virtues he praised.

Donne here defends the pains of praise as being what Izaak Walton would later call 'an honour due to the dead', as well as a vitally efficient method of edification. He sees these as basic to commemoration, while particular detail—which we now treat as the main stuff of remembrance for our own dead—is not. In doing so he follows firm classical precedent. This chapter considers the influence of one of those classical genres of commemoration, funeral oratory, and traces the means by which it comes directly to nourish the exemplary Life, via that flourishing intermediate form, the funeral sermon.

The ancestor and prototype of Renaissance commemorative narration is the Greek *encomium* (ἐγκώμιον), which praises the public dead. Its conventions include the formal exaggeration of virtues, or αὔξησις. Suppression of vice is implied of course, but, as Donne reminds us, your subject is defined as virtuous in being chosen at all. The encomiast is as free to commend chance advantages (such as high birth, or birth into a politically important country) as he is to celebrate virtuous action.[3] His praise, then, must take its cue from contemporary social values. Finally, the encomium is designed as much to display the rhetorical skills of its author as to display the virtues of its subject (the two are not really separable); and so to be rhetorically deft is as important as accuracy.

The Roman *laudatio funebris* inherits these qualities;[4] and its conventions, together with those of the speech of thanks

---

[3] See Alan Wardman, *Plutarch's Lives* (London, 1974), 13. But see also Barbara Lewalski, *Donne's 'Anniversaries' and the Poetry of Praise: The Creation of a Symbolic Mode* (Princeton, 1973), 176, where she argues that Cicero's *De Oratore* alters the balance in favour of virtue.

[4] The complexities attending the Roman inheritance of the Greek form are discussed by J. A. North in a review article dealing in part with the *laudatio funebris*. See 'These He Cannot Take', *Journal of Roman Studies* (1983), 169–74, esp. 169–70.

delivered by a newly elected consul to the Senate and people, known as the *gratiarum actio*, went to help make up the construction of the formal panegyric. An early text which may be defined as panegyrical is Cicero's speech *Pro M. Marcello*, delivered before the Senate in 46 BC. In spite of its title, the speech is not forensic oratory. Cicero was delivering the speech to Caesar shortly after his victory in the civil war against Pompey, thanking him for allowing the recall from exile of Marcellus (who, like Cicero himself, had supported the losing side). Cicero had also been granted a pardon and recall from Caesar that year.

So the speech is one of elaborate and complimentary gratitude, offered to a dictator on behalf of a defeated enemy. Yet it also shows traces of a desire to administer advice to Caesar in the guise of compliment; Cicero had viewed his own role as orator as being, ideally, that of ethical mentor to the powerful, as in the Greek tradition, although he also saw that such a tradition must be severely modified—if not actually crippled—when all political power resided in the hands of one man.[5] The prototype for the formal panegyric, then, already conceals a method for giving policy advice, in which the speaker defends himself from displeasure and its consequences by administering it as praise. The technique has great relevance for Renaissance texts imitating and adapting celebratory classical forms.

For instance, a young, rather poor Erasmus seized upon it gratefully in 1504 when he was writing a panegyric for Archduke Philip, ruler of the Netherlands and duke of Burgundy, celebrating the archduke's return from Spain.[6] His text makes uneasy reading, partly because there is now no reputable literary counterpart to panegyric; but this is not the only reason. Erasmus himself, uncomfortable with a task including (amongst other things) the comparison of the archduke with Alexander the Great to the

[5] For instance, in Cicero's insistence upon the virtues of moderation and mercy to the defeated—virtues linked implicitly to the successful healing of a state wounded by an undesired and divisive civil war. Cicero praises Caesar for displaying these virtues, citing them as evidence that Caesar would not desire war for its own sake. This functions as a recommendation for future policy. See *Pro M. Marcello*, trans. N. H. Watts, Loeb edn. of Cicero's works, vol. 14 (London, 1931), 428–31 and 434–5.
[6] *Panegyricus ad Philippum Austriae Ducem* . . . (Antwerp, 1504); trans. in Erasmus, *Works*, xxvii. 2–75.

latter's disadvantage, was forced to load the form with more moral
freight than it could easily support. Realizing this, he put two
letters with it, to be published before and after the text, in which
he justified what he had done.

In the prefatory letter he admits that 'my own straightforward
nature . . . had some degree of aversion to this whole species of
composition, to which above all, it seemed to me, one might apply
Plato's description "the fourth part of flattery" '.[7] 'Yet', he adds
swiftly, 'the thing is not so much praise as precept; and there
is surely no more effective method of reforming princes than to
present them with a pattern of the good prince under the guise of
praising them.' In the letter following the main text he enlarges
on this, citing Christian as well as pagan precedent for the technique. 'The apostle Paul himself', he argues, used 'this device of
correcting by praising'. Erasmus calls it 'a sort of holy adulation'.[8]
For 'how could one reproach a wicked ruler for his cruelty more
safely, yet more severely, than by proclaiming his mildness; or
for his greed and violence and lust, than by celebrating his generosity, self-control, and chastity, "that he may see fair virtue's
face, and pine with grief that he has left her" '.[9]

And an important new point is made in this second Epistle.
Erasmus discusses the question of audience, arguing that a
panegyric is intended more for the benefit of the commonwealth
(that is, its listening, reading representatives) than of the prince.
From it the people should both learn what qualities make a
pattern prince, and simultaneously believe their own prince to possess them. A panegyric, says Erasmus, should be adapted to the
ears of the multitude 'just as is done in sermons; and the resemblance of a panegyric to these is brought home to us by its very
name, which the Greek derives from a meeting of the multitude

---

[7] Sig. A1ᵛ; trans. ii. 79.

[8] As n. 7 above, sigs. F6–8ᵛ; translation in *Works*, ii. 81. Augustine, Ambrose,
and Jerome are also pressed into service as holy adulators, and their reputation
made to stand against any dubiety in such a practice, almost without further argument (see translation, pp. 81, 83).

[9] Bacon was later to stress the importance of this combination of civility and
severity in his essay 'Of Praise'. See *The Essayes or Covnsels, Civill and Morall
of Francis Lo. Verulam, Newly Enlarged* (London, 1625), 305–6: 'Some *Praises*
come of good Wishes, and Respects, which is a Forme due in Civilitie to Kings,
and Great Persons, *Laudando Praecipere*; when by telling men, what they are,
they represent to them, what they should be.'

at large' (p. 82). Of course, when Erasmus writes 'the multitude at large' we must remember he means in this context only those who can read Latin. His audience is educated, then, but in need of moral instruction (for hidden behind an account of princely duties are the complementary duties of his subjects), and they receive it shaped as a narrative of exemplary conduct. The life described, being that of a prince, must in a Christian principate stand as that of an earthly representative of Christ, the universal exemplar.

By this point it must have become clear that the *Panegyricus* anticipates the arguments of the *Institutio Principis Christiani* in a number of important respects. (And indeed, the relationship between the two is tacitly recognized in that the first edition of the *Institutio* has the text of the *Panegyricus* printed with it.)[10] However, it is not a part of the purpose here to trace the development of that rather different strand of exemplary writing from the *Panegyricus* to the *Institutio*.[11] Advice intended for a powerful living recipient must cast its addressee as the mediator between precept and imitative act, but if you write 'biographically'—and at this point that means writing about the dead—you must take on the mediating role yourself.

Another, even earlier Erasmian oration tackles these specific difficulties of commemoration by becoming just such a mediator. This is the *Oratio Funebris* composed for Berta Heyen, 'a most virtuous widow of Gouda', in 1489.[12] In this text Erasmus is not bound to clothe his precept with *paraenesis* (advice through praise). Berta Heyen is dead, and Erasmus is addressing the living. Instead he alters and manipulates her past into the kind of descriptive narration which tacitly exhorts its audience to imitative acts of virtue. When the exemplary function of commemorative oratory is privileged in this way, the factual status of what is described may become less important than its moral efficacy. Erasmus's audience, in imitating the virtues of Berta Heyen, may, like Donne's readers of the *Anniversaries*, fit themselves to the likeness of his subject, and in doing so make his text properly

---

[10] See Erasmus, *Institutio Principis Christiani* ([Basle], 1516).

[11] For a discussion of this aspect of the *Institutio* see Timothy Hampton, *Writing from History: the Rhetoric of Exemplarity in Renaissance Literature* (Ithaca, NY, 1990), 48–62.

[12] Translated in Erasmus, *Works*, xxix. 15–30.

descriptive of the facts of their own conduct, regardless of what Heyen really did in her own life. The *Oratio* also addresses two distinct audiences. While it is explicitly offered to Heyen's daughters, it also assumes a wider body of readers. When addressing the daughters, Erasmus explains that his aim is 'to console you', but he adds that he also intends 'the edification of all who might read this work' (p. 19). In this way consolation and edification are seen as leading in two different directions for the different audiences. He also invokes different models: while he acknowledges a debt to 'the custom of the ancients' from the outset, he also invokes patristic authority: 'even the famous Jerome used just this literary genre to console . . . Eustochium for the demise of her mother Paula' (p. 17).

Explicitly, he modifies classical convention to accommodate Christian aims. We see him doing this, for instance, when he describes Heyen's dry-eyed fortitude upon the death of another daughter, Margareta. Erasmus allows his own presence as her foil in this anecdote. When he expresses concern for her state of mind, Heyen rebukes him with the words: 'How could I be so shameless as to resent the fact that the Lord has taken away my daughter . . . ?' (p. 26). Partly he means to draw attention to the difference between Berta's response and the response of her classical precursors. 'It is one thing', he argues, 'to ignore the feelings of family love in order to win glory (or, to be more precise, to conceal one's inner distress behind an insincere expression), but it is altogether different to overcome the love she felt for her daughter by means of her exclusive love for Christ and, moreover, even to give thanks for what happened' (p. 27).

The key word here is 'insincere' (*ficta*).[13] Erasmus has previously described examples of Stoical ἀπάθεια ('no passion' or 'no feeling' might be a fair translation for this term), which his ancient heroes exhibit in the face of adversity. In using the word 'insincere' he makes his own position on ἀπάθεια clear; that it is impossible to assume, through the exercise of human will and reason alone, a truly passionless state. It may be affected, but it cannot be entered. Nor is Christian fortitude a version of (divinely assisted) ἀπάθεια, for it is driven instead by an 'exclusive

[13] 'Oratio Funebris in Fvnere Bertae de Heyen . . .', in *Desiderii Erasmi Opervm Omnivm*, 10 vols. (Leiden, 1703–6), viii. 558.

love': passionlessness replaced by passion stronger than grief. As
T. S. Eliot was to point out in 1927 (admittedly with more than
half an eye on Erasmus while he did so), 'stoicism is the reverse
of christian humility'.[14]
     In this way Erasmus measures pagan against Christian defini-
tions of virtue. Since Christian social values—and thus Christian
virtues—are predicated on immortality in a desired afterlife
which is also a type of perfected commonwealth, those definitions
appear to reflect badly on the Graeco-Roman bereaved. Classical
virtue conceals its private grief for the—possibly flawed—*res
publica* (Erasmus's wording (p. 27) implies that concealment was
even a less creditable matter of personal honour), whereas the
Christian virtue of Berta Heyen really rejoices at the entrance of
a soul into a city of perfected souls and resurrected bodies which
is the kingdom of heaven. Yet this is to be deft rather than fair,
since it measures a concept of perfection against the empirically
assessable imperfections of a mortal society, and a hope of
fulfilment against irredeemable grief. It does, however, demonstrate well that the Christian pattern relies on 'exclusive love' if
its fortitude is *not* to mean stoicism. Something has to be stronger
than death.
     Erasmus must also provide specifically Christian precedents
for Berta's ordinary practice of virtue as well as redefining her conformity to classical patterns. Mostly he finds these in Pauline precept. Her marriage, for instance, he describes as having been made
on a Pauline model:

She pondered in her troubled heart the message of the Apostle: 'As for
the rest, those who have wives should live as though they have them not,
etc.' She curbed her fleshly desires with incredible strictness. Whenever
she had the opportunity, she withdrew herself from the troubles of this
worldly life in order to devote herself more calmly to reading and prayer
. . . it almost seemed as though she lived as a maiden, a wife in name only.
(pp. 21–2)

Against this cautious (though authentically Pauline) view of
virtuous married conduct Erasmus sets another of the apostle's
precepts, 'Women, be obedient to your husbands' (p. 22, quoting Ephesians, 5: 22), evidently in order to assuage any fears that

[14] T. S. Eliot, 'Shakespeare and the Stoicism of Seneca', in *Selected Essays*
(London, 1932), 132.

Berta might have made of her piety a channel to the kind
of independence which sets itself against a husband's rights
and authority. 'She was so accommodating to him', he writes
'. . . that you would have believed she was a servant, not a
spouse' (p. 22).

It is pleasant to record that, once widowed, Berta Heyen
appears at last to have come into her own. 'Free of a husband's
authority,' writes Erasmus, 'she immediately devoted herself with
unlimited zeal to every virtuous pursuit, as though she were
at last able, after long, misguided delays, to begin a holy life'
(pp. 22–3). The pleasures of patronage and extensive almsgiving
were evidently potent, for she is described as having decidedly
refused several offers of a second marriage, becoming instead very
active in visiting the sick and destitute. Here Erasmus is able to
cite another precept, this time from the words of Christ: 'What
you have done for the least of my people, you have done for me.
I was sick and you visited me' (p. 24, quoting Matthew 25: 36 and
40). Erasmus has accommodated his classical model, and the
rhetoric of eulogy it properly employs, to a narration of Heyen's
conduct as scriptural precepts in action.

In examining these texts of Erasmus I have chosen to identify
techniques expressing a specifically Christian exemplarity as they
surface in texts explicitly constructed within classical forms. I
would now like to investigate the question from the other way
about: what do the writers of texts presented as funeral sermons
consider their relationship to be with the oration? How is their own
practice modified by its demands, and, most important, what effect
do these modifications have on the presentation of exemplary
biographical material within the sermon?

Erasmus himself identifies the funeral sermon as a form of
demonstrative oratory, but adds that its contemporary practice now differs from classical convention: 'Laudatorum genus
Ecclesiastae, [. . .], fere consumitur in extollendis laudibus dei,
aut divorum. Nam funebres orationes non perinde sunt in usu
Ecclesiastis nuncat que olim fuerunt.[15] ('The eulogistic style of
the preacher is almost continually taken up with singing [lit.
'raising up'] the praises of God or the saints. Funeral orations are

[15] Desiderius Erasmus, *Ecclesiastae, sive de Ratione Concionandi* . . . (Basle,
1535), 151.

not customary for preachers now, as they once were.') He proceeds to identify four possible kinds of laudatory oration, modifying each category in order to accommodate Christian priorities. The aim of Christian oratory, he explains, is to display the glory of God; either by directly praising Him or by narrating the holy acts of His servants. The servants themselves cannot be praised except in so far as they represent the divine virtue, and even this praise is only allowable as a means of reforming the wicked (p. 152). All the examples he cites of such orations have patristic authors: Nazianzen, Chrysostom, Ambrose, Augustine.

A summary follows of the oration's different parts: first the miracles which precede or attend the subject's birth; then his appearance, his country and parentage; and finally his virtuous characteristics (pp. 152–4). One individual can exemplify particular characteristics—there is a safe scriptural precedent: 'in Iob insignis est patientia, in Abraham hospitalitas, fides & obedientia' (Job was remarkable for his patience, Abraham for his hospitality, faith, and obedience.') (p. 154). In this way the reader is offered a selection of exemplars with a tiny range of virtues each, although he is (of course) required to try to display every virtue in his own life conduct.[16] Incidentally, it also staves off full characterizations, a technique which would certainly privilege portrayal above exemplary description.

Nevertheless, the model is problematic for Protestant writers. It tends to praise people rather than simply celebrating the acts and attributes of God. Its details are really biographical, and inevitably the context is laudatory. While the method is usually defended by citing patristic precedent, even the Fathers are seen by some to have been corrupted by the epideictic conventions of their own times.[17] A book of advice on preaching from the mid-sixteenth century which addresses this question is the work *De Formandis Concionibus Sacris*, by Andreas Hyperius (or Gerardus). First published from Marburg in 1553, it was evidently widely influential, finding its way into French in 1563,

[16] See Ch. 2 for a discussion of the comparison, or 'parallel' of the exemplars of different sorts of virtues, as it is employed by Plutarch and his early modern imitators within ecclesiastical proto-biography. See also Erasmus, 'Laudatio per Comparationem', in *Ecclesiastae*, 157.

[17] See Lewalski, *Donne's 'Anniversaries'*, 177–9.

and into English in 1577 under the title *The Practise of Preaching*.[18]

Hyperius's section on laudatory oratory draws some sharp distinctions between traditional practice (in which category he includes both patristic funeral and forensic oratory) and the requirements of the sermon: 'he that wyll prayse eyther a person, or deede, or thing, shall understand that he must somwhat otherwise frame his talke in the Church than the company of *Rhetoritians* is accustomed at the barre, or in the Scholes.'[19] The summary which follows of topics the sermon writer should *exclude* bears a close resemblance to Erasmus's list of things an orator must *include*: Hyperius lists first 'the nation, countrey, lygnage, wounders or miracles that went before the nativitie' of the subject; next, the 'ornamentes of the body, as favour, strength, comliness . . . also the goodes and ornaments of the minde, as witte, docilitye . . . godlines, zeale of religion'; then the subject's social standing and the 'benefites of fortune'; then 'actes done both publickely and privately', with their 'honours, offices, triumphs'; and finally 'all the thinges accomplished in the old age, death . . . opinion after death, signes or wonders going before or following after death' (sig. W8ᵛ). As Hyperius points out, this is essentially a chronological list, running 'through all the degrees of age'. It derives from Quintilian—though it shows some signs of having been tailored to the needs of the pre-Reformation hagiographer, which must have been an element in Hyperius' disapproval. An almost identical list appears in Thomas Wilson's *Arte of Rhetorique* (deriving purely from Quintilian here), where it is presented as an essential part of the rules to be followed by the life-writer.[20] Indeed, it is perhaps fair to say that it is what may be called the biographical element in these instructions which mainly troubles Hyperius. He continues:

---

[18] Andreas Hyperius, *De Formandis Concionibus Sacris; seu de Interpretatione Scripturam Populi* (Marburg, 1553); *Enseignement a Bien Former les Sainctes Predications et Sermons* (Geneva, 1563); *The Practise of Preaching, otherwise Called the Pathway to the Pulpit: Conteyning an Excellent Method how to Frame Divine Sermons . . . Englished by Iohn Ludham . . .* (London, 1577).

[19] *The Practise of Preaching . . . Englished by Iohn Ludham*, sig. W8ᵛ.

[20] See Thomas Wilson, *The Arte of Rhetorique* (London, 1560); reprinted in 1909 and ed. G. H. Mair, 11–14.

But verily the preacher in all this busines useth a much unlike practise. First truely the Church hath not bene accustomed to prosecute with prayses those that be a live, & still subiect to all kindes of temptations and sinnes, as *Orators* have done in puttinge forth their *Panegyricall* and plausible *Orations* uttered in prayse and commendation of men. . . . But it prayseth and extolleth those onely whom all good men trust assuredly to be now translated into the felowshippe and societie of Saintes. (sigs. W8ᵛ–X1)

In this way Hyperius effectively limits all laudatory sermons to praises of the godly dead. However, the godly dead are not to be extolled according to a proto-biographical model. Hyperius states that a preacher 'dealeth very slenderly with those places which wee rehersed, yea so far is it off that he taketh matter of prayse, of the benefits of the body and of fortune, that he scarce toucheth them at all . . .' (sig. X1). For Hyperius all sermons should be exhortatory and exegetical, and the laudatory sermon is no exception. He allows that the preacher may 'by litle and litle' discuss 'one or two, certes not lightly above three' virtues for which the dead man was notable, but this meagre list is a purely illustrative element in an attempt to 'the correctinge and amendinge of mens corrupt maners, and to frame in the mindes of his hearers impressions of true godlynes, also to illustrate and seet forth the glory of the heavenly Countrey' (sig. X1).[21] When he considers exhortation more closely he decides it has two purposes: first, that 'by hearinge the gracious and excellent deedes' of great men, the godly listener will 'be provoked to prayse and

---

[21] The German reformers envisage 'the glory of the heavenly Countrey' as a lasting opportunity to expound the new theology with surprising frequency. Melanchthon, in his funeral oration for Luther, describes him as 'taken out of thys mortal body as out of a pryson, and entred into a Schoole adourned with more excellent doctrine'. See 'Philip Melancthons [*sic*] Oration, Made and Recited for the Funeralles of . . . Martine Luther at Witte[n]berge', in Henry Bennet, *A Famous and Godly History, Contaynyng the Lyves and Actes of Three Renowmed Reformers . . . Newly Englished by Henry Bennet Callesian* (London, 1561), sig. H1ᵛ. This is reiterated in Melanchthon's announcement of Luther's death in the same volume, where Luther is described as having been 'called to God, to the eternal Schole' (sig. G1ᵛ). Wigandus Orthius, in his funeral oration for Hyperius himself, writes: 'Hee hath put off that body of his, subiect to corruption: he loketh now to put on a body immortall and incorruptible. He hath forsaken these *Scoles* of ours: he is admitted into the *Scole* of heaven.' See Wigandus Orthius, 'An Oration as touching the Lyfe and Death of . . . D. Andrewe Hyperius', in *The Practise of Preaching*, sig. Cc.

magnifie GOD'; and secondly, 'that the multitude maye be stirred and enflamed to the imitation of their so notable deedes' (sig. X1ᵛ). As with the oration for Berta Heyen, a distinction is being made between the expected response of an elite audience and that of a wider readership, and in each case the wider readership is expected to come to biographical narration expecting to be edified, and to leave it resolving to imitate what they had read in their own lives.

He is one who disapproves of the funeral oratory of Gregory Nazianzen and Ambrose, calling it 'sticking fast to the rules of the *Rethoritians* . . . repeatinge all thinges [concerning the dead person] from his very childehod even to his olde age' (sigs. X2ᵛ–3). The requirements of the funeral sermon for 'ecclesiasticall Teachers', he writes, should be 'more accordinge to sounde religion':

When they commend a funerall with their Sermon, they handle not prayses curiouslye contrived and couched together, but other places much more holesome and fitte for the enformation of the hearers, such as . . . of preparation unto death, that death is the penaltye of sinne, of the miseryes of mannes lyfe, of the delyveraunce of them by death . . . (sig. X3)

If the preacher feels it will edify the hearers along these lines to commend the life conduct of the dead subject, however,

then add they briefely, and (as ye woulde say) shamefastely some thinge touchinge the kinde of life that he imbraced, and shewe how devoutly he served God therin . . .

Wherby the hearers are given to understande what great industry it behoveth them to employe, to the intent every of them in their callinge . . . may become acceptable to God.

Peradventure also will they commende, and set before them that be alive to be followed, one or other vertue wherin the brother deceased excelled, or some notable act done by him for the behoofe of the Church . . . or his confession of faith made in the very conflicte of death. (sig. X3ᵛ)

But how far were theoretical instructions of this kind, appearing in *artes concionandi* treatises on the writing of funeral sermons, actually followed? The oration delivered at Hyperius' own funeral by Wigandus Orthius, and tucked in at the back of Ludham's 1577 translation of *The Practise of Preaching*, contains a fairly full summary of his life and death.[22] It even begins with a classically elaborate lamentation (sigs. Bb1–2). It is only fair to add that Orthius does observe some of Hyperius' own rules. He assigns Hyperius three notable virtues: learnedness, ability to teach, and 'gravitie and constancye of life and conversation' (sig. Bb5ᵛ). In case any doubt exists as to whether erudition and didactic talent really qualify, he asserts with St Paul that a pastor of the Church needs both to do his work effectively. The last virtue, too, proves Pauline; he cites the third chapter of the first Epistle to Timothy, where the right conduct of a Church elder is set out.[23] It is vital, he goes on to argue, that 'to doctrine and erudition the life and manners may bee agreeable' (sig. Bb6). He manages in this way to imply that erudition presupposes personal rectitude.[24]

By the time the peroration is reached, Orthius has travelled far enough from his opening lamentation to discuss whether the faithful may, at a personal level, legitimately grieve at all. He begins by listing, then assessing, two usual reasons for mourning:

First, forasmuch as [men] . . . suppose them to be evill dealt withall, whom they bewayle being deade. Secondly for bicause they recount with themselves what great incommodities doe redounde by their death, either privately to themselves, or publickely to the commonwealth. The

---

[22] But the title of the oration is explicit about its biographical content: 'An Oration, as Touching the Lyfe and Death of the Famous and Worthy Man D. Andrewe Hyperius, Penned and Pronounced in a Solemne Assemblie of all the States of the Citie of Marpurge, by Wygandus Orthius. And done into English by Iohn Ludham', in Andreas Hyperius, *The Practise of Preaching* . . . (London, 1577). Hyperius also figures in a number of early biographical collections: see Theodore Beza, *Icones*. *Les Vrais Pourtraits des Hommes Illustrees en Piete et Doctrine, Traduicts du Latin*, translated by Simon Goulard, 2nd edn. (Geneva, 1581); Jacobus Verheiden, *Praestantium aliqvot Theologorum, qvi Rom. Antichristum Praecipue Oppugnarunt, Effigies* . . . (The Hague, 1602); Melchior Adamus, *Vitae Germanorum Theologorum, qvi Superiori Seculo Ecclesiam Christi Voce Scriptisqve Propagarunt et Propugnarunt* . . . (Heidelberg, 1612); Jacobus Verheiden and H[enry] H[olland], *History of the Moderne Protestant Divines*, translated by D[onald] L[upton] (London, 1637). This last is simply a translation of Verheiden's *Life* in his Latin collection.
[23] 1 Timothy 3 is, understandably, very often cited in contemporary ecclesiastical narrative. See Ch. 3 (Texts).
[24] A discussion of the relationship perceived to exist between scriptural learning and pastoral efficacy is made in John Morgan, *Godly Learning: Puritan Attitudes Towards Reason, Learning and Education, 1560–1640* (Cambridge, 1986), 95–102.

former cause taketh no place in our heavines: the later ministreth unto us sadnes most sorrowfull. (sig. Cc2)

It hardly needs saying that the first reason is judged inappropriate because the dead man is now enjoying 'eternall felicitie'. But the second is a real concern, and prompts the argument of his final section. Hyperius' loss, he says, as well as being a blow to family and friends, is a blow to the reformed Church, because his didactic virtues were irreplaceable. And he is the latest of a line of significant bereavements: Luther, Bucer, and Melanchthon are dead, and more recently, Peter Martyr and Wolfgang Musculus. Unless the apt in his congregation get to their books, before long there will be no notable teachers, and 'all our religion . . . againe enwrapped in most ugsom darkenes' (sigs. Cc4–4ᵛ). This closing exhortation stands out as a pragmatic central theme.

Orthius' oration, in fact, is something of a mixture—a dash of *encomium* with half a pint of exhortation. In another case— Melanchthon's volume celebrating the life and acts of Luther— we seem to find something closer to Hyperius' specifications:

Albet in thys common sorrow my voyce shalbe troubled wyth dolour & teares: yet I must say somewhat in thys frequent assembly, not (as the Paganes solemne custome was) to sing the Encomye of the dead, but rather to admonish this companye of the marveilous government, & perils of the Church, that we may consider for what causes we ought to be careful & pensive, what thinges we have special neede of, & to what examples we ought to direct our lyfe.[25]

But this is because biographical and laudatory material simply appears in its own right in other sections of the volume. The funeral oration is only the final item in a book which also contains a fairly detailed chronological life history of Luther up to the Diet of Worms, an even more detailed account of the Worms debate, a short narrative describing his last sickness and death, and a number of encomiastic verses on Luther openly modelled on classical practice.[26] And although the oration presents Luther

[25] 'Philip Melancthons [*sic*] Oration', in Henry Bennet, *A Famous and Godly History*, sig. G2ᵛ. Translated from Philip Melanchthon, 'Oratio in Fvnere Reverendi Viri Martini Lvtheri', in *Historia de Vita et Actis Reverendissimi Viri D. Mart. Lutheri, Verae Theologiae Doctoris* . . . (Wittemberg, 1549), sig. E8ᵛ.

[26] In first edition of 1549 (see note above) as follows: 'Historia de Vita . . . M. Lutheri', sigs. A4–C1ᵛ; 'Acta . . . D. Martini Lutheri', sigs. C2–D8ᵛ; 'Philippus Melancthon ad Avditorivm Schola Wittebergensis, Anno 1546. De

as a spiritual leader—along with 'Esay, John Baptist, S. Paule, Austen' (sig. G5)—he is not being held up for imitation. His qualities are discussed in the context of the demands of his own unique position. For instance, Melanchthon cannot decide whether Luther's 'vehemencie' can be counted in the circumstances as a fault. He lists it in company with obvious virtues, and quotes Erasmus as saying (though not, presumably, of Luther) 'God hath given this last age a sharpe Phisician, because of the greate diseases of the same' (sig. G7). His strong implication is that, fault or not, 'vehemencie' had been a very *useful* quality. Like Hyperius' three virtues, it was a practical help at the right time.

Both the last examples have titles which declare them to be part of a tradition of demonstrative oratory. Matthew Parker's funeral sermon for Martin Bucer, however, acknowledges no debt to any classical form on its title-page, declaring its intentions to be homiletic: 'Howe we Ought to Take the Death of the Godly.'[27] While its first section (about a third of the whole) is what it says it is, the other two-thirds take Bucer himself as their subject. This seems to indicate a greater attention to the real man than Hyperius would approve. How does Parker justify his practice?

Conventionally, he begins by condemning the grief of personal loss. 'To bewayle the departure of a rightuous man in respect of hymself we be forbidden, by reason, by nature . . . Against charitie it is and agaynst fayth' (sig. A2ᵛ). Like Erasmus, he then cites pagan examples of fortitude in the face of bereavement, adding that for Christians fortitude should be replaced by real joy (sig. A3). Even in this initial exhortatory section Parker abandons general themes early, arguing that Bucer's death had been a judgement on his Cambridge flock because they had not appreciated him properly, an ingratitude which reminds him, he says, of the disobedience of 'Corah Dathan and Abiram' (sig. B3).[28] Having

Obitu Lutheri', sigs. E–2ᵛ; 'Carmine de Lavde Lvtheri', sigs. E2ᵛ–8 (including 'Gratiarum Actio' sigs. E6ᵛ–8); 'Oratio in Fvnere . . . Martini Lvtheri', sigs. E8ᵛ–F7; Latin and Greek verses for Luther, sigs. F7ᵛ–8ᵛ.

[27] Matthew Parker, *Howe We Ought to Take the Death of the Godly, A Sermon Made in Cambridge at the Buriall of the Noble Clerck D. M. Bucer* (London, [1551]).

[28] See Numbers 16: 1–32; Deuteronomy, 32: 48–52. 'They . . . went down alive into the pit, and the earth closed upon them: and they perished from among the congregation'; also Psalm 106: 17.

engulfed Cambridge's 'murmerours' with this comparison, Parker
concludes the section with prayers of thanksgiving for Bucer's life.
The next part is devoted to Bucer's virtues. Parker finds the
difficulty of reproducing the godly *minutiae* of Bucer's life in
words frustrating: 'To declare before you the holl commen-
datyon of hys lyfe worthely as he deserved to be reported, ye see
ryseth a greate wyde felde to go in, to large for a lytle time to
be walked over' (sig. F3ᵛ). This kind of expression of literary
inadequacy was an oratorical commonplace, and would become
a commonplace of the ecclesiastical Life, but this one is worth
noting for a number of reasons. For instance, Parker perceives
literary skill as a necessary tool with which to record lived virtue,
and assumes that to have an 'artificer' narrating one's life will be
a matter of desert rather than of chance. Also, in Bucer's particular case there is evidence which suggests that his value for contemporaries actually was primarily his conduct. His life, and not
the prolix, clotted prose of the *Scripta Anglicana*, was his most
legible text.[29] A letter from Peter Martyr, published in English
in 1583, in fact describes Bucer instead via a really central
exemplary text, those most popular verses of Pauline precept 1
Timothy 3. As Peter Martyr tells it, Bucer's conduct has brought
the early Church back to life:

Beholde, wellbeloved brethren, in our age, Bishopes upon the earth, or
rather in the Church of Christ, which be trulie holie. This is the office
of a pastor, this is that bishoplike dignitie described by Paul in the Epistles
unto Timothie and Titus. It delighteth me much to read this kinde of
description in those Epistles, but it pleaseth me a greate deale more to
see with the eyes the patternes themselves.[30]

But Paul wrote precept here, not narrative. If Parker in his
sermon decides that Bucer's living actions are his contribution
to the Church, he can only point, can only illustrate precept
through narrative: narrative has become exhortation. Parker is
alive to the implications of writing Bucer in this new Protestant
culture, which regarded with suspicion all works commemorating

---

[29] See Patrick Collinson, ' "A Magazine of Religious Patterns": An Erasmian
Topic Transposed in English Protestantism', in *Godly People: Essays on English
Protestantism and Puritanism* (London, 1988), 503–4.
[30] *Martyrs Divine Epistles*, bound in with *The Common Places of Peter Martyr*,
trans. Anthony Marten (London, 1583), 62–3.

the lives of the dead. So he brings us round the circle. Bucer himself becomes an exhortatory text, a walking precept, in a passage which makes him a compendium of patristic learning at the same time as it skilfully elides Fathers-as-texts and Fathers-in-action:

He was not Bucer only for experience of controversies of our tyme, nor yet syngularly Austen, Athanasius, or Hierom, or any other most expert in there syngular causes and controversies, as thei were specially exercysed in there tymes: But he was an universall Epiphanius in that knowledge, expert in the controversies of all tymes, or rather a boke of common places drawen by long studye and excellent memory out of the store of them all.

This booke[31] is here lost among us of Cambridge, for want whereof we bee dryven nowe to goe agayne to our particular libraries, worthy for our oversyght and neglygence, to be put to more paynes to wandre in them, forstorynge our selfe to stand to our defence. (sigs. E7ᵛ–8)

Parker makes Bucer an erudite type of living 'common places', an active—and unusually complete—patchwork of the writings (which are also the doings) of his sanctified models. Unlike Melanchthon's Luther, Bucer's knowledge and qualities are not praised as simply specific to his time. As far as the past goes, and in his field, he holds every possible reference. His loss, and our over-reliance on his mortal book, drives us from our dependent complacency out into the wilderness of our own libraries, 'to wandre in them' as confusedly as our first parents, or as the Israelites first struggling without an omniscient guide. Only the allusive delicacy of Parker's compliment saves it from its own bold blasphemy. And Parker must, of course, turn his prelapsarian meaning to accommodate an image, a world, full of knowledge of good and evil, a wilderness of texts rather than a world of briars to wander in; so that what we learn from our postlapsarian living book is to make universal books of ourselves 'to stand to our defence' in the contentious world.[32]

One might reasonably expect from this kind of imagery to find Bucer's actions chiefly to be academic discourse. But when

[31] In a copy of this sermon held in the Parker Library at Corpus Christi College, Cambridge, ref. SP 36, the words 'this booke' are underlined in the distinctive orange crayon used by Parker in his annotations.
[32] See below, Ch. 3 (Bodies), for a discussion of men and women as texts in proto-biography.

Parker comes to it, the language he uses suggests something carefully balanced between homily and practical example, accompanied by a strong expectation that its fruits will be in his listeners' performed virtue rather than in mere words: 'What comfort and edificatyon hys nyer aqueyntaunce receyved by hym in hys godlye wordes and communycation: I wolde wysshe for my self that it myghte be better counterfayted in example, than reported in worde' (sigs. F4–4^v). As well as the obvious exemplary intent, this second part carries hints of Bucer's inimitability, germs of grief for the irreplaceable of exactly the kind its first part condemned. Parker refuses, for instance, to narrate any part of the life which he had not known about at first hand because, 'although I applyed my dilygence never so much to spye his nature and learne what was in hym: I perceyved that I could not saye that as yet I ever knewe Bucer. He was not knowen in a daye or two, as most part of men may sone be' (sig. E3^v). It is perhaps typical of the way that life and texts, sayings and doings, constantly melt and interchange that Parker should refer the congregation instead to Erasmus' accounts of Bucer in his Epistles before his move to Cambridge (sig. D2^v). But he does seem himself regularly overwhelmed by a sense that the 'great wyde felde' which was Bucer's life made all attempts to narrate it inadequate. He is reduced twice to emphatic tautology: 'if Bucer was ever Bucer, he was Bucer in Cambridge: that is pithy in learning, and evident in order' (sig. D6). And again, even more plainly: 'In reding and disputing, Bucer was Bucer' (sig. D8^v).

Parker does make a basic decision that Bucer's character had always been consistent. In this way he could assume a description of Bucer's conduct in Cambridge to be representative of his complete life. Although, he says, Erasmus had the greater advantage, having known Bucer over twenty or thirty years, whereas Bucer's Cambridge acquaintance knew him only for 'so lytle a tyme', and that a time when he had been 'broken with syknes', yet Bucer's Cambridge life even so 'may sone declare an evident gesse to us, what he was at home in hys moste quiet, in his strong and perfect helthe' (sigs. D2^v–3).

Parker, then, is clear about the gaps in his picture of Bucer, but nevertheless believes that he can convey something of his essential qualities, which were unchanged by circumstance. And when he finally comes to lament the loss of Bucer to the world, he does so in terms which come clean, and declare him irreplaceable: 'For our desert he is so sone taken from us, and not from us here at Cambrydge onlye, not from the hole Realme only, nor from hys owne Germany: but from the whole worlde of Christendom, from the trew spouse the Catholike churche of Christ here militant uppon earth' (sig. E4^v). As with the orations for those other reformers, Luther and (to a lesser extent) Hyperius, this sermon for Bucer in fact has a dual aim. While concerned to depict Bucer's conduct as an exemplary 'living sermon', Parker's text also shows traces of classically rooted lamentation for an individual loss—a process which naturally elides with a celebratory, commemorative narration fixing the parameters of that loss in speech.

The tensions implicit in the dual aims of exhortation and lamentation continued to pose problems for Protestant orators. While it was possible to exclude the element of mourning by arguing its inappropriateness for Christian believers in the afterlife, this could not automatically exclude the commemorative element. To describe a subject's holy conduct could itself be defined as exhortatory, and the patristic model the form had inherited was problematic, in that the Fathers could be, and were, cited by some to justify celebratory narrative. But on the whole, the consensus after the Reformation, among Catholics as well as Protestants,[33] was that orations like that of Gregory Nazianzen for his sister Gorgonia, or of Ambrose on the death of his brother Satyrus, were too specifically laudatory to belong to the same genre as that of the funeral sermon, because of the weight of classical influence on their authors.[34] Among Protestants, the epideictic nature of the funeral sermon surfaced as an issue in the Admonition Controversy, although it was described in the original Admonition to the Parliament of 1572, which preceded the Whitgift–Cartwright debate, as having its roots in the superstitious (and idolatrous) practice of the 'popish trental'. However,

---

[33] Post-Tridentine decrees address the problem in response to this essentially Protestant unease with epideictic elements in funeral sermons, recommending a shift in meditative focus from the subject to the hearer's life. See Peter Bayley, *French Pulpit Oratory 1598–1650: A Study in Themes and Styles* ... (Cambridge, 1980), 45.

[34] See *Funeral Orations by St. Gregory Nazianzen and St. Ambrose*, trans. R. P. McCauley and others (New York, 1953).

both Thomas Cartwright and (at the separatist end of the debate) Henry Barrow identified the funeral sermon as originating in the encomium and *laudatio funebris*, Cartwright remarking that the practice of Gregory Nazianzen had been (adversely) affected by the funeral conventions of his native Athens. Cartwright eventually conceded that commendation of the godly was acceptable as long as it was separated from the actual preaching content of a funeral sermon.[35] Although Cartwright appears to have purposed a complete severance between sermon and civic oration, in practice it became a convention for funeral sermons to be divided (as with Parker's sermon for Bucer) into a first section which exhorted the congregation with meditations on mortality, often expounding a suitable scriptural text, and a second which specifically commended the dead individual (see Fig. 1.1).

The balance between these two sections varied widely. Some funeral sermons preached in the early seventeenth century, on the whole for civic dignitaries and not ecclesiastics, were fully encomiastic, defending their practice by citing (often defensively) Ambrose, Gregory Nazianzen, and Jerome as proper Christian models.[36] At the other end of the scale, some putative subjects for funeral sermons expressly forbade their preachers to commemorate their life conduct. Such prohibitions could backfire and become an item in a biographical list of exemplary commendations narrated by faithless (or logic-chopping) commemorators.[37] (Arguably it backfired often enough for the whole circular process to look as if it *might* be a species of conventional *occupatio*-in-action: 'do not mention' becoming, effectively, a flag for a literally commendable humility.) For, in general, funeral

---

[35] This aspect of the controversy is discussed in Patrick Collinson, *Godly People*, 518–23.

[36] e.g. [Anthony Nyxon], *London's Dove: Or, A Memorial of the Life and Death of Master Robert Dove* (London, 1612); William Walker, *A Sermon Preached at the Funeralls of the Right Honourable William Lord Russell, Baron of Thornhaugh . . . the 16 of September, 1613* (London, 1614); both cited in Lewalski, *Donne's 'Anniversaries'*, 178.

[37] As in the case of John Carter, who instructed his children to forbid the preacher Samuel Ward to give a funeral sermon which took his virtues as its subject. Ward, however, although he could not preach at Carter's actual funeral, gave his sermon at Ipswich shortly afterwards; and Carter's piety in forbidding it is celebrated by Clarke in his *Lives*, with Ward as one of his authorities. See Collinson, *Godly People*, 520.

But I have troubled you too long with this *Schoole-doctrine* and *pulpit-divinitie* of magnifying *mans merits*, before men, since their *death-bed-divinitie* recants it all; and then, they are all forced, learned and ignorant, utterly to renounce it, and put all their trust in CHRIST's *mercy* and *merits*, as their sure Anchor-head: Of which I have onely this to say; that *merit* may have some place in *their science*, but their owne *consciences*, unlesse they be feared, tells them, there is no true merit, but CHRIST's onely.

Applicatio. I have now done with my Text: and now I apply my selfe and my Text to the present Text, that lies before us: *Vir nec silendus, nec dicendus sine curâ*, A man whose worth may not be passed over in silence, whom all ages with us may celebrate and admire; nor to be spoken of without great care and study: Of whom I can say nothing, but his worth and vertues will farre exceed all mens words. Heere I desire neither the tongue of man, nor Angells: if it were lawfull, I should wish no other but his owne tongue and pen, *Ipse, ipse quem loquar, loquatur*: let him speake of himselfe, none so fitt as himselfe was, of whom I am to speake this day. *Et jam loquitur*, And he now speakes: He speakes in his *learned Workes* and *Sermons*, and he speakes in his *life* and *workes of mercy*, and he speakes in his *death*: And what he taught in his life and works, he taught and expressed in his death. He is the great *Actor* and *performer*, I but the poore cryer, *Vox clamantis*, He was the *Vox clamans*: he was the loud and great *crying Voice*, I am but the poore *Eccho*: and it is well with me, if as an *Eccho*, of his large and learned bookes and workes, I onely repeate a few of the last words.

ring he may do so too. *Oh that men were wise, that they would understand this, that they would consider their latter end!* The Lord teach me and thee, *to number our days, and to apply our hearts unto wisedom.* Amen.

I

I have now done with my Text: But (as I told you) I have another to take in hand, and ye all know it. But something I must tell you, (which perhaps you know not) by way of Preface to what is to be spoken concerning that Reverend person, whose memory we are now to solemnize; Namely, that it was a strict charge of his owne, given to his Son, whom he made his Executor, and inserted into his last Will, That he should be buried privately, without any Solemnity : Which order was agreeable to his known singular modesty and humility. And lest we should seem to transgress that command which we have thus made publick, I must also tell you, that upon intreaty, his consent was obtained, for a Sermon to be preached for him after his Funerals.

FIG 1.1. Showing the textual separation between exegesis and commemoration. Above: from John Buckeridge, 'A Sermon Preached at the Funeral of . . . Lancelot [Andrewes] . . . in Lancelot Andrewes, *XCVI Sermons* (London, 1629). Below: from John Whitefoote, Ἰσραὴλ Ἀγχιθανὴς. *Deaths Alarum, or the Presage of Approaching Death: Given in a Sermon for . . . Joseph Hall, Late Lord Bishop of Norwich* (London, 1656)

pomp was a settled institution, and the preaching of a sermon with a purpose at least partly laudatory was accepted as an element in the convention in which the dying provided in their wills for public and visible signs of their passing.

The first quarter of the seventeenth century seems to have seen a growth in the popularity of funeral sermons, at least in so far as a growth in the number printed is any guide.[38] Corroboration of a circumstantial kind appears in William Fuller's observation, in the dedicatory epistle prefacing his funeral sermon for Gervase Clifton's second wife, Lady Frances Clifton, that whereas his sermon for the former Lady Clifton (preached in 1613) had only been circulated in manuscript, the demand for the present sermon of 1627 had made its printing necessary.[39]

In 1640 a volume of forty-seven funeral sermons by different authors, explicitly intended for general edification, was printed: Θρενοίκος. *The House of Mourning.* Its title continues by making clear the ways in which its contents should be read: *Furnished with Directions for, Preparations to, Meditations of, Consolations at the Houre of Death.*[40] This volume is described by Patrick Collinson as marking 'a kind of apotheosis' of the form, but identified by him also as lacking in 'the motive of "memorial" or "testimonial" '.[41] It therefore seems a good place to inquire how far the

[38] A brief look at STC citations (vol. 1 only) of funeral sermons preached for women and printed between 1591 and 1625 is suggestive. While only one sermon appears for 1591, preached for Anne, Countess of Warwick (STC 4952), four are issued in 1620, for Elizabeth Crashaw (STC 6030), Elizabeth Juxon (STC 6603.5), Lady Phillippa Rous (STC 10940), and Rebecca Crisp (STC 11679). In addition to this, Philip Stubbes's *A Christal Glasse for Christian Women*, written for his wife Katharine, is printed 24 times between 1591 and 1637 (22 of them after 1600), reaching the height of its popularity in 1623, when it is printed twice. I am indebted to Dr Arnold Hunt for this information.

[39] William Fuller, *The Mourning of Mount Libanon: Or, the Temples Teares. A Sermon Preached at Hodsocke, the 20 Day of December, 1627* . . . (London, 1628), sigs. A3ᵛ–4. I am again grateful to Dr Arnold Hunt for bringing this example to my attention.

[40] Θρενοικός. *The House of Mourning; Furnished with Directions for, Preparations of, Meditations on, Consolations at the Houre of Death. Delivered in XLVII Sermons, Preached at the Funeralls of Divers Faithfull Servants of Christ . . . By Daniel Featley, Richard Sibbs, Martin Day, Thomas Taylor . . . and other Reverend Divines* (London, 1640).

[41] *Godly People*, 522.

encomiastic legacy had been modified to accommodate exemplary themes in funeral sermons offered as models of their kind, rather than as commendations for specific public figures.

It would be easy, and partly true, to say that the more 'Puritan' the deceased's affiliations, the fewer were the commendatory and biographical elements in his funeral sermon. Certainly commendation was regarded with caution by many, because of its encomiastic and its 'popish' roots. However, the common topos that the godly life of the dead man or woman had been a living sermon meant that the line between preaching and commendation was ill-defined. It would be unwise to assume a simple correlation between the affiliations of the dead and the commendatory element in his or her funeral sermon. The notable 'puritan' dead might (and often did) receive extensive biographical notice; Clarke's *Lives*, for instance, are often heavily based on the funeral commendations received by his subjects.

I suggest that the relative lack of the 'memorial' element in *The House of Mourning* may actually be due more to the status of its dead. The majority of its subjects are either women or the young, people whose public visibility in terms of individual actions may be assumed to have been low. Freed from the constraints of presenting the (comparatively) individual characterization required by those notable dead, its authors are free to offer a compendium of sermons which are (in every sense) model texts. General meditations on death merge with the presentation of their subjects only as godly patterns, under the pressure of which the lives of the obscure dead dwindle almost to nothing.[42]

But in this volume the subjects' disappearance does seem correlative to their social visibility. One of the few sermons preached for a man, 'Gods Esteeme for the Death of his Saints: Preached at the Funerall of Mr. Iohn Moulson of *Hargrave*, at *Bunbury* in Cheshire, by S.T.', devotes a good deal of space (four pages of a total of eleven) to Moulson's virtues, particularly those

---

[42] This is not, however, a process invariably applying to funeral accounts of the lives of women. The question of how far a self-chosen 'godly' demeanour amongst conformist 'Puritans' may have offered its female professors a measure of self-determination reflected in, and mediated through, the comparative biographical particularity of their funeral commemorations is discussed by Peter Lake in 'Feminine Piety and Personal Potency: The "Emancipation" of Mrs. Jane Ratcliffe', *The Seventeenth Century* (July 1987), 143–65.

associated with the running of his household, in which department he is compared favourably to Bucer (p. 411). Certainly these virtues are given as a formula, listed and numbered, and are too general to be considered as individual commendation, but Moulson is the only subject even to be named in the volume; and very few other subjects receive more than a paragraph of commendation, even of the most general kind.

This is not to say that Moulson is being presented as a notable. He is not; described as having 'made no great noyse in the world' (p. 411), his conduct is offered as a pattern for the ordinary man's imitation. It is simply that the ordinary man, the Christian paterfamilias, is a type which receives more specific attention than the model wife and mother, or the very young man or child. Each of the latter categories tend, in this volume, to be held up as a memento mori for those sections of the congregation who are themselves wives, mothers, young men, or parents, and the emphasis is correspondingly less upon commendation than on warning.[43]

In general, the aim of the collection is well described in its preface to the reader: 'Each Sermon therein being as a severall Legacie bequeathed by those upon the occasion of whose deaths they were preached as by so many Testators, who themselves have made a reall experiment of mortality, and left these for our instruction who survive them' (sig. A3ᵛ). The preacher has become authoritative interpreter for the 'reall experiment of mortality' his subject has entered; the sermon stands for the experience of death. The sermons themselves are explicit as to how their 'instruction' must be read. The author of the sermon 'The Praise of Mourning; or, Mourning Preferred Before Mirth' paraphrases Augustine (without acknowledgement) to make it clear he has no encomiastic intention: 'Funerall Sermons are not intended for the praise of the dead, but for the comfort of the living. Therefore I have chosen such an argument to handle at this time, as might bee of

---

[43] e.g. 'Lifes Apparition, and Mans Dissolution', 495, where the deceased, dead in childbirth, is held up as a 'pattern & example' to 'ye that are Child-bearing women'; 'The Profit of Afflictions, or Gods Ayme in his Corrections', 586, where the deceased is a young man, and described as speaking, in his death, 'in a more speciall manner to you that are young men . . . as a loud Sermon preached unto you . . . to bethinke your selves in your younger yeares of the things that concerne your spirituall and eternall welfare'.

use, and profit to you that live' (p. 52). The same point is made (this time with acknowledgement) in 'The Platforme of Charitie, or, the Liberall Mans Guide' (p. 792). These statements represent a general consensus as to what funeral sermons are for and should do, which conforms with Hyperius' categorization of them as—with martyrological narrative—'Consolatory or Comfortative'.[44] Yet that Hyperius considers them together underlines the difficulty of excluding life conduct from a didactic form, if the life were held to be exemplary.

A number of writers solve the dilemma by using actions in the life to illustrate the sermon's scriptural text. The author[45] of 'A Triall of Sinceritie; or, the Desire of the Faithfull', preaching on Isaiah, 26: 8–9, is one such, carefully distinguishing between the worldly commendation of *encomia* and his own exemplary practice. However, a deft use of *occupatio* allows him to have it both ways:

To passe other circumstances (as that she was descended of an honest, and worthy Familie, and of good qualitie: that Shee had a full and hopefull issue descending from her selfe, and such like circumstances, which I leave for Oratours (as unfit for a Divine) to meddle withall.) All I shall say concerning Her, shall bee out of the Text, in which you may beholde a true picture of her in all the linaments of her: and out of it, you may be able to drawe, and take a good patterne for your selves. (p. 315)[46]

Of course, the preacher is manipulating his commendation to unify his sermon structure. But it is clear from the start that his dead subject has organized her 'text' herself:

The words of the Text, are the sweet Swan-like song of our deceased Sister, which she desired might be her *Funerall Song*, her *Funerall Text*, at this time: and desired it long agoe . . . And I have accordingly pitched upon it: not onely in order to satisfie her desire in a just thing: but . . . because I approve her choyce of a fit Text; there not being in the whole Scripture, a portion that will afford a fitter Character (in my apprehension) for her person. (p. 299)

---

[44] Hyperius, *The Practise of Preaching*, sig. Z7ᵛ.

[45] Identified as Richard Sibbes in a contemporary hand on the title-page of the copy held by Harvard University. See Lewalski, *Donne's 'Anniversaries'*, 193.

[46] For other examples of 'lives' as commentaries upon texts in this volume, see ibid. 194–5.

The claim made at the front of the volume, that the preacher only interpreted and presented the living words of the dead, now appears much more literal. This preacher is simply approver and exponent of a text chosen, long in advance, by 'our deceased Sister'. This sermon is her climactic moment of authority, an authority conferred by her 'reall experiment of Mortality'. The preacher concurs in her self-presentation, for she has not just chosen a text suitable to her death, but selected the instructive 'pattern' of her life from all the scriptural models available to her.

What had happened, in fact, was first that the topos of the 'living sermon' could, and often did, provide a new, impeccably exhortatory rationale for biographical narrative. On top of this, for the more socially visible dead it was perceived as customary that a section be appended to the funeral sermon which was still essentially epideictic. Outside the model sermon, as it is displayed in *The House of Mourning*, something which strongly resembled encomium had been built in as a social norm, together with the hanging of blacks in the church at the funeral, the distribution of mourning gloves and ribbons, and other essentially secular conventions. In a funeral sermon for Humphrey Sydenham, the preacher Henry Byam expresses a strong dissatisfaction with this state of affairs; but he does not break with it. His commemorative section begins:

I make no question, but many in this great Assembly have brought with them itching Ears, and are troubled with the *Athenian Disease*. Act. 17. 21. *They came not so much to learn how themselves might live*; but how this gentleman died, whose *Funerals* we now celebrate: And if I should say no more at the end, then hath been spoken in the beginning: This was the Text which himself gave,[47] and is indeed an *Epitom* of the frequent and fervent prayers, which he used in his sickness; If I should say no more, this were enough to give ample Testimony of his faith, and satisfaction to the Hearer: But I obey Custom, and am ready to render a more full account of what I have both heard and seen.[48]

Byam is actually having to cite his text as an 'Epitom' of Sydenham's last utterances in order to satisfy 'Custom', rather than simply giving it out straight.

[47] Luke 18: 13: 'God be merciful to me a Sinner.'
[48] Henry Byam, 'The Sinner's Legacy: A Sermon Preached at the Funeral of Mr. Humphrey Sydenham', in *XIII Sermons . . . Preached before His Majesty King Charles the II, in his Exile . . .* (London, 1675), 236–7.

John Whitefoote, in his funeral sermon for Bishop Joseph Hall, has the opposite difficulty with the double form. Taking as his text 'And the time drew nigh that Israel must die' (Genesis, 47: 29), he writes:

In the Funeral Sermons of the Antients, the person deceas'd was the only text; and the Sermon nothing but an Anatomy lecture upon the dead mans Life. I have imitated that custome upon this occasion, by taking no other Text, than that of this Saints life . . .
But yet I hold my self by modern custom obliged to chuse another Text, first, or last, and I thought it would be best to give it the Precedence . . . short, and plain, agreeable to the design of my discourse upon it, which must be short, because I have another Text to take up, when I have done with this.[49]

When Hall is himself already a sufficient exhortatory 'Text', a scriptural one on top seems irksome to Whitefoote. Consequently he chooses one that cannot possibly need exegesis, merely complementing his biographical portrait of Hall as a modern patriarch.

Robert Mossom, in the funeral sermon for his predecessor George Wilde, felt the scriptural text to be an obsolete convention. His is virtually abandoned in favour of that living text, Wilde himself, appearing only as an exemplary afterthought to the 'Narrative Panegyrical' of Wilde's 'Life, Sickness and Death'. Mossom's point, such as it is, is applied purely to the imitative virtue of his hearers: 'Let me prompt you to this service', he urges, '. . . that . . . our Lives in imitation write [Wilde's] . . . Epitaph; and if you please, let the Conscription be these words of the Apostle, *Christ is our Life*'.[50]

What seems to emerge from this evidence, as far as the place of classical panegyric and encomium within the funeral sermon is concerned, is this. Although regarded with ambivalence, the epideictic techniques which they employed were nevertheless an almost ineradicable part of funeral sermon convention, along with other kinds of funeral pomp. Attempts to separate the life

[49] John Whitefoote, Ἰσραὴλ Ἀγχιθανής. *Deaths Alarum, or the Presage of Approaching Death: given in a Funeral Sermon . . . for the Right Reverend Joseph Hall, D.D. . . . the 8 Day of Septem. 1656 . . .* (London, 1656), 1–2.
[50] R.[obert] M.[ossom], *A Narrative Panegyrical of the Life, Sickness and Death of George* [Wilde] *. . . Lord Bishop of Derry in Ireland . . .* (London, 1665/6), 19.

narrative associated with their encomiastic techniques from the main exhortatory body of the sermon were instituted, but since the life conduct of the godly was itself perceived as exhortatory, this division tended only to signal a separation between precept and exemplary (therefore celebratory) description. In practice, also, the division would be yoked together by presenting the subject as an active precept, or 'living sermon', exemplifying the preacher's scriptural text.

While this manoeuvre might prove homiletically adequate, it placed severe constrictions on the proto-biographical narrative, already perceived as having great exemplary potential in its own right. An obvious solution was to enshrine the godly life within a form other than the sermon; and here, I think, can be identified one reason for the rise of ecclesiastical biography.

By the time Walton came to write the *Life of Sanderson*, the exemplary requirements of Life and sermon had become distinct: so much so that Walton was able to record Sanderson's dissatisfaction with funeral pomp, and the 'flattery' Sanderson associated with funeral preaching, as illustrative of his subject's unassuming piety. The detail even illustrated Walton's own (apocryphal) scriptural text, 'Mysteries are revealed to the meek' (Ecclesiasticus 3: 19). Because Walton's account was not offered as a sermon, he could safely ignore Sanderson's request that nothing be said of his life conduct that he had not sanctioned, and could even quote the request as an example of the meekness his text expounded. Nor can Walton be seen as flouting Sanderson's wishes (as Samuel Ward had evidently flouted John Carter's) in narrating his wish to remain uncommemorated, since, as Walton renders it, the Will itself expresses a hope that Sanderson's desire for obscurity will itself prove 'exemplary' to the notional hearer. His humility, expressed as a wish to escape biographical commendation, could have been framed already by Sanderson himself for an instructive, proto-biographical purpose:

My will . . . is, That the Funeral Sermon be preached by my own Household Chaplain, containing some wholesome discourse concerning Mortality, the Resurrection of the dead, and the last Judgement; and that he shall have for his pains 5*l*. upon condition that he speak nothing at all concerning my person, either good or ill, other than I my self shall direct . . .

I do very much desire my Will may be carefully observed therein, hoping it may become exemplary to some or other: at least howsoever testifying . . . my utter dislike of the flatteries commonly used in Funeral Sermons, and of the vast Expences otherwise laid out in Funeral Solemnities and Entertainments, with very little benefit to any, which (if bestowed in pious and charitable works) might redound to the private and public benefit of many persons.[51]

[51] Izaak Walton, *Lives*, 410–11.

2

Reading Plutarch, Writing Lives

We know that Izaak Walton read Plutarch. He quotes him (from North's translation) in his own *Lives*, and borrows from him images and situations. He sets his own characters up, very often, in pairs recalling the Plutarchan parallel; a form his friend Henry Wotton and a number of his contemporaries also favoured for the Characters they wrote of public figures. Plutarch is, in any case, the other obvious classical influence on emergent early modern biography, his parallel *Lives* enjoying a large vernacular popularity from the mid-sixteenth century and throughout the seventeenth.[1]

The other monumental biographical precursor is, of course, John Foxe. In preferring to discuss Plutarch, I am following Walton's own circumstantial indications of his models rather than belittling Foxe's massive influence. Walton never mentions Foxe—in pointed contrast to that hotter sort of life writer Samuel Clarke, through whose *Lives* Foxe runs as a constant thread of authoritative reference. Clarke does not merely cite Foxe, but assumes his readers to have a close enough familiarity with the *Acts and Monuments* to understand very glancing

[1] Plutarch's *Lives* were brought into Western culture both by epitome and by piecemeal Latin translation in the fifteenth century (see R. R. Bolgar, *The Classical Heritage and its Beneficiaries* (Cambridge, 1954), 485–7). The major subsequent scholarly translations of the *Lives* were those of Xylander (1561) and Cruserius (1564) in Latin; and of Amyot (1559) in French. Amyot, *Les Hommes Illustres Grecs et Romains* (Paris, 1559), is the major resource of Thomas North. North's translation appeared as *The Lives of the Noble Grecians and Romans* (London, 1579), STC 20065. Subsequent editions, with variants and the later addition of the lives of Philip of Macedon, Epaminondas, and others, are listed in STC 20066–71. Longer discussions of Plutarch's reception can begin most helpfully from R. Aulotte, *Amyot et Plutarque* (Geneva, 1965) and D. A. Russell, *Plutarch* (London, 1973), ch. 9. For the rest of this chapter I cite Plutarch in North's 1579 version (hereafter Plutarch, *Lives*).

allusions to its stories.[2] The authority Clarke grants Foxe is
virtually scriptural in its shape and scope, as it was for so many
Renaissance churches and households.[3] Clarke's *Life and Death
of Master Ignatius Jurdaine* contains the information that he had
read the Bible through 'above twenty times' and Foxe 'seven times
over'.[4] In the *Life and Death of Master Richerd Capel* Clarke
discusses the question of set forms of prayer; in the course of
it he boldly deploys Foxe's account of the Marian martyr John
Bradford as a quasi-liturgical source: 'Doctor *Harris* tells us of
a second *Bradford*, that in time of his distress, was fain to adopt
Master *Bradfords* words, and to spread them before God as his
own, because he had said more for him (as he thought) than he
could say for himself.'[5] Clarke follows this with a description of
a divine who would recite Psalm 51 for his comfort, demonstrating Foxe's Bradford as having become an authority for sacred
utterance comparable to King David. It is difficult to imagine
Walton, whose formal liturgical reverence was naturally much
greater, doing anything quite like this. And, in fact, by the time
Walton was well launched biographically a heavy reliance on Foxe
tended to indicate some nonconformist sympathies, sometimes
with the seventeenth-century Church's role perceived as comparable to the Marian persecutors of the 1550s. This would
certainly explain Walton's silence.

Yet contemporaries do compare both Clarke and Walton to
Plutarch. Before the second part of the *Marrow of Ecclesiastical
History*, congratulatory verses to Clarke say 'Plutarche *cede*'.[6]
Similarly, James Duport's Latin verses on Walton's *Life of
Herbert*, published with the 1675 edition of the *Lives*, describe
Walton as 'Plutarchus *alter* . . . Biograephus';[7] and on the end-
papers of a 1678 copy of Walton's *Life of Sanderson* are found
some Latin verses, in manuscript, which address Walton, 'nove

[2] Clarke, *Lives*, 226: 'Disputations are great trials to the spirits of intelligent
men. Hooper and Ridley were patient Martyrs, but somewhat impatient dis-
puters'; see also Collinson, *Godly People*, 507 n., for other examples.
[3] See William Haller, *Foxe's Book of Martyrs and the Elect Nation* (London,
1963), 221. William Dowsing, the arch-iconoclast, in the extensive annotations
of his book collection, references only Foxe and the Bible.
[4] Clarke, *Lives*, 393.   [5] Ibid. 306.
[6] Clarke, *Marrow*, 2nd part, sig. A3.
[7] Walton, *Lives*, p. 257. James Duport (1606–79) was Master of Magdalene
College, Cambridge. See *DNB*, xvi. 239–41.

o Plutarche Biographe'.[8] Part of the intention in this chapter is to ask whether to call a biographer a 'Plutarch' is to pull a name of a popular classical biographer at random out of a hat of appropriate but imprecise possible compliments, or whether it confers a particular kind of commendation on Walton's practice.

PLUTARCH AS 'SCHOOLEMAISTER'

John Dryden, in the preface to a new translation of Plutarch's *Lives*,[9] suggests one thing it might mean to call someone a 'Plutarch', when succinctly defining the difference between Plutarch's approach and that of other classical life writers:

> *Suetonius* and *Tacitus* may be call'd alike, either Authors of Histories, or Writers of Lives: But the first of them runs too willingly into obscene descriptions, which he teaches while he relates; the other . . . often falls into obscurity; and both of them have made so unlucky a choice of times, that they are forc'd to describe rather Monsters than men . . . Our Author on the contrary, as he was more inclin'd to commend than to dispraise, has generally chosen such great Men as were famous for their several vertues; as least such whose frailties or vices were overpois'd by their excellencies; such from whose Examples we may have more to follow than to shun.[10]

Dryden identifies Plutarch's generosity in commending with a didactic intention to offer his subjects as 'Examples', and this sense that a life written is an example taught is signified in Dryden's caution over Suetonius, whose 'obscene descriptions' might 'teach' vice as Plutarch's commendations taught virtue. Dryden's verb, 'overpois'd', with which he describes the optimum balance between virtue and vice in Plutarch, shows that balance weighted heavily in favour of the 'excellencies' his readers were to emulate. In such a context Suetonius' fault in the *Lives of*

---

[8] *The Life of Dr. Sanderson, Late Bishop of Lincoln. Written by Izaak Walton. To which is added, some Short Tracts or Cases of Conscience, written by the said Bishop* . . . (London, 1678). Copy in Wren Library, Trinity College, Cambridge, ref. K.15.93². The volume (which contains other works canonical to Restoration Anglicanism) is the donation of 'Ed: Rud T.C.C. Soc; 1708'.

[9] *Plutarch's Lives, Translated from the Greek by Several Hands* . . . (London, 1683): see Wing P2633–41.

[10] Dryden, xvii. 276–7.

the Caesars may be identified as moral impartiality, not necessarily as prurience.[11]

A modern critic, Alan Wardman, also contrasts Suetonius' 'readiness to be on equal terms with vice or virtue' with the 'recommendation of virtue' resulting from Plutarch's 'concentration on the good'. The reason he gives for Plutarch's overweighting of the balance incidentally links Plutarch's practice directly with the panegyrists', at least as it was understood by the Renaissance reader: 'if Suetonius's purpose had been the improvement of future Emperors', argues Wardman, 'he would have helped it by giving even more space than he does to the slim virtues of the wicked.'[12] Plutarch's intention is defined, by contrast, as paraenetic; like Pliny, he 'teaches by praising'. To call Walton a 'new Plutarch' is to link him to a virtually pedagogical tradition.

For the Renaissance reader of vernacular translations of Plutarch, his status as mentor was pointed up by the ready availability of didactic works ascribed to him and at that time generally taken to be part of the *Moralia*.[13] Most of the first English translators of Plutarch select just such didactic works: the treatise on good health translated by Erasmus into Latin and by Hales into English, for example; or the treatise on the education of children which, to judge from its printing history, enjoyed considerable popularity.[14] Such separate *Lives* as were translated

---

[11] The only vernacular translation of this work of Suetonius in England before the Restoration is *The Historie of Twelve Caesars Emperors of Rome*, trans. [Philemon Holland] (London, 1606), STC 23422. Two more editions appear in the same year with Holland's name on the title-page, STC 23423, 23424. Holland exhibits some unease in his address 'To the Reader' about Suetonius' methods; while he states that Suetonius had chosen to write about dead emperors in order not to 'incurre the note of Flatterie, extolling above measure the good parts of Princes then living' and calls his account 'plaine trueth', he adds 'if happlie in prosecuting this point, he hath recorded ought that may be offensive to chast and modest mindes, yee shal do well to glaunce over with your eye such places lightly; as I with my pen touched vnwillingly', sig. ¶3.

[12] Alan Wardman, *Plutarch's Lives* (London, 1974), 145.

[13] D. A. Russell, *Plutarch*, 164–72, lists the older canon and indicates its current boundaries.

[14] See e.g. the anonymous translation *The Governaunce of Good Helthe, Erasmus Beynge Interpretoure* (London, 1549?), STC 20060.5. J. Hales's translation is *The Preceptes of the Excellent Clerke and grave Philosopher Plutarche for the Preservacion of Good Healthe* (London, 1543), STC 20062. See also *The Educacion or Bringinge vp of Children . . .* , trans. Sir Thomas Elyot (London,

in manuscript before North also tend to stress Plutarch's didacticism.[15]

Biography itself was presented as instructive. A supposed letter from Plutarch to Trajan, which defined his relationship to the emperor as precisely that of mentor and noble pupil, is included in Amyot's (and consequently in North's) Preface to the *Lives*. While showing some scepticism about whether it was genuine, Amyot is happy to present it as evidence that Plutarch was Trajan's 'schoolemaister'. Purporting to deal with the *Moralia*, it runs (in North's rendering) as follows:

I have set you downe the meanes in writing, which you must observe for the well governing of your common weale, and have shewed you of how great force your behaviour may be in that behalfe. If you thinke good to followe those thinges, you have Plutarke for the director and guider of your life: if not, I protest unto you by this Epistle, that your falling into daunger to the overthrow of the Empire, is not by the doctrine of Plutarke.[16]

Amyot continues by reading Trajan's 'goodnesse and justice' as 'imprinted' in his 'sayings and doings', but their 'paterne and *mowld*' he traces directly to the precepts of the *Moralia*. The (virtuous) life conduct of Trajan has, via the *Moralia*, become another Life by Plutarch. Erasmus' relationship to his addressee

before June 1530), STC 20056.7; another edition 1532, STC 20057; another translation, partly augmented by the translator E. Grant, *A President for Parentes, Teaching the Vertuous Training vp of Children* . . . (London, 1571), STC 20057.5. As well as these, a Greek version of the treatise appears in company with didactic works by Isocrates, *Plutarchi Chaeronei Opusculum de Liberorum Institutione. Item Isocratis Orationes Tres* . . . (London, 1581), STC 20054. This appears in eight more editions between 1585 and 1635, STC 20054.3–20056.5.

[15] See J. K. McConica, *English Humanists and Reformation Politics under Henry VIII and Edward VI* (Oxford, 1965); pseudo-Plutarch's (Donato Acciaiuoli's) 'Life of Scipio Africanus', translated into English by Wylliam Maister, Glasgow University Library, Hunterian MS 466; John Young and Henderson Aitken, *A Catalogue of the Manuscripts in the Library of the Hunterian Museum in the University of Glasgow* (Glasgow, 1908).

[16] Plutarch, *The Lives of the Noble Grecians and Romans. Englished by Sir T. North anno 1570*, ed. W. E. Henley, 'The Tudor Translations VII–XII, 6 vols. (London, 1895–6), i. 21 (unless otherwise stated, subsequent references are to this edition of the *Lives*). Also cited on much the same basis by Dryden in his 'Life of Plutarch'; Dryden, xvii. 266.

Duke Philip in his *Panegyricus* is grounded upon almost identical assumptions.[17]

Plutarch's other, directly narrated *Lives* Amyot defines as having the same close relationship, as it were in reverse, to 'morall Philosophie' earlier in the Preface. As Amyot sees it, the narrative form fulfils essentially the same function as pure precept, but with the advantage that it is more accessible. 'All other learning', he argues, 'is private, fitter for Universities than cities . . . Whereas stories are fit for every place.'[18] As he expands the point, he defines narration as a purely exemplary process, 'forasmuch as examples are of more force to move and instruct, than are the arguments and proofes of reason, or their precise precepts, bicause examples be the very formes of our deedes, and accompanied with all circumstances'.[19] Amyot's argument here closely resembles Hyperius', who considered oratorical technique to be peculiarly suitable to 'Popular' (as distinct from 'Scholastic') preaching.[20] If it is reasonable to locate Plutarch's didactic practice as partly epideictic, then the telling of life stories, according to these definitions, is a popularization of precept through the use of a form which has greater dramatic resources, and so greater appeal. It not merely expounds 'arguments and proofes', but narrates 'the very formes' as they are acted out in lives. Lives, in fact, are the fuller explanation of precept needed by the non-academic reader.

This needs qualifying. Amyot's remark that 'stories are fit for every place' is significantly modified by his assumption that his readers are important enough to need advice on how to make, or help make, civil decisions. He defends writing histories (this includes writing Lives) by claiming them to be a useful aid to

---

[17] See above, pp. 5–7. For the use of Plutarch in another counselling relationship, see the correspondence between Languet and Sidney, as described in E. S. Donno, 'Old Mouse-Eaten Records: History in Sidney's *Apology*', *Studies in Philology*, 72 (1975), 275–98.

[18] Plutarch, *Lives*, i. 7.

[19] Ibid. i. 10. Montaigne, commending Plutarch's use of parallels in the *Lives*, adds: 'He is a Philosopher that teacheth us vertue.' Michel de Montaigne, 'A Defence of *Seneca* and *Plutarke*', in *Essaies*, trans. John Florio, with an Introduction by D. MacCarthy, 3 vols. (London, 1928), ii. 454. See also Dryden, xvii. 274: 'All History is only the precepts of Moral Philosophy reduc'd into Examples.'

[20] Hyperius, *The Practise of Preaching*, sig. B1.

policy decisions: their readers will 'find matter in them whereat
to take light, and counsell thereby to resolve him selfe to take a
part, or to give advise unto others, how to choose in doubtfull
and daungerous cases . . .' (i. 10). Amyot's readers are assumed
to make history as well as to read it—even if the assumption is
partly calculated compliment.

It also accords with Plutarch's tendency to expect his reader
both to understand, and to concur with, educated judgements
on his heroes' behaviour, and to contrast them with the ignorant
assumptions of the 'multitude'. For instance, in the account of
Cicero's enforced exile to Brundisium (Brindisi), Plutarch criti-
cizes him for being miserable about it, and argues that the
Stoic self-control one might reasonably expect from him as a
'Philosopher' had been attenuated by his frequent contact as
a 'common pleader' with the 'passions and moodes' of the 'common people' (v. 347–8). In expecting his reader to take the point,
Plutarch assumes him at least to be acquainted with philosophical discourse. The multitude are there partly to provide a
background of contrast to this assumed knowledge.[21] Cicero's
failing is an *exemplum* to the educated reader which points up the
desirability of a right employment of ἀπάθεια. Again, the relationship between the *Moralia* and the *Lives* surfaces: as historical
events are proper *exempla* for moral philosophical debate, so the
narration of events is properly attended by moral philosophical
commentary.

Both Plutarch and his translators Amyot and North, then,
assume an educated readership who might be expected to deploy
as well as to read Plutarchan counsel. How far does the ecclesiastical life writer, and more specifically Walton, fit with this
assumption? Ecclesiastical biographers apart from Walton are,
almost without exception, university-educated clergymen, and
will therefore have had no difficulty in reading themselves into
the Plutarchan addressee. In Walton's case the issue is more complicated. Neither formally educated nor a clergyman, he should
still be assumed to be well read in his own language, although not
in Latin (and surely, therefore, not in Greek).[22] But philosophical

[21] Wardman, *Plutarch's Lives*, 42–8.
[22] See Novarr, p. 89, for Walton's ignorance of Latin; see also Jonquil Bevan,
'Some Books from Walton's Library', *The Library*, 6th series, 2 (1980), 259–63;

concepts trickled down into the vernacular, variously interpreted and modified by different theological currents; a typical example might be, say, a piece of advice on the governance of the passions which combined Stoicism with the heavenly rewards of self-denial. Books like Charron's *Of Wisedome*, in the English translation by Lennard (which Walton is known to have owned, and which he annotated and underlined extensively) presented such concepts in a comparatively popular and easily digestible form.[23]

But if this solves Walton's social problems as reader, it does not solve them as Plutarchan author. While it is true that *paraenesis* has the author's social inferiority to his subject conveniently built in, you do need to be able to claim some other kind of authority—your great learning—to be a successful mentor. Walton was not a 'schoolemaister'. He made a virtue of his meekness and stressed his ignorance. How could he operate as spokesman for an elite readership?

Walton solves the problem by concentrating on the duties owed by the 'private men' he really represents to the figures of authority he actually depicts—a subject complementary to any discourse addressing the duties of the public man to the private citizen. He also portrays his main protagonists as unpretending exponents of a practical piety—a deft way of administering precept to his betters in the safer dress of example. In this way he characterizes himself, the author, simply as the medium through which his subject, the living precept, is made available to posterity.

Walton's single work of pure exhortation, the 1680 pamphlet *Love and Truth*, is presented on the title-page as the advice of one private man to two others: 'From a Quiet and Conformable *Citizen* of London, to Two Busie and Factious *Shop-Keepers* in Coventry.' In the text, Walton's 'Factious *Shop-Keepers*' are claimed as cousins. He keeps the social distance between 'writer' and 'recipients' deliberately short (though perceptible), because then he can present the former as himself an example of quietness,

the entry for Charron appears on p. 260. A majority of the books owned by Walton are written in English.

[23] Pierre Charron, *Of Wisedome*, trans. Samson Lennard (London, n.d. [before 1612]). The entry for Walton's edition of Charron appears on p. 260 of Bevan's article (n. 22 above).

conformity. Walton speaks here as both of and yet not of the 'multitude', which he, like Plutarch, characterizes as immoderate and passionate in their behaviour; and as both of and yet not of the moderate, grave, and reflective few he holds up as a contrast. He also appears in his own person as biographer—mediator between preceptor and listener—presenting the 'holy life and happy death of Mr. *George Herbert*', 'plainly and I hope truly writ by Mr. *Isaac Walton*', and setting it against the turbulent careers and uncomfortable ends of Hugh Peters and John Lilburne.[24]

Samuel Clarke, that other life writer to whom the comparison with Plutarch was flatteringly applied, also sets the godly few— into which fellowship of saints the reader is included by courtesy —against the ungodly multitude. In doing so he too claims the virtues of moderation for his elite representatives, in a manner so similar to Walton's that it needs stressing that Clarke's 'few' often overlap with Walton's 'many', and vice versa. The puritan divine Samuel Crook meekly endures invasion and persecution from 'bloody minded' royalist soldiers who will not permit him 'quietly to enjoy himself, and his God in his private study' in the 1640s, as Walton's Sanderson is 'visibly disturbed' by parliamentarian soldiers from observing 'order and decent behaviour in reading the Church Service' in the 1650s.[25]

Through this stratagem both Walton and Clarke struggle to justify their respective definitions of a godly elite by characterizing them with the same virtues. The virtues stand in lieu of argument in the narrative, deploying rectitude against a theological opposition which, in many essential respects, actually had little to do with personal conduct. The kinds of virtues claimed have their roots in the Aristotelian mean, the privileging of reason and moderation against the sway of physical passions, but their position in these narratives stems from Plutarchan assumptions and Plutarchan biographical practice. And, for Clarke as for Walton, including the reader amongst the godly and against the ignorant many is another, muted form of 'teaching by praising';

[24] [Izaak Walton], *Love and Truth, in Two Modest and Peaceable Letters* . . . (London, 1680), 37. A copy of this work is held by the Sancroft Library in Emmanuel College, Cambridge, with Walton's annotations. Women and shopkeepers are used as emblems of the passionately immoderate both in the *Life of Hooker*, 186–7, and at intervals throughout *Love and Truth* itself.

[25] Clarke, *Lives*, 211; Walton, *Lives*, 382.

while it confirms his godly status, it exhorts him to an imitative godly conduct.

In the Introduction to his earliest biography, the *Life of Donne*, Walton is especially keen to define where he stands. He wants to clarify the terms of his mediation between Donne's life and his reader's response, and that means demonstrating, or at any rate asserting, a particular social relationship to each. Casting about for one that will fit the case, he invokes an anecdote from Plutarch's *Life of Pompey*. The passage he chooses comes after Pompey's death; Walton tells the story, and sets up his parallels, in two complementary rhetorical questions: 'If I be demanded, as once *Pompeys* poore Bondman was, (whilest he was alone on the Sea shore gathering the pieces of an old Boat to burne the body of his dead Master) What art thou that preparest the funeralls of *Pompey* the great? Who I am that so officiously set the Authors memorie on fire?'[26] Here we see exactly how Walton regards his relation to the Plutarchan hero. He does not have the stature of a Pompey, a Donne: but he is its foil. He asserts that he is creating his commemorative monument in the absence of any fitter person. His function in the vital relationship between *reader* and hero is well exemplified by the same story as Plutarch tells it. There, the person who asks the initial question is an 'old Romane' who, on finding that the bondsman was the only man left prepared to observe Pompey's funeral rites, assists him in making the pyre. For, he says, 'thou shalt not have all this honor alone' (iv. 291–2). In this reading the 'Bondman' author is the humble means whereby the much more worthy reader honours the dead. The reader is the observer who asks the question and who then claims a part of the 'honor'. So Walton subtly combines compliment and demand; only in the act of reading to which we are being invited, not in the act of writing, does Donne receive adequate commemoration.

PLUTARCHAN VIRTUE AND THE CONSTANT MIND

Within the commonplace that defines godly conduct as reasoned, consistent, and moderate, and sets it against the passionate

---

[26] Izaak Walton, *The Life of Dr. John Donne*, in John Donne, *LXXX Sermons*, edited by John Donne the younger (London, 1640), sig. A5[r].

inconsistencies of the ungodly 'multitude', lies a Plutarchan
opposition. For Plutarch, consistency in thought and action
denotes virtue, and vice—active or latent—is heralded by fluctuating irrationalities. How does he establish his oppositions?
And to what use are they put by his Renaissance inheritors?
Plutarch's comparison of Nicias and Crassus shows him drawing his line from inconsistency to viciousness. He narrates how
each got his wealth, and of Crassus he reports that the wealth was
obtained through usury, but spent for the public good. 'Now',
he decides, 'I cannot but wonder at those men, that deny vice to
be an inequality and disagreement of maners, repugnant in it
selfe, seeing men may honestly spend that which is naughtily
gotten.'[27] At the same time he incidentally defines vice as an
intermingling of the good with the bad, rather than as a pure
negative quality. It is a small step from this to identifying vicious
behaviour with a loss of control, the ascendancy of passion over
reason. Crassus' cupidity accounts for the dubious way in which
his wealth is acquired, but his residual nobility explains how he
disposes of it. When Plutarch attempts to narrate the virtuous
life, his concern is primarily to show an agreement of 'maners'
(a word employed by North to indicate moral conduct),[28] and,
as Wardman argues, this leaves him in something of a dilemma
when his subjects move from goodness to viciousness as they grow
older. This is because Plutarch believes virtue to be innate and
permanent; if, therefore, an initially virtuous character behaves
viciously, then either he is finally expressing his true nature, with
all his former virtue only a feint to conceal this original vice,
or else his later evil must be against his really virtuous nature
and forced by a change in circumstances. In the case of Sulla,
Plutarch is noncommittal, though he gives us both possibilities
to think about:

Sylla . . . in the beginning, was very modest and civill in all his
prosperity . . . And being moreover a man in his youth geven to all
pleasure, deliting to laugh, ready to pity, and weep for tender hart: in
that he became after so cruell and bloody, the great alteracion gave
manifest cause to condemne the increase of honor and authority,
as thonly meanes wherby mens maners continue not such as they

[27] Plutarch, *Lives*, iv. 92; Wardman, *Plutarch's Lives*, 37 n.
[28] See *OED*, 'manners', *sb.* 4.

were . . . But whether that alteracion of nature came by chaunging his state and condicion, or that it was otherwise a violent breaking out of hidden malice, which then came to shewe it selfe, when the way of liberty was layed open: this mater is to be decided in some other treatise.[29]

Elsewhere in the *Life of Sulla* Plutarch links Sulla's inconstancy with his passivity in the face of the fortune which favours him: 'it appeareth', he writes of the young Sulla, 'that he did wholly submit himself unto fortune, acknowledging that he did altogether depend on her' (iii. 272). This being so, Sulla's later behaviour is the logical consequence of his dependence on circumstance, and so the responsibility must rest, not with the circumstances themselves, but with Sulla's response to them. Shortly afterwards Plutarch continues, 'Thus have we sufficiently spoken of the trust he had in the favor of the goddes. And furthermore, he seemed to be very contrary in his manners, and unlike to him selfe' (iii. 273). The juxtaposition of the remarks on fortune and 'the favor of the goddes' with the inconstant, self-contradictory self implies a connection between the two, supplied by the passive spirit's readiness to be swayed by internal whim as by external forces. The faults of the later Sulla appear, Plutarch implies, because he will not use his reason either to subdue his passions or his outward circumstances. A dictator to others, he cannot master himself.

On these terms, the Renaissance life-writer must impose uniformity of character and a concordance of qualities on the virtuous subject. Indeed, it swiftly becomes very important to narrate consistent responses and very problematic to explore how circumstances might affect behaviour. To be altered by fortune is to be unacceptably subject to the vicissitudes of the world. The really virtuous overcome fortune with understanding; they may not change events, but they will not be changed (which implies being diminished) by them. Erasmus, in the *Adagia*, includes the saying 'every man's character moulds his fortune' (*sui cuique more fingunt fortuna*). His remarks upon it quote two phrases cited by Plutarch, the first from Menander, 'because the mind in us is God', and the second from Alcman, 'that "Fortune is the sister of Good principles, Persuasion and Foresight"'.[30]

[29] Wardman, *Plutarch's Lives*, 132–5; Plutarch, *Lives*, iii. 311–12.
[30] Erasmus, *Adages*, in *Works*, xxxiii. 205–6.

In the holy Life, where the rewards of virtue are heavenly, its living proofs will appear in its subject's demeanour rather than in worldly success. Alcman's statement adds to this; it recommends intelligent prudence in upright dealings, but acknowledges the necessity of a reasoned and principled fortitude in the unprincipled and treacherous world. This is a version of ἀπάθεια which also surfaces in Justus Lipsius' *Two Bookes of Constancie*, where constancy is defined as

[. . . *a right and immoveable strength of the minde, neither lifted up, nor pressed down with externall or casuall accidentes.*] By STRENGTH, I understande a stedfastnesse not from opinion, but from iudgement and sound reason. For I would in any case exclude OBSTINACIE (or, as I may more fitly term it, FROWARDNES . . .) . . . the true mother of Constancie is PATIENCE, and lowlinesse of mind, which is, *a voluntarie sufferance without grudging of all things whatsoever can happen to, or in a man.*[31]

Lipsius, however, displays some rather Plutarchan reservations about this.[32] Indifference is not virtue: self-command is. In a discussion of the evils of war, he remarks dryly, 'whoso is not mooved with these matters, nor oppressed with the multitude of so manie and manifold miseries, must eyther be very stayed and wise, or els very hard hearted' (p. 17). We find the same distinction drawn when Plutarch describes how Cornelia mourns for her sons, the Gracchi. She is apparently unmoved, he says, adding that 'some writers report' she may have been driven beyond natural sorrow. He has no time for this:

But in deede they were senselesse to say so, not understandinge, howe that to be nobly borne, and vertuouslie brought up, doth make men temperatly to disgest sorow, and that fortune oftentimes overcomes vertue, which regardeth honestie in all respectes, but yet with any adversity she can not take away the temperaunce from them, whereby they paciently beare it. (v. 275)

Plutarch is here objecting to the assumption that external behaviour passively reflects a state of mind: that his human subjects are at the mercy not only of circumstances but of the passions circumstances engender within them. Rather, as he

---

[31] *Two Bookes of Constancie, written in Latin. by Iustus Lipsius. Containing, Principallie, A Comfortable Conference, in Common Calamities . . . Englished by Iohn Stradling . . .* (London, 1595), 9.

[32] See Wardman, *Plutarch's Lives*, 107–8; Russell, *Plutarch*, 84–5.

describes it, the inner self and its passions may actually and actively be subdued by the observance of a seemly outward deportment. The apparent passivity of the sufferer, the 'patient bearer' of misfortune, he reads as a potency virtually divine in its scope, because it demonstrates the limitations of the power of fortune, or worldly 'accidentes'. In this sense, 'character' may control 'fortune', because 'the mind in us is God'.

Lipsius is in accord. Though holding the Stoics 'in estimation & account', the point upon which he differs from Seneca is that he cannot agree to make both God and 'the actions of the will' 'subject to the wheele of Destiny' (p. 45). While human beings must submit to external circumstances, this is because those circumstances are themselves the will of God. A patient endurance of adversity shows the mind embracing its circumstances, and thus partaking of the will of God; still the 'mind in us'—on rather different terms—'is God'.

Martyrology relies for its polemic success implicitly on this argument. In its narrative, the rectitude of the martyr's cause is fully demonstrated by his conduct. So Foxe describes John Bradford as opposing the indignant passion of a (pro-Bradford) mob with his own moderation and reasonableness, even protecting the 'papistical preacher' Bishop Bourne (whose sermon has set them off in the first place) from reprisals:

At length Bourne seing that the people were ready to put hym in peril (of which he was well warned by the hurling of a drawen dagger at him, as he stode in the pulpit) . . . desired Bradford . . . that he would stand in hys place and speake to the people. Bradford dyd so: he spoke to the people of godly and quiet obedience. The people both sawe and hearde hym gladly . . . after they had heard his godly exhortacion, they left of theyr raging, and at leasure quietly departed eche man to hys house.[33]

A little later it is pointed out to Bradford that the man he has preserved will further Bradford's own destruction: 'thou savest him that will help to burn thee.' Bradford's indifference to his own physical safety shows him as master of his fortune—not because he can avert consequences, but because he does not allow them to affect the rectitude of his actions. In Foxe's anecdote the connection between the rational soul and constant rectitude is strongly implied in the epithets the bystanders apply to each: while

[33] Foxe, *Actes and Monuments* (1563), 1173.

Bradford is a 'good . . . man', Bourne is described as a 'botcherlye beast' (p. 1173).

These are not assumptions confined to Protestant martyrology. George Ellyot assumes their ubiquity in using them to discredit Catholic virtue when he describes his betrayal of Edmund Campion. His account (in all other respects short and businesslike) takes time to describe the fear of a young priest named Filbie, captured with Campion:

> About midnight we were put into great fear by reason of a very great cry and noise that the said FILBIE made in his sleep; which wakened the most that were that night in the house, and that in such sort that every man almost thought that some of the prisoners had been broken from us and escaped . . . Master LYDCOT was the first that came unto them: and when the matter was examined, it was found no more but that the said FILBIE was in a dream; and, as he said, he verily thought one to be a ripping down his body and taking out his bowels.[34]

It seems unlikely that Ellyot included this scenario for compassionate reasons. Part of the effect intended is certainly *pour encourager les autres*, but Ellyot is also undermining Filbie, diminishing him by reporting him terrified. Thomas Alfield's account of Campion's death exploits the same relationship in Campion's defence. '*Spectaculum facti sumus deo*', Campion quotes to his condemned companions; 'These are the words of S. Paule, Englished thus: we are made a spectacle, or a sight unto God, unto his angels, and unto men.'[35] By demonstrating such constancy in the face of death, Campion too is clear that his cause is vindicated by the demeanour of its martyrs.

The reverse connection—of inconstancy with vice or error— is also widely assumed. Charron's *Of Wisedome* includes an essay on 'Inconstancie' in which he writes:

> Irresolution on the one part, and afterwards inconstancy and instability, are the most common and apparent vices in the nature of man.

---

[34] George Ellyot, *A Very True Report of the Apprehension and Taking of that Arch-Papist EDMUND CAMPION, the Pope his Right Hand, with Three other Lewd Jesuit Priests*, in *Tudor Tracts*, with an introduction by A. F. Pollard (London, 1903), 464.

[35] [Thomas Alfield], *A True Report of the Death and Martyrdome of M. Campion Jesuite and Preiste, and M. Sherwin and M. Bryan Preistes, at Tiborne the First of December 1581* (London, 1581), sig. C1.

Doubtlesse our actions doe many times so contradict one the other in so strange a maner, that it seemes impossible they should all come foorth of one and the same shop; we alter and we feele it not, we escape as it were, from our selves, and we rob our selves, *ipso nobis furto subducimur*.[36]

Although Charron is writing about behaviour, and not the narration of behaviour, nevertheless he uses an image which suggests the constant self to be a matter of construction, rather than a simple innate quality; contradictory actions, he argues, hardly seem to come from 'the same shop' (using 'shop' to mean a place where artefacts are made as well as sold). Nevertheless, it is the constructed self which is the 'true' one, the one of which we are robbed (as with Plutarch's Sulla) by our own inconstancy, even though we may not 'feele' our alteration. Our conscious self-construction, the action of will and reason upon demeanour, makes a 'real' self, whereas the involuntary alterations of which we are not aware are betrayals, *not* revelations, of this 'real' self.

When this principle is applied to the chronological narration of character—to the writing of a Life—the consistency of the narrated self becomes imperative. Lord Herbert of Cherbury makes this very plain in the opening paragraph of his *Life and Raigne of King Henry the Eighth*:

It is not easie to write of that Princes History, of whom no one thing may constantly be affirmed. Changing of manners and condition alters the coherence of parts, which should give a uniform description. Nor is it probable that contradictories should argue to the Same Person: so that nothing can shake the credit of a Narration more, than if it grow unlike it selfe.[37]

Cherbury is certainly seeing changeableness here as undesirable. His emphasis, though, is on the narrative problems changeableness makes, rather than straightforwardly on its moral implications for the Tudor king. He might not want to insist on these, after all. By taking 'uniform description' as a given, and by using the word 'credit' of the narration—a word implying virtue as well as plausibility—Cherbury suggests that it is 'creditable' to make a consistent artefact out of intractable material. If it is not 'probable' to find 'contradictories' arguing to the 'Same Person',

---

[36] Charron, *Of Wisedome*, 136.

[37] Edward, Lord Herbert of Cherbury, *The Life and Raigne of King Henry the Eighth* (London, 1649), 1.

then narrative 'credit' must become located in the wrenching of those contradictions into a consistent and harmonious pattern, whatever the evidence to the contrary. In effect, Cherbury has first identified his subject as naturally unfitted for exemplary narrative, and has then announced his intention to disguise this fact by forcing his evidence into the consistent pattern exemplary narrative requires.

Cherbury's difficulty—and the dubiety of his solution to it— had already been identified by Montaigne in an essay 'Of the Inconstancie of our Actions', which shows an apprehension of the 'self' as diffuse, infinitely subtler than Charron's imitative essay was to be. Considering 'actions' primarily as narratives of actions, Montaigne locates moral rectitude in the accurate reporting of inevitable inconsistencies, rather than in the deliberate construction of the self as consistent, either before or after its external behaviour might be recorded by a life writer: 'I have thought, that even good Authors, doe ill, and take a wrong course, wilfully to opinionate themselves about framing a solid and constant contexture of us. They chuse a universall ayre, and following that image, range and interpret all a mans actions; which if they cannot wrest sufficiently, they remit them into dissimulation.'[38] Montaigne here dismisses exemplary narration and its needs. 'Dissimulation' is simply a 'wrong course'. Indeed, his use of the word 'image' for the dissimulated text is suggestive. It connects the assumption that actions are transparent, consistent with each other and adding up to an interpretable whole, with iconographic depiction, where holiness is assumed to be visually transmissible. So the comeliness of the features reflects the comeliness of the soul through the employment of conventions which have little to do with the accurate reproduction of an individual face.

Walton's *Lives* are explicitly exemplary. He must, therefore, write consistency into his characters. In the case of Donne, Walton's attempt has led to strictures from later critics that he has suppressed Donne's other, younger, more profane self. Although Walton's text is certainly one slanted in favour of

---

[38] Michel de Montaigne, 'Of the Inconstancie of our Actions', in *Essaies*, trans. Florio, ii. 8. Walton also owned an edition of the Florio Montaigne: see n. 22 above.

Dr Donne, Dean of St Paul's, the conclusion that tends to follow—that Walton's Donne is therefore, in Montaigne's terms, a text he has remitted 'into dissimulation'—should be reconsidered.

Walton is following Plutarch, and later Charron, in assuming there is a 'true self' to be fostered and discovered in each subject. While the virtue of the true self is innate, its discovery involves an effort of will and reason, of self-shaping and self-mastery, on the subject's part. The task of the biographer is to make clear the relationship between innate virtue and the outward striving for it. To 'follow' such an 'image' of virtue is not to obscure the truth of the diffused self; the 'image' is better seen as a map, available to the biographer and the subject (and ultimately to the reader), which facilitates the finding and articulation of a self which is not diffuse, but which corresponds closely enough to the image to appear unified, a product of the 'single eye' of virtue.

In Clarke's *Lives*, while relatively little space is given to early life, that space is given over to the establishment of its subject's innate virtue. This is confirmed by 'conversion'—a word which (especially in a predestinarian climate) tends to mean the considered confirmation of early virtuous traits, not their reversal from bad to good. Clarke's allusions to the process are short, almost casual; his subjects, from showing the promise of virtue, simply choose, in their conversion, to foster virtue in their life conduct. Plutarch's assumption of virtue as innate suits narratives of the elect perfectly. The adult revelation of a 'calling', a radical change of life, is almost criticized in the following passage from *The Life and Death of Master Richard Capel*:

> He saw with a clear eye through all the painted glosses of those that were given to change, and therefore was not moved at all with any thing that was said and done in that kinde; he was true to his Religion [the Church of England], and clave close all along to his first principles, *holding fast the faith that was once . . . and but once delivered to the Saints . . .*
>
> This constant and stable man was set up as a sure Sea-Mark. Let us stand to his step though we stand alone . . . When the wilde humour is spent, men will return home again.[39]

The context makes it clear that the 'wilde humour' is for variations in religious practice. Capel's constancy is set against it, and others 'given to change'. Conversion as revelation strongly

[39] Clarke, *Lives*, 307.

implies radical change. Capel's eye is 'clear', a single eye; the 'painted glosses' represent an (unsuccessful) attempt to obscure this 'clear eye' with images of the self altered by manufactured additions. Montaigne's image is reversed.

I have introduced Clarke's endorsement of constancy, and limitations on 'conversion', as something against which Walton's Donne can be measured. Donne too shows the promise of virtue as a youth, but is 'converted' twice: once at 19, when he chooses the Church of England against Roman Catholicism, and once when he becomes a priest. The first most resembles the kind of 'conversion' experienced by Clarke's subjects, being a reasoned choice and not a spiritual experience. But this is not true of the second. Donne's ordination transforms his life, and the reiteration of the words 'now' and 'new' throughout the passage describing his 'calling' makes this plain.[40] Walton has in fact chosen to represent Donne as subject to momentous change, and this in itself is a reflection on his stability. The narrative prominence of his conversion is an index of the former profanity Walton never openly describes.

For the 'map' of virtue is not, in Plutarchan terms, really equivalent to a formula either for living or its narration. Nicias and Crassus, even Sulla, are not Plutarch's examples of the 'one or two paier' of bad men. Rather, they are offered as essentially virtuous, but with the distinguishing features and faults which make a more individualized characterization possible. Plutarch's characters are analysed in the light of his idea of virtue and judged accordingly, each action as it corresponds—or not—to the idea. In the same way, once Walton has established that virtue was innate in Donne, he is left with a surprising amount of freedom in his characterization.

He chooses a pattern where the original falling-off from the ideal is balanced by a dramatic alteration to holiness in later life, and his reference to the converted Donne as 'a second St. *Austine*' (pp. 47–8) clearly indicates his source for the pattern. The faults obscuring Donne's virtue before his conversion are explicitly identified as faults of passion, a lack of self-mastery, which left him 'unlike himself'. 'Inconstancy', Donne had complained in Holy Sonnet XIX, 'unnaturally hath begot | A

---

[40] Walton, *Lives*, 48; see below, pp. 177–9.

constant habit'; and perhaps Walton had this at the back of his mind when he was combing Donne's own work for bits to use. Yet when he draws attention to Donne's self-contradiction with a Donnean reference, he chooses a far earlier work: 'His marriage', writes Walton, 'was the remarkable error of his life; an error which though he had a wit able and very apt to maintain Paradoxes, yet he was very far from justifying it' (p. 60).

In this way Donne's marriage is made to stand for the ascendance of passion over right reason which characterized Donne's youth, and which made his character a 'Paradox': that is, a life-writer's problem. If this 'error' of Donne's is set against Walton's description of Herbert's marriage, it is perhaps possible to identify marriage itself as being, for Walton, a code standing for a dangerously instinctive impulse to joy, which might undermine the true, the self-constructed self governed purely by will and reason:

> Mr. *Danvers* . . . often and publickly declar'd a desire that Mr. *Herbert* would marry . . . his Daughter *Jane* . . . And he had often said the same to Mr. *Herbert* himself . . . and . . . the like to *Jane*, and so much commended Mr. *Herbert* to her, that *Jane* became so much a Platonick, as to fall in love with Mr. *Herbert* unseen.
>
> This was fair preparation for a Marriage . . . some friends to both parties, procur'd their meeting; at which time a mutual affection entred into both their hearts . . . insomuch, that she chang'd her name into *Herbert*, the third day after this first interview.
>
> This haste might in others be thought a *Love-phrensie*, or worse: but it was not; for they had wooed so like Princes, as to have select Proxies: such, as were true friends to both parties; such as well understood Mr. *Herberts*, and her temper of mind; and also their Estates so well . . . that, the suddenness was justifiable . . . (pp. 285–6)

This passage is hedged anxiously about with provisos. In all respects the marriage is as unlike Donne's as could be, urged initially by Jane's father and not the couple themselves, growing on her side into love carefully defined and acceptably limited by the fact that their physical bodies have not even stood in the same space together. While Herbert himself appears to have needed at least to see his future wife before providing his half of the resulting 'mutual affection', as Walton describes it the main business of the courtship is conducted by the 'friends to both parties'. The suddenness of the marriage shows, not their subjection to the desire of the body, but the absence of it: without a 'Love-phrensie' (or 'worse'), there is no need for courtship. Herbert, unlike Donne, has made a rational marriage, not a passionate one, a marriage based on calculations about 'Estates' and compatibility, and as a result his character remains undivided and consistent, and his conversion is simply a dedicating of his existing powers and virtues to one end, and not a transformation.

Walton, in fact, prefers to depict consistency. In Donne's case he departs from it to a surprising degree to accommodate him, though he translates him into terms which make it possible to read him (more or less) as a Plutarchan exemplar.

PORTRAYING VIRTUE

There has so far been an abundance of visual metaphors, such as Montaigne's 'image'. Biography, after all, is *portrayal*. This requires us to think about the human face: to what extent is the imagery of portraiture used to delineate virtue, or at least moral types; and is this a Plutarchan trait?

At the beginning of the *Life of Pompey* Plutarch describes his hero's physical appearance: 'The cast and soft moving of his eyes, had a certaine resemblaunce (as they sayd) of the statues and images of king Alexander. And bicause every man gave him that name, he did not refuse it him selfe: insomuch there were some which sporting-wise did openly call him Alexander' (iv. 206–7). It is a considered comparison. The reader is not told very much about what kind of 'cast' the two heroes share; only that they share it. This physical resemblance, the details of which are left so doubtful, stands for a different kind of 'cast'—not of the eye, but of the mind. For in the eye's expression the shape of the soul may be read, and Pompey's is identified as one in which 'every man' reads 'Alexander'. Pompey himself accepts the label, with all its (useful) implications for his conduct and actions.

At the beginning of the *Life of Alexander* itself, where Plutarch makes his famous assertion that he intends 'not to write histories, but only lives', a 'life' is characterized as a narrative where individual details are privileged over public events, the 'noblest deedes' often being less expressive of 'mens vertues and vices' than 'a light occasion, a word, or some sporte'. But to clarify this difference of emphasis, Plutarch compares his methods with the techniques of portraiture: 'painters and drawers of pictures', he explains, will ignore the rest of the body in order to 'take the resemblaunce of the face and favor of the countenance, in the which consisteth the judgement of their maners and disposition'. In the same way, he argues, the writers of lives are at liberty to neglect the broad outline for the sake of the significant detail: 'Even so they must geve us leave to seeke out the signes and tokens of the mind only, and thereby shewe the life . . . referring you unto others to write the warres, battells, and other great thinges they did' (iv. 298). Plutarch finds visual portraiture a useful metaphor for the 'signes and tokens of the mind' which he identifies as the distinguishing feature of the Life. When we read that Pompey's expression reminded those around him of Alexander, we are not to assume that Pompey necessarily resembled Alexander's 'statues and images' very closely in other respects; only that the same sort of soul, the 'soul of nobility', gazes out of his eyes.

Plutarch makes the same face-versus-body point in writing about Sulla. The *Life of Sulla*, which charts an unstable mind, is very evidently a *portrait*, not (say) a statue. Plutarch dismisses Sulla's outline in a few words, referring his reader to those 'statues and images' of Sulla which 'yet remain' (iii. 266). This is strongly reminiscent of Plutarch's readiness to send the reader to other historians for accounts of the 'warres, battells, and other great things they did' in the *Life of Alexander*. But he describes Sulla's face in great detail: 'But for his eyes, they were like fire, and wonderfull redde: and the colour of his face withall, made them the more fearefull to beholde. For he was copper nosed, and that was full of white streakes here and there: whereuppon they say that the surname of Sylla was geven him, by reason of his colour' (iii. 266). 'Syl', explains North's marginal note, 'in laten, signifieth oker, which becommeth red when it is put to the fire.' As Pompey's appearance gains him the new name of Alexander, so Sulla too is named and defined by the expression of his eyes and his countenance, 'fearefull to behold'. We are explicitly being invited to read character from this description: Plutarch immediately explains that 'it is not amisse, to search out the naturall disposition of this man by such outward marks and tokens'. Sulla's birthmark and reddened eyes indicate him to be heated by an inner fire. His expression breathes this heat of the mind through his inflamed eyes, and thus his mind is characterized as dominated by passion, as fire is an element of destruction and a symbol of unwilled, unreasoning power.

It is also implicit that the fearfulness of Sulla's countenance, its ugliness and deformity, represents his uncontrolled passions, and so his vulnerability to vice. Certainly Plutarch uses beauty and regularity of feature as an image for virtuous behaviour, as in his description of the popular assessment of Callicratides in the *Life of Lysander*. Callicratides is unpopular because his plain dealing contrasts unattractively with Lysander's opportunistic promotion of any who would serve his own interests. In spite of this, however, the people give Callicratides his due, commending 'the perfection of his vertue, as they would have done the image of some demy-god done after the old facion, which had bene of singular beawty' (iii. 229). Callicratides' political ethics are outworn and do not meet contemporary demands: nevertheless, the image of his unfashionable honesty is an image of 'perfection', flawed only by the passing of time, and originally of 'singular beawty'.[41]

But how does this tendency to use the face as the mind's map, and to read vice or virtue in its features, correspond with Plutarch's assertion, in the *Life of Cimon*, that the 'image and portraiture' of men achieved by the narration of their 'manners and condicions' is 'farre more excellent, then the picture that representeth any mans person or shape only' (iii. 328)? Plutarch seems, perversely, to use visual imagery for inward rather than outward comparisons. As Richard Wendorf points out in an article on the parallel arts of portraiture and biography, Plutarch is here employing a rhetorical commonplace (we find Tacitus making the same point at the close of the *Agricola*, where he asserts the shape of Agricola's mind to be superior to his bronze image),[42] while

---

[41] See Wardman, *Plutarch's Lives*, 31–2, for a slightly different reading of this passage.

[42] Tacitus, *The Life of Iulius Agricola*, published in the Second Part of Tacitus, *Annales*, translated by Richard Greenwey and Henry Savile, 5th edn. (London, 1622), 202 (2nd pag.): 'So I would counsell thy daughter and wife to reuerence the memories of their father and husband . . . recognizing the glory and image of his minde, rather then of his body: not that I dislike of images cut in marble or metall, but . . . the shape of the minde is externall, which wee may represent and expresse, not by matter and Art borrowed abroad, but by our own manners within.' Note again the moralized use of 'manners' in this translation of Savile's (first published in 1591).

his imagery and the specificity of his comparisons make a strong claim that the two arts can employ the same kinds of techniques for the same object.[43] North's translation actually chooses the word 'portraiture' to describe biographical writing, whereas actual drawings, paintings, or sculptures are much more narrowly defined as a man's 'person or shape only'. While the reader is again being offered a distinction between the inexpressive outline and 'facial' (that is, characterized) detail, the use of visual terms like 'portraiture' for characterization modifies the assertion that narration can express more of a man's character than painting can.

Plutarch continues the passage with an analogy between the ways in which character should be delineated in the two arts:

> But like as when we will have a passing fayer face drawen, and lively coun-terfeated, and that hath an excellent good grace withall, yet some manner of bleamishe or imperfection in it: we will not allowe the drawer to leave it out altogether, nor yet too curiously to shewe it, bicause the one would deforme the counterfeate, and the other make it very unlikely. Even so, bicause it is a hard thing . . . to describe a man, whose life should altogether be innocent, and perfect, we must first study to wryte his vertues at large, and thereby seek perfectly to represent the troth, even as the life it selfe. But where by chaunce we finde certaine faultes and errors in their doinges, they are rather to be thought imperfections of vertue not altogether accomplished, then any purposed wickednes proceeding of vice, or certaine malice. Which we shall not neede too curiously to expresse in our history, but rather to passe them lightly over, of reverent shame to the meer frayelty of mans nature. (iii. 328–9)

This is a very clear explanation of the generous way in which Plutarch interprets the rules of representing human beings. The likely is to be balanced carefully against a requirement to delin-eate, as nearly as possible, the 'perfect'—a word which equally denotes moral and physical qualities. To 'represent the troth' in these terms, is to 'wryte' a subject's 'vertues at large'. When the intention is to delineate virtue, then to stress deformity of character and appearance is to be as 'untruthful' as to leave it out altogether. Such an intention is unambiguously exemplary.

However, in an opening passage of the *Life of Pericles* Plutarch implies that, while Lives are always exemplary, real portraits

---

[43] Richard Wendorf, 'Ut Pictura Biographia: Biography and Portrait Paint-ing as Sister Arts', in Wendorf (ed.), *Articulate Images: The Sister Arts from Hogarth to Tennyson* (Minneapolis, 1983), 98–124 (pp. 101–2).

are not. Yet in doing so, he employs a visual image as a moral
metaphor: 'Like as the eye is most delited with the lightest and
freshest cullers', he argues, 'even so we must give our mindes unto
those sightes, which by looking upon them doe draw profit and
pleasure unto us.' He goes on to associate this 'profit and pleasure' with 'an earnest love, and desire to follow' the virtues read
in Lives. And here, he states, is the difference between narration
and visual representation; whereas 'any young gentleman' gazing
on a statue would be unlikely to wish he had carved it—'contrary
oftentimes, when we see the worke, we mislike the worke man'—
the reader of an exemplary Life will automatically be filled with
a 'resolute desire to do the like. And this is the reason, why me
thought I should continew still to write the lives of noble men'
(ii. 1–3). Yet in these terms, it should be noted, the 'worke man'
is equated not with a biography's author, but with its *subject*. The
real carver of a virtuous life is the person who lives it; its
recorder, fascinatingly, is left out of the assessment altogether.

This all shows Plutarch, not unnaturally, to be far more at
ease with visual representation when it is used simultaneously as
moral metaphor. It is not that visual representation as a discrete
art is perceived as necessarily amoral, but that the face—whether
described in words or represented in a portrait—should offer
moral signs which can be read, either of virtue or (as in the case
of Sulla) of particular frailties. But even regarding portraiture as
imaging a metaphor of this kind, especially when it is allied with
a concentration on the generous depiction of imitable virtue, leaves
it open for those Renaissance life-writers influenced by Plutarch
to postulate, and depict, faces which are deemed to express virtue
in their physical characteristics.

It should also be said that the fact of the Reformation, in itself,
could not simply cancel out centuries of iconic depiction, and that
significant remnants of the iconic, re-presented under different
intellectual justifications, also inform the examples which follow.
Thus Foxe includes in his *Actes and Monuments* of 1563 both
a bitter interchange between Thomas Arundel, the unreformed
archbishop of Canterbury, and William Thorpe, where Thorpe
(cheered on by the Protestant reader) condemns all images of the
saints and of the Trinity, *and* a description of Jerome of Prague
'knelinge downe before an Image whiche was like unto the picture of master Ihon Hus' in 'devout prayer' before being burnt,

'bound . . . fast with cordes and chaines of yron to the said Image'.[44]

The chroniclers of the early reformers certainly do not confine their use of the visual to metaphor. Indeed, collections of the lives of the godly, from Beza's *Icones* to Clarke's *Lives*, combine their narratives with actual portraits (often the very same ones used again and again) which are there for the virtually devotional purpose of contemplating different versions of the godly countenance.[45]

This iconic aspect is gingerly defined by Beza in his dedicatory epistle (to a very young James VI of Scotland) appearing before the *Icones*. He acknowledges that to include images in his book is to lay himself open to the accusations of 'les aduersaires (que nous accusons d'estre idolatres . . .)', but argues that 'la pourtraiture, tailleure, & autre telles sciences' can and should be put to 'divers bon vsages'.[46] Why, he asks, should not these 'urais pourtraits' act so that

> nous ne gaignions ce point de pouuoir contempler, &, par maniere de dire, deuiser auec ceux de qui la presence nous estoit honnorable tandi qu'ils viuoyent? . . . Ie puis dire cela de moy, qu'en lisant les liures de tels personnages, & surtout, iettant les yeux sur leur effigies, ie suis autant esmeu, & poussé aussi viuement en sainctes pensees, que si ie les voyois encor preschans, admonestans & reprenans leurs auditeurs. (sigs. (∴) 2^v–3)

For Beza, to possess the faces of the godly is to become included in a community of the departed saints as if there were no divide between living and dead. A kind of afterlife is conferred upon the dead; they are active through the godly thoughts their images inspire. Actually, from the *Icones* it is clear—and not only from the title—that the portraits are the main point. They have, he announces evasively, 'venus en mes mains', and the attendant 'briefue description de la uie & vacation de chascun d'iceux' is just a small extra of his own (sig. (∴) 3).

---

[44] Foxe, *Actes and Monuments* (1563), 143–57 and 248–9.

[45] Cf. e.g. the portraits of John Huss appearing in Theodore Beza, *Icones* (1581), 5; Jacobus Verheiden, *Praestantium aliqvot Theologorum, qvi Rom. Antichristum Praecipue Oppugnarunt, Effigies* . . . (The Hague, 1602), 5; Thomas Fuller, *Abel Redevivus, or the Dead Yet Speaking* . . . (London, 1651), 12.

[46] Beza, *Icones*, sig. (∴) 2^v.

While the portraits of the *Icones* are described as 'urais' (sig. (∴) 2ᵛ), they are, of course, highly stylized. Although the individuals depicted are very distinct from each other (compare Melanchthon, p. 28, with Huss, p. 5) every subject is shown, often in profile, as composed and grave, sometimes (as in the case of Jerome of Prague) actually in the martyr's flames, but with an absolutely self-possessed look and stance. This is, of course, a visible rectitude; Foxe describes Bradford at his martyrdom as dying 'without any alteration of . . . countenance, being void of all feare'.[47]

Even in those collections which privilege written text over image more than Beza's does, the image is often included in the text as a focus for a kind of devotion. The portrait of Berengarius which appears in Verheiden's 1602 collection shows him with his eyes and one hand raised to heaven, and the text begins: 'Ecce Tibi, Spectator, BERENGARIUM illum. Hunc tu suspice, & admirare, qui, coelum ipsum suspiciens dextraq[ue] designans, ostendere videtur locum in quem corpore suo, Apostolis aspicientibus, vere elevatus receptusque est CHRISTUS . . .'[48] When Verheiden's text and the portrait are reproduced in the *History of the Moderne Protestant Divines* of 1637, the translator keeps the sentiment, even though the portrait has been shrunk to the face only and the pointing hand is missing: 'Behold the *Effigies* of this great and worthy Scholler, whose hand and eye poynt towards Heaven, in the sight of his Apostles, whither his Saviour Jesus is ascended.'[49] The upward-pointing hand and eye obviously signify virtue, and surface in Character books which deal with virtuous types. Nicholas Breton's *The Good and the Badde* (1616) says of the 'Good Man' that he is 'the image of God . . . He hath a face alwayes to looke upward', and of the 'Holy Man' that he 'hath an eye to look upward towards God'.[50]

Another visible sign of grace is the 'grave' countenance, which the reader is invited to contemplate in the portrait of Matthew

[47] Foxe, *Actes and Monuments* (1563), 1215.

[48] Jacobus Verheiden, *Praestantium aliqvot Theologorum . . .* , sigs. ?1–1ᵛ.

[49] Jacobus Verheiden and H[enry] H[olland], *History of the Moderne Protestant Divines*, trans. D. L.[upton] (London, 1637), 1–2.

[50] Nicholas Breton, *The Good and the Badde, or, Descriptions of the Worthies and Unworthies of this Age*, in *The Works in Verse and Prose of Nicholas Breton*, edited by A. B. Grosart, 2 vols. (Edinburgh, 1879), ii. 10 and 15.

Parker appearing in the *History of the Moderne Protestant Divines*. 'This countenance speaks Gravity', explains the text, 'and hee was no lesse than he appeares.'[51] Even where a particular aspect of virtue is not specified, the reader is more generally invited to read the signs of grace in an image. Verses on Oecolampadius in *Abel Redevivus* begin: 'Reader, behold the rare-adorned Face | Of him, whose very lookes import a grace.'[52]

Physical description still functions as a moral index even when there is no actual portrait. Beza's *Life of Calvin* mentions his 'forehead so reverende', and states that when dying 'he was of such a countenance, that hys only loke did plainly testify wyth what fayth and hope he was furnished'.[53]

We cannot know how far these stylized signs of the soul are applied with hindsight to men who were deemed to deserve them, rather than known to have possessed them. But many of them are located in gesture, expression, or controllable facial aspects, like the length or abundance of hair, rather than in involuntary and naturally occurring bodily features, and many of them—as with Berengarius' upward-pointing hand—are clearly iconographic conventions which require a static, deliberate pose. We often do not know if their portraits resembled their subjects physically, though in one case at least evidence exists of one that did not. The often-reproduced *Icones* portrait shows John Huss to be a bearded man in middle life. Yet Huss was young at his death, and fifteenth-century pictures of him show him to be clean-shaven, with a round, young, rather forgettable face.[54] Clearly the grave, bearded, implicitly patriarchal image was chosen for its many contemplative advantages.

A much later example demonstrates how inevitably hairiness went with patriarchy. John Whitefoote's funeral sermon for Joseph Hall, bishop of Norwich, takes as its text Genesis 47: 29, 'And the time drew nigh that *Israel* must die'. The sermon is

[51] *History of the Moderne Protestant Divines*, 277 (misnumbered 269).

[52] *Abel Redevivus*, 117–18.

[53] Theodore Beza, *A Discourse . . . Conteyning in Briefe the Historie of the Life and Death of Maister Iohn Calvin, translated by I.S.* (London, 1564), sigs. C5ᵛ and E2ᵛ.

[54] See illustrations in Thomas Fudge, 'Myth, Heresy and Propaganda in the Radical Hussite Movement, 1409–1437', unpublished doctoral dissertation, University of Cambridge (1992), 378–9.

accompanied by a portrait of Hall, neat, grave, with an abundant beard and a little hair showing under his cap. In the biographical portion of the sermon that follows, Whitefoote proposes a 'parallel of the Persons' of Jacob and Hall—an explicitly Plutarchan technique. He extends his parallel to the physical, from which he reads comparisons of temperament: '*Israel*', he writes, 'was a *smooth* man (of body), as himself saith, Gen. 32. 11.'[55] Hall's smoothness is applied to his 'smooth, terse Wit, and Tongue' (p. 65). (Esau, presumably, would have been an unkempt speaker, as well as having hairy hands.) Later Whitefoote has it both ways when he makes it plain that Jacob's smoothness of body will be solely an image for his behaviour (rather than having anything to do with real hair), by reading Hall's patriarchal virtues in his old age into the appearance of his hair and beard. 'He died', writes Whitefoote

in *a good old age*, full of days and full of good works; *Canus Virtutibus*, White with Virtues. *He came to his Grave in a full age, like as a shock of Corn cometh in his season* [marg. *Job* 5.26]. He was crowned with the silver Crown of age in his gray hairs; *Prov.* 16. 31. and now is crowned with the Golden Crown of Immortality. (p. 71)

Here Hall's spiritual crown is invoked in the greying of his hair. His virtues are 'White', the hairy crown 'silver', the hirsute 'shock of Corn' prefigures the 'Golden Crown of Immortality' which will replace and transcend those silver signs of his age. As Plutarch conferred the mark of a hero on Pompey, so Whitefoote has endowed Hall with the mark of a patriarch.

COLLECTION, COMPARISON, AND PARALLEL

While the reading of virtuous signs into the visual image has a strong precedent in Plutarch, he is by no means its only source; the following chapter more appropriately discusses the others. However, Plutarch is the main source for the Renaissance tendency to present, as it were, a conference of portraits, either in

[55] John Whitefoote, Ἰσραὴλ Ἀγχιθανής. *Deaths Alarum, or, the Presage of Approaching Death: Given in a Funeral Sermon . . . for the Right Reverend Joseph Hall, Late Lord Bishop of Norwich . . .* (London, 1656), 67–9.

collections or in the comparison of two virtuous types.[56] Plutarch's distinctive technique was, of course, the parallel, and the use to which the parallel was put by Renaissance proto-biographers is important.

The parallel is rooted in didactic method. It adapts classical rhetorical comparison to narrative. The rhetorical comparison as a laudatory device had a separate Renaissance history in sacred oratory which Erasmus discusses in *Ecclesiastae*, though he has grave reservations about its use. He argues that comparison has given rise in this context to a tradition of competitive praise between different Orders (the Franciscans for St Francis, the Augustinians for St Augustine), escalating to such a degree that its excesses obscure the proper praise of God.[57]

However, Erasmus is alive to its possibilities for non-competitive moral comparison. As Plutarch uses it, differing characteristics (not in themselves necessarily virtues) are assessed as they operate for good within their possessors' different spheres and circumstances. So his comparison of Titus Quintus Flaminius and Philopoemon takes into account that Flaminius 'wanne honor by meanes of the power of Rome, when it florished most', whereas Philopoemon 'made himselfe famous by his deedes, when Greece beganne to stoupe and fall all together'. 'Thus', he concludes, 'the deedes of the one, were common to all the Romaines: and the deedes of the other, were private to himselfe alone' (iii. 108).

Erasmus takes up the method in a letter to Jodocus Jonas, where he compares, in parallel biographical sketches, the Franciscan friar Jehan Vitrier and the divine John Colet, dean of St Paul's.[58] Erasmus intends to provide Jonas with patterns of

---

[56] Melchior Adamus, in the 'Epistola Dedicatoria' [to the Duke of Silesia] prefacing his collection of the lives of German reformers, identifies his three main models as the patriarchal histories in the Pentateuch and elsewhere in the Old Testament, the Gospels and the Acts of the New, and Plutarch's parallel *Lives*. See *Vitae Germanorum Theologorum, qvi Superiori Seculo Ecclesiam Christi Voces Scriptisqve Propagarunt et Propugnarunt* . . . (Heidelberg, 1620), sigs. >:< 2ᵛ–3.

[57] Erasmus, *Ecclesiastae, sive de Ratione Concionandi* . . . (Basle, 1535), 157.

[58] 'Letter to Jodocus Jonas on Vitrier and Colet, June 13, 1521', in *Christian Humanism and the Reformation: Selected Writings*, ed. John C. Olin (New York, 1965), 164–91. The letter was translated by Martin Tyndall in 1533, but no copy now exists, and it may never have been printed. See E. J. Devereux, *A Checklist of English Translations of Erasmus to 1700*, Oxford Bibliographical Society

reform from the conduct of the two men operating from within the Church, and so perhaps acting as a corrective to Luther's more extreme example. Although he does not make this second motive explicit, he does the first, writing that he is offering the sketches 'gladly . . . the rather, from an impression that you are trying to find some eminent pattern of religion by which to regulate your own course of life'.[59]

Jonas had evidently asked only for the sketch of Colet, and the Vitrier is Erasmus' idea; he remarks, 'if I give you two portraits instead of one, you will be the gainer' (p. 165). Variety, he makes clear, is the object:

It will be for you to select from each what you think most conducive to true religion. And if you ask which of the two I prefer, I deem them worthy of equal praise, considering that they were in circumstances so unlike. On the one hand it was a great thing for Colet, in worldly circumstances such as his, to have steadily followed the call not of natural inclination but of Christ. On the other hand, the merit of Vitrier makes yet a fairer show in having attained, amid such conditions of life, to so much of the Gospel spirit as he displayed. It is as though a fish were to contract no marshy flavor, though living in a marsh. (p. 191)

Like Plutarch, Erasmus is using the parallel partly for the freedom it confers to assess context and circumstance through comparison—to make considered, *relative* judgements without abandoning set patterns.

Even outside comparison, some sixteenth-century life-writers show a Plutarchan readiness to consider qualities, not necessarily virtues in themselves, as they proved either explicable or useful in context. Melanchthon's assessment of Luther's 'vehemencie' as a quality helpful to the new Church (although not in itself a sign of Luther's godliness) appeals for its authority to the practice of the 'autentick writers' narrating Lives of 'Hercules, Cimon and other'. Such subjects, he argues, although presented as 'deformed and misshapen', were 'yet apt and upryght in

(Oxford, 1968), 19. Large parts of the letter as it relates to Colet, together with additional information from an epistle on Colet by More, appear in a *Life of Colet*, edited by Thomas Smith and appended to John Colet, *A Sermon of Conforming and Reforming Made to the Convocation at S. Pauls Church in London . . . Writ an Hundred and Fifty Years since* (Cambridge, 1661), 59–80.

[59] 'Letter to Jodocus Jonas', in *Christian Humanism and The Reformation*, 165.

excellent exploites'.[60] Beza, in the *Lyfe and Death of Maister Iohn Calvin*, develops exactly the same point: 'There are others which have reported hym to bee very cholericke, I wyll not make of a man an Angell, yet notwithstanding, bicause I do know how marvellously God hath bene served by that same very vehemencie, I ought not to keepe silent that which is true.'[61] Beza's reasons why Calvin had a short temper, 'besydes his own naturall inclination to choller', are all circumstantial: his 'marvellous prompt' wit which made him impatient of the 'folly of many', the burden of the 'multitude and infinite varietie of the affaires for the Church of GOD', and lastly the graphic list of his 'great and continuall diseases' (sigs. C1^v–2 and D2^v–3).

In the *Icones* Beza presents reformers in complementary pairs. Zwingli and Oecolampadius are such a pair, their portraits appearing together on a double page. Beza takes as his point of contact between the two men that they had 'vn mesme désir de seruir à Dieu', and, more specifically, that they died 'en mesme annee'. This means he can show their very different deaths as comparably holy. Of Zwingli, he writes that he, 'exerçant son ministere en l'armee, fut tué en bataille, & son corps reduit en cendres par l'ennemi'. Oecolampadius, however, dies not by violence but by disease:

Pour le regard d'Oecolampade, peu de temps apres comme il s'employ oit à consoler par la parole de Dieu & par exemples de saincte vie son troupeau griefuement affligé de peste, il fut emporté du monde par c'este maladie, & rendant l'ame paisiblement à son sauueur, alla se reioindre à son frere & compagnon d'armes, dessus les cieux, en vne meilleure vie.[62]

Here they become really complementary: companions in arms who become one through the metaphor of the spiritual battle.

This modifies Plutarchan practice, since Plutarch's pairs are only linked together by their life-writer. But the writer of the early modern Life is likely to want to establish an accord—often presented as a holy friendship—between the different patterns of virtue he compares, depicting them as part of a loving yet varied godly community. So Beza describes Zwingli and Oecolampadius as knit together in a godly relationship, their portraits back

---

[60] Bennet, *Famous and Godly History*, sig. G7^v.
[61] Beza, *Lyfe of Calvin* (London, 1564), sig. C8^v.
[62] Beza, *Icones*, 84–5. The portraits appear on 82–3.

to back on the double page; and Erasmus describes Colet and Vitrier as lovingly aware of the virtues of each other and wanting to meet.[63] In the same way, Walton provides a foil for each of his subjects, a man or woman endowed with different characteristics with whom the subject is intertwined in 'an *Amity* made up of a chain of sutable inclinations and vertues' (p. 265). This is how he describes the relationship between Donne and Magdalen Herbert, each an exponent of a different kind of piety, offered as a pair in order that two equally valid modes of life may be mutually supportive.

George Herbert himself fulfils this role in the *Life of Donne*, so that Herbert's demonstrable private piety reinforces Donne's. In the *Life of Hooker*, the statesmanlike virtues of John Whitgift intertwine with the piety of the scholarly and retiring Hooker to present a more complete and rounded aspect of godly conduct.[64] 'All are not of one Modell', explains the author of a funeral sermon collected in *The House of Mourning*, 'as the bodies of men and women are not of one height and colour . . . but wee esteeme the children of God *according to that they have received, and not according to that they have not received*, as the Apostle speaks.'[65]

Plutarchan comparisons in Lives, then, can make it possible to retain exemplary patterns while adding and comparing variations on the godly theme. In effect, the coexistence of more than one 'Modell' creates a *selection* of imitable patterns. This may be a moving force behind the conglomeration of very different sorts of godliness in collections like Clarke's *Lives*. Erasmus' Colet, for instance, is clearly a prime source for Clarke's *Life of Doctor Collet*, and parts of Clarke's account are simply translations of Erasmus.[66] And although the comparison with Vitrier is no longer there, other Lives more appropriate to Clarke's exemplary agenda fulfil Vitrier's role. He narrates the obscure and saintly life of Richard Greenham in his Cambridgeshire parish within

---

[63] 'Letter to Jodocus Jonas', 176.   [64] See below, pp. 252–3 and 297–9.
[65] 'Abrahams Purchase, or a Possession for Buriall', in *The House of Mourning* . . . (London, 1640), 397.
[66] Cf. e.g. Clarke's account of Colet's reception in London as a young man, with Erasmus' letter (Clarke, *Lives*, 1; Erasmus, 'Letter to Jonas' in Olin, p. 178). Colet's low opinion of Aquinas in Clarke also comes directly from Erasmus' letter (Clarke, *Lives*, 1; Erasmus, 'Letter to Jodocus Jonas', 183).

seven pages of his narration of Colet's eminent one.[67] The reader is offered diverse patterns not only within individual Lives, but in the non-competitive moral comparison invited by the collection of such differing witnesses of the Church of Christ. The function of these diverse patterns is summed up by John Wall and Simeon Ashe in their introduction to Clarke's *Marrow of Ecclesiastical Historie*: 'For which way can we look, or to what condition and concernment of Life can we turn our selves, wherein some Example propounded in this Book, will not aptly suit with our Estates for guidance, comfort, encouragement'.[68]

[67] Clarke, *Lives: The Life of Doctor Collet* is pp. 1–3; *The Life of Master Richard Greenham* is pp. 11–14. Between are the *Lives* of Miles Coverdale and Edwin Sandys.

[68] 'To the Christian Reader', in Clarke, *Marrow,* 1st part, sig d.

3

Godly Prototypes

I have looked at eulogy and at Plutarchan biography, searching for generic prototypes for the kind of biography Walton wrote. This chapter, though, leaves genre for thematic specifics; less concerned with the shape of the tributaries feeding Waltonian narrative, it deals with the commonplaces which are collected, or adapted, or run together, to make their fluid substance. These, of course, provide prototypes in different—in contemporary—terms: they delineate virtuous patterns from which Renaissance readers select versions and components to suit their circumstances. Not to labour the point, they are intended to be exemplary.

So the 'godly prototypes' of the chapter title refers to my own search for *Walton's* generic prototypes, and also to the explicitly 'prototypical' constructions common to every tributary genre. These, though I describe them as 'feeding into' Waltonian biography, are not necessarily its predecessors in any strict sense. Any study of what went to make Walton's work must also be partly a study of his contemporaries; and not only because he had such a long working life. For while, in one sense, Walton's work is certainly the product of a series of experiments in a new genre, it is also emphatically part of the process, and my intention is to show Walton as participating in the flowering and development of the new form's conventions, as well as being its most impressive manifestation.

One major complication in discussing these commonplaces is the extent to which each exemplary image or process in proto-biography is not discrete but interacts with other images or processes. Even the primary division of this long chapter, into 'texts' and 'bodies', attempts the impossible in forcing apart the two halves of the genre's most intimate metaphor, and breaks down even in this (very) rough attempt to use the two sides of the metaphor to demarcate narrative from prescriptive source material.

Accounts which present their subjects as living commentaries on prescriptive biblical texts use not only images which offer those subjects as 'copies' or 'paraphrases' on such texts; they may also (through, for instance, the use of a word like 'draught', applying as it does both to written texts and to pictorial representation) employ the language of portraiture to give their 'copy' flesh. And in an exemplary genre a 'portrait' of a good man may equally be a 'looking-glass'—another sort of 'copy'—in which the godly reader may learn to see his own face. Where physical and moral qualities are made metaphors for each other, the particular description of a subject's facial lineaments or bodily character-istics must function to some extent both as a moral index to his character and as a series of prescriptions for the reader to follow. Thus the printed 'monument' a life-writer may erect to his sub-ject's 'memory' can also function as a prescription to the reader as to how his own bodily behaviour may reflect the Pauline Temple of God.

Again, a godly Life may be described as a 'living Sermon'; but where the actions denoting the godliness of such a life often consist in the frequent writing and preaching of actual sermons, the reader is again brought back to an image of holiness which is as much the academic and theological exposition of a particular text—seen as indispensable to the winning of souls—as it is the performance of charitable and pastoral actions. Even where the narrative emphasis falls on pastoral behaviour, the commonplace of life as sermon is likely to mean that such charitable performances are made to bear a strong resemblance to prescriptive literature— either general character writing or books of advice on preaching and pastoral decorum. So I also use some of this purely pre-scriptive literature for comparison.

Although all the narrative texts considered have a strong biographical element, a number of them first appeared as funeral sermons or as prefaces to works by their subject. The prescrip-tive nature of these works, and of the funeral sermon itself, explains both the narratives' heavy emphasis on metaphors of 'text' or 'word' and their governing assumption that the biographical narrative is *inevitably* exemplary. That Walton's own work has such strong links with genres just as prescriptive as descriptive (and it should be remembered that three of his four ecclesiastical Lives began as prefaces) goes a long way in itself towards explaining their much-criticized didactic emphasis.

I have chosen the (mostly) biographical writings on the list which follows from which to illustrate the commonplaces shaping the ecclesiastical Life. The list itself is by no means intended to be comprehensive, though it might form a starting point for other, more thorough research in the area. Its selection principles (aside from the inevitable arbitrariness of an incomplete initial foray via the STCs) tend to the exclusion of Tacitean models (as, for instance, Paule's statesmanlike *Life of Whitgift* of 1609, discussed in Chapter 5). I have included any Life discussed while excluding comparable entries within whole books: for instance, Foxe's account of Cranmer appears as a typological example, but for obvious reasons I have eschewed listing every account by Foxe of a divine within the period. Again, on a smaller scale, some entries in Fuller's *Abel Redevivus* appear separately because they are discussed separately, but I have not traced and recorded every Life of Fuller's collection. Entries run from sixteenth-century reforming Lives to the decade of Walton's death. I have tried also to show the kinds of genres in which such lives first appeared in print, and where Walton's own writings fit into the list. What does not appear, but should be stressed, is the simple growth in popularity of the form, especially in the years after the Restoration.

Lives

1546 J. Jonas & others, *The Christen Departynge of D. Martyn Luther* . . . , translated by John Bale.

1561 H. Bennet, *A Famous and Godly History, Contayning the Lives of Three Reformers, M. Luther, J. Ecolampadius, and H. Zvinglius. All Set Forth in Latin by P. Melancthon* [sic], *Newly Englished by H. Bennet Callesian.*

1564 T. Beza, *A Discourse . . . Conteyning in Briefe the Historie of the Lyfe and Death of Maister Iohn Calvin,* translated by *I.S.*

1570 J. Foxe, 'The Life, State and Story of the Reuerend Pastour and Prelate Thomas Cranmer Archbishop of Caunterbury . . .', in *Actes and Monuments.*

1609   D. Featley, *Life of the Worthie Prelate . . . Iohn Iewel Sometimes Bishop of Sarisburie*, prefacing John Jewel, *Works*.

1624   See under 1632 (Miles Smith).

1629   J. Buckeridge, *A Sermon Preached at the Funeral of . . . Lancelot* [Andrewes], *Late Lord Bishop of Winchester . . .* , prefacing Lancelot Andrewes, *XCVI Sermons*.

1629   J. Harris, 'A Short View of the Life and Vertves of the Avthovr', prefacing Arthur Lake, *Sermons, with some Religious and Divine Meditations*.

1632   T. Prior, *A Sermon Preached at the Funeral of . . . Miles Smith, Late Lord Bishop of Gloucester . . .* [1624], in Miles Smith, *Sermons*; Preface to Miles Smith, *Sermons* [unsigned].

1640   D. Featley and others, Θρενοίκος. *The House of Mourning . . . XLVII Sermons, Preached at the Funeralls of Divers Faithfull Ministers of Christ*.

E. Leigh and H. Scudder, 'Epistle Dedicatory' and *Life and Death of Mr. William Whateley . . .* , in William Whateley, *Prototypes, or the Primarie Precedent Presidents ovt of the Booke of Genesis . . .*

I. Walton, *The Life of Dr. John Donne*, prefacing John Donne, *LXXX Sermons*.

1641   M. Adamus, *The Life of Dr. Martin Luther*, freely translated by Thomas Hayne.

[S. Foxe], *The Life of Mr. John Foxe . . .* , prefacing Volume 2 of John Foxe, *Acts and Monuments . . .* , 8th edition.

1644   P. Heylyn, *A Briefe Relation of the Death and Sufferings of* [Laud] *L. Archbishop of Canterbury . . .*

1649   J. Taylor, *The Great Exemplar of Sanctity and Holy Life . . . Described in the History of the Life and Death of . . . Jesus Christ . . .*

1650   H. Isaacson, *An exact narration of the life and death of . . . Lancelot Andrewes* [also in Fuller, *Abel Redevivus*, 1651].

[1650s] MS: W. Bedell, 'Life and Death of William Bedell'.

1651   T. Fuller, *Abel Redevivus, or the Dead yet Speaking*.

1653   J. Chetwinde and W. Thomas, *The Dead Speaking, or the Living Names of Two Deceased Ministers of Christ . . . Mr. Sam. Oliver, and Mr. Samuel Crook*.

1656   N. Bernard, *The Life and Death of the Most Reverend and Learned Father of our Church Dr. James Usher, Late Archbishop of Armagh, and Primate of all Ireland*.

J. Whitefoote, Ἰσραὴλ Ἀγχιθανὴς. *Deaths Alarum, or, the Presage of Approaching Death . . . in a Funeral Sermon . . . for . . . Joseph Hall, Late Lord Bishop of Norwich.*

1657 Thomas Fuller, 'The Life of Mr Henry Smith', in Henry Smith, *Sermons.*

1658 I. Walton, *The Life of John Donne, Dr. in Divinity . . .*

1659 S. Clarke, *An Antidote Against Immoderate Mourning for the Dead.*

1660 J. Barwick, Ἱερονίκες, *or the Fight, Victory and Triumph of St. Paul, Accommodated to . . . Thomas* [Morton] *Late Lord Bishop of Duresme, in a Sermon Preached at his Funeral . . . Together, with a Life of the said Bishop.*

1661–2 S. Clarke, *The Lives of Ten Eminent Divines.*
S. Clarke, *The Lives of Twenty Two Eminent Divines.*

1664 S. Clarke, *The Blessed Life and Meritorious Death of our Lord and Saviour Jesus Christ . . .*

1665 I. Walton, *The Life of Mr. R. Hooker.*

1666 I. Walton, *The Life of Mr. R. Hooker*, prefacing Richard Hooker, *Of the Lawes of Ecclesiastical Politie.*

1665/6 R. Mossom, *A Narrative Panegyrical of the Life, Sickness and Death of George* [Wilde] *. . . Lord Bishop of Derry in Ireland . . .*

1669 R. B[addeley]/J. N[aylor], *The Life of Dr. Thomas Morton, Late Bishop of Duresme . . .*

[?1670s] MS: A. Clogie, 'Speculum Episcoporum; or the Apostolick Bishop: Being a Brief Account of the Life and Death of . . . Dr. William Bedell, Lord Bishop of Kilmore in Ireland'.

1670 I. Walton, *The Life of Mr. George Herbert.*
I. Walton, *The Lives of Dr. John Donne, Sir Henry Wotton, Mr. Richard Hooker, Mr. George Herbert.*

1673 I. Basire, *The Dead Mans Real Speech: A Funeral Sermon . . . Together with a Brief of the Life . . . and . . . Death of* [John Cosin] *. . . Lord Bishop of Durham.*
E. Vaghan, *The Life and Death of . . . Dr. Jackson . . . prefacing* Thomas Jackson, *Works.*

1675 S. Clarke, *The Marrow of Ecclesiastical History . . . with the Lives of the Ancient Fathers, School-men, First Reformers, and Modern Divines . . .* , 3rd edition.
I. Walton, *The Lives of Dr. John Donne, Sir Henry Wotton, Mr. Richard Hooker, Mr. George Herbert.*
H. Ward, *The Testimony Given to the Reverend Dr. Henry Byam, at his Burial*, bound with Henry Byam, *XIII Sermons.*

1677	S. Clarke, *A General Martyrologie . . . Whereunto is Added the Lives of Thirty Two English Divines*, 3rd edition.
1678	I. Walton, *The Life of Dr. Robert Sanderson . . . to Which is Added, Some Short Tracts . . .*
1680	W. Burkitt, *The Peoples Zeal Provok't by the Pious and Instructive Example of their Dead Minister . . . Mr. William Gurnall.*
1685	G. Burnet, *The Life of William Bedell.*
1686	I. Walton, *The Life of Dr. Robert Sanderson*, prefacing Robert Sanderson, *XXXVI Sermons . . .*
1688	J. Banks and T. Tully, *The Life of . . . Edward Rainbow, Bishop of Carlisle. To which is Added, a Sermon Preached at his Funeral by Thomas Tully . . .*

Characters

1536?	—— *A Descrypcyon of the Images of a Very Chrysten Bysshop and of a Counterfayte Bysshop.*
1608	J. Hall, *Characters of Vertues and Vices.*
1616	N. Breton, *The Good and the Badde, or, Descriptions of the Worthies and Unworthies of this Age.*
1622	T. Overbury, *His Wife, with Additions of New Characters . . .*, 11th edition.
1633	J. Earle, *Microcosmographie or, A Piece of the World Discovered; in Essayes and Characters*, 6th edition.
1642	H. Browne, *A Map of the Microcosme, or, a Morall Description of Man . . .*
	T. Fuller, *The Holy State.*
1647	R. Venning, *Orthodox Paradoxes, or, a Beleiver* [sic] *Clearing Truth by Seeming Contradictions.*
1658	S. Crook, *Tὰ Διαφέροντα, or Divine Characters . . .*

The commonplaces I shall discuss in this and the following section are: (1) the description of clerical subjects according to scriptural precept (pp. 72–81); (2) the portrayal of subjects in terms of books, texts, or engraved edifices (pp. 81–101); (3) the visible signs of virtue read into the face and body, and into gesture and dress (pp. 102–28); (4) deathbed decorum (pp. 129–52). The chapter finishes with a short examination of one particular work which may legitimately be regarded as a Waltonian prototype: John Harris's 'Short View . . .' of the life of Arthur Lake, Bishop of Bath and Wells, which appeared as a preface to Lake's

Sermons, with Some Religious and Divine Meditations in 1629. This account, as well as bringing together many of the elements I have identified as parts of the Waltonian context, is also explicitly recommended to his readers by Walton in the *Life of Sanderson* (p. 357). In this way the necessary anatomization of this part of the study is at least partly rectified by the study of one narrative in its entirety.

The Scriptural Map

For the clergy, straightforwardly scriptural prototypes were, as it were, supplied neat. Most of these are (or were then thought to be) Pauline: the third chapter of Paul's first Epistle to Timothy, the first chapter of the Epistle to Titus, and (to a lesser extent) the third verse of the fifth chapter of the first Epistle to Peter.

The third chapter of 1 Timothy[1] explains how a bishop should conduct himself. His virtues are to be social and pragmatic; he should be sober, monogamous, hospitable, restrained, a teacher, master of his private household, experienced, well regarded. Then the virtues of gravity, sobriety, and uncovetousness are prescribed for deacons. The polemical attention centred on this text—for instance, as part of controversies about clerical marriage, or about the nature and defensibility of episcopacy—is not itself an issue with which I am directly concerned. However, some of the imagery used in a Reformation tract addressing the question of the function and conduct of a bishop is suggestive. The tract, accepted by contemporaries as by Luther (although no evidence now exists that it was), and titled *A Descrypcyon of the Images of a Verye Chrysten Bysshop and of a Counterfayte Bysshop* (1536?), contrasts the supposed behaviour of reforming and unreforming bishops.[2] The former are identified, by implication, with what the author describes as 'the true Image & forme of a bysshop' as it is laid down by 'the apostle Paule . . . in the thyrde chapytre of the fyrste epystle to Tymothe'. The qualities most opposed to those

---

[1] Kenneth Fincham, in his book *Prelate as Pastor: The Episcopate of James I* (Oxford, 1990), 10–11, stresses the importance of the 1 Timothy text for the Jacobean episcopate.

[2] *A Descrypcyon of the Images of a Verye Chrysten Bysshop and of a Counterfayte Bysshop* (n.p., 1536?). Its STC entry, 16983.5, states Luther's authorship to be unlikely.

prescribed by Paul are, of course, manifest in the 'counterfayte'. Thus, aptness to teach becomes in him the property of being 'excedyngly ignoraunt' (sig. D1^v).

However, the tract's author also addresses the question of how an observer, regarding a bishop as it were from the crowd, could tell by his deportment whether or not he were a 'counterfayte'. How, asks the author, is it possible to distinguish true from false when the false, too, will be careful 'to do all this thyng kepynge the comelynes belongynge to a bysshop' (sig. D2^v)? The problem is solved by asserting that to feign or act the 'gesture' of a true bishop will be beyond the dissembler's skill; 'the whole multytude', he asserts, would associate his attempt with the posturing 'of stage players', and the feigning bishop would be met 'with unmete laughter' (sig. D2^v). Therefore, since his unadorned behaviour will not convince, such a prelate must have recourse to external trappings—gorgeous clothes, a princely household and retinue—the worldly signs of an arrogance which challenges (so the author implies) the dignity which should legitimately be reserved for the secular prince.

Aside from the polemical cunning of this gambit, it is worth noticing that it takes as a basic assumption the improbability of feigning holy behaviour undetectably. The counterfeit prelate must cover his self-betraying body with distracting (and illegitimate) external signs of another kind of greatness. He must remove that body physically from his observant flock, by mounting a horse, surrounding himself with servants. He is, therefore, exceedingly vulnerable to exposure, his virtues donned with his clothes, his beauty not even skin deep. His acting is of the pitiful kind which relies entirely on props. Thus, the bishop's 'image' (a term employed as morally neutral) has become identified with good when it is stripped plain, with evil when it is over-adorned.

For plainness and simplicity are also 'images', and not all part-playing is dissembling. Later the author tells a story in which a 'princely' bishop, out riding, is met by a poor Shepherd who makes him ashamed of his ostentation by asking 'what yf the devyll shulde take and bere awaye the prynce: shall there remayne anythynge of the bysshop?' (sig. K4^v). The moral drawn is that Paul, the bishop's apostolic model, was actually 'a playne symple craftes man' who 'wente some tyme on his feete, and preached the gospell all abrode'. (The tract's author might perhaps have been on safer ground with, say, Peter.) To imitate such simplicity was the only legitimate way to 'playe the Apostle' (sigs. K4^v–5).

In other words, to act the 'playne symple' part *is* to perform, but to perform sincerity is to be sincere. Only the 'royall and pryncely' role exposes its actor to accusations of dissimulation (and a lot of that is because this author wants to distinguish spiritual from secular authority). It is the perceived legitimacy of the model used which confers its moral value. In the 1 Timothy text Paul has provided an 'Image & forme' for the clergy to imitate, and his prescriptions are its lineaments. So episcopal and ministerial 'fitness' is, inevitably, widely assumed to be inherent in a performable deportment—in private conduct and an attention to public reputation. The man and his office are not separable.

When Hyperius cites 1 Timothy in *The Practise of Preaching* he deals squarely with the implications of inseparability. 'Now', he argues, 'that sanctimony of lyfe ought to be required in a Preacher of the Gospell, every man may iudge', because 'a goode life is as it were a scale, whereby sounde doctrine[3] is confirmed in the hearers'.[4] Hyperius expresses the close correspondence between life and teaching through the commonplace of the 'living sermon'. Christ, he explains, is our 'Scholemaster', and his lessons are preached to us 'not onely in worde, but also effectually in deede' (sig. B5). Thus, Christ's preachers, in imitating Christ, must also make sermons of their deeds. And this, concludes Hyperius, is why 'the Apostle most dilygenytlye prescribed what manner of men Bysshops or Elders, & lykewyse Decons with their whole families ought to bee, with what vertues he would have them chiefely garnished and what vices he woulde wyshe them to bee free' (sig. B5). He cites the relevant Pauline texts in the margin: 1 Timothy 3 and Titus 1. These are the unalterable grounds of the cleric's 'living sermon', without which all his verbal preaching would be worthless.

This seems to suggest that preaching is subservient to (or at least dependent on) general godly conduct. But both the scriptural texts cited here define preaching skills as virtues *of conduct*: aptness

---

[3] Titus, 1: 9.

[4] Andreas Hyperius, *The Practise of Preaching . . . Englished by Iohn Ludham* (London, 1577), sigs. B4^v–5.

to teach (1 Timothy 3) and readiness to 'exhort' (Titus 1: 9). So
we find Wigandus Orthius, in his funeral oration for Hyperius
himself, reiterating the same point, using the same Pauline texts,
but heavily privileging preaching ability itself as a living virtue.
Hyperius' three overriding characteristics he cites as having been
his learnedness, his aptness to teach, and last his 'gravitie and
constancye of life and conversation' (sig. Bb6). Orthius points
out that Paul is happy to call the first two characteristics virtues,
and makes his defence of the third dependent on them: 'But no
lesse necessary is this last poynte, namely that to doctrine and
erudition the life and manners may bee agreeable' (sig. Bb6).
This, indeed, is an emphasis which implies reversed priorities,
where preaching becomes the largest element of godly behaviour, and other matters of moral deportment are simply its
complement.

However, Orthius's printed oration is bound in with Hyperius'
preaching manual. It is therefore—as a printed text—a testimony
to Hyperius as the living confirmation of the prescriptions of
his own treatise. Professor Collinson expresses the historian's
problem in determining the relative importance of preaching
and other forms of pastoral conduct succinctly in his essay on the
subject, where he details what contemporary complaints exist
against the bias towards preaching as a main pastoral activity.
'Yet where', he asks, 'were these . . . complaints expressed? In
sermons.'[5]

We find the same difficulty in another popular preaching
manual early in the seventeenth century. Richard Bernard's *The
Faithfull Shepheard* goes through the key Pauline texts point by
point (pp. 90–3), since (he explains) 'a Minister must be a good
Christian in conversation, els hardly will he be so effectual a
Preacher as he ought to be' (p. 90).[6] Again, other considerations
simply attend the minister's preaching skills—but again, the
point is being made in a preaching manual. And in his conclusion
Bernard comes close to arguing that only to the godly behaved
will 'sound doctrine' be revealed by God, and adds that

---

[5] Patrick Collinson, 'Shepherds, Sheepdogs and Hirelings: The Pastoral Ministry in Post-Reformation England', *Studies in Church History*, 26 (Oxford, 1989),
185–220 (p. 189).
[6] Richard Bernard, *The Faithfull Shepheard* . . . (London, 1607).

'Common people respect more a good teachers life, then his learning, and reverence the person, not his preaching so much' (p. 93). This is a paraphrase on the often-repeated commonplace, that 'we live in an Age that hath more need of good examples, than precepts'. I have quoted here Walton's own rendition as it appears in the *Life of Herbert*, but it surfaces in Fuller's *Holy State*, and in Edmund Calamy's address 'To The Christian Reader' which prefaces the first part of Clarke's *Marrow of Ecclesiastical History*, to name only two very prominent sources.[7]

Passing, therefore, from precepts to examples, the main focus of this section: how are these scriptural texts employed in narratives of lives? Taking first an early and prominent account, we find Foxe himself using the text from Titus with some skill in narrating the qualities of that vexed martyr, Thomas Cranmer.

Foxe's 'Life, State and Story' of Cranmer has exemplary intentions, as well as presenting itself as a matter of record.[8] 'Let us take this Archbishop of Canterbury', suggests Foxe ingenuously, 'and trye him by the rule therof, to see either how here he commeth to the description of S. *Paul*, or els how farre he swerueth from the common course of other in his tyme, of his callyng' (ii. 2035). The final qualifier is not accidental. Here as elsewhere in the *Actes and Monuments*, Foxe's two methods complement (or at any rate intertwine) not wholly comfortably: his concern to make his politicized exemplary history a documented one makes more problematic (and more fascinating) reading for the modern historian than a more generically straightforward typological enterprise might.

Foxe uses Titus 1 to characterize the Henrician Cranmer only: it forms part of a section which closes its themes in 1547. Thus Foxe, who writes chronologically but (in the editions of 1563 and 1570) under running heads governed by year of martyrdom, subdivides, without advertisement, into at least two (really into three) Cranmers divided by respective regal policies and vicissitudes. Yet because the whole section appears under 1556, it is

---

[7] Walton, *Lives*, 290; Thomas Fuller, *The Holy State* (Cambridge, 1642), 87; Clarke, *Marrow*, 1st part, sig c.

[8] J. Foxe, 'The Life, State and Story of the Reuerend Pastour and Prelate Thomas Cranmer Archbishop of Caunterbury . . .' in Foxe, *Actes and Monuments* (1570), ii. esp. 2035–9. I am indebted to Professor Diarmaid MacCulloch for bringing this deft and unusual example of the form to my attention.

half-concealed that no act of Cranmer's under Edward VI or Mary I figures in the headings provided by the epistle. (In any case, an apolitical justification for Foxe's silence on at any rate the Marian Cranmer might be that he held no ecclesiastical office under her.)

Cranmer begins by quoting Tyndale's Titus, heading it 'the Rule of a true Bishop': 'A Byshop must be faultles, as becommeth the Minister of God: Not stubborne, not angry, no drunkard, no fighter, not geuen to filthy luker: but harberous, one that loueth goodnes, sober minded, righteous, holy, temperate, and such as cleaueth vnto the true worde and doctrine, that he may be liable to exhort, &c.' (ii. 2035). Each prescription is taken and made into a centred heading except the first, which warrants the margin only in a smaller type, and where 'byshop' is amended to 'minister': 'no manne is without synne', Foxe points out tartly in the main text, 'and euery manne caryeth with hym his especiall vice and fault' 'so yet neuertheles, the Apostle meaneth, that the Byshop and minister must be faultles in comparison of the common conuersation of menne of the world'. It is interesting, all the same, that he chose the absolutist 'faultles' of Tyndale in preference to, for instance, the Genevan 'unreproueable' or even the 'blameless' of Cranmer's own Bishops' Bible (either of which might have been harder to refute).[9]

It is under this head that he describes Cranmer's daily routine of study and work (his only recreations appear to have been walking and chess), linking Cranmer's studiousness with a preceding section on his early concern to raise academic standards amongst the clergy. This is taken both to be an implicitly reformist undertaking and an explicitly virtuous one. Sin and ignorance act almost as synonyms. The point is made with less subtlety under the 'not angry' head, where Cranmer forgives and releases a (papist) priest imprisoned for deriding Cranmer's learning when—it turns out—he himself knows so little he cannot tell him the family relationship between David and Solomon. The anecdote has the incidental advantage of dividing Cranmer's humanity from Cromwell's sternness—Cromwell having been responsible for throwing the priest in the Fleet in the first place.

---

[9] See *The New Testament Octapla: Eight English Versions of the New Testament*, edited by Luther A. Weigle (New York, 1962), 1216–17.

Foxe's most problematic headings are 'not stubborne' and 'such as cleaueth vnto the true worde and doctrine'. He solves both the same way. While agreeing that Cranmer was indeed not stubborn but 'rather culpable of ouer much facilitie and gentiles', he also points out that 'Onely in causes pertayning to God or hys Prince, no man more stoute, more constant, or more hard to be wonne: as in that part his earnest defence in the Parlament house aboue three dayes together in disputing against the vi. articles of *Gardiners* devise, can testify' (ii. 2036). The digression on the grounds of Cranmer's opposition to the Six Articles which follows is, in Diarmaid MacCulloch's characterization, 'rather vague':[10] vaguer, even, than the vexed question as to whether Cranmer was serving God or his Prince most faithfully in opposing them at all.[11] It is reasonable to draw the inference from Foxe's text that he knew the responsibility he attributed to Gardiner for the Articles belonged more properly to Henry himself. Later Cranmer's 'stoutness' as binder of the king's conscience in opposing the Articles is used to illustrate his readiness to 'cleaue fast vnto the true woord of doctrine, that hee may bee able to exhort with wholsome learnyng, and to improue that say agaynst it'. 'He would not', explains Foxe, 'permit the truth in that man [Henry] to be cleane ouerthrowen wyth authority and power' (ii. 2036). It was, as Foxe does not need to say, a tough row to hoe.

John Barwick, in a much later, less problematic, and far less subtle life of Thomas Morton, bishop of Durham, published with his funeral sermon for the bishop in 1660, uses the texts from 1 Timothy and Titus as the sole structural prop for a section called 'A Short Character of his Person and Qualities'.[12] Morton, explains Barwick, lining him up with Paul's requirements point by point, was a '*Paraphrase*' on '1 Tim. 3 and Tit. 1[6]' (p. 141). Indeed, Barwick's Morton is a tissue of textual similitudes: with

[10] D. MacCulloch, *Thomas Cranmer: A Life* (New Haven, 1996), 243.

[11] Ibid. 241–6.

[12] John Barwick, Ἱερονίκης or the Fight, Victory and Triumph of St. Paul, *Accommodated to . . . Thomas* [Morton] *Late Lord Bishop of Duresme, in a Sermon Preached at his Funeral . . . Together, with a Life of the said Bishop* (London, 1660), 141–71. Barwick was Morton's chaplain.

Church Fathers, with his predecessor St Cuthbert, with Bede. No virtue is given without its precedent; and what personal parallels cannot accomplish, Pauline prescription fulfils. It is, he asserts, 'the *Standard* or *Touch-stone* whereby *every Bishop* ought to be tryed and examined' (p. 142).

A second life of Morton, appearing in 1669, its authorship shared between Morton's secretary Richard Baddeley and another chaplain, Joseph Naylor, does much the same thing with the texts, though in prose this time, not in a numbered list. It appears in Naylor's part of the narrative, and he follows Barwick in claiming the *Oration for St Athanasius* by Gregory Nazianzen as a precedent for his use of 1 Timothy 3. Barwick contents himself with citing it, but Naylor quotes the passage:

Now as . . . Gregory Nazianzen saith, in his Oration of that renowned *Athanasius*, the invincible Arch-Bishop of *Alexandria*; so may I, and must I say, of this worthy Prelate . . . *Why should I either trouble you, or my self, to super-rogate unto you the delineation or description of a man, whom* Saint Paul *hath before-hand so compleatly deciphered, partly in the person of that great High Priest, who is entred into the highest of Heavens*, Heb. 4 . . . *and partly in his first Epistle unto* Timothy Chap. 3, *where he doth most exactly and compleatly describe and Characterize a* Bishop, *or man of God, with all his properties and qualifications.*[13]

Naylor then quotes Nazianzen quoting Paul, and concludes triumphantly:

Lo! Here the *Effiges* or *Picture* of a Bishop, drawn by an *Apelles* who could not err: And lo! here a Transcript, or Copy of that Picture in the Person of this Prelate, so lively resembling and representing the Originall, that I dare boldly challenge the most envenomed and foule mouthed Adversary that ever Writ against him . . . to instance in all the aforenamed Episcopall qualifications, positive or privative, wherein this Reverend Prelate Bishop *Morton*, was justly culpable or defective (pp. 171–3).

Naylor's concern, like Barwick's, is to establish an exact correlation between Morton's deportment, 'positive or privative', and St Paul's original complete delineation of what that deportment should be. Having done that, in bald prose, he then strongly

---

[13] R[ichard] B[addeley] and J[oseph] N[aylor], *The Life of Dr. Thomas Morton, Late Bishop of Duresme* . . . (London, 1669), 168–9.

implies that Protestant episcopacy is vindicated in the mere fact of Morton's living imitation of a scriptural (and so an unchallengeable) 'Character'.

This is a standard technique. In many cases its use is even more economical: the narrator lists his subject's scripturally attested virtues, and simply places the relevant reference by the passage in the margin. For instance, Edward Leigh, in his reminiscences of William Whateley, the minister of Banbury, which appear before Whateley's posthumously printed *Prototypes* (a list of examples of good and bad behaviour as they appear in the Book of Genesis), lets his marginal references do a lot of the work for him:

	Oh, with what life and zeale would hee both preach and pray! and how strict and watchful was hee in his whole life!
1 Tim. 3²	being (as every good Minister should be) *Blamelesse, Sober, Just, Holy, Temperate, of good Behaviour,*
Tit. 1⁸ to . . .	*given Hospitality, apt to teach, a lover of good things and*
2 Tim. 2¹⁵	*good to men. Hee studied to approve himselfe unto* GOD, *a workeman that needed not to be ashamed, rightly*
1 Tim. 4¹²	*dividing the word of Truth.* He propounded to
1 Pet. 5³	you the examples of holy Writ, and was himselfe
Tit. 2⁷	while he lived, an Example and Pattern of all good works.¹⁴

Yet the clear point of such references is to stress the exemplary *behaviour* of the clergy; adding to testimonies of eloquent preaching their complement of holy deportment. E. Vaghan, writing the life of Thomas Jackson, dean of Peterborough, thirty years after Leigh, employs precisely the same shift from preaching to private behaviour using a Pauline epistle, making it clear that behaviour validates preaching, not the other way round:

He adorned the doctrine of the Gospel (which he preached and professed) with a suitable life and conversation: Manifesting the signs of a true Apostle. In all things shewing himself a Patern of good works, In doctrine incorruptness, gravity, sincerity, sound speech that cannot be

---

¹⁴ Edward Leigh, 'Epistle Dedicatory' [to the mayor and citizens of Banbury], in William Whateley, *Prototypes, or the Primary Precedent Presidents ovt of the Booke of Genesis* . . . (London, 1640), sigs. A3ᵛ–4.

condemned, that they which were of the *contrary part might be ashamed, having no evil thing to say of him*, Titus 2. 7,8.[15]

It seems, then, that the prescriptive texts from 1 Timothy and Titus are used by the writers of manuals on preaching, and by the writers of lives, in remarkably similar ways—that, in fact, the life-writer can and frequently does regard his subject as a descriptive illustration or proof of a textual point. The growth of the Life out of the funeral sermon is surely partly responsible for this, where the sermon's scriptural text and the commemorative convention were, for the sake of a unity of argument, often mixed with great care, so that the conduct of the dead person's life dealt with by the commemorative section could become an illustration of the text.

Inscribing Holy Characters

The *Lives* of Morton by Barwick and Baddeley/Naylor should not be regarded as rare examples of persons described in terms of texts. Indeed, there is a rich and diverse network of commonplaces based on exactly this premise. This is not just because the funeral sermons which provided so much basic biographical material were built round scriptural texts, though this is important. There are other reasons. For instance, in the passages already cited from Barwick and Naylor, Morton's private conduct is turned into a scriptural 'Paraphrase' or 'Copy', because to make the deportment of a sequestered bishop an illustration (and illustrious imitation) of a text beyond any adversary's criticism is to make a *polemical* point. It becomes a descriptive defence of episcopacy at the evidently critical moment of 1659: not merely a 'living sermon', but a living political argument. Naylor makes this even more explicit when (anticipating the publication of Clarendon's *History of the Rebellion* by some years) he begins his portion of the narrative by adapting the opening words of the Preface of Hooker's *Ecclesiastical Polity*:

If for no other cause, or reason at all, yet that Posterity may not altogether be ignorant what kind of *Superintendents* of cheife choice, and

---

[15] E. Vaghan, *The Life and Death of the Reverend, Learned and Pious Dr. Jackson, Dean of Peterborough* . . . , in Thomas Jackson, *Works*, 3 vols. (London, 1673), i. sig. *6 (misnumbered *5).

Cooperators our Lord Jesus had in his *English Vineyard* . . . even for this cause (if for no other) the life of this eminently gifted, this Orthodox, learned and exemplary-lived Prelate Dr. *Thomas Morton* shall appear unto the world in this plain and naked *Narrative* following.[16]

Naylor's 'plain and naked Narrative' of Morton's episcopal behaviour is being offered as a kind of practical appendix to a central and discursive text which publicly defines the details of the Church's identity. Morton is being used as living proof of the rectitude of episcopacy; while his deportment functions as a 'Copy' of authoritative scriptural texts, the context of Naylor's narrative reveals it explicitly as involved in controversial argument about the nature of the Church Morton represents. Morton himself becomes the scriptural text in action, deployed against the enemies of episcopacy in apparent company with Hooker's arguments. It is not, then, merely the commemorative sermon which lends these Lives their peculiarly textual flavour, but the many treatises of controversy, and the courses of sermons which use the scriptural text as a basis for entering into controversy, which are a part of the pedigree of the ecclesiastical Life. The subjects of such Lives are not merely active examples of godliness, but living arguments, or practical texts, to be deployed in defence of some version or other of the 'Holy State'.[17]

The other genre in the business of making persuasive texts of persons is, of course, the Character.[18] While Character writing was not necessarily exemplary, it is worth noting that it was common to consider persons in terms of types, and formed part of a boy's education in classical rhetoric.[19] And this in its turn meant that

[16] B[addeley]/N[aylor], *Life of Dr. Thomas Morton*, 113–15.

[17] This is not to say that every text personified was scriptural, although scriptural texts naturally predominate. Any instructive work was eligible, with occasionally bathetic results: William Bedell, bishop of Kilmore, is described by his son as so sparing of his speech that it was 'as if God had designed him for a lively and practical edition of Mr. Perkins' treatise of the government of the tongue'. See *Two Lives of William Bedell, Bishop of Kilmore*, edited by E. S. Shuckburgh (Cambridge, 1902), 19.

[18] For studies of the Character which discuss the seventeenth century see B. Boyce, *The Theophrastan Character in England to 1642* (London, 1967) and J. W. Smeed, *The Theophrastan 'Character': The History of a Literary Genre* (Oxford, 1985).

[19] See Smeed, *Theophrastan 'Character'*, 9.

the delineation of moral types was bound to form part of the sermon-writer's argumentative resources.[20] So the exemplary Character, used as a practical persuasion to imitative virtue, inevitably became a considerable type, and in fact the earliest popular book of Characters appearing in the seventeenth century, Joseph Hall's *Characters of Vertues and Vices* of 1608, is written by a future bishop of Norwich and is explicitly didactic. In a preface Hall explains that he has taken as a model those of the 'olde Heathens' who

bestowed their time in drawing out the true lineaments of every vertue and vice, so lively, that who saw the medals, might know the face: which Art they significantly termed Charactery. Their papers were so many tables, their writings so many speaking pictures, or living images, whereby the ruder multitude might even by their sense learn to know vertue, and discerne what to detest.[21]

Hall's 'olde Heathens' are actually Theophrastus, whose 'Characters' in their original form show little concern with moral delineations. However, the editions of Theophrastus available in the seventeenth century included a spurious preface which announced Theophrastus' intentions to be morally instructive, and which was accepted as authentic.[22]

Hall's imagery is largely the imagery of portraiture; and indeed, to write a Character is universally to 'draw' it and the result called a 'sketch'. But the Character writer's imagery is not confined to the visual, and a contributor to that other highly popular collection of Characters begun by Sir Thomas Overbury locates the source of the 'Character' rather in the shaping of word and letter:

If I must speake the Schoole-masters language, I will confesse that Character comes of this Infinitive moode χαράξω, which signifies to engrave, or make a deepe Impression. And for that cause, a letter (as A.B.)

[20] Examples given in ibid. 41–2.

[21] Joseph Hall, 'A Premonition of the Title and Vse of Characters', in *Characters of Vertues and Vices* (London, 1608), sigs. A5–5ᵛ.

[22] See Smeed, *Theophrastan 'Character'*, 20; Isaac Casaubon's edition of Theophrastus, *Theophrasti, Characteres Ethici . . .* (1592)—Greek text, followed by Latin translation and commentary—and John Healey's English translation, *Theophrastus, his Morall Characters* (1616), indicate even in their titles how far Theophrastus was taken to be a moral writer.

is called a Character. Those elements which wee learne first, leaving a strong seale in our memories. Character is also taken for an Ægyptian Hieroglyphicke, for an impresse, or short Embleme, in little comprehending much.[23]

This writer slips in a deft allusion to the alphabet of personal identity under the guise of etymology. Letters and individual characteristics are both impressed upon the mind (by, it is implied, an outside agency) very early; such characteristics form, as it were, the human index by which a person may be deciphered. In the second example he gives, the hieroglyphic provides an image which shares the qualities of word and picture; the 'character' has developed into an 'Embleme', where both the abstraction of the letter and the more graphic visual metaphor combine to offer a more complex representation of a human type. In the sentences which follow this passage he abandons abstract for concrete representation, and fixes the imagery of his development from the bare letter to the full-scale portrait (an imagery which also gently implies a chronological development) by employing the terminology of the artist and the craftsman: 'To square out a Character by our English levell; it is a picture (reall or personall) quaintly drawne, in various colours, all of them heightned by one shadowing' (sig. Q4ᵛ). This portrait still retains some of the qualities of the 'Embleme', being 'heightned by one shadowing' so that one message or set of messages takes precedence over any others which might be offered as part of the 'human index'. Nevertheless, it is complex and flexible enough to delineate both the 'reall' (or general) and the 'personall' (or particular) character. Yet while this example from Overbury assumes a *development* from single letter to full picture, another Character writer, Humphrey Browne, evidently perceives the image of character as letter simply as a convenient adjunct to the commonplace of the world as book—in this case additionally appropriate to the Character he is epitomizing: 'A learned man is the best character in the world, Gods great book in Folio. He is a God in the shape of man, when one that is rude, shut up in the darke dungeon of ignorance, is but a beast in the shape of man.'[24] The context makes it plain that Browne's

[23] Sir Thomas Overbury, *His Wife, with Additions of New Characters, and Many Other Wittie Conceits Never Before Printed* (London, 1622), 11th edn., sigs. Q4–4ᵛ.

[24] Humphrey Browne, *A Map of the Microcosme, or, a Morall Description of Man. Newly Compiled into Essayes* (London, 1647), sig. A11.

'Microcosme' is spiritually rather than physically based; the outward shapes of the 'rude' and the 'learned' men resemble each other physically but, deciphered in 'Gods great book', hold an absolutely different sense and meaning. Here Browne is exploiting what the Overbury writer seems to see as a drawback: the fact that letters do not visually represent their meanings. So it is that, in Browne's book of the world, meanings need not correspond with outward shapes, any more than a book's 'characters' represent pictorially the words they make up.

In biographical writing, where the reader might expect a more particularized portrayal, a Character (combining physical with spiritual qualities) was often introduced towards the end under a separate subheading.[25] Yet these Characters too are often represented as no more than a page from 'Gods great book'—not the world this time, but the Bible. This is what Morton's commemorators did to him, when they described him as a paraphrase or transcript of 1 Timothy 3.[26] John Whitefoote's funeral sermon for Joseph Hall (1656), a more detailed and specific performance than most, employs the same manoeuvre with Job (and at another point with Jacob) as Hall's prototype. 'We have heard of the patience of Job,' writes Whitefoote, 'but never saw a fairer Copy of it, than was in this man.'[27] Thomas Tully, chaplain to Edward Rainbow, bishop of Carlisle, opts for the 1 Timothy text in a funeral sermon for Rainbow which grips convention throughout (1684, printed 1688). In his misdescribed 'very sparing . . . Character' he describes Rainbow as 'Copying out, in the whole tenor and series of his Actions, the Noble draught St. Paul has left us of a good Bishop'.[28] Jonathan Banks, author of the *Life of Rainbow*

[25] Walton only uses this resource once, in the *Life of Donne*. His later *Lives* integrate Character information into the narrative (as in his identification of Herbert with his own clerical 'Character', *The Country Parson*)—a much more subtle and complex approach to delineating the virtuous 'pattern'.

[26] e.g. Barwick, *Life*, 141; Barwick, *Sermon*, 22. Ralph Venning, in a book which presents the 'Character' of a Christian through paradox, quotes a scriptural reference as the basis for each virtuous quality. See e.g. his use of Genesis 32: 10: 'He acounts [sic] himself lesse then the least of all mercies; and yet he lookes on the greatest as his due', in *Orthodox Paradoxes, or, A Beleiver Clearing Truth by Seeming Contradictions* . . . (London, 1647), 48–9.

[27] Whitefoote, *Deaths Alarum*, 70.

[28] *The Life of the Right Reverend Edward Rainbow D.D. Late Lord Bishop of Carlisle. To Which is Added, A Sermon Preached at his Funeral by Thomas Tully . . . April the 1st. 1684* (London, 1688), 11 (2nd pag.).

bound in with Tully's sermon, no less conventionally (but more imaginatively) seizes the textual image as a means to describe Rainbow's living conduct:

> As he inspected the Lives and Manners of his Clergy, and their performance of their Pastoral Charge; so was he not wanting to set them a good Pattern himself, being assured, that nothing won more upon the Minds and Consciences of Men than a good Example, especially in those who attend at Gods Altar, and dispense his Holy Word, and unfold the Sacred Mysteries of our holy Religion. He therefore resoved [*sic*] to set them a Copy as legible as his human Frailties would permit it to be written, that they fairly imitating it, the Laity might be invited to transcribe it from them.[29]

Here the scriptural source for the commonplace has been buried, but the image of man as text which has the scriptural prescription as its source has been elaborated. Rainbow's 'example' has resembled his 'precept' not only in the obvious sense, but in the explicitly hierarchical progression of its planned 'transcription', from bishop to lesser clergy and from them to the laity.

Simeon Ash and John Wall, in a preface to Clarke's *Marrow of Ecclesiastical History*, make the same point (also privileging 'example' over 'precept' with the assertion that 'the common people are more apt to enquire what Ministers do, than what they say'), but naturally do not suggest that the hierarchy stretching from original to imitative copy has any episcopal basis. Rather, the originals are represented as being the holy *Lives* of the *Marrow*, and the reader is appealed to directly as a transcriber of those lives. This reader is exhorted to 'make practical improvements of the Epitomized Lives of these many eminent servants of Christ . . . in this book. These fair Copies we should spread before our eyes, and write after them, until our writing, our living, be like them.'[30]

This theme, that the *listener's* real behavioural response is much of what makes a sermon or preacher 'lively', is actually rather common. When preaching and living are interrelated images linked by textual allusion, action and prescription must elide, and so the preacher's virtues can become curiously merged with his congregation's. Taking the case of Clarke's *Life of Samuel Crook*,

---

[29] See n. 24 above, pp. 66–7 (1st pag.).
[30] Clarke, *Marrow*, 1st part, sig. c3.

Crook's conduct is described as 'one continual Commentary upon his Doctrine, and an exemplary Sermon consisting of living words, or of words translated into works, as will further appear in its due place'.[31] The promised 'translation' is not there, because the *Life of Crook* is really about zeal in preaching, not about pastoral acts. But an indication of the very practical terms upon which he offered his sermons does appear a bit later. Here Crook's own attitude to his preaching is being described: 'If after his preaching he found no mention made of his Sermon, by which he might Collect, that probably some benefit had been reaped by it, he would be much dejected, as if the fault had been in his preaching (even then when he seemed to excell himself,) rather than in his Hearers; and used to say, *That if he had preached better, they would have profited more*' (p. 206). Crook, then, saw a direct relationship between the moral conduct of his hearers and his own preaching skill; perhaps even that the 'words' became 'living words' and 'translated into works' largely in the holy acts of his congregation. Thus, preaching skill becomes itself a holy act, and the minister's private conduct simply a necessary adjunct to his main business of inducing godly behaviour in his flock. The *performed* sermon, too, is a ready analogy for living action—it *is* an act—while its written or printed form, by contrast, can be characterized as empty precept. For instance, Edward Leigh, in the dedicatory Epistle of Whateley's *Prototypes*, justifies his narration of parts of Whateley's life in these terms:

because an *Example* of a Person living amongst you may be more prevalent with some then the Examples of others, though singularly holy, whose vertues they onely read of (as a Sermon delivered, *Viva voce*, doth more affect then the same read out of a Booke). So walke therefore as you had him for an Example, and bee you followers of him, as hee was of CHRIST, in the Graces before mentioned and all holy conversation.[32]

It must have been irresistible morally to delineate people as texts. Texts—not merely scriptures, but the sermons and commentaries based upon them—*really* determined lives. Words were indeed 'translated into works'; the availability of the Word

---

[31] Clarke, *Lives*, 204.

[32] Whateley, sig. A5. Whately, known as 'the Roaring Boy of Banbury', probably lost more than most in his translation from performance to print. See Clarke, *Marrow*, 1st part, p. 460.

in an intelligible form, and the ensuing power to interpret that Word, had after all been a major moving force behind the Reformation. Nor was it necessarily perceived as a simple one-way process where men and women read the prescriptions of the Word of truth and imitated it, because the Word itself was by definition accepted as a means to the *rediscovery* of the true self of its imitator.[33] It was already written in the human heart, and its elucidation by external means was only necessary because of the occluding power of sin. The truthful text defined the man, not the other way about. Bunyan, for instance, describes one act of reading in which the text is the active partner, and he is read by it, saying of Luther's highly influential *Commentarie upon the Epistle to the Galathians* (1575) that 'I found my condition in his experience, so largely and profoundly handled as if his Book had been written out of my heart'.[34] Beza's *Life of Calvin*, written as a preface to Calvin's *Commentarie on the Book of Joshua*, actually personifies the *Commentarie* itself, so that both he and it lament the death of Calvin together: 'And therefore also mine intent hath not bene to recommende him [the Commentary] by thys Testimonie (for what needeth it?) but rather to lament more with him of the death of him, which hath bene as a father, both to him & to mee.'[35]

Such strong links between book and act, or book and person, were further maintained by the status of the learned text—principally the Bible, but also to some extent the works of the early Fathers.[36] The position is summed up by Richard Bernard in *The*

---

[33] Again, the Word was the principal but not the only means to self-discovery. Alexander Clogie, Bedell's chaplain, writes of Bedell that 'he took an account of himself, how he spent every day, by keeping a journal thereof . . . A Christian must study his own book, and so did he.' See *Two Biographies of William Bedell, Bishop of Kilmore*, 156.

[34] John Bunyan, *Grace Abounding to the Chief of Sinners* . . . (London, 1666), 41. For the importance of Luther's *Commentarie* see W. A. Clebsch, 'The Elizabethans on Luther', Jaroslav Pelikan (ed.), in *Interpreters of Luther: Essays in Honor of Wilhelm Pauck* (Philadelphia, 1968), 97–120.

[35] Theodore Beza, *A Discourse . . . Conteyning in Briefe the Historie of the Lyfe and Death of Maister Iohn Calvin, translated by I.S.* (London, 1564), sigs. A3–3ᵛ.

[36] The doctrinal status of the early Fathers in the English Reformed tradition was under severe debate: see e.g. Bishop John Jewel, *Treatise of the Holy Scriptures* (1570), in *The Works of John Jewel*, edited by John Ayre, 4 vols. (Cambridge, 1845–50), iv. 1173–4.

Faithfull Shepheard: 'lastly,' he writes, 'a Minister must haue a good librarie, meanes must be vsed, the helpe of the learned. Extraordinarie Reuelations, are now ceased.'[37]

The image of man as text, or word, finds, of course, its culmination in the person of Christ, the Living Word, expressed through that text of texts, the New Testament. As Erasmus puts it in the *Paraclesis*, the New Testament expresses the person of Christ so immediately that 'you would see less if you gazed upon Him with your very eyes'.[38]

Thus, the imagery employed in exhortations to imitate Christ is also tightly bound up with text and precept. Jeremy Taylor's popular narrative of the life of Christ, *The Great Exemplar of Sanctity and Holy Life* (1649), is also, as its title suggests, a book of precepts, and the descriptive and the prescriptive are bound together at every possible point by textual metaphor. Christ and God are the reader's texts, expressed in the Commandments and the books of the New Testament, and the reader's task with regard to these texts is emphatically not to interpret, but to imitate: 'But GOD who never loved, that man should be too ambitiously buisy in imitating his wisdome (and man lost Paradise for it) is most desirous we should imitate his goodnesse and transcribe copyes of those excellent Emanations from his Holinesse, whereby as he communicates himselfe to us in mercyes, so he propounds himself imitable by us in graces.'[39] But Taylor also makes it plain that the imitative process is not one-way; the text a man reads is that of his own heart, and its imitation is a means to self-knowledge: 'GOD . . . with a great designe of mercy hath writ his Commandements in so large characters, and engraved them in such tables, that no man can want the records, nor yet skill to read the handwriting upon this wall, if he understands what he understands, that is, what is placed in his own spirit' (sig. a2ᵛ). In propounding the life of Christ for imitation, Taylor has, of course, to be careful to make its limits clear. There is only one Redeemer. But, this done, he is free to assert that in every other respect the conduct of Christ was 'even, constant, unblameable, complying with civill society,

[37] Bernard, *The Faithfull Shepheard* . . . , 94.

[38] In *Christian Humanism and the Reformation*, edited by John C. Olin (New York, 1965), 106.

[39] Jeremy Taylor, *The Great Exemplar of Sanctity and Holy Life* . . . (London, 1649), sig. a2ᵛ. Taylor's own model is clearly à Kempis.

without affrightment of precedent or prodigious instances of actions, greater than the imitation of men. For if we observe our blessed Saviour in the whole story of his Life, although he was without sin, yet the instances of his piety were the actions of a very holy, *but of an ordinary life* [my italics]' (p. 6). Having established the clear possibility of imitation,[40] Taylor describes it to be a move from the divine text to the preached (that is, the lived) Word of Christ, and from that to an imitative action in the whole Christian body, 'GOD being the Author, the *word incarnate* being the great Doctor and Preacher of it, his life and death being its consignation,[41] the holy Spirit being the great argument and demonstration of it, and the Apostles being the organs and conduits of its dissemination' (sig. b2).

Inevitably, the Christ of the Gospels—a narrated Christ—mediates absolute precept and the faithful reader's imitative action. But the exemplary (and so biographical) pattern spreads far out from this source, animating a good deal of commemorative, proto-biographical writing. The lives of the godly are written to be an additional proof of the rectitude of their teaching, and in that sense the narrated Life—and particularly the Life which prefaces a subject's Works—also stands mediator between the Author and the multitude of devout recipients, while the biographer plays Apostle.

Within this thinking, both the written Life and the printed Works of the subject are explicitly perceived as an afterlife: hence the strength of Erasmus' hyperbolic assertion that the New

---

[40] J. Sears McGee argues, in his book *The Godly Man in Stuart England* (New Haven and London, 1976), that it was far more common among 'Anglican' divines to propound Christ as direct exemplar; 'Puritans . . . spoke a great deal of the importance of "possessing" Christ or having an "interest" or "portion" in him, but they rarely suggested the use of Christ's actions as a model' (p. 107). See also pp. 110, 196–7. See also D. MacCulloch, 'The Myth of the Reformation', *History Today*, 41 (July 1991), 28–35, and Felicity Heal, *Hospitality in Early Modern England* (Oxford, 1990), 137–9. Heal qualifies McGee's alignment, arguing that in practice acts of charity are less clearly demarcated between works-centred and faith-centred theologies than McGee implies. She suggests rather that 'Anglican' memorialists are more likely to *praise* their subjects for charitable giving than 'Puritan' ones (see pp. 295–6).

[41] See *OED*, 'consignation'. As well as meaning a seal, confirmation, or blessing, the word also suggests the delivery (or consignment) of something to a recipient—a significant definition in this exemplary context.

Testament contained a face of Christ more authentic than the real experience of seeing Him. Its text was the single repository of everything known about Christ. The writings of and about the godly dead also function in this way as a life after death; and a favourite text for the writers of funeral sermons is Hebrews 11: 4: 'By fayth, Abel offered unto God a more plenteous sacrifice then Cayn, by which he obteyned witnes that he was righteous, God testifyinge of his gyftes: by which also he beinge deed, yet speaketh.'[42] The context for this verse is a definition of faith: 'the ground of things hoped for, the evidence of things not seene' (11: 1). Verse 2 adds to this the witness borne by others to the faithful dead of the Old Testament, and verse 3 asserts a fundamental of faith: 'that the worlde was ordeyned by the worde of God: and that thinges which are sene, were made of thinges which were not sene.'

Thus, the progression of the argument runs from a bare assertion of a belief grounded in intangible truths to a written record of the acts of those holding those truths. It then doubles back to the larger assertion that the creation of all things which can be seen was made by the utterance of the Divine Word. Finally it comes to rest in examples (of which Abel is only the first, followed in later verses by others from the Old Testament) of men whose recorded acts, demonstrating an effective belief in the invisible Divinity, prompted a visible Divine approval. The whole chapter, its proofs drawn from written records of the acts of the 'Elders' of the Old Testament, grants an ascendance to the written Word, the Word which bears an exemplary testimony to the acts of the faithful who are now vanished in all other respects from the visible world.

This is clearly a text very suitable to the Renaissance writers of exemplary commemorations of the now-invisible godly dead. In particular, the ambiguous wording of 'he being deed, yet speaketh' can be made to apply with specific force to the dead whose godly utterances had survived them in print or manuscript—especially when those utterances were accompanied by a narrative of their equally godly acts. The King James translation of the phrase also offers as an alternative reading 'he being dead, is yet spoken of',[43]

---

[42] Quoted from Tyndale's 1535 translation.
[43] See *New Testament Octapla*, 1272.

but the consensus in translating the phrase from Tyndale onwards is for the active form.[44]

If a funeral subject had been himself a preacher, he might well be made to give his own tacit sermon on mortality. Barwick's funeral sermon for Morton uses this manoeuvre. 'Let us but imagine', begins Barwick, 'we hear his Hearse preaching now to us: 'Believe it, the *Hearse* of a person of his Sacred order and Exemplary piety, will be a powerful preacher to any devout soul, that duly considers it, and seriously layes it to heart; and therefore do but listen to that as supplying what was so proper and likely for himself to have spoken, and you may have a *Funeral Sermon* (though I should hold my peace) even from the words of my Text.'[45]

Barwick concludes the first part of his sermon—that is, the part which is only textual exegesis and not biographical material—by quoting Morton's own declaration of faith, which he had written and had had signed by five witnesses shortly before his death. This too Barwick describes as Morton's 'sermon'. 'And now', he says, 'you have had *His Sermon* as well as mine . . . I might in this thing fitly compare him to *Abel* before the *flood*, who *being dead yet speaketh*' (p. 52).

Even where the deceased had been no preacher, and had made no recorded declaration, the corpse might become subject to this sort of eloquence. Charles Fitz-Geffry, preaching at the funeral of Lady Philippa Rous in 1620, privileges the corpse's discourse well above his own:

Many Sermons preached to the Eare by the liuing, of the breuity and vncertainty of life, of the meditation of Death, &c. will hardly make so deepe impression in the liuing, as one Sermon preached to their eyes

---

[44] Examples of funeral sermons based on this text and grounded in this premiss are very numerous indeed, but here are some examples: John Chetwinde and William Thomas together produced *The Dead Speaking, or, the Living Names of Two Deceased Ministers of Christ . . . viz. Mr. Sam. Oliver, and Mr. Samuel Crook* (London, 1653); Isaac Basire's funeral sermon for John Cosin is called *The Dead Mans Real Speech: a Funeral Sermon Preached on Hebr. xi. 4 . . . 29th Day of April, 1672 . . . Together with a Brief of the Life . . . Principal Actions, and Sufferings, and of the Death of the . . . Lord Bishop of Durham* (London, 1673); William Burkitt's *The Peoples Zeal Provok't by the Pious and Instructive Example of their Dead Minister . . . Mr. William Gurnall* (London, 1680) has as its running title *The Dead Speaking*.

[45] Barwick, *Sermon*, 3.

by one that is dead or lyes a dying. Wherefore as *Alfonsus* of *Aragon* sometimes said of Counsellors, that the *Dead were the best Counsellors*, (meaning Bookes;) so we may say (in this regard), *the Dead are the best Preachers*,
for what wee preach to your eares, they presse to your hearts.[46]

In both these examples the posthumous message of the body
is very much more prominent a theme than the other afterlife
of the word conferred by print, although this second element is
also present. But John Buckeridge's funeral sermon for Lancelot
Andrewes, printed before his *CXVI Sermons*, presents Andrewes
in a rich variety of articulate and immortal modes:

Now I apply myselfe and my Text, to the present Text which lies before
us . . . A man whose worth may not be passed over in silence, whom
all ages with us may celebrate and admire, nor to be spoken of without
great care and study: . . . Heere I desire neither the tongue of men, nor
Angells: if it were lawfull, I should wish no other but his owne tongue
and pen . . . let him speake of himselfe, none so fitt as himselfe was . . .
And he now speakes: He speakes in his learned *Workes* and *Sermons*, and
he speakes in his *Life* and *workes of mercy*, and he speakes in his *death*:
And what he taught in his life and works, he taught and expressed in his
death . . . he was the loud and great *Crying Voice*, I am but the poore
Eccho: and it is well with me, if as an *Eccho*, of his large and learned bookes
and workes, I onely repeate a few of the last words.[47]

Here the speaking body of Andrewes is at the same time his
corpse—the 'Text which lies before us', and the conduct of his
life and decorous mode of his death, to be commemorated in later
passages of Buckeridge's sermon, and the printed works of which
the sermon is the preface. Buckeridge is careful to indicate both
that his commemorative attempt falls short of the reality of his
subject's eloquence, and that he has not embroidered the truths
uttered by these different aspects of Andrewes.

Nicholas Bernard, in the *Life* of James Ussher which began as
Ussher's funeral sermon, less richly but fully as comprehensively
combines these different commonplaces in the Epistle 'to the
Reader' which serves as its preface:

[46] Charles Fitz-Geffry, *Deaths Sermon Vnto the Liuing. Delivered at the
Funerals of the Religious Ladie Philippe, Late Wife vnto . . . Sr. Anthonie Rovs
. . .* (London, 1620), 13–14.

[47] John Buckeridge, *A Sermon Preached at the Funeral of . . . Lancelot
[Andrewes], Late Lord Bishop of Winchester . . .* , in Lancelot Andrewes, *XCVI
Sermons* (London, 1629), 16 (3rd pag.).

The writing of the lives of Holy and Eminent men departed, *are for us surviving (as a* Father [St Bernard] *saith*, Veluti speculum, exemplum, condimentum, *as a* Glasse *to trimme our lives by, a* Copy *to improve our hands, a* Sauce *to sharpen our tastes* of the heavenly Gift *in them*: *by* which, as after a manner, the Persons themselves live with us after their deaths; so many living, and yet are dead, are incited or reduced to a good life. *And some such fruit may in time be reaped from the following Narration of the* Life and Death *of this Holy and Eminent Primate, by the exemplary application of each passage in his younger years, as elder; like that of* Elisha *to the* Shunamites *Childe*, putting mouth to mouth, eyes to eyes, hands to hands, *the reader may be recovered unto life Eternal.*[48]

Bernard makes the usual plays, but refines the 'dead yet speaking' commonplace by balancing those living in the spirit (or, if you like, in the breath of Divine utterance blowing through them) but dead in body, with those alive in body yet dead in spirit—the unregenerate to whom the Word must reach out. (As one reader of the present book remarked: for dead read living throughout.) Bernard also employs a metaphor of great physicality to vivify exemplary imitation: like Elisha bringing a child back to life as God works through the contact of his body with the child's corpse,[49] so the textual body of holy utterance applies a kiss of Life to the dead souls of the unregenerate living.

Clarke aims for a comparable synthesis of the different modes of afterlife in his *Life of Master Samuel Crook*, combining an exemplary narrative of the conduct of Crook's life and deathbed with extensive quotation from the funeral sermon preached for him, 'the issues of his brain and heart made publick'.[50] The sermon's final word of exhortation, as it is quoted by Clarke, is explicit about the immortality of the utterances of the dead man:

> Remember what he hath spoken while he lived:
> Remember what he yet speaks being dead.

(pp. 213–14)

These words are followed almost immediately by a list of his printed works. That this synthesis amounts to a statement of the subject's immortality in these various modes is expressed clearly, if clumsily, by the filial tribute offered to Clarke in the

---

[48] N. Bernard, *The Life and Death of . . . James Usher . . .* (London, 1656), sigs. A3^r–4^r.

[49] See 2 Kings 4, esp. 32–5.   [50] Clarke, *Lives*, 202–14.

complimentary verses on his *Lives* printed before the 1677 edition
of the first part of *The Marrow of Ecclesiastical History*:

> HOW! LIVES! They're dead. No: death they did evade
> By their good Lives, which them immortal made.
> Death could not take their Lives away, you find
> He took their Bodies, left their Lives behind;
> Which here assembled shew themselves so well,
> As though they strove each other to excell . . .
> Then since good Lives are in this Book so rife,
> I make no doubt to call't a Book of Life.[51]

The clearest statement of such textual immortality is made by
Thomas Fuller's collection of the lives of the eminent godly, *Abel
Redevivus, or, the Dead Yet Speaking* (1651). Here the narration
of each life is followed by a list of works, and frequently accompanied by a portrait; an ensemble encapsulated in its frontispiece,
a speaking skeleton lying in a monument the roof of which is
constructed of books (see Fig. 3.1).

Within such works, or lists of works, the frequent presence
of sermons is a reminder of an important distinction which has
not yet been made explicitly in this chapter, between the sermon
as printed word and the sermon as performed. Naturally, only the
former can be regarded as participating in the commonplace of
textual immortality, but the writers of the printed sermon often
make use of the very clear distinction perceived between the
written and the performed text to denote the difference between
the virtuous life as it has been recorded and the life as it was really
acted. Edward Leigh's remarks, quoted above (p. 87), on the life
of Whateley are a variant on this commonplace. But if we take the
Dedicatory Epistle of John Whitefoote's sermon for Joseph Hall,
he makes it very clear that his work, as it has been printed, falls
far short of the eloquence of the original performance at Hall's
funeral. At the same time as Whitefoote states his commemorative 'Representation' to fall short of the living original, he adds of
the printed version that 'it hath the common disadvantage of all
Writings, which are but the dead Shadows of the living Voyce;
and therefore no marvel, if this wants much of that little Grace
and Vivacity, which it might seem to have in the delivery'.[52]

---

[51] Jo. Clark, 'To his Reverend and much honoured Father . . .', in Clarke,
Marrow, 1st part, sig. e2.

[52] Whitefoote, *Deaths Alarum*, sigs. A3^v–4.

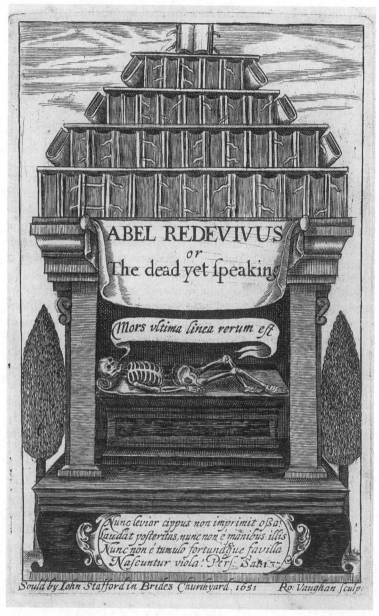

FIG 3.1. Engraved title-page of Thomas Fuller, *Abel Redevivus*
(London, 1651)

While this can look like a conventional modesty topos, it is also worth observing that Whitefoote offers his disclaimer as part of a statement that Hall's living acts could not be reconstructed on paper. Whitefoote, in implying that the spoken word reflects living acts better than the written, also stresses how far both living and preaching are taken as performances.[53] The acted life is indeed being perceived in terms of 'living word', whilst after death a subject can only achieve any significant earthly immortality through print.

When Taylor employs the 'living sermon' commonplace for Christ, in *The Great Exemplar*, the shift of tenses from past to present, and the carefully placed use of the word 'perpetuall' reflects Taylor's assurance of an immortality based on present performance:

Holy and Eternall JESUS whose whole life and doctrine was a perpetuall sermon of holy life . . . give me grace to understand, diligence and attention to consider, care to lay up, and carefulnesse to reduce to practice all those actions, discourses and pious lessons and intimations by which thou didst expresly teach, or tacitely imply, or mysteriously signifie our duty.[54]

Taylor's petitionary prayer, itself arguably a performative form (though I don't propose to argue it here), perceives Christ's acts as becoming the present assistance to the hearer of an imitative virtue.

This last is, of course, not a manoeuvre which may be directly employed for any other being. However, because the resurrection of the body is a general promise, and because the acts and utterances of the godly are assumed to participate in the life of Christ, the written record of those acts and utterances may become a mirror of the subject's resurrection, and thus a promise of eternal life to the imitative reader. The textually resurrected subject charts a means of salvation. Walton's *Lives* of Donne and Herbert function as the most perfectly integrated examples of this technique. Whereas Clarke's *Lives*, Fuller's *Abel Redevivus*, and other similar collections narrate the lives and then simply append lists of their subjects' works to the narrative, Walton builds his subjects' printed utterances directly into their biographies.

[53] Professor Collinson discusses the histrionic (by implication the performative) aspect of sermon delivery in *The Religion of Protestants* (Oxford, 1982), 244–5.

[54] Jeremy Taylor, *The Great Exemplar*, 95.

Sometimes they are represented as direct speech, as when Donne speaks, in a modified form, words from his own sermon for the funeral of Lady Danvers: 'I were miserable, if I might not dye.' Sometimes they are narrated as acts, as when Herbert's *Priest to the Temple* is represented as his own pastoral practice at Bemerton.[55] Works become life, print becomes living speech; the living Donne even utters his own memento mori, in preaching his 'own Funeral Sermon'.[56] Walton's powerful close participates in the resurrection it awards: 'He was earnest and unwearied in the search for knowledge; with which, his vigorous soul is now satisfied, and employed in a continual praise of that God that first breathed it into his active body; that body, which once was a Temple of the Holy Ghost, and is now become a small quantity of Christian dust: *But I shall see it re-animated*' (p. 84).

If we examine the passages following Donne's burial, we discover a deft arrangement of emblems, mutually reinforced, which commemorate the body's death as they signify its resurrection. The first of these is explicit: an 'unknown friend', the day after the funeral, 'writ this *Epitaph* with a cole on the wall, over his grave':

> Reader! I am to let thee know
> Donne's Body only, lyes below,
> For, could the grave his Soul comprize,
> Earth would be richer than the skies.

(pp. 82–3)

While the message is unambiguous, its setting is subtle. As it is described, the verses are written in that most provisional of forms, as a graffito, in that richly symbolic medium, coal. The message in coal, then, is a mortal message which promises immortality beyond the body's death. As such it places the human record in perspective, as a fleeting promise of a lasting good. However, it too has its immortality, in its transcription and insertion into Walton's printed *Life*, ensuring that the words survive the coal they were written in. (It is tempting to wonder whether Walton wrote the epitaph himself.)

Having introduced this first emblem of a textual immortality, words written in dust and then translated into print, Walton

---

[55] See Ch. 4.   [56] Walton, *Lives*, 75.

continues with a second emblem, this time one which more directly represents Donne's now vanished body. This is Donne's 'Monument', a statue of himself built with money donated anonymously, and later discovered to be the gift of his living body's Physician, Dr Fox. While Fox's attempts to preserve that body while it breathed have already been described as having proved unsuccessful and even unwelcome (p. 77), his concealed munificence guarantees another kind of preservation, not in frail flesh but durable marble. This funerary monument is described by Walton as being 'as lively a representation . . . as marble can express'; one, indeed, so 'lively' that 'it seems to breath faintly; and, Posterity shall look upon it as a kind of artificial Miracle' (p. 83). This funeral statue is also an image with a dual function. It both reminds us of the dissolution of the individual body it commemorates, and of the afterlife it preserves by figuring bodily features beyond that dissolution.[57]

Walton's concluding Character of Donne follows his description of the monument. The Character combines physical and spiritual qualities, often reading the latter from the former: 'His aspect was chearful,' writes Walton, 'and such, as gave a silent testimony of a clear knowing soul, and of a Conscience at peace with itself' (p. 83). The juxtaposition of the Character with the statue suggests that to some extent the Character is intended as an articulation of the statue's own 'silent testimony' of Donne's virtues.

The image of the 'monument', both as it appears in Pauline metaphor and as it is employed as an image for commemorative biography, can be used as a spur to virtuous imitation in itself. Robert Mossom exhorts his listeners in these terms in the peroration to his funeral speech for his predecessor: 'Let me prompt you to this service, and I shall readily comply with you in the performance, that our Hearts and Affections may make him a Tomb, and our Lives in Imitation write the Epitaph; and if you please, let the Inscription be those words of the Apostle, *Christ is our Life.*'[58]

---

[57] For further discussion of this point see pp. 175–6 below; see also Nigel Foxall, *A Sermon in Stone: John Donne and his Monument in St. Paul's Cathedral* (London, 1978).

[58] R[obert] Mossom, *A Narrative Panegyrical of the Life, Sickness and Death of George* [Wilde] . . . *Lord Bishop of Derry in Ireland* (London, 1665/6), 19.

Mossom's words also act as a very appropriate summary of Walton's literary intentions. Claiming to have been Donne's 'Friend' (though of a lowly kind), Walton offers the strength of his 'Affections' as a prominent reason for writing the *Life*. The 'Tomb' he makes is the *Life* itself: Walton refers to his work as a 'Monument' in an elegy to Donne, as does Charles Cotton in commendatory verses accompanying the edition of 1675. Its 'Inscription' is the exemplary intentions which run through it, ensuring that the recorded worth of the deceased finds a permanent life in the imitative godliness of each new reader.

Henry Scudder also uses the engraved monument as an image for exemplary biography. He begins his *Life of Whateley* with the remark:

This writing and printing the lives of worthy men, is like the engravings with the point of a diamond, raising up for them an everlasting monument; upon which the light of their Faith and good workes, is made to shine before men that seeing their Faith and holinesse they may follow them; and may also praise God for his Graces in them, and for the good which hath bin done by them, and so glorifie their Father which is in Heaven.[59]

The two examples above demonstrate the 'Monument' to be another, thinly disguised, textual emblem, a kind of more durable page upon which testimonies of worth may be written. The monument enclosing the speaking skeleton of *Abel Redevivus* has a roof of books: the real funerary monument carries an engraved biographical message. And while Walton only makes a delicately implicit link between his *Life* and Donne's actual funerary monument—made explicit later by Cotton in any case—nevertheless his subtler use of juxtapositions in the main text, and his reference to his 'want' of 'abilities | To raise a Monument, as matchless as his worth' in the elegy on Donne, are simply refinements of a common trope. Thus, Banks finishes his commemoration of Rainbow: 'To conclude, May this mean Monument, which I have erected to the Memory of this Right Reverend Prelate, suffice to continue his Name.'[60]

[59] Henry Scudder, *The Life and Death of Mr. William Whateley, Late Minister of the Word at Banbury* . . . , in William Whateley, *Prototypes* . . . (London, 1640), sig a.
[60] [Jonathan Banks], *Life of Rainbow* (London, 1688), 111.

There is one further dimension to the image of the godly man as monument. Walton selects it to sum up the translation of Donne from living body to dead matter, and then to incorruptible spirit. He ends the *Life* with a reference to Donne's body as a 'Temple of the Holy Ghost' (p. 84), and this reference to the living body as temple is also Pauline, taken from 1 Corinthians 3: 16.[61] The same reference is perhaps buried in images which denote the virtuous man—the man whose function is to edify—as part of that great edifice made up of the bodies of the faithful, the Church. 'He is a pillar of our church,' writes John Earle of the 'Grave Divine' in the Character book *Microcosmographie*, 'and his life our religion's best apology.'[62] Thus, the imagery of the virtuous man's actions as essential support for a material structure complements the commonplace that his life in its real performance becomes material proof of abstract arguments. The invisible Church, and the arguments which demonstrate its grounds, are both abstractions which cannot be seen; the seeing of them, the assertion of faith in the unseen, is built into an image of Church as visible edifice, and its tenets as lived actions.

The more 'Anglican' of the life-writers (of whom Walton is one) may even take this one step further and assign real buildings, consecrated to the glory of God, as the visible demonstration of a virtuous man's faith, and as the lasting monument which signifies his immortality beyond, as well as his translation into, 'Christian dust'. Peter Heylyn performs this service for Laud, quoting Sir Edward Dering as his authority: 'Nor need posterity take care to provide his *Monument*. He built one for himselfe . . . it being well observed . . . that *Saint* Pauls *Church will be his perpetuall Monument, and his own Booke* (against the Jesuite) *his lasting Epitaph.*'[63]

---

[61] Donne himself employs the image in his poem 'The Holy Ghost' (The Litanie, III): 'O Holy Ghost, whose temple I | Am, but of mudde walls, and condensed dust'. See *Poems, by J.D.* (London, 1633), 173. See also Joseph Hall, *Characters of Vertues and Vices*, 31, where the 'Humble Man' is described as 'a true Temple of God built with a low roofe'.

[62] John Earle, *Microcosmographie* . . . , 6th edn. (London, 1633), 7.

[63] Peter Heylyn, *Briefe Relation of the Death and Sufferings of* . . . [William Laud] *L. Archbishop of Canterbury* . . . (London, 1644), 27. For Walton's use of real edifices in this way see Ch. 4.

BODIES

Paul's argument that the body, as the Spirit's temple, should be treated as holy, together with the assertion in the first chapter of Genesis that man was made in the image of God, means that the signs of virtue, of the 'image' of godliness, are read into the lineaments of the face, and the everyday actions of the body.

A natural consequence of this kind of attention is that the godly, visually and in narrative, are depicted like (even in terms of) each other.[64] The conventions of godly lineaments, godly carriage and gesture, which I now explore are highly developed, and it is not really possible precisely to determine the extent to which a living man following a godly model will indeed have made his appearance and behaviour conformable to such conventions, and how far he will simply have been described as having done so. I consider some homiletic treatises of advice to ministers in an attempt to discover how much printed encouragement the minister might have had to fashion himself, as part of the practical and visible exemplary duties of his ministry. I deal with the face (pp. 102–15), then gesture (pp. 115–24), then clothing (pp. 124–8), before considering in a separate section the performance of an exemplary death.

The Lineaments of Virtue

'VERTUE', writes Joseph Hall, in the first 'Proeme' to his book of Characters,

is not loved enough, because shee is not seene; and Vice loseth much detestation, because her uglinesse is secret. Certainly, my Lords, there are so many beauties, and so many graces in the face of goodnesse, that no eye can possibly see it without affection, without ravishment; and the visage

---

[64] This can extend to making a description of one godly man serve for another; for instance, Naylor, in the Baddeley/Naylor *Life of Morton* (1669), feels it adequate to describe Bishop Morton by quoting a description of Beza: 'This *Bishop* was, for his own person . . . very much resembling . . . Monsieur *Theodore Beza*, whom I have read thus Characterized and Described . . . of Stature little and cleane, and strong body, an exquisite constitution, comely countenance, constant and seldom interrupted health, quick wit, and solid Judgement, happy memory and indefatigably studious, and on courtesy and condiscension second to none' (pp. 157–8).

of Evil is so monstrous, through loathsome deformities, that if her lovers were not ignorant, they would be mad with disdaine and astonishment.[65]

The passage illustrates how tightly the idea of virtue is bound up with beauty. Hall exploits the association of the two, translating the 'beauty of holiness' into the unambiguously visible. However, Hall is dealing in metaphor; the Characters which follow the 'Proeme' are not, in the main, concerned with actual physical characteristics, but with abstract qualities—'wisdome', 'valor', 'patience'. The extent to which these virtues—or the 'Vices' depicted in Hall's second part—are actually transferred into physical terms is left undefined. As with the Plutarchan use of physical characteristics, beauty and ugliness function well as a moral metaphor, but do not necessarily translate directly into visual representation.

But some physically defined descriptions of beauty can figure virtue. The 'comely' face may perhaps be seen as a kind of compromise between spiritual and physical, carrying as it does connotations of seemliness and decorum as well as its sometimes problematic bodily meanings. Richard Bernard's advice to ministers in *The Faithfull Shepheard* can, for instance, stipulate a 'comely countenance' as important for effective ministry in these terms: 'not lumpish, not frowning or irefull, not light, smiling as too full of laughter: but sober, graue and modest, framed after the godly disposition of the heart.'[66] Bernard here privileges seemly *qualities*, as it were arranged self-consciously on the face, over the natural—or involuntary—gift of physical beauty. In these terms facial expression may truly reflect the 'disposition of the heart'. But his stipulations do not stop here. He also argues that involuntarily ugly or deformed persons should not aspire to be ministers, both because the disgust their features will produce in their listeners will militate against their effectiveness, and—by implication—because such deformed faces are not proper reflections of the image of God, and therefore are more likely to recall vice than virtue to the beholder:

Vnseemelinesse in countenance and gesture, is to be auoided, which deformed persons, either so by defect in nature, or by accident, cannot auoid:

---

[65] Hall, *Characters of Vertues and Vices*, 1–2.
[66] Bernard, *The Faithfull Shepheard*, 88.

and therefore not fit to be set vp in the roome of God, and to stand before
the face of the Congregation, such especially as haue great blemishes in
the face, want of eies, or one eie, a scarre on the mouth, but a peece of a
lippe, a want of a nose, and such like, which cannot be hidden . . .

 . . . it is not laudable that parents should of all their children
thrust such into the Ministerie; as if the woorst were good inough for it.
(p. 89)

While Bernard does (rather grudgingly) acknowledge that there
are some exceptions to this rule who have nevertheless been
'happely blessed therein', in the main it appears that 'woorst' looking recalls 'woorst' acting. (It is perhaps worth noting that the
deformities Bernard lists recall the informal mutilations of brawl-
ing, even perhaps of venereal disease, as well as more distantly the
formal signs of judicial punishment as they appear on the face:
the missing ears and slit noses. He stops short of calling such
'accidents' punishments, human or divine; but only just.) This
adds a new dimension of literalness to Nicholas Breton's statement
in his Character book *The Good and the Badde*, that 'a good man
is the image of God' (p. 15).

The vicious, of course, are desperately ugly. Samuel Clarke,
in the *Life of Gregory Nazianzen* appearing in *The Marrow of
Ecclesiastical History*, comments upon the 'insight' Nazianzen
had 'into mens dispositions by their Physiognomies', and quotes
Nazianzen's description of the emperor Julian the Apostate to
demonstrate his skill at reading faces. Clarke's translation of
Nazianzen runs:

I saw not one sign in him that gave me any hope that ever he would
become an honest man.

He had a running head: his shoulders did never leave waging: He had
winking eyes that continually rouled in his head: His countenance was
staring: He had a sliding and limping pace: his vissage was scornful. He
had a fleering face of his own, the which, his immoderate laughter and
continual scorning did declare. His manner was without all honesty, to
say and unsay: His words came tumbling out with vehemence and stops,
the sentence broken in the midst: His questions and objections were rash
and foolish: His answers were little better, which oftentimes followed one
after another, and as there was little hold of them, so were they proposed
without order.[67]

[67] Clarke, *Marrow*, 1st part, p. 57.

Note the *mobility* of the unfortunate emperor. No part of him is at rest, and when the passage's focus shifts to his mode of argument, it becomes clear that this unsettled countenance and 'waging' body reflect a mind equally shifting and illogical. Clarke lets us draw our own analogy when he follows this with his own description of Nazianzen's expository style: 'diligent, cautious, plain, and without offering violence to the Text' (p. 58). The contrast is pointed; although there is not a single physical detail in Clarke's Character, we helplessly perceive Nazianzen as settled, grave, clear-eyed, in a literal sense self-possessed. Because he has read and known his own spirit through obedience to the Divine Will, his bearing is therefore consistent. Julian's refusal to know God results in a visible lack of self-knowledge which borders on irrationality. The conventional physical signs of his unreason dominate his features, the 'winking eyes . . . that rouled in his head', the 'staring' countenance and 'immoderate laughter'. His sentences are 'broken', his answers disordered and uncontrolled. These are not merely signs of dishonesty, but of the breaking-up of the rational soul whose main impulse is towards the love of God.

Erasmus, in his treatise on manners written in 1530, *De Civilitate Morum Puerilium*, assigns moral characteristics to a number of the features displayed by Nazianzen's Julian:

For the well-ordered mind . . . to be universally manifested—and it is most strongly manifested in the face—the eyes should be calm, respectful and steady . . . not darting and rolling, a feature of insanity . . . nor should the eyes and eyelids be constantly blinking, a mark of the fickle . . . but such as reflects a mind composed, respectful and friendly. For it is no chance saying of the ancient sages that the seat of the soul is in the eyes.[68]

He adds later that 'loud laughter and the immoderate mirth that shakes the whole body . . . is for that reason called συγχόνσιον "discord" by the Greeks' (pp. 275–6).

There is a striking emphasis here on deliberate expression. Erasmus' treatise is virtually a list of stances which will *signify* decency, modesty, intelligence, and so on. For example, he warns his readers not to be seen 'looking down at the ground' (p. 286), because it appears dishonest. And physical description in Lives

---

[68] Erasmus, *Works*, xxv. 274.

and proto-Lives does concentrate on the seemliness of consciously assumed physical traits.

Yet physiognomical signs, natural and assumed, are not treated as infallible. Although Clarke approves Nazianzen's 'insight' in reading faces, the book in which his commendation appears is introduced with a verse which casts doubt on the efficacy of physiognomical skill. The verse appears under an engraved portrait of a studious but rather portly Clarke, and runs:

> The skilfull Physiognomers who scan
> Each line and wrinkle in the face of man,
> Can no more tell what Soul dwell's there, then we
> By seing Starrs can tell what Angels be:
> Then aske not at the doore who 'tis: If so
> This Shadow can not tell thee. Reade and know.[69]

Again, the real face of virtue has become a text; to adapt the *Paraclesis*, in the *Marrow of Ecclesiastical History* you see Samuel Clarke more clearly than if you met him face to face.

A similar ambivalence attaches to the self-conscious adoption of virtuous stances. While it is courteous, necessary, and exemplary to indicate visibly on which side of the moral fence you stand, the very deliberateness of your act makes it an unreliable indicator of your real moral worth. It resembles the sumptuary laws in this, the strengths and the frailties of which it follows and even shares, since messages are sent through clothes as well as gestures. No amount of gravity can well survive a bright red threadbare coat deliberately worn; and wearing sombre colours suggests, rather than guarantees, gravity. The author—possibly Richard Sibbes—of the funeral sermon 'A Triall of Sinceritie' poses the problem by using the image of the visual artist to signify the maker of counterfeits, constructing shadows and reflections of the real:

There is nothing in the world, no shape of any externall thing in the world; but a Painter with his pensill can draw the picture of it, give a resemblance of the thing: and there is no outward action in the world that belongeth to God, or to Christianitie, but it is possible for a Painter, for a base hypocrite to represent them with an artificiall pensill. But the inward acts of life, that no Painter can imitate; he can make shapes, but he cannot put the life into them: he can make outward formes, but he cannot put the inwards to them. Now then this is that intended here: all

---

[69] On the inside of the front cover of Clarke, *Marrow* and id., *Lives*.

those outward actions must be animated actions; not dead actions, actions that have no further bottome then the teeth outwards . . . But they must have the roote in the heart and soule of a man; that must inwardly be carried towards God.[70]

The author has put in a half-submerged pun on 'Painter', suggesting not only the visual artist who makes a separate representation of the features, but also the cosmetic overlay of 'paint' which obscures the real face. In this way two images have been combined which both signify an artificially constructed outward show of virtue's lineaments, two different kinds of painted face. But while the face upon which the paint has been directly applied, the 'made-up' face, is a simple focus of disapproval, the author's attitude to the face's 'resemblance' painted on canvas is more ambiguous. Although such a painting can only portray comeliness from 'the teeth outwards', so that its lineaments, like the mouth of its owner, may be uttering a lie, nevertheless what is being suggested is that the 'inwards', the 'heart and soule of a man', should correspond with the outward signs. So outward signs are in themselves legitimate indicators of the virtuous; the responsibility for a dissembling countenance lies in the heart, not the face. When the author speaks of the 'outward actions' which should be matched to the godly desires of the soul, he does not simply refer to significant acts of *caritas*, but to the deliberate fashioning of the whole 'outward carriage', including the ordinary decorum of a man's everyday habits, the complete aspect of a man of God.

It is not that self-arrangement, then, is sinful: only that self-arrangement must reflect a real inward virtue. Such a stressed self-consciousness makes it more or less inevitable that the sermon writer will employ portraiture images. These stand for the models to which the self-fashioning soul aspires. In the same sermon the author argues that the particulars of godly behaviour are 'limned out' by the prophet Isaiah (p. 312). Of his own deceased subject, he says that she bore the 'Lively image' of God 'graven in her memorie'. But even so highly metaphorical a use of the iconographic must be qualified: her inner 'image' was also 'living in her desires, and (beyond all pictures) moving also in her endeavours to seek after God' (p. 315). In this way the difference between dead image and living soul is denoted by movement

[70] *The House of Mourning*, 305.

and growth; the creature performing the actions of the Spirit has a temporal and spatial freedom denied to the fixed 'externall . . . resemblance' of God engraved on her heart (pp. 305, 314).

Not all commemorative writers are so cautious about the dangers of the icon. As in the case of monuments, a few of the more 'Anglican' of them are able, under certain circumstances, to discard the automatic protection conferred by pure metaphor, and present an exemplary model for their subjects firmly in terms of an actual portrait. But this is a surprisingly infrequent manoeuvre; although all the antecedents of Protestant conformist biography—both 'Anglican' and 'Puritan'—are themselves offered as exemplary *portrayals*, and are frequently accompanied with real portraits, nevertheless few subjects are described as having any truck with exemplary images themselves. But it is not absolutely unknown. Buckeridge's funeral sermon for Lancelet Andrewes contains a slightly odd example, where Andrewes is described as having put up a portrait of his teacher at Merchant Taylors School, Richard Mulcaster, in this spirit: 'And as if he had made Master Mulcaster his Tutor, or supervisor, he placed his picture over the doore of his Studie: whereas in all the rest of the house, you could scantly see a picture.'[71]

This shows Andrewes desiring to conform to a very specific model, where the erudition and teaching skills of Mulcaster are the point, rather than in any direct sense his godliness. But given the tendency to moralize erudition and 'aptness to teach', its iconic function should not be dismissed. It may even be because the morally exemplary function of Mulcaster's portrait is slightly obscured by indirection that Buckeridge felt able to include it without exposing either of them to accusations of idolatry. He is also careful to add that Andrewes displayed almost no other pictures, a statement which serves a double purpose: it guarantees Andrewes's usual aversion to images, and testifies to his regard for Mulcaster.[72]

Given the dangers of showing your subject using real exemplary portraits as a devotional aid, it is not surprising that there are pitfalls in treating the biographical narrative as being itself a kind

---

[71] See Buckeridge, *A Sermon* . . . , 17–18; H. Isaacson, *An Exact Narration of the Life and Death of . . . Lancelot Andrewes* (London, 1650), sig [*]ʳ.

[72] Andrewes's regard for Richard Mulcaster is borne out by the fact that he left his son, Peter Mulcaster, a legacy in his Will. See *DNB*, xxxiv. 275–6.

of exemplary portrait. The self-fashioning virtues of portraiture imagery are also its weak point, because they reveal that imitable decorum demands deliberate artifice on the part of the imitator. If the signs of virtue are humanly constructed, they are not necessarily a Divine signature. For the more Calvinist reader or writer, even the most prominent acts of *caritas* are no guarantee of the doer's real election. By presenting his actions in a narrative explicitly compared to a human act of deliberate artifice—the portrait—a writer also points up the likelihood of a dissembling representation, on the part either of the human subject, or his human biographer, or both.

Samuel Clarke, in a funeral sermon for a 17-year-old, Thomas Bewley, deftly avoids the whole issue by excluding human agency and human effort from his imagery altogether. Clarke's godly subject is indeed an artefact, but his artificer is God Himself:

God deals with some, as a skilful Limner doth with his Master-piece, brings it, and sets it forth to be gazed at and admired by the multitude; and after a while draws a curtain over it, and carrieth it back into his hous again: so God sends souls whom he endows with admirable parts to be looked upon, and wondred at by the world, and then draws the sable curtain of Death over them, and takes them into his own habitation in heaven.[73]

Bewley, though, was young. Never having committed any significant act in the world, good or bad, his kind of virtue must be static, contained in qualities rather than studied acts. Clarke catches a passivity here, an image of perfection frozen on the Divine canvas, entering into no relationship with the 'multitude' who only gaze on it. God alone is active, carrying his 'Master-piece' to and from the place of showing, while the moment of display only allows time for the beholders to admire the still features which can neither be corrupted nor developed, and which, therefore, inspire wonder rather than demanding imitation.

For writers who commemorate the imitable acts of public persons, it is not possible to abolish their own roles as interpreters, mediators between Divine precept and human act, in quite this way. They are the painters of these portraits—although, like Walton, they may represent themselves 'guided' by the 'hand of

[73] Samuel Clarke, *An Antidote Against Immoderate Mourning for the Dead* (London, 1659), 28.

truth'.[74] Consequently, the (very frequent) images of their narratives as portraits are hedged about with limiting devices which stress the painter's fallibility, and thus the provisional nature of the work produced. Whitefoote's sermon for Joseph Hall is one example; and (in common with many others) his caveat has a dual function, both as a disclaimer of his own presumptuous authority in delineating virtue, and as a compliment to the irreproducibly remarkable qualities of the original. In this way, Whitefoote's narrative of Hall becomes 'A short Representation taken in haste; (as all pictures are which are done after the parties death) yet might it have been done nearer to the life, had it not fallen into a very unskilful hand'.[75] Banks offers his portrait of Rainbow on very similar terms, also making a direct link between the draughtsman's skill and the subject's virtuous achievement. He writes: 'I have endeavoured to draw his Picture in Miniature, in Little; tho therein I stand in need of the Pencil of an *Urbin*, or an *Angelo*.'[76] In this way the faults of the portrait are squarely attributed to the workman, not the subject; and at the same time the beauty of Rainbow's holiness is figured aesthetically.

Hamnet Ward's funeral sermon for Henry Byam attempts a slightly more ambitious use of the same convention. He writes: 'And sure I am, the Character I shall present you will be no more fit to be compared with him for worth and excellency, than his Picture now taken by an unskilful Painter, would be like him when he was flourishing in his perfect health and vigour. But such as it is, drawn as well as I can, in water-colours you shall have.'[77] Ward's burial speech, like Whitefoote's, here becomes a funeral portrait; painted after death, it cannot adequately recall its subject's living attributes. As with the graven image of God invoked in 'A Triall of Sinceritie' (p. 314), or as with Whitefoote's 'dead Shadow of the living Voyce', its stasis is being contrasted with the 'active body'. Yet Ward does not leave it at that: he goes on to specify his draughtsmanship as 'unskilful' in order to make it quite clear where the burden of inadequacy rests. Finally, we learn what kind

---

[74] Walton, *Lives*, 21.   [75] Whitefoote, *Deaths Alarum*, sigs. A3^v–4.

[76] [Banks], *Life of Rainbow* (London, 1688), 96. Walton wishes for 'the pensil of a *Tytian* or a *Tintoret*' in the dedicatory epistle (to Sir Robert Holt of Aston) of *The Life of John Donne, Dr. in Divinity* . . . , 2nd edn. (London, 1658), sig. A7.

[77] Hamnet Ward, *The Testimony Given to the Reverend Dr. Henry Byam, at his Burial* . . . , in Henry Byam, *XIII Sermons* . . . (London, 1675), sig. Y1^v.

of portrait Ward is painting. Executed in 'water-colours', it is an impermanent, impressionistic record, washed with tears.

Walton uses portraiture analogies too. In the 1675 revision of the Introduction to the *Life of Donne*, he describes his work as 'the best plain Picture of the *Authors Life* that my artless Pensil, guided by the hand of truth, could present to it' (p. 21). Shortly afterwards he adds:

> But wonder indeed the Reader may, that I who profess myself artless should presume with my faint light to shew forth his Life whose very name makes it illustrious! but be this to the disadvantage of the person represented: Certain I am, it is to the advantage of the beholder, who shall here see the Authors Picture in a natural dress, which ought to beget faith in what is spoken: for he that wants skill to deceive, may safely be trusted.

Walton has refined a common introductory convention. His narrative is characterized as a portrait; and at this point he disclaims his skill with portraits. At the same time he asserts that what skill and beauty the portrayal does possess is only attributable to the beauteous virtue of its subject. So Walton's pun on 'illustrious' points up the difference between his own small skills and his subject's eminence, and this ensures that he takes responsibility for any faults of portrayal at the same as it conveys the compliment. And he turns his weakness to advantage, arguing that his picture must be closer to the truth of its original because of his very inability to dissemble. 'Artless' here stands for a laudable absence of adornment, so that the beholder stands before Donne 'in a natural dress'.

However Walton may insist on his artlessness, he is still presenting a 'Picture', deliberately posed. The represented Donne is not caught unawares. Walton is right to retain (even to insist on) the portrait as an appropriate image for biography, in that both must be *arranged* representations. This is particularly true in the case of narratives of selves fashioned in life by such stringent rules of self-presentation.

A number of exemplary biographies tangle with the additional but related problem of narrating an unworldly self in which many, perhaps all, the virtues must be concealed by their possessor to keep their value. How does the biographer narrate his subject's private prayers, his unrecorded and carefully undisplayed acts of

Godly Prototypes

charity, his unassuming abstinence? As this anecdote by Simeon
Foxe shows, piety can be seriously devalued by display. He writes
of his father John Foxe:

Going abroad (by chance) he met a woman that he knew, who pulling a
Book from under her arme, and saying, See you not that I am going to
a Sermon, Mr. *Fox* replyed, But if you will be ruled by me, go home
rather, for to day you will do but little good at Church; and when
she asked, At what time therefore he would counsell her to go; Then
(answered he) when you tell no body before hand.[78]

In practice, such prayers are overheard, or spoken of by
servants; such acts of charity testified to years later by grateful
recipients; and abstinence, however unassuming, cannot be
concealed from one's chaplain or family. But these are clumsy,
makeshift manoeuvres; and one more thoughtful biographer,
Vaghan, author of a life of Thomas Jackson, dean of Peterborough and president of Corpus Christi in Oxford, finds it
helpful to use an analogy with visual representation to discuss
the difficulties of making his *Life* seem (or even be) an image of
'natural' virtue:

Thus have I presented you with a Memorial of that Excellent Man, but
with *infinite disadvantage* from the unskilfulness of the Relator, and some
likewise from the very disposition of the Party himself. The humble man
conceals his perfections with as much pains, as the proud covers his
defects, and avoids observation as industriously, as the Ambitious
provoke it. He that would draw a face to the Life, commands the Party
to sit down in the Chair in a constant and unremoved Posture, and a
Countenance composed, that he may have full view of every line,
colour, and dimension; whereas he that will not yield to these Ceremonies, must be surprized at unawares, by Artificial stealth, and unsus-
pected glances, like the Divine who was drawn at distance from the Pulpit,
or an ancient man in our days, whose Statue being to be erected, the
Artificer that carved it, was enforced to take him sleeping.[79]

Walton's technique is the one Vaghan uses here for comparison.
He invokes the conventional portrait made with the assent and

---

[78] See [Simeon Foxe], *The Life of Mr. John Fox, Translated out of the Latine*,
in John Foxe, *Acts and Monuments* . . . , 8th edn., 3 vols. (London, 1641), ii. sig.
B6ᵛ. I have taken J. R. Mozley's evidence as to Simeon Foxe's authorship as
conclusive. See Mozley, *John Foxe and his Book* (London, 1940), 1–11.
[79] Vaghan, sigs. **3ᵛ–4.

help of the sitter. His conclusion, though, is different: while he announces that his narrative limns a self-conscious countenance, he asserts that the 'full view of every line, colour and dimension' *does* guarantee a 'face to the Life'.

Additionally (and responsibly), in contrasting the 'faint light' he has been able to throw on Donne's person and actions with the 'illustrious' nature of his real qualities, Walton acknowledges that his composition regards only Donne's partial aspect. Walton here anticipates complaints of later critics (who use 'partial' in both senses); and his much-censured concentration on the later Donne is consistent with the personal knowledge he privileges here, for it too was confined to the latter part of Donne's life.

Walton's imagery of light and shade finds two distinct echoes in the *Life* of Thomas Morton by Baddeley/Naylor. Richard Baddeley's part of the narrative includes a number of passages on Donne, because Morton had been instrumental in persuading him to the priesthood, and in one of these Baddeley anticipates Donne's conversion and ordination in these terms:

> For doubtless the holy Spirit had the greatest stroak and power to incline, and draw him to that sacred Profession: for my selfe have long since seen his Picture in a dear friends Chamber of his in *Lincolnes Inne*, all envel-loped with a darkish shadow, his face & features hardly discernable [*sic*], with this ejaculation and wish written thereon; *Domine illumina tenebras meas*; which long after was really accomplished, when . . . he took Holy Orders.[80]

When Naylor takes up the narrative he applies the same imagery, but to Morton himself. His terms also recall Walton's words on his own *Life of Donne*: 'For in drawing the Picture of this most excellent Prelate, by so rude a Pencill, I know and acknowledge, that there will be indeed so much of the shadow, as will darken and obscure that native beauty and heavenly ornament, which all they that knew him throughly and fully, cannot but attest was lodged in his Person' (pp. 116–17).

Are there direct influences from narrative to narrative? The Baddeley/Naylor *Life* was not published until 1669, although it is clear from its epistle 'To the Christian Reader' that Baddeley's contribution had actually been written some time before, and that his personal knowledge of Morton only extended as far as the Civil

---

[80] B[addeley]/N[aylor], *Life of Dr. Thomas Morton*, 101–2.

War. Naylor's part in the *Life* of 1669 must have been written in about 1650: Naylor comments that Morton (who died in 1659, aged 95) was still going strong at 86 (p. 159). It therefore seems fairly certain (unless he had had access to a pre-1640 manuscript of Baddeley's) that Walton's passage must have been written first. Perhaps Baddeley and Naylor took Walton for a model. Baddeley's shadowy, partly illuminated portrait strongly recalls Walton's image of 1640; and Naylor's 'rude . . . Pencill' and shadowed portrait is even more like Walton's 'artless Pensil' and 'faint light'.

Baddeley's account of the inscribed and emblematic portrait also, however, recalls a later revision of Walton's *Life*. This is the comparison, inserted in 1675, of two actual portraits of Donne— one of them inscribed—as a young man, and dying. Perhaps Walton took the notion of using the portrait as emblem from Baddeley's work of 1669, but he could equally well have decided independently on an 'increasingly iconic' presentation of Donne.[81]

Wherever he got the idea from, Walton uses his portraits much more ambitiously than any contemporary. He makes plain his awareness of the partial and static nature of the portrait in the Introduction; but here he provides, as it were, a series of 'stills', bounded by the two opposed portraits of Donne as a youth and Donne dying, leaving his reader to supply in his own meditations the action and movement between these poles:

And now, having brought him through the many labyrinths and per-plexities of a various life: even to the gates of death and the grave; my desire is, that he may rest until I have told my Reader, that I have seen many Pictures of him, in several habits, and at several ages, and in sev-eral postures: And I now mention this, because I have seen one Picture of him, drawn by a curious hand at his age of eighteen . . . and his Motto then was,

> How much shall I be chang'd,
> Before I am chang'd.

And if that young, and his now dying Picture, were at this time, set together, every beholder might say, *Lord! How much is Dr. Donne already chang'd, before he is chang'd?* (pp. 79–80)

---

[81] See Richard Wendorf, *The Elements of Life: Biography and Portrait Paint-ing in Stuart and Georgian England* (Oxford, 1990), 45–52, for a discussion of these portraits which identifies Walton's intentions as 'increasingly iconic' (p. 46).

Walton speaks here as if Donne were reliving that 'various life' through his narrative; when Walton pauses to consider these portraits, Donne is allowed to 'rest'. Walton stresses the 'various' nature of Donne's experience; prophesies through his early picture a transformatory change; the reader is encouraged to meditate upon his own '*vile . . . changeable body*' and its ultimate dissolution; Donne's own changeableness after his conversion 'both of . . . body and mind' receives comment. The whole effect of the section discussing the portraits is one of mobility. And while the moving images come to rest in Donne's 'spiritual imployment' and serene end, nevertheless Walton has first managed to make a static form 'live, and move'.

'Reuerend Gesture'

In extending a study of the deliberately fashioned visible signs of virtue in ministers from the face to the gesture and actions of the whole body, we meet with new complications in the written evidence. The difficulty of reading prescriptive texts, like preaching manuals, against 'descriptive' Lives (themselves, as we have seen, engagedly concerned to prescribe) is not easy to disentangle. First, we need to attend to the intentions and motives of the writers, taking into account the kinds of works in which they appear. We are handicapped to some extent by our ignorance as to how far preaching skills, and the rhetoric of gesture which properly belongs to them, may have been perceived as a pastoral resource—perhaps deployed in a modified fashion outside the pulpit, perhaps highly dependent on the preacher's effective skill inside it. The generic decorums of preaching are often drawn from classical rhetorical models—notably Quintilian—and filtered through treatises like Wilson's *Art of Rhetorique* (1553). How far, then, may such points be taken as rules for general deportment as well as for pulpit decorum?

Hyperius talks about this in *The Practise of Preaching*, at the beginning of his section on gesture and speech. The way he introduces the subject strongly suggests that he perceives the rules of private and pastoral behaviour to be almost interchangeable with (and at least as binding as) those of preaching:

Howbeit as concerninge comlines in gesture and pronunciation, briefly and truly to speak what I thinke, looke how great care is to bee imployed

in ordering of the life, and dayly conversation, even so great also ought
worthily to bee taken to the due government and moderation of the
speech.

For doubtlesse the speech is a certaine portion of the life, and that
truely not the least . . .

For it is playne and evident that puritie and simplicitie ioyned with
prudence and discretion, like as in life, so also in speech or communication is commended of all men.

Wherefore the Preacher must at all times . . . take diligent heede,
leaste he usurpe any thinge in wordes, in pronunciation, or also in
gesture, which may breede and ingender contempt of his person with the
people.[82]

Ludham's translation perhaps needs some gloss. In his first sentence the 'ordering of the life, and dayly conversation' is balanced
by 'the due government and moderation of the speach'. In the
first phrase, 'dayly conversation' covers all the preacher's actions
and general behaviour; and in the second, 'speech' also implies
gesture and those other physical postures deemed to form a part
of a preacher's rhetorical armoury.[83] In fact, these two words,
which indicate only vocal utterance to a modern reader, are used
here to denote every kind of action, from the minister's actions
of duty, or 'conversation', amongst the flock, to the outward
appearance and deportment which figures out the comeliness
of those actions of duty in a matching decorum.

But Hyperius is also thinking about the auditors' perceptions.
When he says that these qualities are 'commended of all men'
he is not quite saying that they are therefore by any standards
commendable. He is being more pragmatic than that: not so
much explaining how to be good, as how to appear good to a
congregation—and so maintain an effective, because authoritative,
ministry. His concern with 'speech and communication' shows
itself because he considers rhetorical actions—which are visible
as well as audible—to function as a moral index for the beholder.
He is not arguing that these physical signs are necessarily a truthful index, because he is warning his really virtuous preacher against

---

[82] Andreas Hyperius, *The Practise of Preaching* . . . , trans. John Ludham
(London, 1577), sig. Aa1.

[83] I have taken 'conversation' to hold two of the meanings attributed to it by
the *OED*; signifying both the minister's daily intercourse with others in the performance of his duty, and, more generally, his whole behaviour and mode of life.

the possibility that his speech and gesture might be unfavourably misinterpreted. He is, rather, recommending the deliberate performance of speech and gesture which aligns certain tones and actions to certain moral values.

Once a minister loses public respect, perhaps through the most harmless of personal idiosyncracies, he loses his pastoral efficacy: 'we have seene', writes Hyperius, 'them that in the hart of their matter have uttered divers times scarce honest and comely motions' which 'ministred occasion to . . . scoffers and iesters, that . . . thought there could be no fitter thing for theyr turne, then cunningly and plesauntly to represent the wordes, the voyce, the gesture of the Preacher' (sigs. Aa1–1^v).

Hyperius goes on to advise that the preacher should rob profane imitation of its derisive force by assuming the burden of deliberate and solemn imitation himself:

Whosoever taketh in hand the function of preachinge [should] . . . forthwith set before him some one excellent Ecclesiasticall Teacher, whose name is famous and renowmed, and who with singuler [*sic*] grace and dexteritye expoundeth the sacred Scriptures, in all respectes so far as may bee, to be imitated and folowed. (sig. Aa1^v)

Such imitation 'feately and cunningly' pursued, Hyperius argues, will not only command the respect the minister needs, but also engender and develop a real virtue in the imitator: 'he shall at length obteyne some of his vertues, whom he coveteth to bee like' (sigs. Aa1^v–2). He recommends that the process be helped on by placing a critical observer in the congregation, who 'would vouchsafe sometime to admonishe him privately, when he perceiveth any thinge in the speaker, that offendeth either the eares or eyes of the hearers' (sig. Aa2). Again, Hyperius speaks of these faults of preaching style as if they also function as moral deficiencies: 'Wee our selves doubtlesse are more blinde then Beetles in notinge of our own proper faultes . . . but some other truely doe espye many thinges, which escape us, and can wisely discerne what pointes are worthy of reprehension in us' (sig. Aa2).

It seems reasonable to conclude that if points of pulpit decorum were liable to have moral judgements read into them, then the minister's pastoral efficacy was implicated in his effectiveness as a preacher. Moreover, the minister must therefore be required to sharpen all the aspects of his outward decorum, in order that he might provide the proper signs for his flock to read. If he did not, the congregation's urge to imitation would find an outlet in another kind of acting out: the impious caricature. The specificity of Hyperius' concern also suggests that in real life a good many preachers were exciting derision by their mannerisms.

Richard Bernard, in *The Faithfull Shepheard*, follows Hyperius in most of these points, but with an even greater specificity. Of the preacher's physical decorum, he writes: 'A reuerend gesture of the body, is to be observed. The bodie stable and right vp, as nature hath framed it. The head not wagging, the eies moueable, and thy right hand onely as occasion shall be offered, but not alway mouing' (pp. 88–9). An 'upright man' is a righteous man 'as nature hath framed it'. Here (as with the countenance) a deliberately assumed stance is described as 'natural'; and in this instance describes a posture proclaiming our origin as the rational children of God. This equation of godly decorum with 'natural' behaviour is not confined to Bernard: in Overbury's Character book the same assumption is made for 'A Wiseman'—in this case even more explicitly coupled with rationality: 'A *Wiseman* is the truth of the true definition of man, that is, a reasonable creature . . . He looks according to nature; so goes his behaviour.'[84]

In Bernard's passage, the 'reasonable' qualities of the natural posture also show in the way the other prescriptions inhabit a self-conscious middle ground between the excessively mobile and the unnaturally still. So the head is at rest but the eyes alert and lively, while the hand only moves in response to the promptings of the mind's judgement.

We find the same equation of the rational mind with moderate physical actions later in Bernard's prescriptions. He writes this list of possible faults in the preacher's public gestures:

Some there be which haue comelinesse of countenance, and right proportioned of body, yet want seemely gesture: First, either by rash boldnesse, or an inconsiderate zeale at the beginning, and by heat of affection, which haue moued them to violent motions, as casting abroad of their armes, smiting on the Pulpit, lifting themselues vp, and againe suddenly stamping downe very vnaduisedly. Secondly, or by too great feare and bashfulnesse, which causeth hemmings, spitting, rubbing the

---

[84] Sir Thomas Overbury *His Wife, with Additions of New Characters . . .*, 11th edn. (London, 1622), sig. F2.

browes, lifting vp of the shoulders, nodding of the head, taking often hold of the cloake or gowne, fidling with the fingers vpon the breast, buttons, stroaking of the beard and such like toies. Thirdly, or els by acting vpon a stage, who cannot but shew their vaine and phantasticall motions ridiculously in a Pulpit, which they haue vsed in prophane pastimes. (p. 89)[85]

Here every immoderate gesture proceeds from a particular behavioural fault: 'inconsiderate zeale', 'too great feare', and (perhaps worst of all) the 'vaine and phantasticall' dissembling of the stage player. Each, argues Bernard, can be amended by considering what is due to the preacher's office: 'considerate deliberation', 'godly boldnesse' in mediating between man and God, and, for the last, a 'serious consideration of the difference of the actions' (pp. 89–90). When rational behaviour has been defeated through the physical expression of passions, it may yet be re-established through the considered operation of mind and will.[86]

Bernard's argument is complicated by his inclusion of histrionic, as well as unselfconscious, preaching faults. Straight after this passage Bernard, like Hyperius, advises the study and imitation of what is 'comely' in other preachers, also suggesting that 'some faithfull friend' be asked to keep a critical eye on the preacher's own performance (p. 90). A preaching ministry must be histrionic. Bernard stresses that the 'actions' of the stage player and of the preaching minister are different because they are suspiciously similar.

[85] See Patrick Collinson, *The Religion of Protestants*, where further illustrations are given of histrionic preaching styles, including an anecdote from Foxe in which Latimer's opponent William Hubberdyne, whose 'dancings, hoppings and leapings' had led to the collapse of the pulpit, died of his ensuing injuries. The churchwardens, however, pointed out that 'they had made their pulpit for preaching, not for dancing'. See also Erasmus' commendation of Vitrier's delivery in his letter to Jonas, where he says he preached 'with no unbecoming gesticulation, with nothing exciting or declamatory, but perfectly under control, his delivery was yet such that you felt the words to proceed from a fervent and sincere, yet sober spirit withal'. Translation from *Christian Humanism and the Reformation*, ed. Olin, 167–8.

[86] We find the same insistence on moderation in Robert Pricke's tabulation of the duties (in this case) of flock to minister. One of these he defines as 'bodily reuerence or honour', consisting in 'Gesture and Speech'. He prescribes a deportment which may 'declare and manifest the inward reuerence of their harts toward his ministery', while deploring the two extremes of 'no reuerence at all' and excessive deference 'as kneeling, &c.' See *The Doctrine of Svperioritie, and of Subiection* ... (London, 1609), sigs. F4–4ᵛ.

Nor is it a process confined to the pulpit. Holy performance is a constant imperative, requiring the kind of attention to detail which will signify an equivalent attention paid to the inner virtues. 'All these vertues of his', writes Simeon Foxe of his father, 'were fenced about, as with a Bulwark, by a singular modesty and integrity of life; which suffered not any thing to enter into his manners, or to break forth in his actions, but what was first with much diligence searched into, and examined, whether it might beseem him, or not.'[87] This elision of the seemly with the virtuous also finds its echo in Barwick's two works on Morton. He refers in the funeral sermon to Morton's 'exquisite carriage in matters of morality' (p. 29); and in the *Life*, this figurative use of the word 'carriage' to mean 'conduct' is translated into significant physical terms, as 'a Decorum in his motion, walking, habit, and speech' (pp. 155–6). This very common employment of the word 'carriage' in its two meanings of physical decorum and moral conduct is also beautifully exemplified in the sermon 'A Triall of Sinceritie', where the author's figurative usage still recalls outward deportment. 'God is a holy overseer of all our wayes', he writes, 'a spectatour of all our carriage and behaviour, how we do carry our selves, and approve our selves to him.'[88] And John Moulson's 'grave deportment and carriage' are commended by the author of his funeral sermon as that 'sage gravity' which 'commands respect from the beholders' and which ensures that 'his very presence was such, as would discountenance the rude and prophane'.[89]

The deliberate artifice biographers employ for outward forms lends itself well to histrionic imagery, just as the self-composed countenance lends itself to portraiture images. So Whitefoote sums up Hall's life as 'well acted',[90] and Buckeridge, more boldly, says of Andrewes, 'he is the great *Actor* and *performer*, I but the poor cryer'.[91] Daniel Featley introduces St Peter (in a sermon given at Robert Wright's ordination to the See of Bristol) by bringing

[87] [Simeon Foxe], *Life of Mr. John Fox*, sig. B3ᵛ.
[88] See *The House of Mourning* . . . (London, 1640), 312. Also see *OED*, 'carriage', *sb.* 12–15. The earliest citation of this moral meaning of 'carriage' is 1590.
[89] *The House of Mourning* . . . (London, 1640), 408.
[90] Whitefoote, *Deaths Alarum*, 79.   [91] Buckeridge, *A Sermon* . . . , 16.

him 'upon this holy Stage'.[92] But, although a common resource, this imagery underlines that what can be resembled, can also be dissembled.

A great deal of contemporary literature, specifically the sermon and the moral Character, is exercised to determine palpable differences between resembling and dissembling: to borrow Bernard's phrase, a 'difference in the actions' of the sincere Christian and the hypocrite. The very popularity of the issue as a didactic subject indicates how vexed the question is, especially as hypocrisy is distinguished from all the other vices as perniciously invisible.[93] 'Neither Man nor Angel can discern | Hypocrisie,' asserts Milton in *Paradise Lost*, 'the only evil that walks | Invisible, except to God alone' (iii. 682–4).

Nevertheless, outside Milton, attempts are made to identify its visible signs. Samuel Crook, in a treatise adapted from a series of sermons on the difference between the sincere and the dissembling Christian, argues that the hypocrite will be exposed by a falseness of gesture, a palpable artificiality in his deportment, which reflects to the discerning eye the equivalent falseness of his heart. In doing so, Crook too calls up comparisons with the stage, but all on the wrong side of the debate. His reasoning is etymological: 'the name of *hypocrisie*, and *Hypocrites* are borrowed from the Greek, In which tongue they primarily signifie the profession of a *Stage-player*, which is to express in speech, habit and action, not his own person and manners, but his whom he representeth.'[94] Thus, he explains, the hypocrite is 'Indeed a very *Stage-player*, acting the part of a member of Christ, without any portion of sound or saving grace'. Crook goes on:

The hypocrites part lies most in mimical countenances, guises and gesticulations, by which he endeavours to proclaim himself Religious . . .

---

[92] Daniel Featley, *Clavis Mystica: A Key Opening Divers Difficult and Mysterious Texts of Holy Scripture* (London, 1636), 131.

[93] Smeed's list of Characters to be found in sermons (Smeed, *Theophrastan 'Character'*, 45) contains a significant number on the hypocrite: e.g. Thomas Adams, *The White Devil, or the Hypocrite Uncased* (1614); John Rawlinson, *The Unmasking of the Hypocrite* (1616).

[94] Samuel Crook, *Τὰ Διαφέροντα, or Divine Characters . . . Acutely Distinguishing the More Secret and Undiscerned Differences Between . . . the Hypocrite . . . and the True Christian . . .* (London, 1658), 6. Crook's treatise was also originally a course of sermons.

He covers a fowle heart under a fair face, an ulcerous soul under neat cloaths, a wanton heart under a modest habit, and a world of spiritual wickedness under an affected gravity of carriage and behaviour: yet, as the absurd Actor (when he thinks to do best) commits a solicisme with his hande; so this hypocrite, with his face. (p. 62)

At this point Crook runs into difficulties. When he makes his comparison of dissembling behaviour with the 'outward comelinesse' proceeding from true 'inward holinesse' (p. 63), he cites exactly the same signs that he has detailed for the hypocrite; humble looks, modest attire, a grave and sober deportment. Nor can he distinguish them very clearly by stating the dissembler to be '*what he is by imitation*', since the true Christian is also 'not abhorrent from all imitation of others; as well knowing that, as in rhetorick and oratory, so in Religion, there is a commendable use of *imitation*' (p. 64). Crook too falls back on 'natural' gesture as the unselfconscious reflection of the godly soul, but has no notion of universally natural deportment; for he asserts that purely national fashions make gestures 'natural' to the Spaniard 'uncomely' to an English imitator:

And as for his [the true Christian's] gestures, he will have them grave, not affected . . . Natural gestures become well enough, which being affected prove ridiculous; the cast of the eye, the bowing of the head or body, when not done to deceive, or in an apish imitation of strangers or other Nations to whom it is natural, are not to be slighted, or censured. The Spanish gravity and slow pace in them is not unseemly . . . but in an English man, uncomely and odious. (p. 65)

Crook must define 'natural' gesture as largely directed by social convention. It is an *acquired* deportment. This undermines his attempts to establish such gesture as the unstudied expression of the inner man. He has, therefore, to make a distinction between an acceptable set of gestures affected with laudable intentions, and the same gestures affected with false intentions, by applying heavily loaded terms to the differently intended imitations. 'This hypocrite', he concludes, 'will be every mans ape, but no mans follower', whereas 'the Christian is every good mans follower, but no mans ape' (p. 65). No distinction relying on impalpable motives can be that satisfactory. Those who, like the anonymous writer of the biographical preface for Miles Smith, bishop of Gloucester, discerned the difference between 'the elect Child of

God' and 'the bastard cast-away' through acts of visible charity
to the brethren, were on much safer ground—except, perhaps,
theologically.[95]

Crook's easy definition of stage-playing as being in itself a proof
of insincerity is not shared by all his contemporaries. I have already
demonstrated that the deliberate, practised performance of the
signs of virtue can be considered a useful discipline, through which
a real possession of the virtues imitated may gradually be acquired.
The most striking example of this process may be found in the
Ferrar community at Little Gidding. Within the community
was a group known as the 'Little Academy', the function of which,
as Nicholas Ferrar explains it, was 'euery day at a sett houre to
conferre together of some such subiect, as should tend either to
Information of the Vnderstanding or to the Exciting of the
Affection to the more ready and fervent prosecution of vertues'.[96]
While each member of the 'Little Academy' was given an alternative name descriptive of his or her function, several of its
younger women were assigned names also intended as characterizations of the kinds of virtues they were perceived as needing
to acquire. For instance, the seven young women making up
the group's core—Mary and Anna Collett, Susanna Collett
Mapletoft, Hester Collett Kestian, Margaret Collett Ramsay,
Joyce Collett Wallis, and Judith Collett Mapletoft—became,
respectively, the 'Chief' (later 'Mother'), the 'Patient', the
'Goodwife', the 'Cheerfull', the 'Affectionate', the 'Submisse',
and the 'Obedient'.[97] Ferrar refers to the participants as 'Actors'
(p. 6) and they are distinguished, in the carefully polished
accounts of the dialogues which survive, by their 'characters'
of 'Submisse', 'Affectionate', and so on. In one of the dialogues,
'On the Retirement of Charles V', the terms upon which the
names were conferred is made plain: 'There's none here perhaps
answeares to their Names, as an expression of their Natures, or
Conditions; but as a testimonie of their desires & endeavours, that
they would fain bee such as they are called' (p. 136). What these
people were requiring of each other (or at any rate of their young,

---

[95] See Preface to Miles Smith, *Sermons* (London, 1632) sig ¶4ᵛ.

[96] *Conversations at Little Gidding*, ed. A. M. Williams (Cambridge, 1970), 5.

[97] Some of these identifications are only probable, and I have given the final
married names of all the participants where these apply, although they were not
all married at the time the dialogues were made. See ibid., pp. xxix–xxxiii.

female members) was a deliberate acting out, in character, of the
virtue of which it was felt each was most in need. It is striking how
many of the virtues assigned to (and therefore presumably felt
to be lacking in) these young women are passive: patience, sub-
mission, obedience. The dialogues themselves show several of
the speakers in some species of revolt against their 'characters';
the unfortunate 'Submisse', for instance, causes a good deal of
consternation amongst the other members for her unsubmissive
stance, including her refusal to wear a habit (pp. 136–8).

This is not to argue that the acquisition of virtue through the
acting of its 'character' was imperative only for these more junior
members. It was, perhaps, an explicit exercise which formally
expressed an implicit aspect of the self-training the more authoritative and senior members may have applied privately to themselves. Peter Peckard, Master of Magdalene College, Cambridge,
and author of a late-eighteenth-century life of Nicholas Ferrar,
comments on a manuscript copy of Fuller's *Holy State* found
among the Ferrar papers, which he consequently believed to
be Ferrar's own work.[98] Its existence, laboriously transcribed
into Ferrar's own handwriting, and its function (according to
Peckard) as a daily reading resource over dinner, suggests that the
older members attached a similar importance to the assimilation
of 'character' to 'life'.

The 'Body's Body'

There is a final aspect to bodily decorum in contemporary commonplace: dress. It is Erasmus who calls dress the 'body's body'
(*corpus corporis*) in *De Civilitate*, neatly demonstrating clothes both
to encase and to mirror the shape and condition of the soul. Like
the body itself, its clothes participate in the ambivalence of all visible signs: the 'ulcerous soul' of Crook's hypocrite is concealed
under 'neat cloaths' and a 'modest habit' (p. 62), but his real
Christian is equally identifiable by his modest attire (p. 63). In the
Ferrar dialogue 'On the Retirement of Charles V', the refusal of
'Submisse' to wear a religious habit is seen by one interlocutor

---

[98] The MS was lost by Magdalene College, Cambridge, some time in the
nineteenth century. I am indebted to the Pepys Librarian of Magdalene College,
Dr Richard Luckett, for this information. See Peter Peckard, *Memoirs of the
Life of Mr. Nicholas Ferrar* (Cambridge, 1790), 190–4.

as modest and lowly, indicating her sense of her unworthiness, and by another (who in the end gains his point) as being 'no necessarie proof of more humble Affections', but rather

out of Ambitious fancies & hopes to better her estate in those things, wherein shee accounts Respect & Honour perhaps cheifely to lie, Fine cloathes, Brave Company, Iolly conversation, & the like appurtenances and imployments of this kind of life. The conceited delights whereof make her loathe, I feare, the sobriety of that tyre, which her Sisters weare; howeuer it may bee she deceiue herself in the thought, not onely vs in the allegation, That a vayle is too stately a Couer for her head; which being full of Changeable phancies can no waies brooke so solemne a Dress . . . (p. 138)

Although this speaker, the 'Guardian' John Ferrar the elder, sees his niece's refusal as a conscious or unconscious deception, he reveals her objections to have some force. While he takes her 'Changeable phancies' as a symptom of vicious desires which denial and suppression will rectify, she clearly treats them as facts to be acknowledged. In doing so, paradoxically she asserts a constancy between her inner and outer self, a refusal to dissimulate, whatever her motives. She does not accept that the dissimulation of virtue will help her to acquire real virtue.

Even if Ferrar's characterization of her refusal as 'Ambitious' rather than merely 'Changeable' were just, 'Submisse' is not alone with her fault. Walton's Herbert also has a weakness for dressing elegantly: 'his cloaths', writes Walton of the young Herbert, 'seem'd to prove, that he put too great a value on his parts and parentage' (p. 270). The point where Herbert changes 'his sword and silk Cloaths for a Canonical coat' (p. 291) is one of genuine transformation. He is not assuming this attire in the hope that it will help change him: rather, the inner change, already complete, is emblematized by his change of habit. But whereas Herbert reaches this point after long and careful consideration, for his wife the case is different. Immediately after this passage Herbert returns to her, already transformed in dress and function, and announces to her: '—You are now a Ministers Wife, and must now so far forget your fathers house, as not to claim a precedence of any of your Parishioners; for you are to know, that a Priests Wife can challenge no precedence or place, but that which she purchases by her obliging humility.' Walton then narrates her falling in

cheerfully with her altered state, which he presents to show her
'unfeigned love' and 'serviceable respect'. He adds, 'this love
followed her in all places, as inseparably, as shadows follow sub-
stances in sunshine'. For Jane Herbert, then, her function changes
with her husband's, and the only decision she is empowered to
make is whether she should acquiesce in his. Walton's image of
her love as a shadow following her substance is extremely appropriate. As her state shifts, from the secular dignity held in the person of her father to the priestly function of her husband, Jane
herself is discovered a shadow, falling behind the choices made
for her by the 'substance' for which she lives, the man who has
a controlling interest in her. In such a context, Jane Herbert's
dissimulation of a humility she might not altogether feel would
be more seemly a choice than a refusal to participate in her husband's decision. It is such a dissimulation, such an outward acqui-
escence in the decisions made for her by her familial superiors,
which 'Submisse' will not make in the Ferrar dialogue, in refusing to wear a religious dress.

Thus far these examples are as it were material, where the
real clothing of the godly exhibits visible signs of the inner self.
In a society so aware of sumptuary meanings, we do not lack
examples of godly individuals who either insist on retaining
certain significant types of dress, or who, like Herbert, relinquish
worldly finery. Barwick relates approvingly of Morton that during the Civil War he retained his 'habit Episcopal, even then when
it was hazardous to be seen in a Clerical garment'.[99] Barwick also
shows in the same passage that the unassuming way Morton wore
his clerical dress forms part of his entire demeanour, and so tells
us a good deal about his whole conduct. Having devoted five pages
to Morton's 'Moderation', Barwick continues by praising his
modesty, a quality which he declares to have 'so much affinity'
with moderation 'as to view it in the next place' (p. 155). The Latin
word *Ornatus* ('dress') is cited, and Jerome's gloss on it rendered
as 'a *Decorum* in . . . *motion, walking, habit and speech*'. This, continues Barwick, 'is all comprised in our English phrase in that
place, *A person of good behaviour*'. Seemly dress evidently figures
'good behaviour', walking the tightrope between over-austere
and flamboyant. Barwick follows Jerome in choosing dress to

[99] Barwick, *Life*, 155.

demonstrate his point, and cites other patristic precedent: 'With S. *Augustine*, he was *neither too spruce nor too mean in his bodily apparel . . .* and with St. *Cyprian* (besides the *comeliness* of his *Apparel*) there was *in his carriage such an exact mixture of gravity and courtesie, as carried him in an equal line between pride on the one hand, and mean-ness of spirit on the other*' (p. 156).

Dress also surfaces as a metaphor for the assumption of godly attitudes. Some of these are approving, where pious clothing figures a genuinely devotional mind, and some pejorative, indicating the ease with which the fickle can alter the dress of the soul. A striking use of the latter is made by Naylor:

> We know that an *English-man*, in former times, was wont to be drawn beyond seas (by way of a jeare) to shewe his inconstancy and fickleness in his apparrell, with a bundle of Cloth upon the one Shoulder, and a payre of Taylors Sheares hanging on the other, to cut out a new fashion for himselfe every moneth, or week, as his fancy should lead him, for the clothing and apparrelling of his body. But now alas! he may be Pictured more scornfully, and yet (God knows) more properly and truely, in respect to his Religion (which is, or ought to be, the apparrell of the soule) with a sheet of blanck Paper in the one hand, and a Pen full of Inke in the other, to Write every day what religion he most fancieth, *Papist* or *Protestant, Presbyterian* or *Independent, Quaker* or *Dipper, Arrian* or *Atheist, Anabaptist* or *Adamite*, or what is most in fashion, or sway with the times.[100]

Naylor's image of 'Religion' as the 'apparrell of the soule' here demonstrates its own defects, for he first employs it to denote the changeableness of fashion, whereas his later metaphorical use should not carry connotations of frequent alteration. This may be why Naylor abandons his image halfway through the passage, replacing it with the 'sheet of blanck Paper' on which different kinds of religion may be written 'every day'. Walton also uses fashion as a metaphor for religious fickleness in *Love and Truth*; he narrates an anecdote in which three girls receive a patrimony of ten pounds to spend on dress, in order to help them get husbands. Two of them spend it on 'very fantastical Cloaths'; the third saves it, assuming instead 'a new fantastical opinion in Religion . . . thereby to get admirers, and as many as they [the other two girls] should; and it proved so'.[101]

[100] B[addeley]/N[aylor], *Life of Dr. Thomas Morton*, 142–4.
[101] Walton, *Love and Truth* (London, 1680), 29.

Joseph Hall deploys an approving image of the appropriately clothed soul in characterizing the 'Faithfull man'. Hall's image, unlike Naylor's, is not hampered by the easiness with which the 'body's body' can be put on and off, because he makes changing clothes into an occasional and ceremonial, but regular act. 'When he goes in, to converse with God', he writes of his Character, 'he weares not his own clothes, but takes them still out of the rich Wardrobe of his Redeemer.'[102] Here Christ is at once repository and justification for every ceremonially pious attitude, as well as a welcome covering for the naked soul. 'Put ye on the Lord Jesus Christ', writes Paul in Romans 13: 14; and Jeremy Taylor enlarges the point:

The *Word Incarnate*, [is] the great example of all the Predestinate . . . And therefore it was a precept of the Apostle, and by his Doctrine we understand its meaning: *Put you on the Lord Jesus Christ* [*marg. Rom. 13.14*]. The similitude declares the Duty; as a garment is composed and made of the same fashion with the body, and is applyed to each part in its true figure and commensuration. So should we *put on Christ*, and imitate the whole body of his Sanctity, conforming to every integral part, and expresse him in our lives, that . . . we may be acknowledged for sons when we have the tire and features, and resemblances of our elder Brother.[103]

Taylor is not interested in fashionable variation. For him clothing's distinguishing characteristic is that it is made to fit the shape of the body. Yet Christ is our garment because we fit ourselves to his cut, which for Taylor is not at odds with the previous assumption because Christ is deemed to have a truer knowledge of our soul's shape than we do. His 'whole body' of sanctity—a useful phrase incorporating the scriptural books and the precepts of the invisible Church as well as being an image of Christ's self— fits round ours, we 'inhabit' his body; and the result is that we are seen, not literally clothed with Christ, but wearing his clothes, and with his 'resemblances' stamped on bodies under those clothes. And bearing in mind the exactly corporeal nature of those resurrected bodies, it becomes very clear that the imitative and even histrionic process required of the godly person is by no means simply a matter of external decorum, but a fundamental means of salvation.

[102] Hall, *Characters of Vertues and Vices*, 20.
[103] Taylor, *The Great Exemplar*, 4–5.

DEATH

'Dyenge Well'

Any examination of the conventions attending exemplary decorum must include that most crucial of exemplary public acts, the godly death. While other sections in this chapter have dealt principally with the commonplaces associated with each issue, this one (though it does discuss commonplaces) also tries to make some tentative assessment of the function and significance of the godly deathbed in proto-biographical narrative.

Of all the biographical acts considered in this book, its assessment of deathbed narratives is perhaps the most politically polarized. My attention in all areas is really conformist because I write about Walton; but what 'conformist' means is problematic, especially for the sixteenth century when many of these biographical models are built, and when 'nonconformity' as it is historically understood barely exists outside the Church. Yet throughout the period I discuss there is usually a surprising degree of consensus between the 'Anglican' and the 'Puritan' exemplary imperative, which I have tried to indicate, for instance, in my decision to use the word 'godly' comprehensively.

Having said all this, though, it is much less true that there is a consensus in deathbed narrative. There are real differences between those narratives (especially from the turn of the seventeenth century) written out of the Calvinist disciplines of self-examination and the really tormenting debate on assurance, and those which construct the exemplarily serene deaths which appear in earlier deathbed accounts (as of Luther and of Calvin himself), in the martyrologies, and in the later biographical prefaces for Church dignitaries. Some of this expresses a division between lay and ecclesiastical deaths (the agonies preceding the last-minute assurance of *The Life and Death of Katharine Brettergh*[104] would surely never find expression in the latter

---

[104] See W. Harrison and W. Leygh, *Deaths Advantage Little Regarded, and the Soules Solace against Sorow. Preached in Two Funerall Sermons, at the Buriall of K. Brettergh . . . whereunto is annexed the Life of the Said Gentlewoman . . .* (London, 1602); W. Harrison, *The Life and Death, of Mistris K. Brettergh* (London, 1612). Work in this area is being done by Mr Jason Yiannikou of Queens' College, Cambridge, whose doctoral thesis 'Puritanism and Practical

context even if they were felt), but deathbeds expose, as no other part of a Life, upon what side of the debate on assurance its subject and even more its writer stand.

The narratives of deathbed doubt are a considerable sub-genre closely related to a confessional tradition which uses exemplarity in radically different ways from Walton, and goes therefore beyond my remit in this book. Walton's subjects die assured; and they are all priests. To a great extent, therefore (though not exclusively), in considering his influences I assess the tradition as it flowers into the exemplary, conformist ecclesiastical deathbed.

Some other kinds of dying, for example, all species of martyrdom, are very obviously in a tradition of edifying public performance and might therefore more plausibly be considered part of my remit. But the martyrological tradition is also very considerable, and again very specific; its relationship to Walton's interests is skewed partly because of the growing identification of Foxe with the 'nonconformist' interest during the seventeenth century, which makes Foxe so conspicuous by his absence from Walton's writing. In any case, Walton's subjects died to a man in bed (even if they are said to have missed dying in the pulpit by a hair). English Protestant conformist martyrs after 1558 are few, whereas dissenters and Roman Catholics have spectacularly greater opportunities to ransack the traditions of violent exemplary death as they emerge from Eusebius, Voraginus, and others[105] (whether filtered through Foxe or via the Douay formula disseminated by John Wilson and Thomas Worthington).[106] I have made here another (possibly arbitrary) decision not to consider martyrological influence in this section, except very briefly as it

Divinity in England *c.*1570–1620', currently in preparation, considers death as a topic within divinity, *passim*. He also identifies pamphlet narratives of lay deaths as the main area in which last-minute grace is the triumphant culmination of a deathbed struggle with the Devil over assurance; whereas clerical deaths (in Clarke as in Walton) tend to be exemplary and celebratory.

[105] Not to mention the New Testament.
[106] See Thomas Worthington, *A Relation of Sixteene Martyrs Glorified in England in Twelve Monethes* (Douay, 1601); Thomas Worthington, *A Catalogue of Martyrs in England; for Profession of the Catholique Faith, since the Year of our Lord, 1535 . . . unto this Year 1608* ([Douay], 1608); J.[ohn] W.[ilson] *The English Martyrologe, Conteyning a Summary of the Lives of the Saints of England, Scotland and Ireland. Collected and Distributed into Monethes* (St Omer, 1608).

informs the century's most politically contentious ecclesiastical 'martyrdom': the execution of Laud.

Peter Heylyn's account of the death of Laud shows Heylyn, as elsewhere, to be easy with stage imagery, his single reservation being that he can only describe Laud's 'last act':

It is a preposterous kind of writing to begin the story of a great mans life, at the houre of his death, a most strange way of setting forth a solemne *Tragedie*, to keepe the *principall Actor* in the *tyring-house* till the play be done, and then to bring him on the stage onely to speake the *Epilogue*, and receive the Plaudites. Yet this must be the scope of the following papers. To write the whole life of . . . the Lord Arch-Bishop of Canterbury, would require more time then publique expectation can endure to heare of.[107]

Heylyn's talk about shortness of time is pragmatic (though it also calls up an arrogant echo of the close of the Gospel of John).[108] His martyr's version of Laud's death must get into print at least as fast as rival versions. But rhetorically it works, in that by confining his account to Laud's deportment only in that final act Heylyn implicitly vindicates all his other acts without having to mention them. He died well: he must have lived well.

Laud himself pays the same anxious attention to his performance (and to its dissemination in print) in his sermon preached at the scaffold. He knows its potency in vindicating his earlier performance as the Church's principal representative. In the printed account of this sermon, the title-page specifies that it was 'all faithfully written by *John Hinde*, whom the Archbishop beseeched him that he would not let any wrong be done him by any phrase in false Copies'.[109] This means that on the scaffold itself Laud took the time to safeguard his final text by checking the presence and faithfulness of his stenographer. And the sermon itself is an explicit performance. Laud begins by apologizing to the crowd for using notes, because he knows their critical appreciation is important,

[107] Heylyn, *Briefe Relation* . . . (London, 1644), 1.

[108] Heylyn was to write a full life of Laud, extraordinarily biased even for so partial a century. See *Cyprianus Anglicus, or, the History of the Life and Death of the Most Reverend and Renowned Prelate, William* [Laud] . . . *Lord Archbishop of Canterbury* . . . (London, 1668). See also John 21: 25.

[109] *The Archbishop of Canterbury's Speech: or His Funerall Sermon, Preacht by Himself on the Scaffold on Tower-Hill, on Friday the 10. of Ianuary, 1644* . . . (London, 1644).

but the effect is to highlight his remarkable self-possession. '*Good People*', he begins, 'You'l pardon my old Memory, and upon so sad occasions as I am come to this place, to make use of my Papers, I dare not trust my self otherwise' (p. 6). Upon coming to the end of his address, he dictates the timing of the executioner's part, specifying precisely where in his final prayer he should lift the axe to strike (about halfway through): 'The Executioner desiring him to give some signe when he should strike, he answered: Yes, I will, but let me fit my selfe first . . . And when he said, *Lord receive my soule* (which was his signe) the Executioner did his office' (p. 19).

Such histrionic elements are a standard feature of public deaths (Marvell's 'Royal Actor'); and since they are by their nature public occasions, it is almost inevitable that they should become edifying spectacle in certain hands. This is not a point which needs to be laboured. But what about the godly individual's private deathbed? Is this, too, an occasion for the patterned and edifying performance? The very great attention given to the manner in which a subject dies, and the proliferation of texts offering advice on how to die well, are evidence that it is.

Those *ars moriendi* treatises written at the very outset of the Reformation stress the extent to which a 'good death' only follows a holy life (although at the same time it is always emphasized that nothing can be inferred from the mode of death, as distinct from the demeanour of the dying person). An evident gladness and eagerness for dissolution identifies the godly patient, but sudden death (for instance, a stroke) or a mind disordered as a result of disease must not be taken as evidence of divine displeasure, but as accident. Thomas Lupset, in a treatise published about 1534, *The Waye of Dyenge Well*, brings out both these points,[110] suggesting also that the aspirant to a godly death should study and imitate notably godly predecessors (specifically, Paul, Peter, and Jerome): 'This lesson to lerne the way of dyenge well, hath nede to have a mayster, the whiche knoweth both what our life is, and what the losse of the same is. Nor no man in mynde can effectuously teache the way to dye well, except he be one that knoweth the way to lyve wel' (sig. A3). Erasmus' *Preparation to Deathe*,

---

[110] Thomas Lupset, *A Compendiovs and a Very Frvtefvl Treatyse, Teachynge the Waye of Dyenge Well* . . . (n.p. 1534), sigs. B3ᵛ, C4–5.

Englished in 1538, has the same message. He also makes use of stage imagery in his Preface, incidentally pointing up the extent of the beholder's (or reader's) attention to the decorum of dying only implied in Lupset: 'Ye provoke me to adde to my former bokes some lytle thynge, teachinge howe a man ought to prepare hym to deth. For this is of mans lyfe the last part (as it were) of the playe, wherof hangeth eyther everlastynge blysse of men, or everlastynge damnation.'[111] For Erasmus, the effectual proofs of salvation after death are all textual; he refers to the 'handwriting of grace' with which Christ 'hath annulled & cancelled that fyrst handwrityng, whiche Adam vnhappily had described vnto vs'.[112] This 'handwriting' he identifies as the 'innumerable testimonies of prophetes, apostels, martyrs, and virgins, whiche with their blode alsoo haue subscribed'. He continues:

If ye aske where this chyrograph or handwryting that assureth vs, remaineth: I answer in the canonicall scriptures, in whiche we rede the wordis of god, not of men. To these nolesse credence is to be youen, than if god had spoken theym vnto the, with his owne mouth, Yea I dare boldli say somwhat more largely. For if god had spoken vnto the by some created lykenes, perchaunce, accordinge to thexample of certayne good men, thou woldest haue doubted, whether there were any disceite in the thynge. But al this doubte the perpetuall consent of the catholyke churche, hath cleane take away frome vs. Than in this handwriting to studye all our lyfe, is the best preparation to dethe. (sig. A8)

This is again the same image that surfaces in the *Paraclesis*, where the face of Christ is seen more truly in scripture than it could be in fact. But here Erasmus is building on his text from Colossians 2: 14: not only the 'canonicall scriptures' but also later testimonies sanctioned by the Church are to be given this kind of credence; and not only the death of Christ, but the testimonies of 'martyrs, and virgins' are its proofs. The testimonies of godly deaths, then, are not only exemplary, but a wholly legitimate part of the direct and instructive 'wordis of god', and the specifically textual nature of those testimonies, if they also appear with the sanction of the

[111] *Preparation to Deathe, a Boke as Deuout as Eloquent, Compiled by Erasmus Roterodame* (London, 1538), sig. A2.

[112] His image is from Colossians 2: 14, where Christ, 'blotting out the handwriting of ordinances that was against us . . . took it out of the way, nailing it to his cross'.

Church, are the fundamental proof of their reliability. Erasmus seems tacitly to sanction the writing of a kind of 'new scripture', one which the emergent reforming churches will develop, in which the decorum in death of their new leaders takes on both an exemplary function, and one which publicly validates their acts and conduct in life.

Here a considerable importance attaches to the first great Protestant death: the death of Luther. Narrating Luther's death is itself a major tradition in English Protestant writings.[113] The first eyewitness account of it, written by Justus Jonas, Johannes Aurifaber, and Michael Coelius, was translated into English by John Bale in 1546. Melanchthon's account, which draws on this 1546 testimony of Jonas *et al.*, was translated into English by Henry Bennet in 1561 as part of his *Famous and Godly History*, and part of Bennet's translation appears as a document by Melanchthon in Foxe's account of Luther in the 1563 *Actes and Monuments*. Melchior Adamus also used the 1546 account as a major source for his Latin life of Luther appearing in the 1618 *Vitae*. This was subsequently translated into English by Thomas Hayne and published separately in 1641, and was incorporated by Fuller in 1651 into *Abel Redevivus*.[114]

I propose to look at the first of these, the 1546 *Christen Departynge of D. Martyne Luther*, identifying points at which the account is deliberately patterned into a kind of Gospel narrative. Shaping Luther's death into an edifying performance was a task not without difficulties, since Luther died comatose. But there are real signs that, while capable, Luther participates in this attempt

---

[113] For historical and generic context to this tradition see Robert Kolb, 'Burying the Brethren: Lutheran Funeral Sermons as Life Writing', in D. R. Woolf and Thomas R. Mayer (eds.), *The Rhetorics of Life-Writing in Early Modern Europe* (Ann Arbor, Mich., 1995), 97–113.

[114] Justus Jonas (and others), *The True Hystorye of the Christen Departynge of D. Martyne Luther*, trans. John Bale (Marburg, 1546); *Historia de Vita et Actis Reverendissimus D. Mart. Lutheri, Verae Theologiae Doctoris, Bona Fide Conscripta a P. Melanchthon* (Wittemberg, 1549); Henry Bennet, *A Famous and Godly History* . . . (London, 1561); Foxe, *Actes and Monuments* (1563), 415–17; *Vitae Germanorum Theologorum, qvi Superiori Seculo Ecclesiam Christi Voce Scriptisqve Propagarunt et Propugnarunt. Congestae & Ad Annum Usqve* [1618]; *Deductae a Melchior Adamo* (Heidelberg, 1620), 101–70; Thomas Hayne, *The Life and Death of Dr. Martin Luther* (London, 1641); Thomas Fuller, *Abel Redevivus, or the Dead Yet Speaking* (London, 1651), 23–56.

to 'authorize' the piety of his demise. My examination will, therefore, include the earlier stages of his last illness. But I begin with the death itself:

In peace
And by that tyme he waxed very pale in the face. Hys fete and handes were deadlye colde, and from the hart warde he sumwhat panted, but it was so softlye that we verye lyttle perceyved it. In the whych lyght breathynge he gave over hys lyfe to God, without any payne to all our iudgementes. For he neyther moved hande nor fote therin. Neyther was there anye of us (as we testyfye here in conscience both before God & man) that coulde perceyve hym anye perturbacyon, dolour or other unquyetnesse of body in hys departynge. But quyetouslye and swetelye with all gentylnesse of sprete he rested in the lorde. Like
Symeon
as olde Symeon sayd. Now letyst thy servaunt depart in peace, accordynge to thy promes. So that thys saynge of Christ in the viii. of Johan may wele be veryfyed on hym. Verelye I say unto yow, he that kepe my worde shall never se deathe.

Thys text out of the viii. of Johan, was the last clause that in thys lyfe he wrote wyth hys owne hande, about x. dayes afore he departed. And for a memoryall he regestred it in the Byble of huldrick hans hys frynde, whych was there the rent mastre of that cytie. And he laft it after thys sort. Never to se deathe. What an incredyble
Joann. 8
speakynge is thys, if it be conferred with manyfest & common experyence? Yet he whych is the veryte it selfe, hath so spoken it. Trulye whan a man hath thys sentence in seryouse remembraunce, stedefastlye belevinge it, and departeth hens therin, he must plesauntlye passe awaye, and not fele the harde panges of deathe. And undoubtedlye blessed is that man in that word of beleve whych hath so remembred in the verye death. Herunto he thus subscribed. Martynus Luther Doctor, 1546. die 7 februarii.
Hys bodye
After thys was hys dead bodye wrapped in a newe white lynen vesture . . . (fos. 8^v–9)

The passage divides into four sections, corresponding roughly with the marginal headings. The first is the final moments—that is, from the beginning of the extract up to the words 'rested in the lorde'. The second cites the biblical texts, up to the words 'se deathe'. The third is the exegesis, reported as being Luther's last written remarks, of the John text, up to '7 februarii', and the fourth is the account of the laying out (here omitted).

The first section is headed '*In peace*', and is dominated by Luther's breathing. The word 'pant' loses its distress with the qualifier 'softly' and with the amplified description in the next sentence: 'light breathing'. Yet in spite of his unconsciousness, he is granted the conscious acceptance of his own death in the assertion that while breathing he 'gave up hys lyfe to God'. It is a 'good death' because it is embraced by the dying man. In this case, though, his acceptance is assumed by the authors without Luther himself giving any visible assent, for a formal testimony is given in brackets, that the dying man did not move and exhibited no symptoms of distress or indeed anything else. The authors invest his inertia with the passive qualities of sweetness and gentleness of spirit, and his lack of 'perturbacyon', 'dolour', and 'unquyet-nesse of body' become guarantees of his virtue.

The second section begins with the *Nunc Dimittis*. It is linked with the previous section through the words 'depart in peace': 'in peace' heads section one, and 'departure' is used for 'death' throughout. It is the proper text for a perfect finish, central to Vespers and to the English reformed Evening Prayer. The 'so that' link between it and the text from John is disingenuous: nowhere in the *Nunc Dimittis* is it suggested that to 'depart in peace' means to be unconscious of your passing. Simeon's own departure was conscious, deliberate, and not before time.

The interpretation of the second text is, anyway, disconcertingly literal. It may be assumed that the more usual reading of it, as a promise of everlasting life through the Atonement and Resurrection, is being relied on here to overlay the account's much more idiosyncratic one. It relies on context, too, for its authority, suggesting Luther to be the first unconscious dying person for whom unconsciousness could be a promise of immortality.

The reason for these exegetical acrobatics almost certainly lies with the Reformed abandonment of the Sacrament of extreme unction. The effect upon early Protestants of this loss cannot be overstressed. The mechanical efficacy of the ritual was both the decisive factor which occasioned its rejection, and its greatest virtue for those who were able to believe in it. It was a visible guarantee of salvation for the dying, which meant that the Roman Catholic hagiographers who provided the models for the first Protestant Lives were able to offer a certainty of their subjects' heavenly destination by citing it. Their Protestant successors, while feeling an equal need to offer such certainties, were effectively prevented from doing so, and were instead forced to fall back on interpreting the conduct and attitude of each subject to his imminent death, and on scriptural assurances, neither of which was conclusive evidence of salvation. In this context, the attempts of Jonas *et al.* to assure their readers of the salvation of a crucial Reformation figure via the scriptural assurances acceptable to Protestant theology become much more explicable, and prefigure a much greater and more urgent attention to death decorum in exemplary Lives than had been necessary before the Reformation.

The third section contains Luther's exegesis of the John text. Presented in order to back up the previous interpretation, it still has a slightly different emphasis. The euphemisms of a 'good death' punctuating the rest of the account are here too— 'departeth hens', 'plesauntlye passe awaye'—but are set uncompromisingly against 'the harde panges of death' and the 'verye death'. Here it is as if the gift of unconsciousness may be divinely granted as the result of faith. The magnitude of the gift is denoted by a paradox—'incredible speaking' having issued from Him who is the 'veryte it selfe'. In this way not only does the text from John become a licence to ascertain Luther's salvation, but Luther himself is enabled, through his accepted stature as a theologian, to guarantee it for himself. The language of the commentary is the language of authority, imitating the Gospel text stylistically. 'Trulye' (says the commentary), 'whan a man hath thys sentence in seryouse remembraunce . . . he must pleasuntlye passe awaye'; 'Verelye' (says the text from John), 'I say unto yow, he that kepe my words shall never se deathe.'

Even so, the account's authors do not simply rely on the authority of Gospel language. They also add Luther's signature to the commentary, and stress that it is the last 'clause that in thys lyfe he wrote with hys owne hande'—a bid for a further authority. The curious inclusion of the words 'in thys lyfe' also appears to suggest that Luther's gift for exegesis was one certain to continue to be useful once he reached his heavenly destination. To his followers, he was obviously headed for a truly permanent position as heaven's theologian.[115] Luther's reforming status is part of his immortality; and it, as well as his soul, must survive the death of the body.

It is clear that this 'eyewitness account' has been self-consciously shaped. Unobtrusively the reader is invited to identify the document as a latter-day scripture—the Gospel of Luther according to Jonas (and others). Luther himself is pressed into service as a circumstantial exponent of the holiness of his own death, through a deft use of the private exegesis written so soon before it in Huldrick's Bible. It is hardly surprising that the fact of his actual death is not stressed. It was not, in any case, either a welcome or a well-timed event: of it Melanchthon made the bald public statement, 'we have received heavy newes, which have so augmented my dolour, that I am in dout if I mai continue hencefoorth in scholasticall profession, and exercise of teachyng'.[116] It was urgent that Luther's death should quickly be converted into a public text carrying the stamp of an authority as nearly Divine as could be contrived. That way it might be read, not only as exemplary, but as literally inspiring: infusing its readers with the Spirit's comfort and a renewed zeal.

The account offers us a number of 'Gospel' vignettes. For instance, the business Luther conducts before he takes to his bed is reported twice: once, in a dry paragraph of public chronology; but then, in the second paragraph, the same time-span is described again in rather different terms:

From the aforesayd xxix. daye of januarye to the xvii. of februarye, manye a wonderfull sentence came out of hys mouthe, and manye confortable wordes did he utter. Manye hard places of the scriptures he opened in the presence of those noble princes both at their tables and other where else, wherof a boke is now compyled and imprented. And amonge all other, he oft tymes complayned of hys age, and sayd, if it pleased God that he came agayne to Wittemberge, he wolde desyre no longar to lyve, but depart in the lorde. (pp. 3–3ᵛ)

These are activities not so much apostolic as Christlike; and presented iconographically—'manye a wonderfull sentence came

[115] See also E. Disley, 'Degrees of Glory, Protestant Doctrine and the Concept of Rewards Hereafter', *Journal of Theological Studies*, 42, (1991), 77–105; also ch. 1, p. 13 n.

[116] Bennet, *Famous and Godly History* . . . , sig. G.

out of hys mouthe'. Other traces of an iconographical viewpoint appear in this part of the account—for instance, he is described as praying 'standynge ryght up agaynst the windowe'. It is not clear how far Luther is consciously presenting his behaviour as a spectacle; but it is reasonable to assume him to be as aware as any other public figure of the importance of public decorum, and acute enough to image his behaviour as a holy function. The formal stages of his leavetaking are a series of funeral portraits; when he takes to his bed, he gives audience to each of his followers in turn: 'And as he had done of hys clothes, and was layed in the bedde, he gave to yche one of them hys hande, and sayde fare wele to yow all swete bretherne in the lorde' (p. 6). This is certainly self-orchestration. Such formal audiences were already well established as part of deathbed decorum, and form a prominent element in other early accounts of the deaths of reformers. Beza's narrative of the death of Calvin includes a similar scene, and the convention was to survive into accounts of much later deathbeds: for instance, into Daniel Featley's translation of Laurence Humphrey's Latin account of the death of Bishop Jewel, and, of course, into Walton's own narrative of the death of Donne.[117]

There are also strong hints of a sacramental narrative, as in the reference that follows to Luther's 'confortable words'. And when Luther finally takes to his bed, he speaks the real 'confortable words' incorporated by Archbishop Herman of Cologne after the Absolution in the Strassburg Mass of 1524 (and, later, taken from there by Cranmer for inclusion in the *Book of Common Prayer*):[118]

So hath God loved the worlde, that he hath geven it hys onlye sonne, that non whych beleve in hym shuld perysh, but have the lyfe everlastynge. For God sent not hys sonne into the worlde to condempne the worlde, but that the worlde through hym, myght be saved. He that beleveth on hym, shall not be condempned. (John 3: 16–17, quoted p. 7ᵛ)

Here Luther acts both priest and people—comforting himself, and comforting others by example, in the words of a new part of

---

[117] Beza, *Life of Calvin*, sigs. D6ᵛ–7ᵛ; Daniel Featley, *The Life of the Worthie Prelate and Faithfull Servant of God Iohn Iewel Sometimes Bishop of Sarisburie*, in John Jewel, *Works* (London, 1609), sec. 34; Walton, *Lives*, 80–1.

[118] See *Liturgy and Worship: A Companion to the Prayer Books of the Anglican Communion*, ed. W. K. Lowther Clarke and assisted by Charles Harris (London, 1932), 144–5 and 153–4.

a traditional sacrament. This may perhaps be seen as two docu-ments—the exemplary account of a significant death and the new Eucharist—legitimizing the other, although in each case the main legitimation is scriptural.

The reader is encouraged—by Luther as well as by his chroniclers—to connect the dying Luther with the dying Christ. Luther says 'Into thy handes, o lorde, I commend my sprete' at three different times, apparently trusting that one of them will actually accompany the point of death. (None do.) But this three-fold repetition also strongly recalls the Compline liturgy: and Compline, the last devotion of the day before night falls, is con-structed to remind us of the close of our life. It is filled with the parallels between sleep and death, between darkness and death, and where the people commend their spirits to God three times, in the words from Psalm 31 which Jesus cried from the cross, they do so in anticipation of two different kinds of sleep. Luther is not, therefore, claiming more Christlikeness than any other wor-shipper. Whether the Compline parallel was openly admissible in a reformed climate is another question; that it would be well under-stood in the 1540s seems certain.

Luther's beholders and historians, then, ensure, in the absence of the Sacrament of extreme unction, that his last words—after his stroke—are an assent to a declaration of faith made for him by Jonas and Coelius (p. 8).

In one set of accounts drawn from this document—the one which traces its descent from Adamus' Latin version (1620) to Hayne's free translation (1641), and which finally found a place in Fuller's *Abel Redevivus* (1651)—the narrative takes its sacra-mental echoes even further. While the Adamus/Hayne account of Luther's death is paraphrased straight from Jonas, there is one significant difference. Jonas's narrative is personal as well as pub-lic, and when its authors record that Luther 'receyved' medicine 'to the quantyte of a spone full' (p. 7ᵛ) in the midst his final words, it reads only like a faithful detail. But Hayne's translation of Adamus' summary puts it like this:

He [Luther] added moreover. *God so loved the world, that he gave his onely begotten Son, that every one, who beleeveth in him should not perish, but have life everlasting.* And that in the 68. Psalme. *Our God is the God of salva-tion: and our Lord is the Lord, who can deliver from death.* And here taking a medicine, and drinking it, he further said. *Lord I render up my spirit*

into thy hands and come to thee. And again, Lord into thy hands I com-
mend my spirit, thou, O God of truth, hast redeemed me. Here as one falling
asleep and without any bodily pain, that could be discerned, he departed
this life.[119]

The Eucharistic significance of the 'medicine' here is absolutely
clear. After this Luther's three quotations of the last words of
Jesus (separated by appreciable gaps of time in the original) are
conflated so that they are all said together and at the right time.

That Adamus/Hayne should have *heightened* the sacramental
elements here is particularly interesting, because earlier in the *Life*
an Italian libel of Luther's death (written while he was still alive
to refute it) is recorded in full: that Luther, 'when he saw that he
must die . . . requested that his body might be set upon the Altar,
and be adored with divine worship' (p. 105). Clearly there are
acceptable limits of identification with the Christ figure.

While a sacramental aspect may not be said to have survived in
any explicit or deliberate form into the seventeenth century, the
importance of a decorous death is even more prominent. Fuller,
in his 'Epistle to the Reader' prefacing that popular and crucially
death-centred set of exemplary biographies *Abel Redevivus*, really
privileges decorum in the following passage:

. . . The *Roman Gladiators*, set forth and designed to Death, when
despairing to come off alive, tooke all their care; *honeste decumbere*, to fall
down in a decent posture; so contriving their Bodies into a Modest
method, that no uncomlinesse might therein be discovered. So was it in
these Martyrs (and ought to be in us, if called unto their condition) all
their sollicitousnesse was, taking leave of life to entertain Death with
so sweet a deportment, that they might betray no unworthinesse or
meannesse in minde, in their latter end.[120]

'Sweet deportment' here virtually guarantees salvation, and
certainly invites imitation. Not that martyrdom is a prerequisite
for an edifying death. Natural death, being rather commoner,
gets just as much public attention. A deathbed was an occasion
for edifying the living, as well as validating the dying person's
claim to godliness; and the widespread assumption that the dying
would, as it were, perform a holy death for the benefit of (at the
very least) their nearest relatives is neatly exemplified by Simeon

[119] Hayne, *Life and Death of Martin Luther*, 110.
[120] Fuller, *Abel Redevivus*, sig. A3ᵛ.

Foxe, when he laments his father's refusal to do this office for his sons. Foxe writes:

Ere he had quite passed through his 70th year he dyed, not through any known disease, but through much age. Yet did he foresee the time of his departure, nor would suffer his sonnes (which notwithstanding he entirely loved) to be present at his death, but forbad the one at any hand to be sent for, and sent the other on a journey three dayes before he died. . . . whether he thought them unable to bear so heavy a spectacle, or would not have his own minde at that time troubled with any thing that might move him to desire life. Which to me and my brother was the most grievous of all chances, that thereby we could neither come to close his eyes, to receive his last blessing and exhortations, nor satisfie our mindes with that last sight of him. Perchance we could, with more patience have endured to see the fainting approahces [*sic*] of his death drawing in, then to have lost in him so good an example how to die.[121]

Simeon Foxe barely conceals a tone almost of hurt or blame. The anxious parenthesis, 'which notwithstanding he entirely loved', betrays the extent to which he feels his father's deception might be interpreted as a lack of love. Foxe is clear that he feels he has lost a unique chance for edification; he has no 'last blessing and exhortations' to lay up or to publish for the wider instruction of his readers, and his own, particular opportunity directly to witness an exemplary deathbed has been denied him. Surely John Foxe was departing from a widely established convention, to have left such a sense of loss with his sons. For it centres not so much on the fact of the sons having been absent when their father might have needed them (Simeon rather implies that his father was almost selfish in wanting them absent for his own reasons), as on the fact that they felt witnessing the educative and exemplary decorum of their father's death to be a right due to them from him.

The kind of attention which close relatives would pay to the final actions of the dying, and the relation between this attention and the construction of exemplary narrative, can to some extent be traced in accounts of the deathbed of William Bedell, bishop of Kilmore until the Irish Rebellion.[122] The earliest of these appears in a life written by his son—another William Bedell—but it, and

[121] [Simeon Foxe], *Life of Mr. John Fox*, sig. B6ᵛ.
[122] Walton gives a sketch of Bedell in the *Life of Wotton*: see Walton, *Lives*, 114.

the next biography, composed by his chaplain Alexander Clogie, remained in manuscript until the nineteenth century.[123] However, extensive use of these manuscripts—Clogie's in particular— was made by Bedell's third biographer Gilbert Burnet, who printed his *Life of Bedell* in 1685.[124] Each narrative devotes some time to Bedell's deathbed, and Bedell's dying exhortation to his family is written out in full. (The two later accounts naturally follow the younger Bedell's closely here.) Burnet goes on to explain how these final words had come to be preserved. He writes, 'on the fourth day he apprehending his speedy change, called for his Sons, and his Sons Wives, and spake to them at several times, as near in these Words as their memories could serve to write them down soon after'—and the exhortation follows (p. 210).

The first part of Burnet's sentence is a simple paraphrase of Clogie, but the final clause is an addition of Burnet's own.[125] He is stressing that it was felt appropriate to memorize, and then to record, Bedell's departing exhortations. The text of his final speech as it appears in the younger Bedell's account (and thus also in Clogie and Burnet) is coherent and highly polished; and if it were not known that the account was written by an eyewitness, it might seem that it was simply one of those invented speeches to which early modern historians are so prone. Burnet's remark tells us it was not.

Although Burnet seems to suggest that grieving relatives were making notes almost as soon as they were out of the room, he may simply refer to the younger Bedell's narrative. Either way it raises an interesting point about the whole process of fixing a loved person's death in writing. What, for instance, is the extent of Bedell's own collaboration with the process? Did he, like Laud, hope for an accurate stenographer? If his exhortation is indeed recorded in the form (or even fairly close to the form) in which

[123] Alexander Clogie, *Memoir of the Life and Episcopate of William Bedell. Printed for the First Time ... from the Original Manuscript in the Harleian Collection, British Museum*, ed. W. W. Wilkins (London, 1862); *Life of Bishop Bedell, by his Son*, ed. J. E. B. Mayor (Cambridge, 1871).

[124] Gilbert Burnet, *The Life of William Bedell, D.D. Bishop of Kilmore in Ireland* (London, 1685).

[125] For Clogie's version see *Two Biographies of William Bedell, Bishop of Kilmore ...*, ed. E. S. Shuckburgh (Cambridge, 1902), 198–9. All further references to Clogie's and to the younger Bedell's biographies are cited in this edition.

it was delivered, he must have devoted a significant amount of his failing energies to its composition. These are not broken remarks, but a miniature sermon. If Bedell was articulating his final speech in order that it might be recorded, for whom was it intended—the family alone, or a wider audience of possible readers? Although the younger Bedell's narrative never reached print in his lifetime, this is not to say that it was not composed with an eye to a wider public. One most popular biographical funeral sermon, Philip Stubbes's *A Christal Glasse for Christian Women*, which commemorated his wife Katharine, records her making a long and very self-possessed dying speech. Katharine was 20, and dying of puerperal fever; did she compose her words, and if so for whom? In the event, they went into multiple editions.[126]

Even if the family were intended to be the only readers, it still seems possible to extrapolate from Burnet's remark and Bedell's son's account that the element of deliberate shaping in Bedell's whole behaviour was deemed peculiarly suitable for exemplary narrative; and also that, in committing Bedell's decorous and self-possessed embrace of his final scene to writing, his son was ensuring that an exemplary decorum in life could be made to survive the death of the body, in instructing a new generation of the living.

Some clue to the centrality of deathbed decorum in seventeenth-century accounts of godly lives may be found in the controversy about its significance surfacing in funeral sermons. The issue is this: how far could an evidently patterned, performed, and decorous deathbed be taken as a proof of real godliness in the deceased; and conversely, if someone were to die badly—with evident fear, or very suddenly, or with a disordered intellect— would this negate all signs of godliness in the life preceding it? 'A Holy life', writes Jeremy Taylor in his discourse on preparing for death in *The Great Exemplar*, 'is the onely preparation to a happy death.'[127] Yet he evidently regarded the 'happy death' as something to be deliberately, even painfully acquired, for his *Holy Dying* (1651) is a whole course of mental exercises preparing

---

[126] Philip Stubbes, *A Christal Glasse for Christian Women* (London, 1591). Printed 24 times altogether between 1591 and 1637 (STC 23381–95).

[127] Taylor, *The Great Exemplar*, 145.

for this event, coupled with a multitude of rules of behaviour in sickness. His assertion in *The Great Exemplar* could be turned on its head; it being as true to say that a continual preparation for death is a necessary sign of a holy life.

Even without making death preparation so explicit a component of holy living, a number of writers are prepared to assert a causal connection between pious conduct and a successful deathbed performance. Samuel Clarke, in *An Antidote to Immoderate Mourning*, not only argues that the 'good' death of his subject Thomas Bewley was ensured by the works of charity he had performed in life, but even implies that its comparative painlessness was a Divine reward for them. He writes: 'Its no marvel that this charitable frame of heart contributed so much towards the comfortable end of this our deceased brother. I remember what *Hierom* saith . . . I do not remember (saith he) that I ever read of any one that died an ill death that was frequent in works of charity.'[128] Clarke's (or Jerome's) statement seems to be a bribe as much as a promise: give to the poor and you too can have a death like this. And while Clarke's words can be defended to some extent, in that if Bewley's 'comfortable end' referred only to the serenity of his behaviour, he could have constructed for himself a holy decease as deliberately as he had given to the poor, this does not address the accidents of death: pain, delirium, protractedness. It is perhaps significant that Jerome explicitly refers to *written* deathbeds; only in narrative, where the conventions of holy dying are clear cut and its circumstances manipulable, can an easy death be guaranteed to the good; and even in this context an easy death is rather prayed for than expected, with the extent to which it might be a reward for good conduct left necessarily vague. For example, in the course of describing the death of Miles Smith, bishop of Gloucester, the anonymous author cites both a narrative precedent and an eyewitness account for his subject's easy departure:

They write of *Lanfrancus*, sometime *Archbishop of Canterbury*, that he often prayed and obtained to dye such a death, that neither hindered speech, or memory; this blessing God afforded our Reuerend Bishop; for as I am certified (by one most deare to him, and worthy to be beleeved

---

[128] Clarke, *An Antidote Against Immoderate Mourning for the Dead* (London, 1659), 46.

[marg. *Mistris K. Smith*]) when he was leauing this life, he looked on her, and on the rest of his children in the chamber present, and said, *Christ blesse you All*. And like that old Patriark *Jacob*, he moued himselfe vpon the bed, and cryed *Christ Jesus helpe*, and so Christ tooke him, and *conclamatum est*.[129]

The issue is raised discursively in a number of funeral sermons. The author of 'Peace in Death, or the Quiet End of the Righteous' asserts 'a comfortable, quiet, and peaceable departure' to be one of God's promises to his children.[130] Yet having said this (at some length, with examples), he inserts a caveat removing the burden of proof from visible signs:

Now here some may object first, Wee see many worthy men, that have made a great, and an extraordinary profession of Religion in their lives, and which have also carried themselves unblameably, yet to give appearance of much anguish and perplexity, and even of a kind of despaire in their death. How can wee say then, that all good and holy persons have a peaceable departure?

I answer first, Wee ought to remember the Rule our Saviour gives, *not to judge according to the outward appearance*. It is a very weake argument to say, that this, or that man dyeth without peace, because to the standers by hee makes not shew of peace. Certaine it is, that as a man may have peace with God, and yet himselfe for a time [*sic*], by reason of some tentation not feele it; so a man being sicke, or going out of the world may feele it, and yet others that behold him cannot perceive it. (p. 685)

This is Erasmus' reasoning, offered with an almost identical analogy a hundred years later.[131] The same sophisticated distinction between the visible signs of holiness in the dying and the real case of things is made by Donne in *Deaths Dvell*;[132] but Donne himself nevertheless performed his own deathbed with extraordinary, exaggerated artistry, even (according to Walton) closing his own eyes as he died, and arranging his 'hands and body into such a posture as required not the least alteration by those that came to shroud him'.[133] Why should Donne—and why should

---

[129] Thomas Prior, *A Sermon at the Fvneral of . . . Miles Smith, Late Lord Bishop of Gloucester*, in Miles Smith, *Sermons* (London, 1632), 304.

[130] *The House of Mourning*, 684–5.

[131] See *Preparation to Deathe*, sigs. E3–4.

[132] *John Donne: Complete Poetry and Selected Prose*, ed. John Hayward (London, 1929), 751–3.

[133] Walton, *Lives*, 82.

the subjects of a multitude of other deathbeds—have paid such enormous attention to its decorum if the consensus was that visible signs were not important?

Perhaps the reason lies in a distinction between educated consensus and popular belief. That the point is made so often itself suggests constant attempts to uproot a general assumption about painful, ugly, or sudden deaths. This is brought out very explicitly in a funeral sermon preached some time before 1639 for a man who had died of a stroke during a dispute with some neighbours. Here the preacher is at some pains to lay to rest parochial gossip that God had deliberately struck him down for being quarrelsome. 'I know you desire to heare of his death', he says, 'and it hath much afflicted my soule, to heare what unjust aspersions have beene on the manner of it.'[134] The preacher does call the man's illness 'a sudden stroke indeed of Gods hand', and even acknowledges that 'if hee had uttered one word of falshood to helpe his cause, if hee had used one word of imprecation, wishing any curse to himself; then it had beene peradventure, a just thing with God, to have taken him at his word' (p. 475). Therefore, he is not arguing that to believe in the supernatural manifestation of God's judgement is itself superstitious. What he does instead is to argue that the deceased's demeanour (which he had witnessed, arbitrating the dispute) had been too temperate and too pious, and that his acceptance of approaching death too dutiful (for the man had not died immediately, although he had lost his speech) for God's actions in striking him down to be seen as a judgement on his morals. Rather, he suggests, it should be regarded as one of God's mysterious actions, into which it was presumptuous to inquire:

He did plead his cause, but with that meeknesse of spirit, with that quietnesse, with that sweet temper, and that Christian moderation, as more could not be required in any Saint of God . . . Brethren, considering these things that I have told you before, I beseech you judge not, that you not be judged . . . You owe a dutie to the truth . . . stoppe the mouths of all them that shall either bee forgers, or spreaders of such notorious lies: though it pleased God it were by a sudden stroake of his hand; and how often hath he done it, when men have beene worse busied? hee was but seeking to worke peace. (p. 476)

[134] 'The Saints Longing for the Great Epiphanie', in *The House of Mourning*, p. 475.

He narrates the man's last moments, establishing first that he had command of his senses: 'I perceived by the lifting up of his hand that hee knew mee.' He then describes presenting the man with a series of questions, 'I asked him whether he beleeved those promises of God', 'I asked him . . . if hee found any assurance of Gods favour in Christ', to which the man assents each time by lifting his hand. The preacher concludes finally from these motions of assent and from the passivity with which he meets the moment of expiry, that the dying man's behaviour reliably indicated that he had died in faith (pp. 476–7).

This narrative establishes a clear distinction between external accidents and deliberate conduct. Its author makes a great deal of the extent to which, within his limits, the dying man had ordered his behaviour in conformity with the conventions of a godly death. These are presented to the congregation as proofs of godliness strong enough effectively to eradicate the impressions they (by implication, very naturally) had received from the context and manner of his final illness. They are, in fact, gestures which convince a watching, reading, or listening public; in themselves, perhaps, not efficacious, but extremely valuable as rough-hewn assurances to a less educated populace hungry for visible signs of salvation.

Perhaps for priests, the Church's acknowledged exemplars, the histrionic piety of the performed deathbed was felt to be required by their function. If your whole demeanour was constructed didactically, surely your most crucial and final act should be fashioned to be specially exemplary. Neither does Donne (nor anyone else) ever argue that, because some good people had not for some reason or other managed to perform an edifying deathbed, therefore it was any less incumbent on themselves to do so if possible.

If Donne were to believe that his priestly duty included an exemplary deathbed, then his private conviction that the manner of his death was of no importance as between himself and God would be irrelevant. He would be performing a kind of pastoral office—strengthening the faith of those who, like Thomas, had difficulty with 'things unseen'. Nor was this an unreasonable expectation. In Donne's own case, he was already a public enough figure to warrant some printed recognition of his passing, and in general the lives and deaths of ecclesiastical dignitaries were being put into narrative form with increasing frequency, often with the knowledge and consent of their subjects before they died. Thomas Morton is a case in point; it is clear from internal evidence in the accounts of Barwick, Baddeley, and Naylor (all secretaries or chaplains of Morton's) that his Life was being written long before he died, and that Baddeley at least was submitting his account for Morton's approval as he wrote it.

If this kind of performed deliberation was being fashioned by *subjects*, this must alter how we read biographers. Narrative conventions, from being deliberate manipulations of material, could be seen as simple records of highly patterned real behaviour. But to detect stylized patterns in someone's real living cannot remove the need for patterns in narrative. Rather, it must mean that the real performers (our 'Walking Texts') are seeing themselves *as a story*. We cannot be sure who is prime storyteller: subject or biographer. What we can say is that they shared their literary models.

The prime model, and the one carrying most automatic authority, was Holy Scripture itself; and I propose here to look at a deathbed which manipulates scriptural allusion to great effect. Daniel Featley's *Life of the Worthie Prelate and Faithfull Servant of God Iohn Iewel Sometimes Bishop of Sarisburie* first appeared in English as a Preface to Jewel's *Works* in 1609. It finishes with an account of Jewel's death identified by the modern historian Kenneth Fincham as influential enough to have given rise to at least one widespread deathbed commonplace, 'that there was no fitter place for a bishop to die than the pulpit'.[135] Featley's narrative is a very successful reduction and translation of a Latin Life of Jewel, Laurence Humphrey's *Iohannis Iuelli . . . Vita et Mors*, which was printed in 1573. But Featley's version is a work of art within the genre in its own right, and its publication in the vernacular reveals it aiming for a broader readership than Humphrey's work, one that would include the educated layman. Featley himself, in a letter to Thomas Morton, saw his narrative as linked with, but distinct from Humphrey's: he calls the Latin source 'a large sampler whence I have taken some principall flowres', and adds, 'the filling set[t]ing and whole working was mine own'.[136] Featley's own feeling about the result is hard to

[135] Featley, *Life of . . . Iewel . . .*, sec. 33; Fincham, *Prelate as Pastor*, 12.

[136] Bodleian Library, MS Rawlinson D 47 (Daniel Featley MS) following Featley's MS copy of 'The life and death of B. Jewell . . . anno 1609' (fos. 194ʳ–209ᵛ), fo. 209. I am grateful to Professor Patrick Collinson, and to the late

gauge. In the same letter he performs a curious pessimistic reversal of the 'living text' commonplace, in calling it his 'late now
formed, yet deformed dead Life of B. Jewel', and argues that the
very violence of his involvement in this 'chylde of his fancy' gave
it 'a kinde of deadnes through the whole body it came from the
stupour of his griefe that made it'. Yet in spite of this apparently
complete acceptance of authorial responsibility—in spite, if you
like, of Featley's pained recognition and mimesis of the death
of his subject—within a very few sentences he is ascribing
characteristics to his narrative which properly belong to the living Jewel himself. Unexpectedly, he claims Jewel's collaboration
in fashioning the narrative. This is what he says: 'If it be . . .
obiected that a narration should be like a cleare streame fountaine
but that this a stream troubled with the flood of affections My
answer is this life of whome I treate was for the many changes in
it, a troubled streame and the image much be like.' In spite of
these passionate doubts, the *Life*'s success is demonstrated by the
fact that Featley's text was reprinted in Fuller's *Abel Redevivus*
in 1651.[137]

Featley's account of Jewel's death is woven about with scriptural allusion. It depicts Jewel as active participant in its conventions, collecting his own scriptural garlands, and nudging his
deathbed companions into positions which will underline the piety
of his own decorum. When 'shrinking and failing', Jewel calls 'all
his household about him' (section 34). This ensures an audience
for his performance who are both his witnesses and his recipients.
They articulate a need for comfort and assurance which implicitly places the reader in their company. Jewel provides for them
(for us)—verbally, and also implicitly in his whole deportment.
He then makes a speech which Featley presents as his best and
final sermon, his swan-song: 'Cantator cygnus funeris ipse sui.'
The speech that follows is conventional; he affirms his faith,
declares his desire to die in terms that suggest he would have

Jeremy Maule for bringing a fascinating (and baffling) description of Featley's
motives and biographical practice to my attention. Perhaps it could only have
been done with a man who had subscribed under Mary.

[137] Laurence Humphrey, *Ioannis Iuelli, Episcopi Sarisburiensis Vita et Mors
eiusque; Vera Doctrina Defensio* (London, 1573). Fuller acknowledges Featley's
authorship in his dedicatory epistle in *Abel Redevivus*, sig. A3ᵛ. I have followed
Fuller in giving Featley as author in the text.

preferred martyrdom (although the events of his life suggest this was not always his preference), condemns the pope and all his works, prays for the queen, asks forgiveness from any present he may have offended, and requests the help, through prayer, of his auditors in the difficult business of dying faithful. Everybody present is invited to sing Psalm 71, and Jewel joins in 'as well as he could with them' (section 35). He adds to the singing a number of personal reflections on the words, and some 'thicke and short prayers, as it were pulses', which end in broken renderings of the usual quotations which identify Jewel both with the dying Christ and with his dying servants in the New Testament: 'Lord take from me my spirit; Lord now let thy servant depart in peace: breake off all delayes; Suffer thy servant to come unto thee; Command him to be with thee: Lord receive my spirit' (section 35). The very fragmentary nature of these quotations is what makes the narrative moving. They might suggest that it was Jewel who decided on their inclusion in his deathbed scene, and not his chronicler. Featley's description of Jewel's ejaculations as 'pulses' also introduces a Latinate pun; the word derives from *pulso*, which can mean to knock at a door, to play on a harp, and to hurt, all fit meanings.

This is not the end. One of the bystanders makes the happy mistake of praying for Jewel's recovery. Since Jewel's recovery is not the point, he is rebuked sharply 'in the words of Saint Ambrose: 'I have not lived so, that I am ashamed to live longer, neither do I fear to die, because we have a mercifull Lord . . . This is my To day: This day quickly let me come unto thee: This day let me see the Lord Jesus' (section 36).[138]

His actual death is attended by poetic images of the expiring body which draw heavily on Ecclesiastes 12. These are set against prosaic and peripheral details which lend them a powerful particularity:

With these words the doore was shut by the bas sound of the grinding, and the daughters of singing were abased, the silver cord lengthened no

---

[138] See also Thomas Prior, *Sermon at the Fvnerall of . . . Miles Smith*, in Miles Smith, *Sermons* (London, 1632), 303: 'Non ita inter vos vixi, ut pudeat me viuere; nec timeo mori, quoniam Dominum bonum habemus; I haue not so liued among you, that I am ashamed to liue, neither am I afraid to dye, because our Lord is good.'

more, the golden ewer was crackt, and the pitcher broken at the well; yet the keepers, though with much trembling stood erect, and they that looked out of the windowes, though darke, yet were fixed towards heaven, till after a few fervent inward praiers of devotion, and sighs of longing desire, the soule returned to God that gave it. M. *Ridley* the Steward of his house shut his eies in the yeere of our Lord 1571. Sept. 22 about three of the clocke in the afternoone. (section 36)

Featley and Jewel, then, have collaborated here (as Luther had done with his chroniclers) in the construction of a kind of latter-day scripture, an edifying spectacle saturated with textual references, and itself arguably constructed with an eye to its eventual shaping and distribution as a text from the moment that Jewel began to act it.

'LIFE, TRULY WRIT'

This section attempts to reassemble the anatomized components of the godly biography into one 'Life, truly writ'. I quote Walton's *Life of Sanderson*, where he commends John Harris's account of the life of Arthur Lake, bishop of Bath and Wells, 1616–26.[139] Harris's narrative appeared as a preface to Lake's *Sermons* in 1629, and is the Life I read here.

While Walton's phrase defines Harris's work as a full biography, Harris himself calls it only 'some of the obseruable passages . . . which returned to my minde upon the publishing of this worke' (sig. ¶4). How far, then, should we expect biographical fulness? Three of Walton's four ecclesiastical Lives (which do command such an expectation) were also issued as prefaces. What a 'Life, truly writ' might be is clearly still fluid—though Harris is also probably treating modesty as the better part of valour.

Harris begins his account with a personal introduction. Lake, he explains, was a 'rare and eminent' man, 'whom if thou knewest not in his life time, I suppose it concernes thee to bee acquainted with now' (sig. ¶4). The printed meeting is here given the weight of a real one; but he qualifies this quite quickly, postulating a hypothetical 'able Historian' who would have done a better job of

---

[139] Walton, *Lives*, 357; [John Harris], 'A Short View of the Life and Vertves of the Avthovr', in Arthur Lake, *Sermons, with some Religious and Divine Meditations* (London, 1629).

making Lake real. It is a conventional disclaimer, as common in Lives not characterized as prefaces as in those that are,[140] but it is not Harris's only reason for drawing our attention to his omissions. 'If the lawes of a Preface did permit so much,' he says, 'I suppose it would be a labour worth thy acceptance, to give thee a iust storie of his life, whereof there is no part but would yeild thee good matter of imitation'. Harris regrets the larger scope for exemplary narrative in a whole biography, but cannot feel it appropriate to a preface. But we know, because he tells us, that what remains has been included as a 'dutie'; it is what *cannot* be left out. And it explicitly works in tandem with (and claims the same importance as) Lake's own sermons: the 'attentiue' reader of the Preface should, explains Harris, expect to be 'as well edified, as by the Worke it selfe' (sig. ¶4ᵛ).

A short summary of Lake's education and preferments follows, but no account is given of his birth, parentage, or early life. Harris begins instead with his placement at Winchester School, and takes him in one (lengthy) sentence all the way to his bishopric. He asserts, incidentally, that this rapid rise to 'the heighth of Episcopall dignitie' (reflected here in the rapidity of the narrative) had not been a result of Lake's 'ambitious suit or seeking . . . but by the speciall, and I had almost said; immediate prouidence of Almightie God'. (In point of fact Lake's preferment had not been quite that swift or providential—evidence exists in Lake's correspondence that he had been 'angling for high office from the early years of James I's reign'); but it can be argued that Harris was employing hyperbole meant to suggest that Lake's interest was genuinely pastoral rather than crudely ambitious.[141]

Harris doubles back here for a more leisurely tour through Lake's preferments. He frames it carefully with Lake's modesty, describing his 'naturall inclination' to be 'priuate and retired'. Then, using sartorial alterations to stand for his changing employments, Harris asserts that he 'continued the same in his Rotchet, which he had beene in his Schollers gowne' (sig. ¶5). His public offices could not alter the fundamental shape of a 'retired' character. Noticing that he has therefore suggested a disparity

<hr>

[140] See below, pp. 256–9, where George Paule's employment of the modesty topos in his separately published *Life of Whitgift* (1612) is discussed.
[141] See Fincham, *Prelate as Pastor*, 33; *DNB*, xxxi. 408–9.

between the outer and the inner Lake, he wards off its dangers by a speedy use of stage imagery: 'his vertues', writes Harris, 'were vertues indeed . . . hee vsed them not as Stage-players doe their vizards, only to act a part in, which being done, they pull them off, and cast them into a corner.' Harris is pointing out that as far as what he calls the 'personall' virtues are concerned (sig. ¶4), Lake's performance was rightly consistent, and therefore sincere, in every context. The virtues themselves, however, are identified with the players' 'vizards'; although personal, they are also visible and deliberately assumed properties of the public self, their genuineness guaranteed only by the fact that they were never discarded.

Here Harris abandons chronology for a numbered list of Lake's exemplary qualities; first those defined by Harris as 'priuate and personall' (sig. ¶6ᵛ)—humility, affability, tranquillity of mind, and temperance—and then those he calls '*publike or Pastorall*'—munificence, 'Magnanimitie and Courage', 'Contempt of Wealth'. Finally, Harris comes 'yet more nearely to the discharge of his Episcopall Function' (sig. §1ᵛ) by attributing to Lake (of course) the episcopal virtues of 1 Timothy 3—'Abilitie to teach', hospitality, the effective rule of his household and (by extension) diocese (sigs. §1ᵛ–3ᵛ).

Taking the 'priuate and personall' list first, it is observable that Lake's humility is characterized as an acquired, or 'studied' virtue (sig. ¶5). Lake's later career puts his humility at risk, but, asserts Harris, he was never tempted to abandon this 'fruit of true Christian mortification' for any higher-prized self-estimate. His second private virtue, 'Affabilitie', emerges out of this acquired humility, but arises naturally from it 'from the goodnesse of his nature'. It is on the 'priuate' list, but is pastorally effective: Lake is almost constantly available (except in his 'times of devotion') to all comers down to 'the meanest person'.

Lake's third private virtue, 'rare Tranquillitie and Contentednesse of minde', is a kind of Plutarchan virtuous constancy. 'Hauing first framed' his mind to be indifferent to the accidents of fortune, Harris comments of Lake:

whatsoeuer outwardly befell him either to the better or the worser part, he seemed uery little to be affected, surely nothing disquieted therewithall. A strange serenitie of minde in him; whereof I take it also to haue beene a good argument, that (as I haue often heard him say) so long as he was in perfect health of his bodie, he did neuer dreame. (sig. ¶5ᵛ)

To master conscious desires is to master unconscious ones. Harris gives Aristotle and Plutarch as authorities for this association between dreamlessness, and serenity. They are explicitly obtained, he explains, through 'Temperancie'. Lake, austere in diet, dress, and daily habits which include the writing of regular meditations on scripture, has an 'intellectual part' which 'had the predominancy ouer his sensuall, or rather indeed . . . grace ruled them both; and . . . the Man in him was subordinate to the Christian (sig. ¶6). It is not just that dreamlessness is a *deodatus* of self-discipline. The Stoically based virtues, which can be summarily defined as the ascendance of reason over passion, become the ascendance of the new man, the rational soul, operating under grace, over the old man subject to the sins and irrational desires of Adam.[142]

Coming to Lake's *'publike or* Pastorall' virtues, we find first liberality, which 'vpon the increase of his fortunes hee improved . . . euen to a kind of *Magnificence*' (sig. ¶6ᵛ).[143] While Harris includes 'largesse to the poore at his gates, and in the streets', his examples are on the whole academically focused; the endowment of 'Exhibitions' (scholarships to poor scholars), the maintenance of two regular lectures at New College, Oxford (in Hebrew

---

[142] For a converse example of this belief, see William Prynne, *A Breviate of the Life of W. Laud* . . . (London, 1644), where Prynne publishes Laud's private diary, which includes his dreams. Prynne's intentions are malicious, of course, and condemn the sleeping Laud (whose dream narratives are authentically anxious, uncontrolled, and random) as surely as if he had been in full conscious command of his faculties. See esp. pp. 6, 10: '*August.21.* [1625] I stayed at *Brecon* in *Wales*: that night in a dreame the Duke of Buckingham seemed to me to ascend into my bed; where he carried himself with much love towards me, after such rest wherein wearied men are wont exceedingly to rejoyce: And likewise many seemed to me to enter the Chamber, who did see this . . . *Febr.7.* I dreamed in the night that I was sick of the Scurvey, and that all my teeth were sodainly loose, especially one in my lower jaw-bone, which I could hardly keep in with my finger . . . *March 8.* I came to *London*. The night following, *I dreamed I had been reconciled to the Church of Rome*: this distracted me, and I wondred much whence it hapned, being troubled at the Scandall . . . Thus troubled in my dream, I said with my selfe, that I would presently goe, and making confession, aske pardon of the Church of *England*. As I was going to doe it, a certaine Priest met me, and would hinder me: but being moved with indignation, I went on my way; and when I had wearied my selfe with wayward Cogitations, I awaked. I felt such impressions, I could scarcely beleeve I had dreamed.'

[143] For the function of hospitality amongst the post-Reformation episcopate see Heal, *Hospitality, passim*, and 277–95.

and Mathematics), and the founding of two libraries in the
Cathedrals of Wells and Worcester.[144]

His second public virtue Harris also puts in an academic
context: that 'Magnanimitie and Courage' which 'appeared well
in the gouernment of the Uniuersitie, that one yeare wherein he
bare the office of *Vicechancellour*' (sig. §1). Evidently this was
a tough job. Harris compares his labours in subjecting the
well-known 'animosity' of his fellow-academics to 'the ancient
Discipline there', to Plutarch's description of Alexander sub-
duing his horse to a 'due temper and pace'. For, explains Harris,
horse and scholars shared the same temperament, for good and
evil, being 'generous indeed, and fit for great seruices', but 'fierce
and vntractable for the time', and so requiring 'no lesse then an
Alexander to curbe them'. The reference is given in the margin;
and the swiftness with which a biographer would turn to
Plutarch's *Lives* for his imagery is perhaps exemplified in this
remarkable comparison.

Lake's next characteristic, 'Contempt of Wealth', is a part of
his 'Magnanimitie', but also includes his refusal to make ecclesiastical appointments and decisions on the acceptance of bribes.
This is Harris's bridge to a final set of virtues: those which 'come
more nearely to the discharge of his Episcopall Function' (sig. §1ᵛ).
They follow 1 Timothy 3; and the academic emphasis of Lake's
foregoing 'Pastorall' virtues is supported by one on Lake's
'Abilitie to teach' (1 Timothy 3: 2) and his worthiness for the
'double honour *which Saint* Paul *allowes to such as doe* not onely
rule well, but also labour in the Word and Doctrine' (1 Timothy 5).
Harris characterizes Lake not merely as a living text, whose
'ordinarie Discourses were . . . as good as Lectures to those that
heard them', but as a collection of texts to which any 'Scholler'
could resort: a 'liuing librarie' (sig. §2).

He deals next with hospitality. For 'it is required of a Bishop',
explains Harris, quoting Paul 'that hee should *pascere cibo* too as
well as *verbo*'. A list of Lake's regular entertainments follows; not
only the charitable donation of 'constant, solide and substantiall
meales' to the inmates of the hospital at St Cross when he was its

---

[144] In point of fact Lake founded neither, although he contributed to the one
at Wells and gave three volumes of Chrysostom to the one at Worcester in 1616.
See David Pearson, 'The Libraries of English Bishops, 1600–40', *The Library*,
6th series, 14 (Sept. 1992), 221–57 (p. 246).

master, but also his feasts given for 'the better sort' while dean of Worcester; and not only his public entertainments, but his habitual private table of family, friends, and visitors which 'did commonly consist of at least fiftie persons' (sig. §2^v).[145]

This magnificence is tempered with another Pauline quality which ensures that we here see bounty, not waste or disorder: Lake is characterized as 'ruling . . . his house well: *and hauing those that are vnder him* in subiection with all grauitie' (1 Timothy 3: 4). Harris explains his success in keeping an orderly house on two counts: because he has modelled himself on Paul's advice to Timothy, and because he trained (Harris's word) his household himself to the practice of 'true pietie and deuotion' (sigs. §2^v–3). Lake's insistence on regular household prayers, on family prayers which he conducted himself, and on having portions of Scripture read to him while he ate, 'according to the ancient fashion of Bishops', are all actions commonly described (with slight variations) in comparable accounts of ecclesiastical Lives.[146]

---

[145] See Walton's praise of Archbishop Whitgift's hospitality at the Croydon almshouse he built in the *Life of Hooker*, where the tone is very similar: 'whensoever the Queen descended to that lowliness as to dine with him at his Palace in *Lambeth* (which was very often) he would usually the next day shew the same lowliness to his poor Brothers and Sisters at *Croydon*, and dine with them at his Hospital; at which, you may believe, there was Joy at the Table' (Walton, *Lives*, 196). Whitgift seems to have used his episcopal duties of hospitality to political effect in the style and frequency with which he entertained the Queen. See Heal, *Hospitality*, 276.

[146] See also e.g. Foxe, 'The Life, State and Story of . . . Cranmer', in *Actes and Monuments* (1570), ii. 2038, where Foxe combines a celebration of Cranmer's episcopal munificence in hospitality with a dual defence against accusations of overspending and miserliness by stressing his personal asceticism and careful household routine at the same time; Featley, *Life of . . . Iewel*, sec. 29, where Featley describes Jewel's hospitable care for the 'young scholars, whom he maintained at his table', his household prayers and subsequent exhortations to his servants, and his habit of listening 'some part of an Authour, read vnto him by the gentleman of his bed-chamber'; B[addeley]/N[aylor], *Life of Dr. Thomas Morton*, (in the section written by Baddeley), 86–8, where Morton is described as habitually reading or listening to some 'choice or usefull book' while 'travelling in his coach', and as conducting regular devotions 'in publique with his Family, and afterwards more privately by himself; his bed-chamber servants . . . reading some other pious books, or some Church History unto him, till such time as acceptable sleep stole upon him'; Bedell, 'Life of William Bedell', in *Two Lives . . .* , ed. Shuckburgh, 19–20, where Bedell's habit of conducting family and household prayers and catechisms on Sundays is described in detail, 'so truly was he God's vice-gerent in his family'.

Harris (in common with the younger Bedell) takes this as a starting-point for describing another kind of quasi-paternal rule: diocesan administration. He devotes time and detail to Lake's practice; his care in examining ordinands personally; his pastoral concern for those already ordained, especially the 'weaker sort' (by which the more uneducated are clearly meant); his firm but benign treatment of offenders; and his frequent visitations to his parishes. The space Harris devotes to these details is suggestive, in the light of his opening remarks. Since he has only included those parts of Lake's life he judges relevant to the reading of his works, but has presented those parts as being as edifying as Lake's works themselves, this emphasis on episcopal practice argues that Harris sees it as relevant to the value of Lake's preaching. Walton's judgement, in the *Life of Sanderson*, on Lake's life in the light of Harris's narrative reveals a similar emphasis on pastoral practice, stating that 'he made the great trust committed to him, the chief care and whole business of his life'.[147]

But where, in that case, does Harris place the reading layman in his exemplary narrative? Perhaps we can locate it in the final pastoral scene before Lake's death. Here Harris says he must 'adde but one thing more of the cariage of this man in his Episcopall Function'. The 'thing' is a detail, unlike the large picture the rest has been (sig. +1ᵛ). He draws a habitual scene: Lake, in Wells Cathedral, standing at the end of the service 'whether it were so that himselfe preacht or no', and blessing the people 'after the example of the High Priest in the Old Testament, *Numb.* 6.23'.[148] Harris continues:

Which thing he performed like himselfe, that is to say, in a most graue and fatherlike manner; so any man that had but seene with what atten-tiue and deuout gestures the people receiued it, what apparant comfort they tooke in it, and how carefull euery particular man was not to depart from Church without it; could not but conclude that there is a secret vertue in the Prayers and blessings as of naturall so of spirituall Parents. (sig. +1ᵛ)

---

[147] Walton, *Lives*, 357.
[148] In fact Numbers 6: 24–6. These words of Moses to Aaron and his sons are used as a traditional Jewish blessing. While not in the Anglican liturgy, it is still currently used as a pastoral blessing.

He uses the same word to describe the people's deportment that he has initially applied to the reader, 'attentiue'. Like Lake's congregation, we are blessed by his words, by the words of his acts.

On this valedictory note, Harris leaves Lake's life for his death. He begins, though, with a defensive affirmation of Lake's Protestantism which may in part be explained by the recent flurry over whether Bishop King of London had converted to Romanism on his deathbed in 1621.[149] Harris expresses a fear that Lake's virtues might be appropriated for the wrong Church, adding darkly that this was a common Roman trick.[150] He then argues that Lake's vulnerability to a charge of secret Catholicism was exacerbated because

> it is true that of his own disposition . . . he was . . . of a most peaceable and milde temper, apter to reconcile differences then to make them, and to interpret the sayings euen of the Aduersaries where they were ambiguous in the better part: in regard whereof if there be any hope left of sowing vp those innumerable rents which Faction hath wrought in the seamlesse coat of Christ . . . I think he had beene such a man as is hardly found amongst many to bee imployed in that seruice. (sigs. +2–2ᵛ)

Some further light is perhaps thrown on this by David Pearson's remarking on the presence of 'contemporary Roman Catholic authors' in Lake's library (as well as in the libraries of Lancelot Andrewes and Samuel Harsnett). While some of these Pearson identifies as texts which a controversialist would acquire purely for purposes of refutation, others in his judgement indicate 'a genuine respect for the learning of the major Roman Catholic commentators' (p. 229). Harris, as Fellow of New College, Oxford, and later prebendary of Wells Cathedral, was certainly in a position to have seen Lake's books, which at his death were in the main divided between these two institutions.

---

[149] See H. King, *A Sermon Preached at Pauls Crosse, Touching the Supposed Apostasie of J King, late Bishop of London* . . . (London, 1621); G. Muschet, *The Bishop of London his Legacy. Or Certain Motives of D. King, late Bishop of London, for his Change of Religion* (St Omer, 1623). The same concern surfaces subtly in the anonymous biographical preface to Miles Smith's *Sermons* (London, 1632), sig ¶¶, and less subtly in Thomas Prior's funeral sermon of 1624 for Smith, bound in with the same volume, pp. 303–4.

[150] Vaghan, sig. *1ᵛ; [Banks], *Life of Rainbow*, 4; Barwick, *Life*, p. 55; Whitefoote, *Deaths Alarum*, 78–9; Daniel Featley to George Paule, Bodleian Library, MS Rawlinson D 47 (Daniel Featley MS), fo. 19.

Harris takes his conclusive proof of Lake's Anglican faith from his Will, which he quotes at length. But, apart from the disposition of his books, Harris says little about bequests, claiming his greatest parting gift was intangible: 'Only a name hee hath left behind him, and that more precious then any ointment a name that filleth the Church for the present, with the sweet sauour thereof, and I trust that euen Posteritie also shall be refreshed by it' (sig. +3ᵛ). This is an adaptation of Ecclesiastes 7: 1, an understandably common funeral text ('a good name is better than a precious ointment; and the day of death better than the day of one's birth'). Harris is not alone in using it biographically. Vaghan was to deploy it in his *Life of Dr. Jackson* of 1673, Jonathan Banks to apply it to the behaviour of Edward Rainbow's father Thomas in 1688, Barwick to use it as a title-page text for his *Life of Morton* in 1660, and Whitefoote to make elaborate use of it and related texts in his funeral sermon for Joseph Hall in 1656. Featley too uses it casually, as a mutually familiar code, in his letter to George Paule after the publication of Paule's *Life of Whitgift* in 1612: 'This your embalming your deceased master with the sweet ointment of a good report cannot but be gratefully accepted of all that wish well to this See.'[151] Whitefoote is as explicit as Featley in linking the Ecclesiastes text to the actions of the woman who anointed Jesus with spikenard before the Last Supper (described in Mark 14: 8 and Matthew 26: 7–12); as Jesus identifies her action in Matthew's version as an honour 'for my burial' (verse 12) so Whitefoote asserts that he too is perpetuating the odour of Hall's good name through his words as an honour due to him as part of his funeral rites. This meaning is implicit in Harris's use of the text, for he too stands in relation to Lake as the woman stood to Jesus, pouring out words rather than perfume, in recording Lake's exemplary life for 'Posteritie'.

Harris devotes a paragraph only to the 'manner' of Lake's death, because, he explains casually, 'any man might guesse at it that hath beene acquainted thus farre with the passages of his life, (for seldome doth a mans life and his end varie)' (sig. +3ᵛ). Harris sees virtually no need to spell out the connection between a good

---

[151] The anonymous biographical preface to the *Sermons* of Miles Smith also employs examples of 'ioint harmony', including (this time) Nazianzen and Basil, sig ¶¶; later, the image from Daniel is also used, sig ¶¶3ʳ.

death and a good life, or even to insist on the visibility of its signs.
Only the word 'seldome' betrays any consciousness that holy
living and holy dying did not invariably concur. Harris mentions
Lake's final confession to the bishop of Ely, Nicholas Felton, and
describes Felton as assisting 'to the last gaspe' with 'comfortable
and heauenly prayers' until Lake 'speedily yeilded vp his soule to
God' (sig. +4). He notes the proximity of Felton's own death to
Lake's, and describes the friendship between the two men in life
in terms which surely prefigure directly Walton's accounts of holy
friendships, and in particular that between Donne and Magdalen
Herbert. Harris writes that Lake and Felton had

> liued many yeares in a most entire league of friendship, not unlike that
> which Saint *Chrysostome* describes to haue beene betwixt himselfe and
> Saint *Basil* . . . so I doubt not but they are now vnited and incorporated
> together in a farre more firme and vndiuided societie, euen that of the
> *first-borne* which are written in Heauen . . . and as they were heere . . .
> a paire of Lights of our Church . . . so they haue by this time receiued
> the reward . . . euen to be *Stars in the Firmament for euer and euer,
> Dan.* 12.3. (sig. +4)

Walton says of Donne and Magdalen Herbert that they were
bound in an '*Amity* made up of a chain of sutable inclinations
and vertues; an *Amity*, like that of St. *Chrysostoms* to his dear
and vertuous *Olimpias* . . . Or . . . like that of St. *Hierom* to his
Paula'.[152] He adds that although the 'Hymns' written by Donne
for Magdalen Herbert 'are now lost to us', yet 'doubtless they were
such, as they two now sing in *Heaven*'. It may be even that an echo
of the last image of Harris's account may be traced in a phrase
appearing in Walton's Introduction to the *Life of Herbert*, where
he refers to the 'Conjunction' of his subjects Donne, Wotton,
Hooker, and Herbert in his Collected *Lives* 'after their deaths'
(p. 259). Like Felton and Lake, these four are measuring out the
heavenly dance.

Harris follows Lake's death with reflections on his terrestrial
afterlife in epitaphs and monuments. 'An Epitaph', he begins
'is a good mans due after his departure'; but Lake has no need of
one, 'because he yet liues in the mouthes and hearts of all that
knew him' (sig. +4). However, Lake, though dead, yet speaks
when Harris quotes the epitaph he wrote for himself, engraved at

---

[152] Walton, *Lives*, 265.

his request upon his funeral monument.[153] Lake's sentiments are exemplary: a product, explains Harris, of 'his charitable desire of their good that should suruiue him' (sig. +4ᵛ). Harris finishes by introducing Lake's own writings as 'another Monument of his own making too. A Monument of his wit shall I say, and of his Learning? or rather of his Pietie and Deuotion?' Lake's writings are all these; they are 'an exact *Idea* of the true forme of a Sermon' (sig. A1ʳ).

Harris describes Lake's writings as exact rather than elaborate. He does it through a pictorial image from Plutarch's 'On Listening to Poets' in the *Moralia*:

For whereas speech is fitly compared by the ancients to a picture, in the framing whereof the chiefe thing that requires the Artisans skill, is to draw his lines in their iust number and proportion, so as may expresse all the parts of the thing described, and the postures of them: which when it is done, it is no hard matter to adde the colours thereunto: it follows that the principall point of art likewise in making of a Speech or Sermon is the delineation of the parts of it, and the apt connecting of them together, or opposing them one to the other: whereupon the seuerall exornations of them with words and sentences, does either of it selfe follow or is without any great difficultie put too. (sigs. A1ʳ⁻ᵛ)

Harris links the pictorial with the verbal with that versatile word 'delineation'. He is arguing for the centrality of argument and structure to ecclesiastical oratory, and thus for the peripheral nature of 'colour' ('it were not his fashion to lay on much colour', explains Harris of Lake's writing)—a word which signifies the elaborations of rhetoric while also recalling the pictorial. Later he implies that the scriptural text is itself a picture on which the preacher gazes as he deciphers it, stating that Lake's two main expository tools, 'Logicke, and skill in the Tongues', may be seen as 'the two Spectacles, that I may not say eyes, that enable a man to looke exactly and distinctly into a Text' (sig. A1ᵛ).

Harris's last long paragraph deliberately replaces his own narrative with Lake's text following: 'I had rather thou shouldest discouer these things . . . by thy owne iudgement and obseruation, then by my aduertisement' (sig. A1ᵛ); and at the same time summarizes the exemplary nature of Lake's life (stressing that it lives

---

[153] In fact it was not engraved: see P.Hembry, *The Bishops of Bath and Wells 1540–1640* (London, 1967), 220.

in his own writings rather than dying with his body) by linking life and works together. When reading Lake, writes Harris,

if thou bee indued . . . with the same spirit of grace and regeneration, that the Author was, thou shalt find thine affections kindled and stirred vp thereby to a reall practice of Pietie and good Workes . . . And these things when thou hast found by thine owne experience: I doubt not but thou wilt bee moued together with me and all others that haue receiued benefit by the godly example and pious labours of that learned man, to glorifie that great God and Father of Lights, who . . . doth daily raise such excellent Instruments as he was, for the . . . œdification of his Church. (sig. A2^r)

In concluding his own narrative by introducing the *Sermons* themselves, and in linking the life-labours of his subject with his written words, Harris, as well as locating Lake's posthumous exemplarity in his writings, has incidentally justified his characterization of Lake in his title (and again in this passage) as living 'Avthovr' rather than dead subject. Lake has indeed constructed his own monument; Harris, whose own name is nowhere on the title-page, is only the mediator through which the concomitant details of Lake's living behaviour may be built into our 'attentiue' reading of his godly exhortations to us.

PART II

Walton's *Lives*

4

Walton's *Lives* of Donne and Herbert

Daniel Featley, in the *Life of Jewel*, asserts that in biography the 'truth of love' should not 'preiudice' the 'love of truth'.[1] While this privileges truth-led over love-led information, it also asserts that love contains a truth of its own, and identifies love's truth as the kind which most challenges the truth of intractable fact. This neat summary of the delicate tensions of principle a biographer must govern is altered for Walton the layman, particularly in the two biographies discussed in this chapter, which had no external commissioner. Its balance is pulled awry because this means he must stress his affectionate relationship to his subject in lieu of more formal authority to speak. The 'truth of love' is his major justification for venturing into print.

It has, in this last century in particular, been perceived as historically irresponsible to ascribe truth of any kind to the written impulses of love; though we also recognize objectivity, like factual perfection, to be no more than a concept against which the imperfect narrative will be measured. Yet there can be virtues as well as artistic freedoms in the clear acknowledgement of the claims of love. It requires an authorial presence which makes its standpoint visible; and so the reader can allow for that in her work of interpretation. Walton made himself particularly visible because his position was unusual and so needed defining. Had it occurred

---

[1] Daniel Featley, *Life of Iewel*, in Jewel, *Works* (London, 1609), sec. 18. Featley himself saw his *Life of Iewel* as a work with an *agendum* narrower and more partial than a biography need have; he calls his text 'a comment upon the title which is *Of the life* etc. not the life because all of it is not the life though all be of the life of Bp Jewel first Bishop then Jewel'. He goes on to give explicitly political reasons for stressing the prelate over the man in the sentences which follow. See Featley to Thomas Morton, Bodleian Library, MS Rawlinson D 47 (Daniel Featley MS), fo. 209.

to him, he would have felt it irresponsible to follow a policy of deliberate (but practically impossible) self-exclusion in the service of 'objectivity'.

I argue that Walton's authorial presence, his manifest partiality, makes his (essentially literary) manipulation of fact defensible because it limits and alters the aims of his work. Since he is openly subjective, it is redundant to complain that he heightens some aspects of Donne's character to the exclusion of others. He would never have attempted a complete Donne: that he would have judged presumptuous, as well as impossible. All he could do was to offer an interpretation of the bits he knew.

THE *LIFE OF DR. JOHN DONNE*

Walton as Donne's Author

What are the specific terms upon which Walton offers his portrait? Since there were four versions of the *Life*, and Walton's terms alter as his reputation increases, it may be useful first to rehearse the circumstances surrounding each. It first appeared in 1640, as a preface to Donne's *Sermons*. In 1658 it was revised, expanded, and printed separately, a venture upon which Walton embarked at the request of its original printer, and Walton's friend, Richard Marriot.[2] In 1670 yet another version appeared in company with the *Lives* of Wotton, Hooker, and Herbert as a collected volume. This collection was issued again in 1675, with further revisions. Marriot was the printer of all four versions.

The first paragraphs of the *Life* of 1640 explain how Walton became Donne's life-writer. The projected author of Donne's life had been Sir Henry Wotton, and Walton had been collecting information for him, but Wotton had died before he had time to write it. Walton says of this:

that learned Knights love followed his friends fame beyond the forget-full grave, which he testified by intreating me (whom he acquainted with his designe) to inquire of certaine particulars that concerned it: Not doubting but my knowledge of the Author, and love to his memory, would make my diligence usefull. I did prepare them in a readiness to

[2] Novarr, 68.

be augmented, and rectified by his powerfull pen; but then death prevented his intentions.

When I heard that sad newes, and likewise that these Sermons
were to be publisht without the Authors life (which I thought was rare)
indignation or griefe (I know not whether) transported me so far, that I
re-viewed my forsaken Collections, and resolved the world should see
the best picture of the Author that my artlesse Pensil (guided by the hand
of Truth) could present to it.[3]

Clearly Walton is not writing from a position of authority.
The first indication that the life-writer justifies himself through
friendship refers not to himself but to Wotton—'that learned
Knight' who had followed Donne's 'fame beyond the forgetfull
grave'. Walton only knew about it because Wotton had asked
him to 'inquire of certain particulars' for him. Walton himself is
witnessing the friendship between Wotton and Donne expressed
by Wotton's desire to commemorate Donne's life in print. And
while Walton goes on to suggest that what made his own 'diligence
usefull' was specifically his 'knowledge of the Author, and love
to his memory', the punctuation of the paragraph suggests that
this was a fact of which *Wotton* had no doubt. Apparently, in 1640
Walton did not have the confidence to suggest that his own love
and knowledge of Donne were enough of a biographical qualification by themselves. While he did consider them to be an asset
when it came to collecting material for someone else, he was
relying on Wotton to 'augment' and 'rectify' what he had provided.

Walton appears primarily to be doubting his literary ability;
but he is also deferring to Wotton's greater claims of friendship.
Walton's knowledge of Donne was not a friendship of equals, and
Wotton's was. Walton had known Donne only in the last years
of his life during Donne's deanship of St Paul's, when he had been
Donne's parishioner in his subsidiary church of St Dunstan's-in-
the-West.

When, in the second quoted paragraph above, Walton argues
for his own fitness for the position of life-writer, he bases it firmly
on his knowledge and love of Donne, while reiterating his
literary deficiency in the reference to his 'artlesse Pensil'. But
this is clearly less important to him than the fact that his own

---

[3] Izaak Walton, *The Life of Dr. John Donne*, in John Donne, *LXXX Sermons*,
ed. John Donne the younger (London, 1640), sig. A5.

unskilled hand was guided by 'the hand of Truth'. In context, this reference to the Divine hand surely identifies Walton's specific knowledge of Donne as a fundamental reason for choosing Walton as its instrument.[4] Yet he never suggests that this 'Truth' will make his *Life* comprehensive; the most he promises is that he will present the 'best picture' of Donne of which he is capable.

The edition of 1658 shows Walton with his literary confidence greatly increased. After all, he had since published his *Life of Wotton* in 1651 and *The Compleat Angler* in 1653, both of which had met with public approbation and both of which had already gone into second editions. David Novarr, in his excellent and comprehensive study *The Making of Walton's* 'Lives', also provides evidence suggesting that Walton had continued to collect material relevant to his Life of Donne between 1640 and 1658 with a view to its revision and expansion. This suggests that Walton had entertained hopes of the *Life*'s dignification to a separately published work.[5]

His increased confidence shows in a revision made to the opening paragraphs quoted above. Where he had originally written that he hoped to present to the world 'the best picture' of Donne 'that my artlesse Pensil . . . could present to it', he now replaced the word 'picture' with 'narration' and 'Pensil' with 'pen'.[6] Evidently Walton felt that his pictorial imagery implied that he was being tentative about the scope of his perceptions. Novarr identifies this change as being consistent with a number of others which formalized the *Life*'s language,[7] and concludes his section on the 1658 revision by saying: 'The revision of 1658 made the Life a work of art. The parts had been shaped in 1640. The phrases and words were shaped in 1658' (p. 96). This seems a very fair summary of Walton's development from his original position, where he only felt able to offer his 'love' of Donne as a qualification for writing his *Life*, to one where he also considered his literary ability to be equal to the task. The 1658 edition also shows Walton as offering 'you, that shall become my Reader' a summary of the principles upon which the *Life* had been written. He states that

---

    [4] See above, p. 111.   [5] Novarr, 68 and 71–2.
    [6] Izaak Walton, *The Life of John Donne, Dr. in Divinity &c.*, 2nd edn., corrected and enlarged (London, 1658), 3.
    [7] Novarr, 86.

in that part of this following discourse, which is onely narration, I either speak my own knowledge, or from testimony of such as dare do any thing, rather than speak an untruth. And for that part of it which is my own observation and opinion, if I had a power I would not use it to force any mans assent, but leave him a liberty to disbelieve what his own reason inclines him to.[8]

Walton has no intention of excising his opinions from his text. Rather, their visibility allows the reader 'a liberty to disbelieve what his own reason inclines him to'. He does not claim a comprehensive view for himself: only the reader's critical interpretation can make his text complete. The passage also demonstrates a touching faith in the integrity of his informants, a faith which was to dictate Walton's hierarchy of source material in this and later *Lives*, and was, I shall argue later, directly responsible for the inaccuracies of his depiction of Hooker's marriage in the *Life of Hooker*.[9]

The collected editions of 1670 and 1675 both contain a separate Introduction to the *Life of Donne*, as well as a General Epistle 'To the Reader' which prefaces all four of the *Lives*. In this context the differences between the two later editions are immaterial: I quote from the final revision of 1675. The Epistle omits Walton's 1658 summary of his practice just discussed, but retains its opening address to 'you that shall become my Reader'. In place of the summary Walton writes: 'when I sometime look back upon my education and mean abilities, 'tis not without some little wonder at my self, that I am come to be publickly in print.'[10] 'Walton's modesty', remarks Novarr dryly, 'grew with his ability.'[11] And certainly this humble self-congulating has *replaced* what was essentially a defence of his practice.

In the Epistle's final paragraph Walton writes:

And now, I wish that as that learned *Jew, Josephus* and others, so these men had also writ their own lives: but since 'tis not the fashion of these times, I wish their relations or friends would do it for them, before delays make it too difficult. And I desire this the more: because 'tis an *honour*

---

[8] *Donne*, (1658), sig. A10. Pagination begins after this page; sig. B1 appears on p. 5.

[9] See Ch. 5.

[10] Walton, *Lives*, p. 5. All further page references to this edition appear in the text.

[11] Novarr, 97.

due to the dead, [and] *a generous debt to those that shall live, and succeed us: and, would to them prove both a content and satisfaction* . . . And, though I cannot hope, that my example or reason can perswade to this under-taking, yet, I please myself, that I shall conclude this Preface, *with wishing that it were so.* (p. 7)

It emerges from this that Walton sees a *Life* written and informed by the 'truth of love' to be the next best thing to the perfect autobiographical narrative; and that he assumes the main function of biography to be exemplary.

This means that Walton's perfect *Life* cannot include details its subject might prefer suppressed; and this is worth bearing in mind when considering the slant of the *Life of Donne.* Walton is assumed to bear full responsibility for keeping the profane poet to the minimum (and that shot through with hints of a virtuous future); but if he was writing the exemplary *Life* which he (surely correctly) deemed Donne, dean of St Paul's, to have wanted, then Donne himself should perhaps bear some of it; and if not Donne in particular, then the form's exemplary requirements and the respect due to Donne's function should certainly be taken into consideration.

Walton's preference for autobiography informs his tendency to use his subjects' own words or phraseology. His tendency to extrapolate autobiographical details (often unsuitably) from their public writings seems to be an attempt to come as close to medi-ating a kind of posthumous autobiography as he could. (It is curious, though, that in his praise for it he never considered autobiography's huge drawback: no deathbed.)

However, as Walton says, autobiography was not 'the fashion of these times', and so he chooses the second option; that great men's 'relatives and friends should do it for them'. In adding that this should be done 'before delays make it too difficult', Walton privileges personal memories and oral testimony over records, for memory is the direct source material of the 'truth of love'. Walton sees biography chiefly as a way to preserve memory; earlier in the Epistle he writes: 'I humbly conceive writing to be both a safer and truer preserver of mens Vertuous actions, then tradition, especially as 'tis manag'd in this age' (p. 6). Were 'tradition' a more reliable witness to virtue, he implies, biography would be less necessary.

Who was he writing to instruct? Evidence internal to the *Lives* suggests that his view of posterity was relatively short-term. To take only one of Novarr's examples, a reference in the *Life of Donne* to Henry King, bishop of Chichester, adds that he is 'now living' in the earlier revisions, and 'lately deceased' in the versions of 1670 and 1675.[12] Within the passage I have quoted, Walton defines posterity as being 'those that shall live, and succeed us' (p. 7), which does not imply that he was writing for a distant generation. Evidently Walton's sense of the immediacy of his own generation's political needs precluded a concern for the more remote future— or perhaps he was, really, modest.

The Introduction to the *Life of Donne* (first appearing in 1670) is expanded from the opening paragraphs of the *Life* of 1658. In it Walton seems able to offer the *Life* as truly his, rather than a pale copy of Wotton's far better (if unwritten) biography. In 1640 Walton had described his intention to give his material to Wotton to be 'augmented and rectified'.[13] Here the unflattering word 'rectified' is replaced by the more neutral 'compleated' (p. 21).

Walton also makes a significant reversion to an earlier reading. In 1658, as I have said, he replaced the word 'picture' with 'narration' and the word 'Pensil' with 'pen' in the 1658 edition. In 1670, however, and again in 1675, Walton writes that he 'resolv'd the World should see the best plain picture of the *Authors Life* that my artless Pensil, guided by the hand of truth, could present to it' (p. 21). Judith Anderson, in her discussion of this reading in her book *Biographical Truth*, points out that 'Walton revises continually, but virtually never does he restore earlier readings. The word 'picture' must have seemed to him the more fitting choice'.[14] She argues that Walton and his critics use analogies with portraiture so often because his aim is more than narration: it is the creation of a 'picture'—what she calls a 'manipulation of appearance and effect' (p. 55). In Walton's restoration of this reading, in which the significant word 'plain' before 'picture' is the only addition, Anderson sees his own recognition of this.

[12] *Donne* (1658), 81 and Novarr, 104; Izaak Walton, *Lives of Dr. John Donne &c.* (London, 1670), 57; *Lives*, 63 and Novarr, 104.

[13] *Donne* (1640), sig. A5.

[14] Judith Anderson, *Biographical Truth: The Representation of Historical Persons in Tudor-Stuart Writing* (New Haven, 1984), 55.

When Walton does pursue the portraiture analogy later in the Introduction, he actually denies that he 'manipulated' at all. He writes: 'Certain I am, it is to the advantage of the beholder, who shall here see the Authors Picture in a natural dress, which ought to beget faith in what is spoken: for he that wants skill to deceive, may safely be trusted' (p. 21). What you see, he seems to be saying, can be the truth, as what you are told might not be. Besides, he adds, having it both ways, his very lack of literary skill makes it impossible for him to manipulate his material: 'for he that wants skill to deceive, may safely be trusted'. Since his literary skill, even to him, was not any longer in doubt, this statement should be regarded with caution. The 'natural dress' in which he clothed Donne was artfully arranged.[15]

But it is not fair simply to dismiss his insistence on the plain truth and simple expression of his portraiture. Walton concentrated deliberately on those aspects of Donne's character he knew; and, where he did not, he used a version of Donne's own words if he could. And although he had now acquired a literary confidence, it was accompanied by an apparently entirely serene sense of his own social and intellectual inferiority to his subject. It is possible to read the passage as meaning that he acknowledged his picture of Donne to be lacking in some of the complexities of its original, but that nevertheless on its own terms—as a labour of love by a far more ordinary man—it had a validity. His alteration of 'best picture' to 'best plain Picture' certainly suggests that he thought his talents suitable only for, as it were, the layman's viewpoint. Walton always looks up; his subjects look down. The Introduction finishes:

And if the Authors glorious spirit, which now is in Heaven; can have the leasure to look down and see me, the poorest, the meanest of all his friends, in the midst of this officious duty, confident I am, that he will not disdain this well-meant sacrifice to his memory; for, whilst his Conversation made me and many others happy below, I know his Humility and Gentleness was then eminent; and, I have heard Divines say, those Vertues that were but sparks upon Earth, become great and glorious flames in Heaven. (pp. 21–2)

---

[15] See above, pp. 102–15, for a discussion of the place of pictorial imagery in life-writing, and for a reading of this passage informed by that context.

Donne 'looks down', not just because he is 'in Heaven', but because he was, and so is, humble: that is, condescending (not, for Walton, a pejorative word). Walton's expressed confidence that the heavenly Donne would approve his *Life* is heavily qualified; Donne will only even notice it if he has the 'leasure'; the approval is presented in the negative form 'will not disdain'; and Walton's own description of the Life as a 'well-meant sacrifice' does not suggest that he thought Donne would find the *Life* adequate, only that he would appreciate the love that prompted it and the labours which sustained it.

Judith Anderson suggests that the versified address to Walton by Charles Cotton, which precedes the *Lives* in the collected edition of 1675, shows a 'considerable insight into the purpose of Walton's biographical efforts'.[16] She quotes Cotton pointing out that the written works of Walton's subjects, which he calls 'Monument[s]' (p. 10), are not in themselves enough for posterity. Anderson puts it that Cotton 'explains that the works of these men are an incomplete measure of their virtues because they fail to show "*how th'Almighties grace*" by various ways "*Brought them to be the Organs of his praise*" '.[17] In Cotton's view, then, Walton's *Lives* complement his subjects' works in providing for them an interpretative context. As such, each *Life* itself acts as a lasting 'Monument' which performs a useful posthumous office in informing, with 'true friendship' (p. 11), posterity's reading of their works with a description of their virtuous occasions. Walton also refers to the *Life of Donne*, in an elegy of his own printed with it in the editions of 1670 and 1675, as a 'Monument' which he 'want[s] abilities' to make 'as matchless as his [Donne's] worth' (p. 89). The *Life* itself contains another, real monument to Donne, as a 'lively . . . representation' of a 'dead Friend' (p. 83). Cotton also refers to Donne's statue, which was damaged by the Great Fire of 1666, and links it to Walton's *Life*, calling it:

> *A Monument! that, as it has, shall last*
> *And prove a Monument to that defac't.*

(p. 9)

---

[16] George Saintsbury's edition of the *Lives*, which is based upon the revision of 1675, follows it in misprinting 'Wotton' for 'Cotton' (p. 10). And see Anderson, *Biographical Truth*, 56–7.

[17] Anderson, *Biographical Truth*, 56.

Monuments simultaneously celebrate the particularity of one life in perpetuating a version of the real features of a real body, while yet reminding us of the death of that body. Cotton means Donne's statue here, but he could mean his corpse, too: the temple of his body defaced by corruption. Walton feels that the monument he raises is necessary, and that raising it is an exemplary act; but he mourns Donne's real loss in drawing attention to the shortcomings of his inscription, of the stone features of the image. Cotton is in complimentary mode: he chooses to see only the resurrection figured in the erected, written monument. Yet both lament and compliment are animated by the motives of love: by the desire to have preserved, in some form, the qualities, imitable and inimitable, of the dead man. And this recreative process is, in both senses, partial.

Donne as Walton's Author

How did Walton use Donne's own writings? Cotton saw the *Life* as animating the exemplary messages of Donne's works; Walton used those works to invest his biography with the preserved life of Donne's own words. How did he select, and what did he alter? Since he could not be Donne, how did he invoke his aid in imagining his own partial 'picture'?

It seems at first sight curious that there is no direct discussion of the sermons in Walton's text, especially as the original version of the *Life of Donne* was a preface to his *Sermons*. Novarr suggests that Walton 'had all his life a dislike for abstruse speculation' and 'cared little for close exegesis'.[18] Perhaps Walton also felt (or was?) unqualified to discuss them in any detail. Exegesis is in any case relatively rare in prefatory notices of the century, being usually replaced by less specific praise. Only an author's adversary tended to indulge in detailed criticism.

Walton does not, in fact, exclude sermons; but his only direct references to them are from the auditor's standpoint. He sticks to what he knows (and perhaps, unlike the writer of an exegetical work, assumes lay limits to what his readers know). So, while eschewing discussion of the theological content of Donne's sermons, he would discuss the effects of those sermons upon their auditors because he had been one, and was addressing others.

[18] Novarr, 61.

Take his description of Donne's 'first Sermon . . . at *Paddington*' (p. 48). Walton puts us in the congregation, where we experience

> a Preacher in earnest; weeping sometimes for his Auditory, sometimes with them: always preaching to himself, like an Angel from a cloud, but in none; carrying some, as St. *Paul* was, to Heaven in holy raptures, and inticing others by a sacred Art and Courtship to amend their lives; here picturing a vice so as to make it ugly to those that practised it; and a vertue so, as to make it be beloved even by those that lov'd it not; and all this with a most particular grace and an unexpressible addition of comeliness. (p. 49)

The passage's most extravagant image—the preacher as descending angel—is Donne's. It is not from a sermon, but from the poem 'To Mr. Tilman after he had taken orders'. The lines Walton used when first composing this passage for the 1640 edition read that preachers, 'As Angels out of clouds, from Pulpits speake'.[19] Perhaps Donne himself took it from the fifth book of Hooker's *Ecclesiastical Polity*, where the author asks, 'for what is thassemblinge of the Church to learn, but the receivinge of Angels descended from above?'.[20]

Since Walton tended to regard his subjects' writings as more prescriptive than descriptive, and also assumed they would certainly follow their own prescriptions, Donne's own words on preaching were an absolutely authoritative medium for describing how Donne himself preached. Donne's poem is addressed to a man newly ordained, and so serves perfectly to describe Donne just after his own ordination. Walton's passage forms part of a section of the *Life* which celebrates how completely Donne's new calling had changed him. The section begins, 'Now the *English Church* had gain'd a second St. *Austine*' (pp. 47–8), and the urgent, transformatory word 'now', together with the word 'new' is reiterated several times in the next paragraph:

[19] John Donne, *Complete Poetry and Selected Prose*, ed. Hayward, 305.

[20] Richard Hooker, *Of the Laws of Ecclesiastical Polity*, Book V, ch. 23.1, in *The Folger Library Edition of the Works of Richard Hooker*, 6 vols. (Cambridge, Man., 1972–93), ii. 110. And see also H. Isaacson, *An Exact Narration, of the Life . . . of Lancelot Andrewes* (London, 1650), sigs. [**3]ᵛ–[**4]ʳ: 'in this faculty [preaching] he hath left a pattern unimitable. So that he was truly stiled *Stella perdicantium*; and an Angell in the Pulpit.' Isaacson presumably found Walton more imitable than Andrewes.

And now all his studies which had been occasionally diffused, were all concentred in Divinity. Now he had a new calling, new thoughts, and a new imployment for his wit and eloquence: Now all his earthly affections were changed into divine love; and the faculties of his own soul, were ingaged in the Conversion of others. (p. 48)

Anderson argues that the repetitions of 'now' and 'new' are intended to lend 'increasing immediacy' to what she sees as a Waltonian attempt to imagine Donne's own responses to his priesting. 'In the excitement of Walton's rhetorical moment', she adds, 'we might overlook the fact that this rendition of Donne's renewal, in all its melodrama, is clearly Walton's. There is really nothing to make us think otherwise.'[21] But it depends on what you mean by 'clearly Walton's'. There are echoes of Donne's poem from the beginning of the whole section on his transformation from layman to cleric, long before the direct borrowing appears in the passage on Donne's preaching. This is how it begins:

> Thou, whose diviner soule hath caus'd thee now
> To put thy hand unto the holy Plough . . .
> What bringst thou home with thee? . . .
>   . . . Dost thou finde
> New thoughts and stirrings in thee? And as Steele
> Toucht with a Loadstone, dost new motions feele? . . .
> Thou art the same materials, as before,
> Onely the stampe is changed; but no more.
> And as new crowned Kings alter the face,
> But not the monies substance; so hath grace
> Changed onely Gods old Image by Creation,
> To Christs new stampe, at this thy Coronation.[22]

The words 'now' and 'new' are everywhere, lending a transformatory urgency to Donne's images. The argument, stripped of its imagery, also resembles Walton's. Donne invokes the belief that to take Orders is to become filled with Christ, to become Christ's representative. As Donne regards it, the change from layman to cleric is one where the essential materials of the man are not different, but their function is transformed by the process.[23]

[21] Anderson, *Biographical Truth*, 63.
[22] Donne, *Complete Poetry and Selected Prose*, ed. Hayward, 304.
[23] The reading I have given of ll. 7–8 gives them as a statement rather than (in conformity with the preceding lines) as a question. This is the reading given in the 1635 edition of *Poems, by J.D.* . . . , 369, which Walton may have helped edit,

Walton also represents Donne's faculties as unchanged, but dedicated to new and sacred uses. In doing so, those faculties, and by implication Donne's own person, become sacred too.

There is circumstantial evidence that Walton did use the Tilman poem to inform this part of the *Life*. It figures in his notes for the 1658 revision as they appear on the flyleaf of Walton's copy of Eusebius' *Ancient Ecclesiasticall Histories*:

> At his conversion take out of Jeremy the ways of man are
> not in his owne powr
> loke doc dones letter to Tilman.[24]

Walton clothes his Donne's imagined reponse to conversion, in a version of the real Donne's words, the real Donne's images. On its own terms, this is a bid to invest his imagined subject with a kind of verifiable reality. It does mean that Walton assumes that Donne's poem expresses a deeply felt opinion on what it meant to take orders, when it is as possible that Donne was simply taking an appropriate stance on it. But the latter possibility, which implies that the demands of art are not always moralized, or even truthful, is not one that Walton would be eager to recognize. He very seldom does recognize it. If, as Cotton suggests in his verses, Walton's *Lives* exist as exemplary portraits to support readings of their subjects' works, then it is logical for Walton to assume that the works would also express clearly exemplary messages on virtue, which must complement his own work, and would furnish its examples.

The second sermon reference supports a description of Donne's grief at the death of his wife. It first appeared in 1658. In 1640 the description consisted of a passage owing some of its sentiments and phraseology to Donne's poem 'A Valediction forbidding mourning', and some to a variety of biblical references where Donne's feelings are expressed in paraphrases from Job

and is adopted by Hayward in the Nonesuch Donne (*Complete Poetry and Selected Prose*). Helen Gardner's edition, *The Divine Poems of John Donne*, 2nd edn. (Oxford, 1978), 32, gives them as a question, acknowledging the variant in a note. In Gardner's preferred MS reading, then, Donne is less certain about the stasis of Tilman's 'essential materials'.

[24] Quoted in Novarr, 72–3 and see 499–502. Walton's copy of Eusebius is held by Salisbury Cathedral Library.

and the Psalms.[25] These are discussed in more detail later in this chapter. In the versions of 1658 and after they are followed by this passage:

Thus he began the day, and ended the night; ended the restless night and began the weary day in *Lamentations* . . .

His first motion from his house was to preach, where his beloved wife lay buried (in St. *Clements* Church, near Temple-Bar *London*) and his text was a part of the Prophet *Jeremy*'s Lamentation: *Lo, I am the man that have seen affliction.*

And indeed, his very words and looks testified him to be truly such a man; and they, with the addition of his sighs and tears, exprest in his Sermon, did so work upon the affections of his hearers, as melted and moulded them into a companionable sadness. (p. 52)

Again, we are in the congregation. The auditors' reactions as they are described apparently provide a factually based support for the passionately imagined depiction of Donne's grief which precedes them. (Novarr points out, though, that no evidence survives that such a sermon was preached at that time and place; the only sermon existing on Jeremiah's text was preached at St Dunstan's and shows no signs of having any personal application.)[26]

Given or not, the passage demonstrates Walton's tendency to extrapolate biographical detail from texts which are absolutely not autobiographical. If Walton did invent the details of time and place, this suggests that he preferred to back up his insertions of Donne's texts with some unexceptionable matters of fact, even if those facts were untrue. If this is a passage which deliberately invents significant details, it demonstrates at the same time that Walton regarded simple facts as more persuasive than biographical speculation.

Walton's last direct sermon reference is the famous description of Donne's last sermon. Here too, we are in the congregation:

. . . when (to the amazement of some beholders) he appeared in the Pulpit, many thought he presented himselfe, not to preach mortification by a

---

[25] *Poems, by J.D.* . . . (London, 1633), 193–4 (misnumbered 164); *Donne* (1640), sig. B2ᵛ.

[26] Novarr, 78. A personal application might (at a pinch) be read into the fact that Donne rendered this text into verse, 'The Lamentations of Ieremy, for the most part according to Tremelius'. See *Poems, by J.D., with Elegies on the Authors Death* (London, 1633), 306–23.

living voice, but mortality by a decayed body and dying face. And doubtlesse many did secretly ask that question in *Ezekiel, Doe these bones live?* Or can that soule organize that tongue to speak so long time as the sand in that glasse will move towards its center, and measure out a houre of this dying man's unspent life? Doubtlesse it cannot. Yet after some faint pauses in his zealous Prayer, his strong desires inabled his weak body to discharge his memory of his pre-conceived Meditations which were of dying; The Text being, *To God the Lord belong the issues from death.* Many that saw his teares, and heard his hollow voice, professing they thought the Text Prophetically chosen, and that D. *Donne* had preacht his owne Funerall Sermon.[27]

This is not exegesis, or even summary. When Walton takes the liberty of articulating the listeners' 'secret' questions, though, he borrows from Donne's text. Donne's version of Ezekiel's question runs: '*God* seemes to haue caried the declaration of his *power* to a great height, when hee sets the *Prophet Ezechiel* in the *valley of drye bones*, & sayes, *Sonne of man can these bones liue?*'[28] When the observers think that 'D. Donne had preacht his owne Funerall Sermon', they recall the Epistle to the Reader of *Deaths Dvell*'s first edition of 1632. It is explained on its title-page that the sermon was delivered '*at White Hall, before the* KINGS MAIESTY . . . *and called by his Maiesties household* THE DOCTORS OWNE FUNERALL SERMON'. Its first lines run

This Sermon was, by Sacred Authoritie, stiled the Authors own funeral Sermon. Most fitly: whether wee respect the time, or the matter. It was preached not many dayes before his death; as if, hauing done this, there remained nothing for him to doe, but to die: And the matter is, of Death; the occasion and subiect of all funerall Sermons.

This is surely Walton's evidence for the congregation's 'secret' thoughts—stamped and named with the king's 'Sacred Authority', putting its new title beyond question.

Walton's narrative of Donne's death borrows from this Epistle, and from the sermon text. The Epistle's phrase 'there remained nothing for him to doe, but to die' introduces the deathbed, becoming 'Now he had nothing to doe but die'.[29] The *Life*'s

[27] *Donne* (1640), sig. B6.

[28] John Donne, *Deaths Dvell, or, a Consolation to the Soule, Against the Dying Life, and Liuing Death of the Body. Delivered in a Sermon at White Hall, before the Kings Maiesty, in the Beginning of Lent, 1630* (London, 1632), 22–3.

[29] *Donne* (1640), sig. B6ᵛ.

famous final cadence also harbours part of Donne's reading of
the Ezekiel passage. This is Walton's version:

> that body, which once was a Temple of the Holy Ghost . . . is now
> become a small quantity of Christian dust.
>   But I shall see it reanimated. (p. 84)

Donne writes

> If we say, can this dust liue? perchance it *cannot*, it may bee the meere
> *dust* of the *earth*, which never did liue, never shall . . . This death of *incin-
> eration* and dispersion, is, to naturall *reason*, the most *irrecouerable death*
> of all, & yet . . . *vnto God the Lord belong the issues of death*, and by *recom-
> pacting* this *dust* into the *same body*, and *reanimating* the *same body* with
> the *same soule*, hee shall in a blessed and glorious *resurrection* giue mee
> such an *issue from* this *death*, as shal neuer passe into any other *death*,
> but establish me into a life that shall last as long as the *Lord of life*
> himself.[30]

Walton takes the image of the dead body as dust, and affirms
his belief in its resurrection by bringing to life Donne's word
'reanimated' as his last word on Donne. In the 1640 *Life* he gives
the word as 're-inanimated': a form peculiar to Donne.

But Donne does not use it in *Deaths Dvell*. It is true that in 1660
his passage from *Deaths Dvell* was printed with 're-inanimating'
in the place of the 1632 'reanimating'. (Walton's own copy of the
sermon, the second edition of 1633, uses the rather ordinary word
'remaining'.)[31] To find 're-inanimating' before 1640, we need
instead to go to Donne's sermon in St Paul's for the evening of
Easter Day 1626. Donne has (of course) taken a Resurrection text:
1 Corinthians 15: 20: 'Else what shall they do that are baptized
for dead? If the dead rise not at all, why are they then baptized
for dead?' It is a complementary text to the text of *Deaths Dvell*
from Psalm 68: 20: 'to God the Lord belong the issues from
death'—itself a statement which holds within it the answer to
Paul's rhetorical question.

The 1626 sermon celebrates and scrutinizes the particularities
of bodily resurrection, as *Deaths Dvell* takes a typically vermicular

---

[30] *Deaths Dvell*, 23–4.

[31] See *Donne* (1640), sig. C1; 'Deaths Dvell', in John Donne, *XXVI Sermons*
(London, 1660), 405; *Deaths Dvell*, 2nd edn. (London, 1633), 17. For the word's
uniqueness to Donne, see *OED*, 're-inanimating'.

look at dissolution. The 1626 sermon also uses the Ezekiel text; and its peroration also, and famously, animates Christian dust in phrases which prefigure very exactly its sister passage from *Deaths Dvell*: 'God that knows in which Boxe of his Cabinet all this seed Pearle lies, in what corner of the world every atome, every graine of every mans dust sleeps, shall recollect that dust, and then recompact that body, and then re-inanimate that man, and that is the accomplishment of all.'[32] Donne was presumably borrowing his own words of 1626 in this parallel passage of 1630. In both the human body moves from scattered dispersal, to recompaction, to a final reanimation. Yet the 1626 sermon must be another, separate source for Walton. The unique form 'reinanimate' confirms this. Walton has underwritten Donne's death with his own sermon on death and affirmed his coming resurrection in a reiteration, a re-utterance, of his earlier words on everlasting life. Being dead, he yet speaketh. Walton himself mimics and celebrates the divine act of recollection in his own recompaction and reanimation of Donne's textual dust.

As we read Donne's death, we read an account permeated with the promise of resurrection which we assume to take much of its force from the fact that it was made as he was dying. While *Deaths Dvell* certainly makes this promise, the 1626 sermon celebrates it with as little ambivalence as Donne can ever affirm. This is really not true of *Deaths Dvell* as a whole. Walton allows the promises and phraseology of each sermon to pervade his narrative of Donne's death, but alters the balance in favour of assurance by this characteristic conflation of sources. Yet he allows Donne himself an articulate authorship in his dying process beyond the histrionic shaping of his bodily deportment Walton narrates for him. Donne's *Life*, like his last sermon, shows him preaching at (or simply preaching) his own funeral.[33]

These are all the sermons which Walton describes Donne preaching. But there are a couple of verbal echoes from the *Sermon of Commemoration of the Lady Danvers*, which he was to narrate Donne preaching in the *Life of Herbert*. Here, for instance, he quotes Donne as saying, on his deathbed, 'I were miserable, if

[32] See *The Sermons of John Donne*, ed. Evelyn M. Simpson and George R. Potter, 10 vols. (California, 1953–62), vii. 116, and (for Ezekiel text), 115.

[33] For the commonplaces associated with this idea, see Ch. 3 (Death).

I might not die'.[34] Donne writes, 'wee were more miserable if wee might not die'.[35]

Walton uses one other substantial prose work of Donne's: *Pseudo-Martyr*. He draws, unsurprisingly, on its Preface in narrating Donne's reasons for becoming a Protestant. Walton has chosen the obvious text for this purpose, and he reproduces its relevant points fairly faithfully, indicating in the margin where he quotes Donne.[36] He rearranges Donne's words; but when Novarr writes that he 'selected, he regrouped, he added to make the passage his own', he may be attributing the wrong motive to him.[37] Walton shows the signs of someone presenting a difficult subject with tact. As Anderson argues, Walton's intended readership, unlike Donne's, is not 'The Priestes, and Iesuits, and . . . their Disciples in this Kingdome', but a general one.[38] And the political climate was different from what it had been in 1610. Indeed, even between 1640 and 1658 Walton became uneasy with his description of Cardinal Bellarmine as 'learned' (a word implying 'wise' as well as 'educated'), and deleted it.[39]

This is Walton's account of Donne's decision:

He was now entred into the nineteenth year of his age, and being unresolved in his religion (though his youth and strength promised him a long life) yet he thought it necessary to rectifie all scruples which concerned that: And therefore waving the Law, and betrothing himself to no art or profession, that might justly denominate him, he began to survey the body of Divinity, controverted between the Reformed and Roman Church. And *as Gods blessed Spirit did then awaken him to the search, and in that industry did never forsake him, (they being his owne words)* So he calls the same Spirit to witness to his Protestation, that in the search and disquisition he proceeded with humility and diffidence in himselfe, by the safest way of frequent Prayers, and indifferent affection to both parties. (sig. A6)

Walton puts Donne's 'youth and strength' in brackets to let us know that Donne had a pious anxiety to settle the religion question even though he had plenty of time left to live. Donne's reasons are not put so disinterestedly: his 'irresolution', he explains,

---

[34] *Donne* (1640), sig. B6ᵛ.
[35] Donne, *A Sermon of Commemoration* . . . , (London, 1627), 160–1.
[36] *Donne* (1640), sig. A6.   [37] Novarr, 60–1.
[38] Anderson, *Biographical Truth*, 59.
[39] *Donne* (1640), sig. A6; *Donne* (1658), 11.

'not onely retarded my fortune, but also bred some scandall, and *endangered my spirituall reputation*'.[40] Donne's reasons, therefore, have a lot to do with the public constructions which could be put on his 'irresolution'—not to mention its public consequences. Walton, narrating irresolution, has the same problem about how it will be publicly received. Like Donne, he lets this affect what he is prepared to say about Donne's religious dilemma.

Walton's Donne first abandons the idea of any profession 'that might justly denominate him'; he could not consider furthering his worldly prospects until he had resolved his spiritual allegiance. This seems a fair assessment of Donne's real position. The paraphrase of Donne's own words begins with the words 'he began to survey the body of Divinity', and continues until the end of the passage. Walton acknowledges this in brackets halfway through the paraphrase. Anderson feels Walton's use of the third person makes it clearly a paraphrase, rather than just a misquotation.[41] Walton has a different audience, and needs more freedom than quotation would give him. So, where Donne bluntly calls his 'frequent Prayers, and indifferent affection to both parties' the 'ordinary meanes' to determine doubts, in Walton they become, more cautiously, the 'safest way'.

Walton's reference to 'Gods blessed Spirit' dignifies Donne's assertion that throughout his 'search . . . God, which awakened me then . . . hath never forsaken me in that industry' (sig. B3). A 'typical Waltonism', says Novarr, which 'introduces a more religious tone into the passage'.[42] But it is not an empty piety: it highlights Donne's own identification of the will of God as operating through Donne's actions. Walton has added nothing except in invoking God more precisely in the Person of His 'blessed Spirit'; for those who utter the will of God do so through the actions of the Spirit.

Both Donne's sentence, and Walton's rendering of it, imply that God, in willing Donne to embrace the Church of England, was a Protestant. This is something Walton would wish to emphasize; Donne, however, would only need to mention it. His Roman Catholic readership (which included not only his acquaintance but members of his family) would be unlikely to miss the point. In

---

[40] Donne, *Pseudo-Martyr* (London, 1610), sig. B3.
[41] Anderson, *Biographical Truth*, 59. [42] Novarr, 61.

the same way, and surely for the same reasons, Walton renders Donne's 'affections' to each Church as 'indifferent', but not, as Donne does, as 'equall and indifferent'. But then Walton had no Catholic acquaintance to conciliate, and his aim was to represent the strength of Donne's calling to the Church he did in fact embrace. This surely makes Walton's alterations of emphasis a little more defensible. And he gives his source: he is letting us check.

Walton also acknowledges an accurate source in his reproduction of parts of Donne's Will and his ledger of end-of-year accounts, where the remainder was given over 'to the poor and pious uses'.[43] These demonstrate Donne's generosity, his charitableness, and (in the case of the Will) his readiness for death. He uses them rather in the spirit he uses *Pseudo-Martyr*, and his deft manipulations of detail are all to be found in Novarr.[44] It is Walton's *selection* of accurate source-material, the fact that his attributions are most specific in support of aspects of Donne's character which he most wishes to stress, and much vaguer if he does not, which is most irresponsible by modern standards. However, he also makes free on occasion with the sources themselves, and what he does is worth discussing.

Take his use of the dedicatory epistle addressed to the king in *Pseudo-Martyr*. Donne writes:

Of my boldnesse in this addresse, I most humbly beseech your Maiestie, to admit this excuse, that having observed, how much your Maiestie had vouchsafed to descend to a conversation with your Subiects, by way of your Bookes, I also conceiv'd an ambition, of ascending to your presence, by the same way, and of participating, by this meanes, their happinesse, of whome, that saying of the Queene of Sheba, may bee usurp'd: Happie are thy men, and happier are those thy servants, which stand before thee alwayes, and heare thy wisedome.[45]

Walton lets this passage mean that the king and Donne had met and had discussed 'many of those Arguments urged by the Romanists', adding that the king had been so impressed by Donne's answers that he had urged him 'bring his Reasons to him in writing' (*Pseudo-Martyr* being the putative result).[46] Yet Donne clearly meant a 'conversation' between *texts*, with

---

[43] *Donne* (1640), sig. B5.   [44] Novarr, 54–6.
[45] *Pseudo-Martyr*, sigs. A3–3ᵛ.   [46] *Donne* (1640), sig. B1ᵛ.

Pseudo-Martyr as a part of this discourse, not commissioned as a result of it. This is manipulation by any standards.

My second example is more complicated. In 1670 Walton added two letters of Donne's to the main text. Their point is to stress the misery of Donne's existence in Mitcham, where he lived after the disgrace of his marriage. Walton calls them 'an extract collected from some few of his many letters' (p. 36). This is literal, but misleading; two letters are printed, but they conflate phrases and passages from no less than seven separate sources. They are certainly 'letters' by Donne; indeed, the greater part of the source letters were reprinted by Walton himself, as an appendix to the 1658 *Life*. In 1670 this appendix disappears, to be replaced by this far more artful use of parts of its content.

Precise ascriptions are given by R. E. Bennett in his article 'Walton's Use of Donne's Letters'.[47] The first 'letter' comes from one written by Donne in 1614, some years after he left Mitcham. Walton's version paraphrases Donne's beginning, but leaves out an initial preamble and a longer passage referring to purely practical details, so that all that is left is Donne saying that he had not answered his correspondent's last letter, because 'it found me under too great a sadness' (p. 36). (Donne writes 'under very much sadness'.)[48] The paragraph that follows in Walton's version appears rather later in the original letter, but is rendered fairly faithfully, with no significant departures from Donne's text. It is one of unrelieved misery, a narration of deaths and sicknesses in the family. Walton breaks off here, where Donne moves to more cheerful subjects, remarking 'I will mingle no more of my sadness to you'.[49] Walton acknowledges his omission though: he ends with an unfinished sentence followed by a dash: 'As for ——' (p. 36). The date, 'Aug. 10', and the appended address, 'From my hospital at *Micham*', are taken from an entirely different letter of Donne's.[50]

The second letter is made up from five different letters, but is mostly from two which Walton had printed in his 1658 appendix. The date, 'Sept. 7', is an invention. Walton does tell us it is a conflation: 'Thus he did bemoan himself', he writes, 'And thus

---

[47] R. E. Bennett, 'Walton's Use of Donne's Letters', *Philological Quarterly*, 16 (1937), 30–4.
[48] John Donne, *Letters to Severall Persons of Honour* (London, 1651), 151.
[49] Ibid. 153.   [50] Ibid. 207–8.

in other letters' (p. 36). Walton's method is simple: if it is melancholic, he keeps it, if cheerful or practical, he deletes it. Donne's remark that 'I doubt not but next week I shall be good news to you, for I have mending or dying on my side, which is two to one', appears in Walton without the final joke.[51] Bennett minds this: 'perhaps [Walton] did not comprehend its sheer whimsicality', he wonders, adding that 'if Walton has erred' it is in losing sight of the fact that 'Donne always kept his melancholy under control'. He concludes: 'the apparent facts which Walton used are likely to be true only with reference to the larger purpose for which he employed them.'[52] What is so interesting about Bennett's summary is that he allows something to be a truth in context which is not, in isolation, that true at all: when read as part of Walton's 'larger purpose' his 'facts', explains Bennett, are 'likely to be true'. Anderson, in discussing Walton's use of Donne's letters, puts it that Walton has drawn a 'likeness' of Donne, which is 'imaginative and perceptive' and which 'portrays a truth about Donne's character'.[53]

Walton himself calls on the letters as being 'a part of the picture' of Donne's 'narrow fortune', which also shows an attention directed to context and impression. He certainly convinced George Saintsbury, who, in his preface to the 1927 World's Classics edition of the Lives, identifies the second 'letter' as beautifully demonstrative of Donne's style, 'scarcely . . . surpassed even in the Sermons' and a welcome contrast to the 'harmonious . . . simplicity of Walton's prose' (p. ix). And indeed, virtually every word is Donne's. Novarr complains that Walton has no 'representative and undistorted' extract. Walton tells us we are getting 'part of the picture'. These are all different moral readings of a process recognizably *exactly the same*.

Then there are Donne's poems. I have already mentioned Walton's borrowings from 'A Valediction forbidding mourning' which appear as part of Walton's description of the death of Donne's wife. Edmund Gosse thinks this passage has the stamp of Donne's, rather than Walton's, style; perhaps he is recognizing Donne's utterances buried in the sentences.[54] In the 1640

---

[51] *Letters to Severall Persons*, 37.
[52] Bennett, 'Walton's use of Donne's Letters', 33–4.
[53] Anderson, *Biographical Truth*, 60.
[54] Edmund Gosse, *Life and Letters of John Donne*, 2 vols. (London, 1899), ii. 101–2.

edition Walton describes Donne as having buried 'all his sublunary joys' with his wife.[55] In 1658 'sublunary' is replaced by
'earthly', but a sentence is added later: 'now his very soul was ele-
mented of nothing but sadness.'[56] Both phrases can be traced to

> Dull sublunary lovers love
> (Whose soule is sense) cannot admit
> Absence, because it doth remove
> Those things which elemented it.[57]

Again, Walton says that Donne had shared with his wife 'so many
pleasant sorrows, and contented fears, as Common-people are not
capable of'. This may be a prose rendering of

> T'were prophanation of our joyes
> To tell the layetie our love.

> (p. 193)

Novarr thinks this poem is one which Walton tended to associate
with Anne Donne, and in the 1675 edition Walton's narration
of Donne's vision of his wife is followed by the poem in full, and
evidently from memory. It differs in small respects from any other
printed version, and Walton calls it 'A Valediction, forbidding to
Mourn', which is a unique rendering of its title (pp. 43–4). This
again demonstrates Walton assuming a piece of Donne's writing to have a particular autobiographical relevance, on no very
obvious evidence. Another identification on Walton's part of the
addressee of Donne's love poems with Anne Donne also appears
in his narration of the vision. He says of Anne Donne that when
she heard that Donne must leave her to go to France 'her divin-
ing soul boded her some ill in his absence' (p. 39), which clearly
takes its attribution from these lines of the 'Song' beginning
'Sweetest love, I do not go':

> Let not thy divining heart
> Forethinke me any ill.[58]

Walton cannot think that Donne's love poetry could have any other
recipient—or no recipient. Assuming this, which is consistent with
Walton's tendency to read all his subjects' writings as autobiographical, then using Donne's words to lend verisimilitude to

---

[55] *Donne* (1640), sig. B2ᵛ.   [56] *Donne* (1658), 52–3.
[57] *Poems, by J.D.* . . . , 194 (misnumbered 164).   [58] Ibid. 207.

his feelings for his wife, and hers for him, is on its own terms more responsible than simple invention.

Apart from this example, Walton reserves acknowledged reproductions of poems by Donne for his summary of Donne's life. The summary appears after Donne's penultimate sickness, and before the deathbed (pp. 60–7). Walton uses poetry three times, each time as evidence of an aspect of Donne's character. The first of these is Donne's 'Hymn to God the Father', which is printed in full. It demonstrates his continuing involvement with divine poetry, and counteracts the effect of Walton's previous paragraph, which deals, rather cautiously, with 'the Recreations' of Donne's 'youth' (pp. 60–2). The only one of these 'Recreations' which Walton is prepared to describe is his poetry, but in that description is implied his other, and unacceptably profane, activities. The divine poetry exhibits Donne's holiness in later life as certainly as the secular indicates the profanity of his earlier years. Walton puts it that

> though he was no friend to them [the early verses], he was not so fallen out with heavenly Poetry as to forsake that: no not in his declining age; witnessed then by many Divine Sonnets, and other high, holy and harmonious Composures. Yea, even on his former sick-bed he wrote this heavenly *Hymn*, expressing the great joy that then possest his soul in the Assurance of Gods favour to him when he Composed it. (p. 61)

The poem follows the passage to reinforce the point.

In the editions from 1658 onwards it is made to serve another purpose. Walton adds that Donne had the poem 'set to a most grave and solemn Tune, and to be often sung to the *Organ* by the *Choristers* of St. *Pauls* Church, in his own hearing' (p. 62). This allows Walton to defend the use of church music as an aid to worship, with Donne as potent ally.

From the 1658 edition onwards Walton uses the poems as part of an 'enumeration' of Donne's significant friends (p. 63). Walton employs a device; he describes Donne as having made a number of commemorative seals or rings to be given upon his death to his dearest friends. As Novarr points out, the seals are there to record the friends, and not vice versa, since Walton includes in his list a number who had 'put off mortality, and taken possession of the grave' before Donne, and could not be included in his benefactions (p. 63). Of all these, George Herbert is given particular prominence; as a man well known to be of 'primitive

piety' his close acquaintance with Donne sanctifies him further
by association (p. 63).[59] The poems which follow are Donne's
complimentary verses which accompany his gift of the seal to
Herbert, and Herbert's equally complimentary reply. Walton says
explicitly that the verses are included as 'some Testimony' to their
'happy friendship', which 'was still maintained by many sacred
indearments' (p. 64).

They also remind us that Donne was a holy writer of holy verses.
Walton illustrates the point again immediately: 'I return to tell the
Reader, that besides these verses to his dear Mr. *Herbert*, and that
Hymn that I mentioned to be sung in the *Quire* of St. *Pauls Church*;
he did also shorten and beguile many sad hours by composing
other sacred Ditties; and he writ an Hymn on his death-bed, which
bears this title' (pp. 65–6). What follows is 'Hymne to God, my
God, in my sicknesse'.[60] Whether it was, as Walton says, composed
on Donne's deathbed is doubtful: Walton's date, '*March* 23.
1630'—eight days before Donne's death—was not added until
1658, and the poem exists in another manuscript collection bearing the date 'Deceb. 1623'.[61] After weighing the evidence, David
Novarr concludes that 'Walton's date was dictated by artistry
rather than accuracy' (p. 101). Accuracy apart, citing a date so close
to the author's death certainly gives weight to Walton's reading
of the verses as a form of devotional autobiography.

Walton omits the development of its major conceit, printing only
the opening and closing stanzas, and two and a half lines of the
second stanza. It reads:

> Since I am coming to that holy room,
> Where, with thy Quire of Saints for evermore
> I shall be made thy musique, as I come
> I tune my Instrument here at the dore,
> And what I must do then, think here before.
>
> Since my Physitians by their loves are grown
> Cosmographers! and I their map, who lye
> Flat on this bed ——
>
> ——————————
>
> So, in his purple wrapt receive me, Lord!
> By these, his *thorns*, give me his other *Crown*:

[59] Novarr, 74.

[60] Donne, *Complete Poetry and Selected Prose*, ed. Hayward, 320.

[61] See Novarr, 99–101.

And, as to other souls I preach'd thy Word,
Be this my Text: my Sermon to mine own.
That, he may raise; therefore, the Lord throws down.

(p. 66)

In this version the first stanza is well over a third of the poem.
Walton wants it because it is self-aware, *ars moriendi* imagined and
practised. At the same time its conceit shows Donne employing
music as versatile spiritual metaphor: his dying body as divine
instrument, through which, perhaps, the breath of God is blown.
This 'musique' is harmony, a perfected image of order available
to Walton as to Donne; and much used by both.

Walton, ever practical, brings the metaphor into the actions of
the world immediately, defending the use of 'high raptures and
illuminations' in worship, and particularly those of sacred music.
He brings on some eminent corroborators: Prudentius, who 'not
many days before his death' had required his soul to 'present his
God each morning and evening with a new and spiritual song',
'King *David*', whose own 'spiritual songs' are neither given, nor
need, further description, and finally 'the good King *Hezekias*',
who had 'paid his thankful vows to Almighty God in a royal
Hymn' (p. 66).

By contrast, the second stanza starts a new conceit far less
malleable to such a personal reading. Its elaborate geographical
analogy, which is developed in the three and half stanzas which
ought to follow these lines, shows Donne playing with the idea of
his own dissolution. Even granted his remarkable self-possession,
his manifest interest in pure *technique* sits oddly with deathbed
urgency. Not that Donne was not capable of verbal play all the
way to his final breath (1623, the alternative date, takes us close
to the illness in which he wrote the *Devotions on Emergent
Occasions*); but Walton is aiming at a warmer, more imitable
narrative of self-possession than these cool, highly wrought
cosmic gambollings allow for.

Walton tells us there are lines missing. He is honest enough to
broach the conceit before breaking the stanza off abruptly with
two long dashes. Having made this gesture towards textual
responsibility he is free to cut straight to the final stanza, which
reads in context as simple, direct, and assured. At the same time
it shows Donne 'preaching to himself', as Walton has described

him doing in the pulpit (p. 49). Donne's self-admonition acts as a spiritual challenge to the living man through the written medium of his biography. Walton refines the technique by using Donne's own words; here again, Donne is author of his own deathbed exhortation. All Walton has to do is demonstrate that the Donne writing these words was really dying to invest the stanza with an unassailable authority. The disputed date is that demonstration.

He alters the word-order of the final cadence. Donne's rendering, 'Therfore that he may raise the Lord throws down',[62] becomes 'That, he may raise; therefore, the Lord throws down' (p. 66). Presumably Walton is doing this to clarify the line's sense (or perhaps he was just working from memory). His version certainly privileges the divine promise of bodily resurrection. The words 'That, he may raise' are pointed by the punctuation which surrounds them, and take precedence over the academic and explanatory 'therefore'.

Possibly Walton's most wholesale use of Donne's work is when he supports an assertion that even in 'the most unsetled days of his youth' Donne had studied from four until ten every morning (p. 67), by citing the 'visible fruits of his labours' as 'testimonies of what is here written'. A list follows, the contents of which are based upon the papers found in Donne's study after his death: 'the resultance of 1400 authors, most of them abridged and analysed with his own hand', 'sixscore . . . Sermons', the treatise on suicide *Biathanatos*, papers on contemporary affairs, and letters and cases of conscience 'that had concerned his friends, with his observations and solutions of them' (p. 68). No doubt Donne had written a number of them when young (*Biathanatos* is a case in point[63]) but it is not a full proof of his study habits at that age which Walton produces; it is a whole life's work. Novarr demonstrates that Walton may well have had access to most of Donne's unpublished papers after his death, and that he must certainly have seen some of them, since *Biathanatos* was not published until 1646–7.[64]

[62] Donne, *Complete Poetry and Selected Prose*, ed. Hayward, 321.

[63] Probably written around 1611. See John Carey, *John Donne: Life, Mind and Art* (London, 1981), 32.

[64] Novarr, 26–9.

Donne's Will follows naturally. Walton cites it as proof of an assured readiness for death; that he, as he puts it, 'did prepare to leave the world before life left him' (p. 68). But the date—'Decemb. 13 1630'—is a slight embarrassment. It is just too close to the final illness to show Donne to be quite prepared enough. On the other hand, a date substantiates the Will's real existence very satisfactorily. Walton left the date out of his 1640 *Life*, but it appears from 1658. Novarr sees its inclusion as part of Walton's later attempts to authorize the narrative by adding small factual details. He argues that since Walton cites the Will some time before he describes the deathbed, the reader will unconsciously assume a greater time-lapse between them than there really was.[65]

This is plausible, and impossible to prove. What is certain, is that to add this inconvenient date is to privilege fact over impression. Without it the Will acts as satisfactory evidence that Donne prepared for his death with 'mature deliberation'; with it, Walton's assurance that Donne made his Will 'when no faculty of his soul was damp'd or made defective by pain or sickness' looks doubtful (p. 68).

The Will serves another purpose too. It is documentary evidence for Donne's charities. The bequests, like the commemorative seals, also mean a list of Donne's significant friends, as well as offering proofs of his care for his family. Once Walton has quoted the Will, he adds a number of his charitable actions in life—firmly in the tradition of a commemorative notice, then as now. They range from the gifts of alms to prisoners at 'all the Festival times of the year' to his support for his own mother (pp. 70–1). Walton supplies a separate piece of documentary evidence for Donne's charity during his lifetime: his end-of-year account books, which demonstrate that the remainder of his revenue was given over to 'pious uses', and commended to God in a Latin prayer.

Donne's Death

With this last piece of evidence in the form of Donne's 'own words' (p. 72) Walton ends his summary of Donne's life, and begins to tell his death. Like Featley before him in the 1609 *Life of Jewel*, Walton starts by describing someone who deliberately, even

[65] Novarr, 90 and 56.

wantonly, sacrifices his health to his priestly duties. Featley, though, takes two paragraphs over it. The first comes as Featley discusses Jewel's 'divination' of his death, and says:

> Thus being forewarned to leave this hold of his body . . . he did not, after the custom of most men, seeke by all meanes as it were violently to keepe possession beyond the day, and by all kinde of naturall aliments and medicate potions to surfet the senses, and stop all the passages of the soule: No, but by fasting, labour and watching he openeth them wider, that he might be readier to entertain death Gods harbinger, and to meet his Saviour.[66]

The second paragraph appears a little later:

> By . . . restlesse labors and watchful cares he brought his feeble body so low, that as he rode to preach at *Lacok* in *Wiltshire*, a gentleman friendly admonished him to return home for his health's sake . . . To whom he replieth, It becommeth best a Bishop to die preaching in the pulpit . . . Wherefore, that he might not deceive the people's expectations, he ascendeth the pulpit, and now nothing but spirit (his flesh being pined away and exhausted) reades his text out of the fifth to the Galatians, *Walke in the spirit*, and with much paine makes an end of it. (Section 33)

Featley's image in the first of these paragraphs is of the temporal body as a house leased by God for the soul. Jewel is a man who will not question the terms of the lease, but in refusing medical help assists the will of God that soul and body should be parted. Thus Jewel welcomes death as 'Gods harbinger'. So does Donne, when he utters one of his own funeral sermons in the words 'I were miserable if I might not dye'.[67] And we can find almost every other strategy Featley employs for Jewel's death in Walton's account of Donne's.

Walton begins his last section by reporting a rumour that Donne would be unable to preach before the king as he had done for 'almost twenty years' because he was already dead (p. 73). This gives him the chance to quote from a letter of Donne's which, apart from expressing some gratification at the general sorrow his 'death' had occasioned, also (in Walton's version) contains these lines:

---

[66] Daniel Featley, *Life of Iewel*, sec. 32.

[67] Donne, *A Sermon of Commemoration for the Lady Danvers* . . . (London, 1627), 160–1.

one writ to me that some . . . conceived I was not so ill as I pretended, but withdrew myself to live at ease, discharged of preaching. It is an unfriendly, and God knows an ill-grounded interpretation; for I have always been sorrier when I could not preach, than any could be they could not hear me. It hath been my desire, and God may be pleased to grant it, that I might dye in the Pulpit; if not that, yet that I might take my death in the Pulpit, that is, dye the sooner by occasion of those labours. Sir, I hope to see you presently after *Candlemas*, about which time will fall my *Lent-Sermon* at Court, except my *Lord Chamberlain* believe me to be dead . . . as long as I live, and am not speechless, I would not willingly decline that service. (pp. 73–4)

This is a more elaborate version of Jewel's 'it becommeth best a Bishop to die preaching in the pulpit'. By the time Donne writes it, though, it has become a commonplace; Walton, in quoting it, has his author's own attestation that he is dying in this tradition.[68]

Walton manipulates Donne's text, of course. He quotes a version of the letter published in an edited form in 1635, and some evidence exists to suggest that he had also had a hand in the original editing.[69] Whether he did or not, he took no steps to revise the version in the *Life of Donne* when the original letter was published in full in 1651.[70] The 1635 version served his biographical purpose much better. It omits a passage where Donne makes it plain that, Lent Sermon notwithstanding, he has delegated his Christmas sermon at St Paul's to 'one of my fellowes'. Perhaps he is only prepared to 'die preaching' a really prestigious sermon; perhaps he is using a commonplace not wholly seriously. No wonder Walton never put the passage back.

I have suggested in my previous chapter that an exemplary death might be a minister's final pastoral act, disseminated, usually in written form, to widen the scope of its effect. To some extent John Earle backs up this theory in the concluding passage of his 'Character of a Grave Divine'. He writes: 'His death is the last

---

[68] See Fincham, *Prelate as Pastor*, 12, which identifies this remark as the beginning of a narrative topos in episcopal biography. Other examples of its use are given in a note on the same page. See also R.[obert] M.[ossom], *A Narrative Panegyrical of the Life, Sickness and Death of George* [Wilde] . . . *Lord Bishop of Derry . . . as it was Delivered at his Funerals* . . . (London, 1665/6), 12: 'And thus though he died not standing in the Pulpit, yet he died studying of the Sermon; and blessed is that servant, whom his Lord, when he cometh, shall finde so doing.'

[69] *Poems, by J.D.* . . . , 2nd edn. (London, 1635), 288–9, and see Novarr, 43–8.

[70] *Letters to Severall Persons*, 241–4.

Sermon, where, in the Pulpit of his Bed, he instructs men to die by his example.'[71] Earle's concern is with typical behaviour; we can assume, then, that a minister's deathbed was widely assumed to be a 'Sermon' of this kind. Yet the popularity of 'dying preaching' as exemplary theme can also be explained as a perfect mirror-image of Earle's commonplace. The preacher's deathbed is his pulpit; and his pulpit, his deathbed. On a deathbed, actions and demeanour preach as well as words; in the pulpit, the scope of a last sermon also extends beyond the verbal to the preacher's deathlike appearance and deportment. So Jewel, preaching on the Spirit, appears physically 'nothing but spirit' to his beholders.

Walton certainly follows Donne's letter with a description of his final sermon which concentrates above all things upon his appearance. And he includes a scenario remarkably similar to the second of Featley's passages. He writes:

Before that month ended, he was appointed to preach . . . he . . . had in his sickness so prepared for that imployment, that as he had long thirsted for it: so he resolved his weakness should not hinder his journey . . . At his coming thither, many of his friends (who with sorrow saw his sickness had left him but so much flesh as did only cover his bones) doubted his strength to perform that task; and did therefore disswade him from undertaking it, assuring him however, it was like to shorten his life; but he passionately denied their requests. (p. 74)

Like Jewel, Donne encounters friendly individuals so strangely and pointedly ignorant of *ars moriendi* conventions as to advise him not to preach just because he has been seriously ill. Like Jewel, he takes the opportunity they offer to state his intentions clearly. Both Walton and Featley describe the appearance and demeanour of their subjects in terms which recall the text of their last sermon. Featley's Jewel is a 'spirit' preaching on the Spirit. Walton says of Donne that his sickness 'had left him but so much flesh as did only cover his bones', and adds that, of his congregation, 'many did secretly ask that question in *Ezekiel; do these bones live?*'; both Donne's sermons (of 1626 and 1630) include an exegesis of the passage in Ezekiel concerning the 'valley of drye bones'.[72]

---

[71] John Earle, *Microcosmographie, or, a Piece of the World Discovered*; in *Essayes and Characters*, 6th edn., augmented (London, 1633), sig. B7ᵛ.

[72] *Deaths Dvell*, 22–3.

Walton's Donne and Featley's Jewel both take to their beds
straight after the sermon, and then give a declaration of faith from
it. While Jewel's only looks forward to his death, Donne's also
includes a summary of the spiritual events of his life. Walton has
Donne quote the Preface to the first edition of *The Temple* as a
part of it, which tells us something, perhaps, about how far Walton
identified Donne's piety with his friend Herbert's. The Preface
says that Herbert's 'Motto', with which 'he used to conclude
all things that might seem to tend to his own honour', was 'Lesse
than the least of Gods mercies'.[73] Walton's Donne says: 'at this
present time, I was in a serious contemplation of the providence
and goodness of God to me: to me *who am less than the least of his
mercies*' (p. 76). Perhaps they both independently took it from
Genesis 32: 10, where Jacob says to God, 'I am not worthy of the
least of thy mercies'; but the two passages bear a verbal similarity to each other as well as to their common source.

Donne's declaration of faith is followed by a refusal to take
medicine, very like Jewel's. Walton writes:

his old Friend and Physitian, Dr. *Fox* . . . came to him to consult his
health, and that after a sight of him . . . he told him, *that by Cordials,
and drinking milk twenty days together, there was a possibility of his restaura-
tion to health*; but he passionately denied to drink it. Nevertheless,
Dr. *Fox*, who loved him most intirely, wearied him with sollicitations,
till he yielded to take it for ten days; at the end of which time, he told
Dr. *Fox, he had drunk it more to satisfie him, than to recover his health;
and, that he would not drink it ten days longer upon the best moral assurance of having twenty years added to his life: for he loved it not; and was
so far from fearing death, which to others is the King of terrors: that he long'd
for the day of his dissolution.* (p. 77)

Walton's account is a detailed anecdote, which lends it a greater
apparent authority than Featley's. Donne's evident distaste for
'Cordials, and drinking milk' implied in the aside 'for he loved it
not' sounds silly enough to be true.

The reiteration of the phrase 'he passionately denied' recalls the
earlier passage demonstrating Donne's determination to preach
his last sermon, where 'he passionately denied' the request that
he should return home for his health's sake. His passions, it seems,
are reserved for posthumous joys: Walton, never comfortable with

---

[73] See Hutchinson, 4–5. The 'motto' is taken from 'The Posie', in ibid. 182.

the idea of passion, has at last found a suitably bounded focus for them. It is Featley's sentiment, where holy desire leaves the world and searches out heaven: where the (feminized) holy desirer 'did not . . . by all kinde of naturall aliments and medicate potions . . . stop all the passages of the soul . . . but . . . openeth them wider, that he might be readier to entertain death Gods harbinger'.

Then comes the famous description of the scene in which Donne poses for his portrait wearing his winding-sheet, 'with so much of the sheet turned aside as might show his lean, pale, and death-like face'. The finished portrait is then placed by his bedside, where it serves as Donne's memento mori, 'his hourly object until his death' (p. 78). This incident was not included in the *Life* until 1658—perhaps, as Novarr suggests, because of the 'vainglory' it implied.[74] Walton certainly introduces the incident with a certain caution, making it plain that Donne was persuaded into having the portrait painted, and arguing that 'a desire for glory and commendation' is a universal human characteristic, of which 'we want not sacred examples' (pp. 77–8). Besides this, Donne's 'hourly' contemplation of his dead self is exemplary, reminds us of our deaths; yet also exists to record Donne's inimitability.[75]

---

[74] Novarr, 78–9. See also Helen Gardner, 'Dean Donne's Monument in St. Paul's', in René Wellek and Alvaro Ribeiro (eds.), *Evidence in Literary Scholarship: Essays in Memory of James Marshall Osborne* (Oxford, 1979), 29–44, for a discussion on the accuracy (or lack of it) of this 1658 addition.

[75] Donne's action is not without narrative precedent. See the anonymous *Life off the 70. Archbishopp of Canterbury Presently Sitting Englished and to be Added to the 69. lately Sett Forth in Latin* ([Zurich], 1574). This is a pirated translation of the Latin Life of Matthew Parker written by his secretary John Josselin under his guidance, and intended for Parker's history of British archbishops, *De Antiquitate Britannicae Ecclesiae et Privilegiis Ecclesiae Cantuariensis* (London, 1572). In it Parker (still living at the time of writing) commissions his tomb 'off blacke Marbell' partly that he may use it as an instrument and focus for contemplating his own death during his lifetime, and partly to demonstrate to 'posteritye' after his death his worldly consequence while living: 'And this Tombe off purpose he caused to be made of noe exquisite worke/ but smothe/ streighte/ and plaine/ thinkinge it enoughe if being represented to the eie/ it mighte serve eyther for him selfe, while he lived/ as a token/ or monumente off his uncertain estate/ or when he was deade/ as a testimonye to his posteritye/ what principall place by the bounty of his Prince he obteyned in Christe his commonwealth' (sigs. C2v–3). Parker was more than usually concerned, in an age obsessed with monuments, to leave tangible emblems of his existence and 'principall place'. See e.g. Parker Library, Corpus Christi College, Cambridge, MS 582, which

The 1675 edition then has a digression, in which Walton compares Donne's funeral portrait with an earlier picture of him 'drawn by a curious hand at the age of eighteen' (p. 79). Novarr identifies this picture as being an engraving by William Marshall affixed to the 1635 edition of Donne's poems, and it shows the young Donne in martial costume, 'with his sword and what other adornments might then suit with the present fashions of youth, and the giddy gayeties of that age' (p. 79). The motto under the Marshall engraving reads 'Antes muerdo que mudado', 'sooner dead than changed'.[76] Walton renders this ingeniously as

> *How much shall I be chang'd,*
> *Before I am chang'd.*

(p. 79)

In the comparison which follows of 'that young, and his now dying picture' Walton comments that

every beholder might say, *Lord! How much is Dr. Donne already chang'd, before he is chang'd?* And the view of them might give my Reader occasion, to ask himself with some amazement, *Lord! How much may I also, that am now in health be chang'd, before I am chang'd? before this vile, this changeable body shall put off mortality?* and therefore to prepare for it.—— (p. 80)

Walton realizes that his exhortation to the reader uses the contrasting pictures as a general memento mori. But he is not willing that this should be his only message; as well as offering the pictures as a lesson to the reader, he requires them to offer specific information about Donne himself. He therefore adds:

But this is not writ so much for my Readers *Memento*, as to tell him, that Dr. *Donne* would often . . . mention the many changes both of his body and mind . . . and would as often say, *His great and most blessed change*

contains ' "the testimony of the guiftes of Matthue Archb of Cant." [Attested] by . . . the Masters and Fellows of Corpus Christi College, Gonville and Caius College and Trinity Hall, recording Parker's gifts and good deeds to themselves and others . . . compiled by Parker, probably in 1574'. Recorded in *Transactions of the Cambridge Bibliographical Society*, 3 (London, 1963), 120. The entry relates to Parker's presentation copy to the College, not (as the *Transactions* has it) the 'Black Book'. I am indebted to Mrs C. P. Hall, Library Archivist, for drawing my attention to this; information given in square brackets indicates her MS corrections of the printed entry.

[76] Novarr, 118–19.

was from a temporal, to a spiritual imployment: in which he was so happy, that he accounted the former part of his life to be lost. (p. 80)

Novarr says that Walton 'turned an audacious motto of four words into a testimonial of Donne's inherent religiosity and even into a meditation on man's journey through life'. Walton has done something subtler. He alters the motto's sense. Donne will be 'chang'd' while in the body, before his final 'change' from life to death. In the passage Walton identifies this change as being 'from a temporal, to a spiritual imployment', and adds that 'the beginning of it' was 'from his first entring into sacred Orders'. Walton has said that Donne 'accounted the former part of his life to be lost', which implies that he became dead to his earlier, secular self, before his bodily death. He was indeed 'sooner dead than changed', but that death was a death to the world, marked by his ordination, the occasion of his right to enjoy a spiritual immortality. This reading of the motto also, incidentally, supports Walton's own depiction of Donne's life, which concentrates upon Donne as priest. By showing that Donne regarded his secular youth as lost to him, Walton enlists his posthumous approbation for the portrait Walton draws of him as primarily concerned with matters of the spirit. Donne's 'entring into sacred Orders' is indeed perceived as transformatory.[77]

Donne's last moments follow. He takes 'a solemn and deliberate farewell' of his acquaintance, appoints a time-limit for his servants to consult him about worldly business, after which he refuses to discuss or consider such things any more, announces to his Maker that he is now ready for his 'dissolution', and then lies in readiness for it for a full fifteen days (pp. 80–1). With a refreshing originality, he murmurs on his deathbed not the *Nunc Dimittis* but a line from the Lord's Prayer, 'saying often, *Thy Kingdom come, Thy Will be done*' (p. 81). When he loses the power of speech, Walton imagines it as having 'dyed before him, for that it was then become useless to him that now conversed with God on earth, as Angels are said to do in heaven, *only by thoughts and looks*' (p. 81). The suggestion that Donne's silent passing exhibited the certainty of his heavenly destination is delicate, but

---

[77] See Richard Wendorf, *The Elements of Life: Biography and Portrait-Painting in Stuart and Georgian England* (Oxford, 1990), 45–52 for a perceptive discussion of the portraits in the *Life of Donne*. See also above, pp. 111–15.

definite. The artistry of the life-writer has come a long way
since Jonas's articulation of a complicated scriptural 'proof' that
Luther's final coma functioned as an assurance of his salvation,
but the message is essentially the same.

Unlike his speech, Donne's self-possession does not enter
heaven before him. Even as he dies, Donne is shown closing his
own eyes, and arranging 'his hands and body into such a posture
as required not the least alteration by those that came to shroud
him' (p. 82).

Some evidence exists that Walton was present at Donne's
deathbed. Before printing the *Life of Hooker* in 1665, he sent
a letter to Henry King, bishop of Chichester, enclosing the
manuscript and asking for permission to print King's reply in
his book. King agreed, and the letter as it was printed in the first
edition of the *Life of Hooker* includes these words:

I shall begin with my most dear and incomparable friend Dr. *Donne*, late
Dean of St. *Pauls* Church, who not onely trusted me as his Executor,
but three days before his death delivered into my hands those excellent
Sermons of his now made publick: professing before Dr. *Winniff*,
Dr. *Montford*, and I think yourself then present at his bed-side, that it
was by my restless importunity that he had prepared them for the Press.[78]

King was writing thirty-four years after the event, and may have
remembered incorrectly; but he sounds fairly sure that Walton was
there. It is not impossible that Walton might have edited himself
out, just as he never mentions the bloodstone seal Donne gave
him in the list of commemorative gifts (and eminent friends) he
makes earlier in the biography. This might be his own version
of 'objectivity'—though, if so, he abandons it in the *Life of
Sanderson*, where he appears as a witness to Civil War events.
He seems to have decided, at any rate, not to interfere here in his
own voice one way or the other. He prints King's letter without
contradicting, and without confirming, its speculation. However,
that Walton was closely involved with the disposal of Donne's
posthumous papers, to which he clearly had access, is certain.[79]
It seems fair to say that, even if Walton were not actually present
at the deathbed, he at least had access to very reliable information
about Donne's last days.

[78] Izaak Walton, *The Life of Mr. R. Hooker* (London, 1665), sig. A2^v.
[79] Novarr, 26–9.

Conclusion

In the *Life of Donne* Walton was writing as his subject's personal friend, and the reasons he gives for his efforts owe a great deal to this fact. The *Life* is animated by the demands of 'the truth of love', and I have attempted to show where Walton allowed these demands to affect his presentation of factual details, or 'love of truth'. In his extensive but somewhat free use of Donne's own writings may be seen an attempt to reconcile these two imperatives. The result may not always be accurate,[80] but it does show Walton developing the conventions available to him with skill and subtlety, and according to consistent principles. Their very consistency shows Walton to have, on his own terms, a sense of historical responsibility.

THE *LIFE OF MR. GEORGE HERBERT*

Of all Walton's *Lives*, this was the one most vivified by the truth of love. Walton describes it, in his Epistle to the Reader affixed to the collections of 1670 and 1675, as 'a Free-will-offering, *that it was writ, chiefly to please my self*' (p. 6).

Walton here makes more use of his subject's own writings (and in this case especially the poetry) than he does in any other biography, including *Donne*. In the section which follows I shall discuss this, and the terms of Walton's claims to be Herbert's life-writer when he had no immediate personal knowledge of Herbert himself. ('I have only seen him', he wrote in his Introduction).

Walton had no reason, besides inclination, to write Herbert's life; he was not paying a debt of gratitude to the memory of a friend, as he was with the *Lives* of Donne and Wotton, and nor had he been urged to it by any acquaintance to whom he had an obligation, as with the *Lives* of Hooker and (to a lesser extent) Sanderson. Why, then, did he do it?

---

[80] See e.g. R. C. Bald, 'Historical Doubts Respecting Walton's Life of Donne', in Millar MacLure and F. W. Watt (eds.), *Essays in English Literature from the Renaissance to the Victorian Age* (Toronto, 1964), 69–84; Gardner, 'Dean Donne's Monument in St. Paul's', cited in n. 74 above.

Walton as Herbert's Author

Walton had been interested in Herbert for years. He had quoted him approvingly in the 1653 *Compleat Angler*, and the 1658 *Life of Donne* has an admiring reference to Herbert as a 'man of primitive piety' and to *The Temple* as a book which 'hath raised many a dejected and discomposed soul, and charmed them into sweet and quiet thoughts'.[81] Donne quotes on his final sickbed the words given as Herbert's motto in the Preface to the 1633 edition of *The Temple*, themselves taken from Herbert's poem 'The Posie'. There is also evidence internal to the *Life* that Walton had begun his research for it years earlier. For instance, Walton uses the testimony of Arthur Woodnoth, a friend of Herbert's, to substantiate a number of facts. Since Woodnoth had died by 1651, and had in all probability forfeited Walton's friendship before that by supporting the parliamentary side during the Civil War, Walton must have collected the information twenty years or more before the *Life*'s publication.[82]

Herbert's life and writings, then, had an attraction strong enough for Walton to make biographical inquiries years before writing the *Life*, and to quote Herbert himself a number of times in other works of his own. This is not surprising. Herbert's contemporary reputation was as much or more that of exemplary priest as poet, and the Preface to the 1633 edition of *The Temple*, which was written by Nicholas Ferrar, describes him as 'a pattern or more for the age he lived in'. Ferrar also states that Herbert's poems 'bear witnesse' to the intellectual course, or 'inward enforcements', of Herbert's decision to lead a holy life, implying that their value lay largely in their function as virtually autobiographical religious testimony.[83] Walton was an exemplary biographer; and he would use his subjects' writings as a direct, though sometimes inappropriate, source for his narrative. Ferrar's Preface, then, indicates Walton's biographical approach to be especially suited to writing Herbert.

Herbert's own tendency in his poems consciously to use self and experience via a psalmic confessional mode means that the way Walton uses his subjects' writings is well suited to Herbert's

---

[81] *Donne* (1658), 81–2.　　　[82] See Novarr, 301–7.
[83] See Hutchinson, 3–5.

chosen artistic model.[84] And although it is not possible to define the conduct of Herbert's life exclusively as an artistic performance any more than it would be to read his poems solely as devotional models, Walton, in blurring the distinction between the two, is still following a literary precedent set by Herbert himself. It is therefore no surprise that the *Life* uses Herbert's writings so much.

Why, given all this, did Walton hesitate for so long? Perhaps the answer lies in his own criteria for biographical fitness. In the Introduction to the *Life of Donne* Walton says that his personal knowledge of Donne, together with his sense that the Donne's *Sermons* ought in all decency to have a *Life*, were the only compelling reasons for his presumption (pp. 20–1). For the later project the circumstances were different. Walton did not know Herbert, and Ferrar (who did) had already introduced *The Temple*.

By 1670, though, Walton had an established biographical reputation. In the *Life of Hooker* he had also shown that he could write a stranger's Life 'personally' simply by citing a number of acquaintances or relatives he and his subject shared. During that time he had also met Christopher Hervey, whose imitative (and uneven) collection *The Synagogue* was to be published with *The Temple* as a package for the next 200 years.[85] Reasons why Walton may have felt unable to meet his own criteria to be Herbert's life-writer in the 1640s and 1650s, had largely disappeared, then, by the time the *Life of Hooker* appeared in 1665.

This is what Walton says about it in his Introduction:

. . . I did lately look back, and not without some content (at least to my self) *that I have endeavour'd to deserve the love, and preserve the memory of my two deceased friends, Dr.* Donne, *and Sir* Henry Wotton, *by declaring the several employments and various accidents of their Lives: And though Mr.* George Herbert (whose Life I now intend to write) *were to me a*

---

[84] See Barbara Lewalski, *Protestant Poetics and the Seventeenth Century Religious Lyric* (Princeton, 1979), 301–2.

[85] Walton is likely to have met Harvey after 1640 but before 1655, when Harvey's commendatory verses for the *Compleat Angler* appeared in its second edition. In the commendatory verses Walton wrote to appear before the 1661 (fourth) edition of *The Synagogue*, he makes it plain that they are already friends, but that he knew Harvey's verses before he knew him personally. They may have met through Sir Robert Holt of Aston, to whom Walton dedicates the 1658 *Donne* and in whose gift Harvey's living was. Walton apparently knew Aston when young. See *DNB*, xxv. 78–9; *Selected Writings of Izaak Walton*, ed. Jessica Martin (Manchester, 1997); *Donne* (1658), sigs. A3^r–9^r.

stranger as to his person, for I have only seen him: yet since he was, and was
worthy to be their friend, and very many of his have been mine; I judge it
may not be unacceptable to those that knew any of them in their lives, or do
now know them by mine, or their own Writings, to see this Conjunction of
them after their deaths; without which, many things that concern'd them,
and some things that concern'd the Age in which they lived, would be less
perfect, and lost to Posterity.

For these Reasons I have undertaken it, and if I have prevented any
abler person, I beg pardon of him, and my Reader. (p. 259)

The Introduction was intended by Walton for the collected
edition of the *Lives* of 1670, and this shows in its rhetoric.[86] He
assumes that the *Life of Herbert* will be read together with the *Lives*
of Donne and Wotton. He advances his personal knowledge of the
latter two, and the 'content' he felt upon contemplating their *Lives*,
as part of his justification for writing the *Life of Herbert* at all. He
is able to fulfil his own requirement that he should have been
Herbert's friend, even though he was 'a stranger as to his person',
by citing his friendship with two men who really were Herbert's
friends, and his more general knowledge of 'very many' more. And
even the worthiness of Herbert as subject is described in terms of
his worthiness to be the friend of Donne and Wotton.

Walton clearly believes that his biographies make it possible
for posterity fully to 'know' his subjects. This means that he sees
himself as an appropriate, indeed an entirely transparent, mediator of the essential details not merely of the 'accidents' of their
lives, but of their reasons for living. This explains his very stringent application to himself of criteria which comprise a series
of personal and ideological compatibilities before embarking
upon any of the *Lives*. That he also perceives his subjects' writings
to hold forms of autobiographical knowledge is shown by his
parenthetical reference to 'mine, or their own Writings'. Walton,
as ever, will not make a distinction between the practical pursuit
of virtue and its written expression.

I would also suggest that, for Walton, personal friendship
guaranteed more than simple liking. It proved a spiritual compatibility. He had already supported his delineation of Donne's
piety by stressing his friendship with Herbert; now he would use

---

[86] It probably first appeared, without Walton's sanction, prefacing the separate edition of the *Life of Herbert* (1670) which acted as a kind of flyer for the
Collected *Lives* of the same year. See Novarr, 510–12.

his success in writing the *Life of Donne* (a *Life* firmly and openly based upon personal knowledge) to justify writing a *Life of Herbert*.

Walton gives one public reason for his *Herbert*: 'respect to posterity'. He explains that, although Herbert 'was not a man that the next age can forget; yet, many of his particular acts and vertues might have been neglected, or lost, if I had not collected and presented them to the Imitation of those that shall succeed us' (p. 6). Its didactic intention aims at 'posterity', qualified as those who will live in 'the next age' and who will 'succeed us'. The same 'respect to posterity' receives due notice in the passage from the Introduction to the *Life* itself as I have quoted it above. Here Walton assumes that the personal friendship he demonstrates between Donne, Wotton, and Herbert (and thus himself) guarantees the identical didactic concerns, not only as regards the specific virtues of their specific lives, but also with respect to 'the Age in which they lived'. Spiritual amity, for Walton, ensures political compatibility.

Walton's own agenda deals with one particular interpretation of the Church's fall under the Commonwealth. He uses the pious accidents of Herbert's life to attempt to correct an opinion, prevalent among a number of moderate churchmen from the Commonwealth onwards, that part of the responsibility for the Church's fall in 1649 must be taken by the Church herself. Specifically, this responsibility was seen to rest in the low status accorded to priests because of a general failure on their part to discharge their pastoral responsibilities properly.

As far as Walton was concerned, full responsibility for the events and instability of the Civil War lay with the nonconformists; but an important source of his, the Revd Barnabas Oley, was not so sure. Oley had edited Herbert's *Remains* in 1652, affixing a 'Prefatory View' of Herbert upon which Walton drew heavily when he came to write his *Life*.[87] Oley, in issuing the *Remains*, had a particular aim. A large part of it comprised Herbert's *Countrey Parson*, which Herbert himself describes like this:

I have resolved to set down the Form and Character of a true Pastour, that I may have a Mark to aim at: which also I will set as high as I can, since hee shoots higher that threatens the Moon, then hee that aims at a

---

[87] *Herbert's Remains*, ed. Barnabas Oley (London, 1652).

Tree. Not that I think, if a man do not all which is here expressed, hee presently sinns, and displeases God, but that it is a good strife to go as farre as we can in pleasing of him, who hath done so much for us. The Lord prosper my intention to my selfe, and others, who may not despise my poor labours, but add to those points, which I have observed, untill the Book grow to a complete Pastorall. (sigs. A3ᵛ–4ᵛ)

Herbert wrote a manual of advice to himself, which he would try to follow, and which might incidentally be of help to other country priests. He saw its publication as a way of receiving advice, too, which could go into later editions 'untill the Book grow to a complete Pastorall'. He appears to be suggesting that its contents describe the ideals of pastoral care, rather than being a set of rigid prescriptions setting out a required minimum of duties.

Oley's view, though, was that Herbert, in indicating how a priest in a rural benefice should behave, also incidentally laid bare some of the common abuses and irreverences of priest and people in the years before the Commonwealth. His republication of the *Country Parson* was clearly intended as a tactful means to 'help on in the the [*sic*] way of Repentance, by the discovery of former mistakes or neglects', adding transparently that the text 'being writ nigh twenty years since, will be lesse subject to misconstruction' (sig. c6ᵛ). And by citing Herbert's priestly and personal virtues, Oley could prove that previous shortcomings had not been universal. He writes: 'I hope no man will think . . . that I give him leave to construe my words Mathematically, *as if there was not an atome, or hair of a good man, or man of God in our Church. There were divers* primitive . . . holy, *and* heavenly souls, *vessels chosen and fitted for the service of the Sanctuary*' (sigs. a8ᵛ–9). Oley cites three: Thomas Jackson, Nicholas Ferrar, and George Herbert. He describes them as having 'that inseparable Lot and signe of Christ and Christians . . . To be signes of Contradiction (or spoken Against) men wondred at, and rated at by the world' (sig. a10). This certainly suggests that he saw them as the exception rather than the rule. He uses their example to argue that the disrepute into which the priesthood had fallen should not undermine the essential dignity of the calling. So he makes a lot of Herbert's 'Noble, and Ancient Family', and of the secular honours accorded to him before he made the priesthood his vocation. Of his Oratorship in the University of Cambridge he writes that 'propably [*sic*] he might, I have heard (as other Orators) have had a Secretary of States place' (sig. b8). But who would be a mere secretary of state when he could have a rural benefice?

In the *Life of Herbert* Walton opposes the main thrust of Oley's argument using Oley's own evidence. His Herbert becomes a living example of the general holiness and diligence characterizing the ministry of the 1620s and 1630s. He cites the nobility of Herbert's family, and his secular eminence when young, to demonstrate the naturalness of a priestly calling for an aristocrat. The *Country Parson* is treated as an autobiographical record.

Here Walton ignores Herbert's own characterization of the *Country Parson* as a 'Mark to aim at', with its implication that Herbert felt himself to have fallen short of his own prescriptions. For Walton, it described rather than animated Herbert's actual pastoral practice. Yet he evidently realized that even a credulous reader would find the resultant record of unremitting piety hard to swallow, for he breaks off his narrative just before describing Herbert at his last parish of Bemerton, to 'bespeak the Reader to prepare for an almost incredible story, of the great sanctity of the short remainder of his holy life' (p. 288). Walton knows that he is writing a kind of hagiography.

'Eloquence' and 'Sincerity'

The *Life* is not simply animated by general exemplary intentions. Although Walton continues the exhortation to the reader which I have quoted above with a lamentation that so 'few of the Clergy lived like him then, and how many live so unlike him now', he adds that his 'design' is not to 'censure', but 'rather to assure the Reader, that I have used very great diligence to inform my self, that I might inform him of the truth of what follows; and though I cannot adorn it with eloquence, yet I will do it with sincerity' (p. 289). This asks to be read as a declaration of researcher's accuracy, accompanied by its characteristic denial of literary skill. As with *Donne*, Walton actually gauarantees 'the truth of what follows' by a denial of this kind: clever people obscure facts, simple ones cannot. The contemporary definition of 'sincerity' as meaning the genuineness or actual existence of a thing should be borne in mind when considering Walton's use of the word.[88] But, having said this, we need to remember that Walton treats

[88] See *OED*, *sb*. 15.

Herbert's own writings biographically, and that this must alter his definition of research, and indeed of what the 'truth' of Herbert's holy life might be. He is not talking about the ethics of modern scholarship.

His denial of eloquence is, of course, itself rhetorical. Throughout the *Life* he uses all the literary resources he can command to delineate the 'sincerity' he asserts. For Walton, biography is not a science but an art, and he approaches it with artistry. In any case, the rhetoric of literary inadequacy he employs reflects Herbert's. Take 'The Forerunners', for instance, or 'Jordan (I)': they wind themselves into a skilful, semi-Calvinistic rejection of their own skill as a fit expression of praise.[89] If faith is not justified by works, and if the poem, being a made thing, is a work, it may therefore only acquire worth through the grace of God. Consequently, poem after poem is skilfully and beautifully discursive on the subject of its own worthlessness as an object of skill and beauty. Walton has appropriated not only Herbert's own words for 'sincerity', but also Herbert's own disclaimers as to the worth of the human artefact offered in order to celebrate the works of God.

Edification

His appropriation is partial. Walton sees himself as mediator of the achievements of other men holier and more skilled than he is. He is a celebrator, not a creator. Also, he is a ceremonialist, and remarkably untouched by Calvinism. His theology allows him to regard skill and beauty as proper ways to praise. The civilized artefact—religious music and poetry, the beautified church building, liturgy and ritual—may be used as ceremonial structures for his own work. Besides, he can treat Herbert himself (and Walton's Herbert necessarily embodies his written work as well as the events of his life) as this kind of edifice, whereas Herbert in his own writing is in the painful position of having himself as subject, and cannot therefore exhibit a Waltonian confidence in the matter.

The *Life* is constructed out of significant edifices. It has been pointed out by Clayton Lein that the civilized artefacts which bear a relation to Herbert are used as its props, as well as symbols for

---

[89] Hutchinson, 176 and 56.

virtue.[90] It begins and ends with the destruction by the 'late rebels'
of two such artefacts—Montgomery Castle (the Herbert seat)
at the beginning (p. 260), and Herbert's 'private Writings' at the
end (p. 321). In between these two poles, Herbert himself rebuilds
two churches, Leighton (p. 278) and Bemerton (p. 287). Walton is
at pains to present these churches as beautiful, even allowing to
Leighton an unparalleled, though probably fictional wainscoting,[91]
and describing the church itself as 'being, for the workmanship,
a costly *Mosaick*' (p. 278).

Walton had got his last phrase by misreading Oley, who
wrote that the Church owed to Herbert '*the reparation of a*
Church-materiall, *and erection of that costly piece (of Mosaick or
Solomonick work)* The Temple; *which flourishes and stands inviol-
ate, when our other Magnificences are desolate, and despised*' (sig. b9).
Oley's readiness to mix real with textual edifices, as he mixed
Leighton, the 'Church-materiall', with *The Temple*, clearly gener-
ated a fortuitous (though possibly accidental) transfer of epithet.

Walton treats the rebuilding of Bemerton Rectory suggestively
too. Having rebuilt it 'at his own Charge' (he is insistent on this
point), he writes that Herbert

caus'd these verses to be writ upon, and ingraven in the Mantle of the
Chimney in his Hall.

> To My Successor.
> *If thou chance for to find*
> *A new House to thy mind,*
> *And built without thy Cost:*
> *Be good to the Poor,*
> *As God gives thee store,*
> *And then my Labour's not lost.*

(p. 293)

This rationalizes the importance of building edifices associated
with the Church; Herbert rebuilds 'at his own Charge' and leaves
his successor's money free for alms. But their source is interesting. They are adapted from Fuller's 'Character of the Faithfull Minister' in *The Holy State*; and the precepts exemplified
by Fuller's character surface a number of times as Herbert's

---

[90] C. D. Lein, 'Art and Structure in Walton's Life of Mr. George Herbert',
University of Toronto Quarterly, 46 (1976–7), 162–76.
[91] See Novarr, 342.

actions in the *Life*.[92] Perhaps Walton's insertion of Fuller's verse acknowledges this; no such engraving has ever been discovered at Bemerton. (But written exhortations, painted to look as if they were engraved in stone and affixed to the inner walls of its buildings, were a feature of the Little Gidding community.)[93]

The Herbert of Walton's *Life* insists upon catechism and short sermons, and so does Fuller's 'Faithfull Minister'. More specifically, Fuller's minister is said not to make 'odious comparisons betwixt prayer and preaching',[94] and Walton says Herbert made, at Leighton, the 'Reading Pew, and Pulpit' of an 'equal height' in order that '*Prayer* and *Preaching*, being equally useful, might agree like brethren' (p. 278). But both these borrowings can be traced to other sources; the insistence on catechism and short sermons could equally have come from the *Country Parson*,[95] and the arrangements at Leighton also recall those made by the Ferrar community.[96]

Clearly Walton's Herbert is almost flawlessly exemplary: the embodied 'Faithfull Minister'. But Walton firmly acknowledges himself to be inside a widely used exemplary tradition. This is not manipulation or falsification in any straightforward sense, because a consensus exists as to how it should be read—not to say acted on. His Herbert, too, is specific about the pastoral efficacy of his carriage:

I will be sure to live well, because the vertuous Life of a Clergyman, is the most powerful eloquence to perswade all that see it, to reverence and love, and at least, to desire to live like him. And this I will do, because I know we live in an Age that hath more need of good examples, than precepts. (pp. 289–90)

Walton could have taken this from Fuller, 'our minister lives sermons', or from a multitude of other sources.[97] Since 'eloquence'

[92] Thomas Fuller, *The Holy State* (London, 1642), 87. See also above, pp. 99–101, for a discussion of the common characterization of written works as edifices.
[93] See Novarr, 336; A. L. Maycock, *Nicholas Ferrar of Little Gidding* (London, 1938), 149–50.
[94] *The Holy State*, 81.   [95] Hutchinson, 236 and 235.
[96] See 'A Life of Nicholas Ferrar', in *The Ferrar Papers*, ed. B. Blackstone (Cambridge, 1938), 27–8.
[97] *The Holy State*, 81. See also 'Lying on his deathbed he bequeaths to each of his parishioners his precepts and example for a legacie' (p. 87). And see Ch. 3 (Death), for a discussion of this commonplace.

could (and often did) mean 'speaking actions', it seems just as appropriate that Walton should translate such actions back into narrated speech like this. To take only one testimony that Herbert framed his life according to its precept, we have the words of his brother Edward in his *Autobiography*: 'his life was most holy and exemplary; insomuch, that about Salisbury, where he lived, bene-ficed for many years, he was little less than sainted.'[98]

The passage above tells us one more important thing about Herbert's status within Walton's work. His life is described as 'the most powerful eloquence to perswade' others to virtue. The 'eloquence', then, to which Walton professes himself to be unequal, becomes a 'powerful' persuasion when it just means moral action. But Walton has also established himself to be an appropriate chronicler of Herbert's actions, and assumes a reading knowledge of his *Lives* to be equivalent to knowing his subjects. By using a word more appropriate to the employment of literary techniques than to the pursuit of a pious vocation, Walton has therefore acknowledged a need for an 'eloquence' in his record of Herbert's life that will match the 'eloquence' of the life itself. For since the 'vertuous life of a Clergyman' is being offered as the perfect artistic performance, it follows that Walton, in order to achieve the 'sincerity' in his account that he claims for it, must match the real Herbert's moral perfection through the employment of his own faultless style.

Music

Walton images Herbert's perfections via another art, dedicated to the service of God and offered as an expression of divine qualities: church music.

Walton had already tried this manoeuvre out in the 1658 *Life of Donne*, where he describes Donne as having had his 'Hymn to God the Father' set to music and sung in St Paul's (p. 62). Walton here quotes Donne saying 'to a friend'

The words of this Hymn *have restored to me the same thoughts of joy that possest my Soul in my sickness when I composed it. And, O the power of Church-musick! that Harmony added to this Hymn has raised the Affections of my heart, and quickned the graces of zeal and gratitude; and I observe, that I always return from paying this publick duty of* Prayer *and*

---

[98] Quoted in Hutchinson, p. xxxvi.

Praise *to God, with an unexpressible tranquillity of mind*, and a willing-
ness to leave the world. (p. 62)

Walton then defends church music himself, arguing that 'after
this manner have many devout Souls lifted up their hands and
offered acceptable Sacrifices unto Almighty God', and lamenting
the 1656 proscription of the use of music in church services.

Novarr sees such passages as constituting 'rather easily recog-
nizable partisan opinion', which, of course, they do.[99] On the other
hand, Walton built his biographies from the belief that the dedi-
cation of art to divine purposes was to offer one of the highest expressions of love of which God's creatures were capable. It is not
possible to imply that the biographies would have been better
stripped of opinion without either the point of the biographies,
or the point of the judgement, collapsing into meaninglessness.
It says, in effect, that someone else should have written something
else; or it suggests either that Walton could hold beliefs about
ceremony which were apolitical (which he could not), or that the
fact that they were political should have made them detachable.
Actually Walton had no detachable beliefs whatever, and thought
politicians argued about truth. In the same way music always
operates as a spiritual metaphor for him, not, I suggest, just
because there was already a literary precedent for it, but because
he really thought that music lifted the spirit.

Walton depicts Herbert's love of music doubly: both as a
neutral personal trait and as a quality of devotion. In the same sentence he describes it as 'recreation' and as a 'heavenly Art' (p. 303).
He quotes Herbert saying that 'his time spent in Prayer, and
Cathedral Musick, elevated his Soul, and was his Heaven upon
Earth'. There is no reason to doubt that Herbert did indeed practise music in this spirit. For one thing, Walton takes Herbert's
description of music as 'Heaven upon Earth' from Oley; and Oley
is uneasy enough about it to add immediately that nevertheless
Herbert's 'chief delight was in the Holy Scripture, one leafe
whereof he professed he would not part with, though he might
have the whole world in Exchange'.[100] Oley's reluctance (which
at least supports the truth of the statement; for why should he
make up something he would clearly rather have suppressed?)
is a low-church caution about ceremonial trappings, which is

therefore countered with a remark which makes Herbert's primary concern the Word of God.

Walton, of course, wants instead to demonstrate that Herbert's piety upheld a tradition of worship in which ceremony aided, rather than obscured, devotion. Firmly echoing (for instance) the Renaissance theorist Johannes Tinctoris in the *Complexus Effectuum Musices*, he asserts 'musica animas beatificat'.[101] Though these are pre-Reformation assumptions, they are firmly present in a Protestant tradition—as in this letter of Bishop Jewel's, who wrote to Peter Martyr about the new practice of singing in churches:

> Religion is somewhat more established now than it was. The people are everywhere exceedingly inclined to the better part. Church music for the people has very much conduced to this. For as soon as they had once commenced singing publicly in only one little church in London, immediately not only the churches in the neighbourhood, but even distant towns, began to vie with one another in the same practice. You may now sometimes see at Paul's Cross, after the service, six thousand persons, old and young, of both sexes, all singing together and praising God.[102]

Hooker praises church music in the *Laws of Ecclesiastical Polity*, characteristically defending it with the assertion that it was 'a thinge which all Christian churches in the world have received' and 'which alwaies heretofore the best men and wisest governors of Gods people did thinke they never could commend enough'.[103] And both Donne and Herbert frequently employ the idea of music as *speculum*, which makes it appropriate for Walton to do it too.

In Walton, music becomes a metaphor for piety as well as a form piety takes. So Herbert's charitable actions 'prove Musick to him

---

[101] Quoted in John Stevens, *Music and Poetry in the Early Tudor Court* (London, 1961), 64.

[102] Quoted in a modified form in Nicholas Temperley, *The Music of the English Parish Church*, 2nd edn., 2 vols. (Cambridge, 1983), i. 43. Foxe represents the opposite camp with the martyr Thomas Bilney. Bilney, apparently, could 'abide no swearinge, nor singing. Comming from the church where singing was, he wold lament to his schollers, the curiositie of their deinty singing, which he called rather a mockery with god, then otherwise. And when Doct. Thurlby Bishop after, then scholler lieing in the chamber underneath him, wold play on his recorder (as he wold often do) he would resort straight to hys prayer.' *Actes and Monuments* (1563), 466.

[103] *Polity*, Book V, ch. 39.4: see *Folger Edition*, ii. 158.

at Mid-night', and to have omitted them would have 'made discord in his Conscience' (p. 305). Once the connection has been made between music and sanctity, Herbert's private pursuit reinforces his public role. He therefore becomes both player and instrument in an artistic performance, for he both enacts the will of God and is also the instrument through which God Himself acts. Thus an apparently chance preference of Herbert's for chamber concerts becomes, without a word of rational argument, another proof of his holiness.

With Herbert, as with Donne, Walton shows his subject becoming God's instrument at the point of death, quoting each time a poem which employs this conceit. Donne writes the 'Hymn to God, my God, in my sickness' apparently on his final sickbed, in which he writes 'I shall be made thy musique' (p. 66). Herbert rises from his bed 'The *Sunday* before his death' and calls for 'one of his Instruments'. Before he plays, he dedicates his performance with words which are a modified version of part of 'The Thanksgiving':[104]

> My God, my God,
> My Musick shall find thee,
>   And every string
> Shall have his attribute to sing.
>
>   (pp. 316–17)

Walton celebrates the climactic nature of these deaths in a combination of arts: music and poetry. He locates those arts in the expiring bodies of his subjects, by choosing devotional poetry they themselves made, and by making their bodies therefore, and in more than one sense, the instruments of praise. Whether Herbert actually sang, or Donne actually wrote, on each deathbed becomes less important than whether Walton's narrative corresponds in the perfection of its own artistry with these essentially aesthetic symbols of sanctity. Yet the symbols are not originally Walton's, however congenial he finds them. They belonged to Donne and Herbert first. That is why they are there.

It is becoming clear that the mixture of aesthetic and moral principles which animate *The Life of Herbert* require Walton

---

[104] Hutchinson, 36.

to maintain a stylistic consistency not necessarily matched by historical fact. But there is a further question, too: what sort of consistent narrative is appropriate to what sort of moral perfection? If Walton is writing pure hagiography, then Herbert should be presented as inimitable, uniquely gifted, a focus for a piety impossible for ordinary people. If, on the other hand, Walton is following Oley, he should present Herbert as an entirely imitable exemplar whose clerical conduct provides a pattern to follow. That Ferrar, at least, had recognized a potential problem in presenting the extreme piety of Herbert's life as imitable is indicated by the fact that his 1633 Preface to *The Temple* described Herbert not just as a pattern for 'the age he lived in' but as 'a pattern or more'. He also stated that Herbert was 'justly a companion to the primitive saints'.[105] Walton, in offering the conduct of Herbert's life as 'A Mark' for his readers 'to aim at', has also to ask those readers to 'threaten the Moon'.

For he attempts to maintain both attitudes. Herbert's inimitability is left very largely implicit in his 'edification': the linkage of events and accidents of his life with other, more material cultural edifices, so that Herbert himself becomes an edifice too. Walton's more straightforwardly didactic intentions, on the other hand, are to be found in his largely successful attempts to present Herbert as a man endowed from birth with worldly eminence and prospects who nevertheless devoted his energies to a vocation which had no use for such things. Thus, the conduct of Herbert's life becomes a powerful argument for the essential nobility of the priesthood.

Walton's double aim pervades the first section of the *Life*, up to Herbert's installation at Bemerton. His early piety is indicated by, for instance, the poem written by Herbert at 17 attacking the convention of addressing verses to women rather than to God (pp. 268–9). His worldly eminence is vested partly in his family (since in that context eminence and piety need not conflict) and in the lists Walton makes of the powerful men Herbert knew: the king, Sir Henry Wotton, Lancelot Andrewes, Francis Bacon (pp. 273–4). The most interesting pointer as to the sort of man Walton conceived a secular Herbert might have been like is his information that the king had given him a sinecure which 'was the

---

[105] Ibid. 3.

same, that Queen *Elizabeth* had formerly given to her Favourite
Sir *Philip Sidney*; and valued to be worth an hundred and twenty
pound *per Annum*' (p. 274). In much the same way, Walton supports the impression he wishes to give of the extreme piety of the
latter part of Herbert's life by stressing his 'holy friendship' with
Nicholas Ferrar, and inserting a long digression on the pious habits
of the Little Gidding community (pp. 309–12).

This does indeed show a regard for narrative consistency
which takes precedence over the vagaries of fact; for instance, there
is no record of Herbert ever having accepted the sinecure once held
by Sidney,[106] and the facts he gives about Ferrar and the Little
Gidding community are vague.[107] But there is one point in the
Life where Walton, startlingly, abandons consistency in order to
attempt to assimilate facts not previously considered.

This happens in his 1675 revision, where Walton describes a
dispute between Herbert and the Scottish nonconformist Andrew
Melville, called by Walton 'Andrew Melvin'. The episode occurs in
the *Life*'s secular half (half, that is, of Walton's account, but taking
up thirty-four of Herbert's thirty-nine years). Walton seems to be
putting it in to display concrete evidence of Herbert's 'great affection to that Church in which he received his *Baptism*' during his
years of relative spiritual barrenness at Cambridge (p. 271).

This is what Walton's 1670 version said. 'Melvin' had written
'malicious bitter Verses' against 'our *Liturgy*, our *Ceremonies*,
and our *Church-Government*' which he had scattered in 1605 at
the Hampton Court Conference (p. 271). Herbert, filled with
ecclesiastical loyalty, had answered these verses 'to the satisfaction of all un-ingaged persons'.[108] Walton goes on to suggest that
Melville was imprisoned in the Tower from 1607 to 1611 for
writing the verses which Herbert had answered.

Melville was not at the Hampton Court Conference of 1604 (not
1605 as Walton gives it), but did scatter verses at Hampton Court
in 1606 when English bishops met Scottish Presbyterians.[109] In
1603–4 Melville had written a different set of satirical verses,
the *Anti-Tami-Cami-Categoria*, which attacked the Universities'

---

[106] See Hutchinson, pp. xxxii.   [107] See Novarr, 352.

[108] Izaak Walton, *Life of Mr. George Herbert* (London, 1670), 24.

[109] Dr Peter McCullough has suggested that Walton may be confusing
Melville's actions of 1606 with those of Patrick Galloway, James I's Scottish
chaplain, in the Conference of 1604.

hostile response to the Millenary petition. Walton mixed up the two sets of verses as well as conflating the two Conferences and splitting the difference as to the date.

Herbert was born in 1593. Even given the speed at which children grew up, and the intensity with which they were educated, he was not likely to be taking on distinguished Scottish theologians before he was 13. The truth of it is that there were two waves of replies to the *Anti-Tami-Cami-Categoria*: one when they first appeared, and another in 1620. Herbert's reply, the *Musae Responsiorae*, was in the second wave.

Walton leaves it where it is (that is, in his 'Herbert at Cambridge' section) for the 1675 revision, adding only the hopeful phrase that the verses 'were therefore brought into *Westminster-School*' (p. 271). He says that Herbert made answer to them 'then, and often after',—a last-ditch attempt to make the incident work in the right bit of chronology while still maintaining Herbert's part in putting Melville in the Tower.[110] The reference to Westminster is bewildering, because it is out of context. Walton has jeopardized the narrative consistency or 'credit' of his text with a gesture towards a historical accuracy prefiguring the ethics of modern biographical practice.

Herbert as Walton's Author

This is not a typical gesture. Walton is firmly concerned to ensure the truth of what he writes, but he locates it in a different place. With *Herbert* (as with *Donne*, but more so) he finds his authoritative sources in his subject's own written words. He paraphrases these words, or quotes them selectively, with and without acknowledgement, all through the *Life*. As I have argued, this involves quarrying biographical details from work not necessarily intended autobiographically. Walton's use of passages from the *Country Parson* to describe Herbert's daily life at Bemerton is a case in point. For instance, in Chapter XIV Herbert writes of parishioners in general that 'they labour profanely, when they set themselves to work like brute beasts, never raising their thoughts to God, nor sanctifying their labour with daily prayer'.[111] Walton turns a criticism of a general parochial failing into a narrative where Herbert's own parishioners do precisely the opposite. He writes:

[110] See Novarr, 345–7.   [111] Hutchinson, 247–8.

'some of the meaner sort of his parish, did so love and reverence
Mr. *Herbert*, that they would let their Plow rest when Mr. *Herbert's
Saints-Bell* rung to prayers, that they might offer their devotions
to God with him' (p. 302).[112] Walton's picture of an essentially
medieval rural piety indicates his debt to a version of history where
the practices and traditions of the pre-Reformation Church are
appropriated and commended to lend the new Protestantism
historical continuity. Herbert's 'Saints-Bell' is the *sanctus* bell, rung
at the consecration of the Host. In England, before the reforms
of the mid-sixteenth century, the *sanctus* bell accompanied the
elevation of the Host in the Eucharist—specifically proscribed by
the 1552 Book of Common Prayer, and vilified by Cranmer (to
name but one) as an act of idolatry.[113] The elevation had indeed
all but vanished: the bell, it seems, retained some customary power.

In this too Walton is arguably following Herbert's lead.
Patrick Collinson identifies the *Country Parson* itself as committed to a form of pastoral ministry he calls 'both pre-protestant
and a-protestant'. He points out, also, that Herbert's stress on
door-to-door visitation and other bits of practical charity was not
confined to 'Anglican' practice but appears in accounts of conformist 'Puritan' ministry. Collinson implies these practices to
be (at their best) a continuation of pre-Reformation patterns,
adapted to contemporary circumstances. Walton may again be
seen here as reflecting in narrative an ideal ministry, the traditional
contours of which were shared, not only by Herbert, but by a
significant body of contemporaries, priest and lay, on both sides
of the Anglican–Puritan divide.[114]

Walton uses Chapter VI of the *Country Parson* with rather
less subtle didactic intentions. He takes a reproof of Herbert's,
directed again in general terms at the behaviour of parishioners,
and transfers its object from the parishioners to the clergy.
Herbert writes that a congregation at prayer should make their
responses, 'not in a hudling, or slubbering fashion, gaping or

---

[112] See Novarr, 339.

[113] See Patrick Collinson, 'Shepherds, Sheepdogs and Hirelings: The Pastoral
Ministry in Post-Reformation England', *Studies in Church History*, 26 (Oxford,
1989), 185–220. Note especially pp. 196–8 and 211–16. See also Heal, *Hospitality*, 291–2, where Herbert's pastoral principles (may) find a practitioner in William
Bedell.

[114] See Gregory Dix, *The Shape of the Liturgy* (London, 1945), 620 n.

scratching the head, or spitting even in the midst of their answer, but gently and pausably, thinking what they say'.[115] The specificity of these criticisms argues that Bemerton was not always the ideal community. Consequently, Walton makes it a more general criticism, not so much of the indifferent lay people as of the (liturgically) indifferent minister. He writes: 'if he were at any time too zealous in his Sermons, it was in reproving the indecencies of the peoples behaviour, in the time of Divine Service; and of those Ministers that hudled up the Church-prayers, without a visible reverence and affection' (p. 301). Walton is not necessarily making a strongly partisan statement here. Conformists of both kinds could identify a set form of prayer as a focus for corporate worship, in which case the thoughtful delivery of such prayers must operate as a visible sign of piety in the minister, and as an example to the congregation for equally devout corporate response. As a point about godly behaviour, it could span a number of differing views about individual points of ceremony, and could expect to receive a generally approving response in all but extremist puritan circles. When Walton makes the point again in his 1680 pamphlet *Love and Truth*, using virtually the same words, he actually presents it as a point of accord with his nonconformist addressee. 'And I wish as heartily as you', he writes to his 'busie and factious' shopkeeping addressees, 'that they [ministers] would not only read, but pray, the Common Prayer; and, not huddle it up so fast, (as too many do) by getting into a middle of the second Collect, before a devout hearer can say Amen to the first.'[116]

Herbert's poems are used to inform an interpretation of the more private events of his life. This is hardly surprising, given the contemplative nature of many of them. Yet Walton's selection of quotations and the wording of his paraphrases are both very careful, for he is anxious to avoid any serious suggestion of internal theological or moral conflict. The poems appear at moments of spiritual crisis, but Herbert's victory over temptation is never in doubt. 'Affliction (IV)', which is paraphrased into Herbert's reported speech, and 'Affliction (I)', which is selectively quoted

[115] Hutchinson, 231.

[116] *Love and Truth: in Two Modest and Peaceable Letters. Concerning the Distempers of the Present Times. Written from a Quiet and Conformable Citizen of London, to Two Busie and Factious Shop-keepers in Coventry* (London, 1680), 2.

(pp. 275–6), are used to demonstrate Herbert's dissatisfaction with his life in Cambridge.[117] At Herbert's induction into Bemerton, 'Content', 'The Odour', and 'The Pearl' all appear in paraphrase as Herbert's reported speech, 'The Pearl' and 'The Odour' cited, and 'The Pearl' quoted (pp. 289–91).[118] Shortly before Herbert dies he makes a speech which owes a good deal to 'The Quip' (p. 316).[119] And, as I have said, he quotes some lines from 'The Thanksgiving' and sings a stanza of 'Sunday' (p. 317).[120] While Walton does not give the titles of either of these last two, he does ensure that Herbert sings the stanza of 'Sunday' on 'the *Sunday* before his death' (p. 316).

I want to discuss the group of derivations which cover Herbert's induction into Bemerton, since every way that Walton uses the poems is represented here. I am assuming throughout that Walton regards Herbert's poems as autobiographical, and my analysis of Herbert's text is slanted accordingly.

This is Walton's paraphrase of the copious list of worldly temptations in 'The Pearl'. Herbert is reported to say: '*I can now behold the Court with an impartial Eye, and see plainly, that it is made up of* Fraud, *and* Titles, *and* Flattery, *and many other such empty, imaginary, painted Pleasures: Pleasures, that are so empty, as not to satisfy when they are enjoy'd*' (p. 289). Compare this with the third stanza of 'The Pearl' itself:

> I know the wayes of Pleasure, the sweet strains,
> The lullings and the relishes of it;
> The propositions of hot bloud and brains;
> What mirth and musick mean; what love and wit
> Have done these twentie hundred yeares, and more:
> I know the projects of unbridled store:
> My stuff is flesh, not brasse; my senses live,
> And grumble oft, that they have more in me
> Then he that curbs them, being but one to five:
>   Yet I love thee.

Walton presents his list of temptations partly to remind us of Herbert's social position, something Herbert himself does not need

---

[117] Hutchinson, 90 and 46–8, and see Novarr, 333.
[118] Hutchinson, 68–9, 174–5, and 88–9, and see Novarr, 334–5.
[119] Hutchinson, 110–11, and see Novarr, 335.
[120] Hutchinson, 36 and 76.

to stress. Having made his point, Walton is then forced to invert the scale of what constitutes worth (God's aristocracy being the only real one) and is also careful strenuously to exclude all the vividness in the poem's descriptions. So 'hot bloud' becomes merely 'painted', and emptiness is twice made pleasure's overriding quality, in striking contrast to Herbert's 'projects of unbridled store'.

Both writers, although their lists are copious, decline to offer very specific description of the characteristics of each item. Instead, their terms are spacious ones—wit, mirth, 'aspiring thoughts'—but their spaciousness is used to very different ends. In Herbert's case it is the sheer weight of possibility which prevents him from enlarging upon what precisely 'mirth and musick mean'. The intention is to present the difficulty the narrator finds in making his final choice. In the lines 'I . . . fully understand | Both the main sale, and the commodities', Herbert's claim is startling because of, rather than in spite of, the plenitude of the pleasures of the world.

Walton, on the other hand, excludes specificity as part of a simple policy of reduction. He lists the possibilities simply in order to make sure that no worldly value escapes the effect of this policy. For practical reasons—a concern to present an imitable Herbert—Walton has to make his choice appear easy. Consequently, when he has Herbert say 'I can now behold the Court with an impartial Eye', the word 'impartial' means, quite literally, one that is not partial, if not positively hostile. Yet the word's more usual meaning suggests to the reader a more balanced view, and the particular quality of this 'impartiality' is only made clear on examining the terms with which these court-pleasures are described. 'Fraud' and 'Flattery' are exclusively pejorative; 'Titles' becomes so in its juxtaposition with the other two words. The 'fulness of all *joy* and pleasure' to which Walton alludes after the passage I have quoted, is only in God's gift. At this point, at least, Herbert's image of 'thy silk-twist let down from heav'n to me' vanishes behind this unspecific and all-pervading abundance.

When, a short while later, Walton cites 'The Pearl' he wants it to demonstrate Herbert's 'unforc'd choice to serve at Gods Altar' (p. 290). In one sense, of course, it is appropriate enough, since in the words 'I fully understand' and in the assertion 'Yet I love thee' Herbert demonstrates the essential freedom of his narrator's choice. However, in the language of the poem—and particularly lines 7 to 9 of the third stanza—there is a sense that there is (in the words of Ferrar's Preface) 'inward enforcements' to his choice,[121] because of the ease and longing of the description of what he rejects, and because of the vivid logic of the fleshly voice:

> My stuff is flesh, not brasse; my senses live,
> And grumble oft, that they have more in me
> Than he that curbs them, being but one to five.

But Walton's paraphrase of the poem reduces all fleshly longing until it vanishes entirely into the phrase 'He knew . . . upon what terms he declined all these [pleasures] for the service of his Master JESUS' (p. 290). He then quotes the poem's last four lines, offering his readers the benefit of the resolution without the trouble of the conflict.

By this time the context has rendered Herbert's image of the 'silk twist' very little more exotic than the commonplace of the 'narrow way'. Although it is still possible to grasp the ambiguity of the word 'twist' for thread, since it is still juxtaposed with 'labyrinths', the voluptuous nature of the 'silk' is minimized out of context. Instead, Walton offers us a small, subtle paradox of his own; for, following the quotation with a description of Herbert's actions on the day after his induction, he includes the detail that he changed his 'silk Cloaths into a Canonical Coat' (p. 291).

Both 'Content' and 'The Odour' are used rather less in the same passage. 'Content' is used least. Its first phrase, 'Peace mutt'ring thoughts', is recalled in the first words of the Waltonian Herbert's speech: 'I now look back on my aspiring thoughts' (p. 289). Again, the tone of Herbert's poem is such that it is as if the resolution of its final cadence is only in response to its formal requirements:

> He that by seeking hath himself once found
> Hath ever found a happie fortune.

The predominant tone is rather injunction, or request—'Peace mutt'ring thoughts', 'Gad not abroad', 'Give me the pliant minde',

[121] Hutchinson, 3.

'cease discoursing soul'—and the effect of the repetition is, as so often in Herbert's poetry, to suggest a desperate and unsatisfied demand. Walton again takes the final cadence as his point of reflection: 'I . . . think my self more happy than if I had attain'd what I so ambitiously thirsted for' (p. 289). The poem's title, then certainly describes the Waltonian Herbert's state of mind, but a critique operates upon Walton's interpretation by the poem itself.

'The Odour' is both cited and selectively paraphrased by Walton, but phrases from it are put into Herbert's mouth since this enables Walton to use the poem's existence to verify the sincerity of Herbert's speech. By extension, the sincerity of Herbert himself is established at the same time. For instance, he is reported as saying '*I will* . . . *alwaies call* [Christ] . . . Jesus my Master'. Walton adds 'And that he did so, may appear in many parts of his Book of *Sacred Poems*; especially, in that which he calls *the Odour*'. It is an effective circularity which, although at first sight it seems hardly fair, nevertheless operates, in Walton's terms, as a more or less responsible citation of an irreproachable source.

It may be seen from this analysis that Walton consistently uses those parts of Herbert's poems which present their narrator as tranquil in his certainty of God's love. Although this involves a strenuous exclusion of any serious spiritual conflict, it should be said that Walton does acknowledge that Herbert felt such a conflict, for he writes that when Herbert considered the question of his vocation, 'in which time he had some resolutions to decline . . . the Priesthood . . . He endur'd (as he would often say) such spiritual Conflicts, as none can think, but only those that have endur'd them' (p. 287).

I suggest that this statement is a cautious allusion to those aspects of the poems which Walton excludes from the *Life* rather than being a report of a piece of hearsay from an informant, for this would be entirely consistent with his practice. It also seems reasonable to conjecture that Walton, being himself evidently not subject to a Herbertian doubt, had chosen to offer a portrait of Herbert which, like his portrait of Donne, concentrated on those aspects of his character which Walton felt himself best qualified to present. It is notable that Walton's Herbert is practically passionless, and calm under almost all circumstances—though he does show signs of agitation on his deathbed when the weeping of his nieces disturbs his concentration. Yet Herbert's brother,

Edward, Lord Herbert of Cherbury, describes him in his *Autobiography* as 'not exempt from passion and choler'.[122] There is no reason for Walton to have known Herbert had a short temper; he certainly could not have read it in the *Autobiography*, which did not appear in print until the following century. He was working on a combination of likelihood and didactic usefulness.

   Viewed in this light, Walton's remark about Herbert's 'spiritual Conflicts' reads like an admission of the limitations of Walton's perception. Just as he would not narrate the life of a man with whom he had no personal connection, so he also would not attempt to narrate experience which he could not understand. His concern was with the outcome of Herbert's inward struggles, which outcome he evidently (and defensibly, given his aim) felt far exceeded in importance the details of the struggles themselves. The *Life of Herbert*, therefore, like the *Life of Donne*, should perhaps be seen as a partial picture of its subject, a portrait of those aspects of Herbert which Walton felt would best edify his readers and which he was most fitted to present. Upon these terms Walton's somewhat reductive use of Herbert's poetry appears far more defensible.

---

[122] Edward, Lord Herbert of Cherbury, *Autobiography*, ed. Sidney Lee (London, 1888), 11.

5

Walton's *Lives* of Hooker and Sanderson

The *Lives* of Hooker and Sanderson could be called Walton's Restoration biographies. By this I mean that, in rather different ways, they both struggle to make sense of the Civil War, and the events which led up to it, from a perspective which locates a happy outcome to a sad history in the restored Church and monarchy of 1660. The *Life of Herbert*, published between *Hooker* (1665) and *Sanderson* (1678) in 1670, is a different case: its political lesson to the restored Church is primarily about the fundamental nobility of the priesthood, not directly about the war or its causes. It notably lacks foreboding or anticipation. In some ways, indeed, it has little historical particularity, because it is really a legend of pre-Reformation devotional pastoral.[1] But *Hooker* and *Sanderson*, in different ways, ponder a divided nation through narratives which present the events of 1660 as the perfect (if not the final) resolution of that discord. In *Hooker* the late-sixteenth-century dissensions Walton describes are the terrifying seeds of a war that will happen halfway through the next century. In *Sanderson*, the war itself, a cacophony to be harmonized in 1660, is a warning figure of the approaching Exclusion Crisis. We suffer the internal dissensions with which each biography makes its events, in order to celebrate the (brief) historical moment of 'Jerusalem . . .

---

[1] For how far that legend may have been performed as much as imagined, see Patrick Collinson, 'Shepherds, Sheepdogs and Hirelings: The Pastoral Ministry in Post-Reformation England', *Studies in Church History*, 26 (Oxford, 1989), 185–220.

at unity with it self', as Walton's Hooker puts it.[2] And whereas Hooker's words appear in a context where they deplore the disunity of the 1590s, this Hooker himself, carefully compared with St John the Baptist at significant points in the narrative, also cries a future where unity will come to pass.[3] He is a prophet.

What both biographies also have in common is that they are commissioned, and so respond to an external interpretation of contemporary politics, imposed on Walton from above. Gilbert Sheldon, then archbishop of Canterbury, with George Morley, the bishop of Winchester, are likely to have approached Walton about the Hooker biography; and Morley may also have been the commissioner for *Sanderson*. This chapter looks at what Walton did to reconcile the requirements of his commissioners with his own perspectives, both political and literary.

THE *LIFE OF MR. RICHARD HOOKER*

Hooker as Restoration Text

Like the *Life of Donne*, the *Life of Hooker* was primarily intended as a preface to its subject's works, although it first appeared separately in 1665. There resemblance between the two ends. The edition of Donne's *Sermons* for which his *Life* was written was simply a posthumous publication of material never published before. There were no specifically political reasons either for the book's appearance, or for the choice of Walton as Donne's life-writer. The *Life of Hooker* was a different matter.

To understand why, we need first to look at the reasons for its commission, and the circumstances for which it appeared. Walton's *Life of Hooker* prefaced the second of two editions of Hooker's *Works* appearing in the decade after the Restoration. The first edition appeared in 1661/2, and made a good deal of its claim to have printed, for the first time, a version of all eight books of

---

[2] See Walton, *Lives*, 207; adapted from Psalm 122: 3 (AV), 'Jerusalem is builded as a city that is compact together'. Walton recalls the Book of Common Prayer wording: 'Jerusalem is built as a city: that is at unity in itself.' The 'with' that Walton substitutes for 'in' implies a concord between differentiated parts; 'in itself' suggests an organic whole characterized by the 'unity' it modifies.

[3] See *Lives*, 166 and 216.

the Lawes of Ecclesiastical Polity. It was edited by the new bishop of Exeter, John Gauden, a moderate with reservations about ceremonial who supported episcopacy at the Restoration. Gauden also wrote the long (and long-winded) *Life* of Hooker which went with it.[4] The second edition appeared in 1666 (Walton's biography appeared separately, as a kind of flyer for it, in 1665). Gauden was still named as editor but Walton's *Life* had replaced his, and Walton had written a little note before it saying that Gauden had made a few unavoidable mistakes which he, Walton, had had the respectful temerity to correct. The main text of Walton's *Life* was also propped at both ends by different kinds of letters and testimonies signed by a selection of reasonably senior clergymen, all apparently devoted to asserting that Hooker's text following was regrettably corrupt and unreliable, and that whole chunks of the later books probably hadn't been written by Hooker at all.

Why were there two editions of Hooker, both emphasizing the *Polity* and the prefatory biography, so hard on the heels of the Restoration? And why did Walton's biography replace Gauden's in 1666, in an edition which went to such lengths to cast doubt on the very text the first edition had made so much of publishing —the full text of the *Polity*, including the last three books? The strongly biographical emphasis of these two Restoration editions is important to these questions. The biographical form (especially in so far as it is explicitly exemplary) is suited to replacing argument with narrative; and while the arguments of Hooker's text could be (and were) problematic in ways I will discuss shortly, his symbolic presence in 1660 might be most useful. A textual body for that presence was certainly necessary, and this could be supplied by a match of the new texts of Books VI–VIII with a prefatory narrative which, as it told its author, also instructed the reader of Hooker's words as to how they should, and how they should not, be read. The reason why this happened twice, with different prefatory narratives for the two editions, was arguably because Gauden, the author of the first biography, instructed his reader to a version of Hooker which was at odds with the intentions of

[4] John Gauden, *Richard Hooker . . . An Account of his Holy Life and Happy Death*, in *The Works of Richard Hooker* (London, 1662). There are two dates given in the volume; the frontispiece is dated 1661 and the title-page 1662. Gauden's Epistle to Charles II is dated 'Jan. 1. 1661' (i.e. new style 1662). The two dates suggest a printing delay, which is discussed below, pp. 238–9.

the edition's patron Gilbert Sheldon (at that point still bishop of London)—or at least of his intentions by 1662. Sheldon, since elevated to Canterbury, along with Winchester's Morley, brought in Walton to make good the damage.

This reasoning assumes that what 'Hooker' symbolized (quite apart from what he actually *argued*) was both powerful and more than usually politically fluid. For why this might have been so, it is perhaps worth considering the claims of the opening words of the Polity's famous Preface:

> Though for no other cause, yet for this, That Posterity may know we have not loosly through silence, permitted things to pass away as in a Dream, there shall be for Mens information extant thus much concerning the present state of the Church of God, established among us, and their careful endeavour which would have upheld the same.

Hooker's passage defines experience as ephemeral until it is uttered. To write down circumstances, on the other hand, is to simulate eternity. This is all in a framework where Hooker's tenses seem to express a doubt about the continuance of the Church of England: 'their careful endeavour which would have upheld the same'. Hooker is, therefore, making a promise of a kind of permanence, a fixity, located quite explicitly in a textual form which seems at first sight to promise the coherence of narration, rather than the discursive speculations that belong to argument.

But Hooker was not, himself, writing narrative. Broadly, he was discussing, in a very particular polemical context, what kinds of criteria could legitimately be used to establish the limits of conformity in the *adiaphora*[5] of religious practice within the Church of England. This he was doing in the very different context of the polemical engagement between conformists and Presbyterians at the end of the sixteenth century. This is not to say that Hooker necessarily conceived his exposition of church discipline as defined by its inevitable participation in dispute—on the contrary, part of his claim to authority was vested in an assertion that he sought a stable consensus between the parties. But he implies that he is more likely to define than discuss, and his reference to

---

[5] Or 'things indifferent'. The term was used to refer to those matters of church-government about which there was no explicit scriptural command and therefore human judgement had to be used. Whether e.g. episcopal government actually came into this category was, of course, a fundamental point of contention.

posterity offers to take his definitions beyond contemporary needs and make them durable and universal. Authoritative and universal definition: firm, narrow, and unambiguous, and (best of all perhaps) not very recent, might look very attractive to a restored episcopate (so long as it upheld the power of episcopacy and the sacred nature of monarchy). All that remained was to assert that Hooker did indeed do this.

We know that the authoritative promises of Hooker's Preface were appropriated at the Restoration on these terms, because they were borrowed and tacked on to the front of a number of monarchist texts which are, as Hooker's treatise is not, historical narratives. Most famously, of course, there is Clarendon's *History of the Rebellion*, which imitates Hooker's Preface in its own first lines; but there are also certainly two episcopal biographies (published in 1660 and 1663 respectively) which quote it, in an adapted and unattributed form, as part of a justification for their own acts of narrative record in support of the restored episcopate. The first of these is the opening to Joseph Naylor's 1660 narrative of the life of Thomas Morton, bishop of Durham, already quoted on pp. 81–2; the second, the anonymous life of Robert Sanderson called *Reason and Judgment* of 1663, which makes exactly the same manoeuvre as Naylor:

> . . . I cannot take his portraicture, nor recount his memorials so exactly as I could wish, and you may expect: yet for no other cause then for this, 'That Posterity may know we have not loosely through silence permitted things and persons to pass away as in a dream'; there shall be thus much extant concerning this excellent person, for his own honour, and the honour of the Church he was bred in, That he was a Bishop, and a man of most sound Judgement, of most deep Learning, of a vast Apprehension, of an holy and unspotted Life, of an unsuspected Integrity, a great Friend, a faithful Servant, a valiant Champion of the Church.[6]

Hooker's promise of permanence is recognized and adapted from 'things' to 'persons' in these passages by Naylor and the anonymous author of *Reason and Judgment*. Since the words themselves are memorable and authoritative, the process is mimetic: not

---

[6] See B[addeley]/N[aylor], *Life of Dr. Thomas Morton*, 113–15; *Reason and Judgment* ([Oxford/London], 1663), 4; above, pp. 81–2.

merely the promise, but its expression, guarantees its powerful survival into the future. In adapting Hooker's words, Naylor *et al.* were borrowing authority from a text already acknowledged to possess it. Hooker, in the process, became of course by implication a powerful spokesman for the monarchist view; but it is notable that the appropriation process should have relied, in every case, on the shift of emphasis from things (or argument) to persons (or narrative) for its force. (It is worth noticing, too, how Sanderson is made to bear Hooker's distinctive title of 'the Church's Champion'.) In the two Restoration editions of Hooker's *Works* between 1660 and 1666, the only difference made was in the substitution of Walton's biography for Gauden's. No attempt was made to suppress the text.

What, then, were the messages which surrounded the biographies of Hooker contained in the two editions? The title-page and frontispiece to the editions of 1662, 1666, 1676, and 1684 (reproduced, Figs. 5.1, 5.2), tell us how the *Polity* was intended to be read. Word, Church, and King (a figure not unlike James I) equally receive the divine illumination; and Charles II is named as the edition's dedicatee on the title-page, in a sentence which tells the reader how useful his late royal father had found Hooker for settling the 'Publick Peace of this Church and Kingdom'. In some circles this would not have been a recommendation. John Gauden's prefatory 'Epistle to the King' also describes the *Polity* in clear and prescriptive terms which match the messages of frontispiece and title-page, and which were not erased in the later editions as his more ambivalently targeted *Life* of Hooker would be:

this noble *work, and* durable *defence* . . . is indeed at once (as the Tongues of Eloquent Princes are to themselves, and their Subjects) both a Treasury & an Armory, to inrich the friends, and defend against the Enemies of the Church of England: A rare composition of unpassionate Reason, and unpartial Religion; the mature product of a judicious Scholar, a loyal Subject, an humble Preacher, and a most eloquent Writer: The very abstract and quintessence of Laws Humane and Divine; a summary of the grounds, rules and proportions of true Polity in Church and State: upon which clear, solid, and safe foundations, the good Order, Peace, and Government of this Church was anciently settled, and on which, while it stands firm, it will be flourishing. All other popular and specious pretensions being found by late sad experiences, to be, as novel and unfit, so factious and fallacious, yea, dangerous and destructive to the peace

THE WORKS
OF
Mr. Richard Hooker,
(That Learned, Godly, Judicious, and Eloquent Divine)
Vindicating the
CHURCH of ENGLAND,
As truly Christian, and duly Reformed:
In Eight Books of
ECCLESIASTICAL POLITY.
Now compleated,
As with the *Sixth* and *Eighth,* so with the *SEVENTH,*
(touching *Episcopacy,* as the Primitive, Catholick and Apostolick
Government of the Church) out of his own Manuscripts, never
before Published.

With an account of his *Holy Life,* and *Happy Death,*
Written by Dr. *John Gauden,* now Bishop of Exeter.

The entire *Edition* Dedicated to the Kings Most
Excellent Majestie,
CHARLS the II.

By whose ROYAL FATHER (near His Martyrdom) the former Five Books (then onely extant) were
commended to his dear Children, as an excellent means
to satisfie Private Scruples, and settle the Publique
Peace of this Church and Kingdom.

James 3. 17. *The wisdom from above, is first pure, then peaceable, gentle, easie to be intreated, full of mercy and good works, without partiality and hypocrisie.* Plut.

Multi tales investigabiles veritatis ad proximos divertunt errores. Min. Fel.

London, Printed by *J. Best,* for *Andrew Crook,* at the *Green Dragon* in *S. Pauls* Church-yard. 1662.

THE
WORKS
Of that Learned and Judicious Divine,
Mr. Richard Hooker,
IN
EIGHT BOOKS
OF
Ecclesiastical Polity,
Compleated out of his own Manuscripts;

With several other Treatises by the same Author, and
an Account of his LIFE and DEATH.

Dedicated to the Kings most Excellent Majesty,
CHARLES II.

By whose ROYAL FATHER (near His
Martyrdom) the former Five Books (then only extant) were commended to his Dear Children, as an excellent means to satisfie Private Scruples,
and settle the Publick Peace of this CHURCH and KINGDOM.

JAMES 3. 17. *The wisdom from above, is first pure, then peaceable, gentle, easie to be intreated, full of mercy and good works, without partiality and hypocrisie.* Plin.

Multi tales investigabiles veritati ad proximos divertunt errores. Min. Fel.

LONDON,
Printed by R. *White,* for Rob. *Son,* Tho. *Basset,* John *Wright* and Rich. *Chiswel,*
and are to be sold by Robert *Boulter* at the *Turks Head* in *Cornhil.* 1 6 7 6.

FIG 5.1. Title-pages of Hooker, *Works* (1662 and 1676)

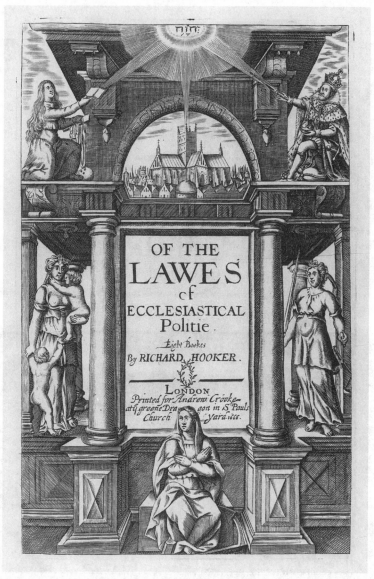

FIG 5.2. Engraved title-page of Hooker, *Works* (1666)

and prosperity of this Church and Kingdom, whose inseparable happiness and Interests are bound up in Monarchy and Episcopacy.[7]

'Anciently settled', the phrase used here for the Hookerian foundations of Church policy, claims, of course, 'primitive' authority for a comparatively recent work discussing the polity of a scarcely less recent establishment. More subtle is the way Hooker's tongue, via a deft simile, ventriloquizes an 'Eloquent Prince' who nourishes and defends his grateful subjects. Notable too is the absence of any suggestion of discursive material in the words 'abstract', 'summary', 'grounds, rules, and proportions' as they are applied to Hooker's text. Hooker's own preaching is carefully described as 'humble' and his reasoning as 'unpassionate'. He writes a 'defence'; he does not engage in dispute. All this tells us a good deal about the political location of confident, lengthy, and enthusiastic argument.

On the other hand, we are given some clues as to the limits of Gauden's tolerance for the ceremonialist view. His disapproval of 'Club-masters *and* Tub-ministers' is confined to those who '*sought not fairly to obtain Reformation of what might seem amiss, but violently and wholly to overthrow the ancient and* goodly Fabrick *of this* Church and Kingdom' (sig. A3ʳ). He also had visible hopes that what he called '*The still* crazy Church *of* England' might rise from her ashes minus extraneous plumage, pleading that '*sober severity*' might characterize her ceremonies and be not '*shaken or sacrificed to any private varieties and extravagancies*' (sig. A3ᵛ). His agenda is observably one which sought to influence policy through a concessionary rhetoric intended for the ascendant party which he mixed, not always happily, with imperfectly camouflaged caveats.

Hooker's Text

The text Gauden had chosen to preface in this way was not just a revival of one which had had a different relevance in the 1590s, now altered by the events of 1642–59. Bits of it had actually never been seen before at all. It was, partly, a new text.

Books I–IV had first appeared in 1593, and Book V in 1597. David Novarr[8] argues that Edwin Sandys financed the printing

<hr>

[7] Hooker, *Works* (London, 1662), sigs. A3ʳ⁻ᵛ.   [8] Novarr, p. 208.

of Books I–V, and did so in the first place in order that he might use Hooker's arguments in defence of a Bill he presented to Parliament in March 1593 which advocated the enforcement of conformity over dissenters as well as Roman Catholics.[9] Though Edwin Sandys may not, in fact, have been the presenter of the Bill, he certainly financed the *Polity* when Hooker was having difficulty finding a publisher who would take it on. There was little demand for books on church discipline (particularly on the bishops' side of the debate), and it may be that Edwin Sandys saw an opportunity to present, and perhaps to influence, a summary of the case for a conformist polity by financing it.[10] We only have Walton's word for it that Whitgift supported Hooker in writing the *Polity* (which would argue Hooker to be spokesman for Whitgift's politics), and Hooker's academic method is more discursive than this implies at least as far as the book's inception is concerned. But if he was taken up by a conformist sponsor midway through the *Polity*, this might explain the difficulties he had in completing the projected eight books.

For Books VI–VIII had a more vexed history; and, not coincidentally, they deal with politically vexed issues. Book VI, which discusses the limits of lay powers in ecclesiastical jurisdiction, also contained a tract on private confession. Book VII (not published until 1662) talks about the origins and limits of episcopal power, defending episcopacy on grounds of history and custom rather than apostolic succession, about which Hooker has doubts. Book VIII sets the cat firmly among the pigeons in a discussion of the civil prince's ecclesiastical jurisdiction, the terms of which were almost more congenial to the Presbyterian than the conformist.

---

[9] See J. E. Neale, *Elizabeth I and her Parliaments 1584–1601* (London, 1958), 280–97, esp. 284. It has since been argued that the bill was presented not by Edwin but by his uncle Miles Sandys, on the grounds that Miles was a much more experienced and senior Parliamentarian. See P. Collinson, 'Hooker and the Elizabethan Establishment', in A. S. McGrade (ed.), *Richard Hooker and the Construction of Christian Community* (Tempe, Ariz., 1997), 149–181, esp. 162–3; W. B. Richardson, 'The Religious Policy of the Cecils', unpublished D.Phil. dissertation, Oxford (1994), 88–111.

[10] See W. Speed Hill, 'The Evolution of Hooker's *Laws of Ecclesiastical Polity*', in *Studies in Richard Hooker* . . . (Cleveland and London, 1972), 117–58, esp. 117–34, for a useful discussion of the arguments for and against Hooker as official and commissioned spokesman for conformism. See also Walton, *Lives*, 208–13.

They certainly are not a straightforward defence of *iure divino*. All are incomplete.[11]

A brief look at the arguments Hooker uses on this most vexed issue can give us some sense of the (politically rather than academically) problematic nature of his method. Peter Lake has defined this method to have been 'an attempt to explicate a set of common assumptions' and from them to draw logical inferences on the debated issues of *adiaphora* which would therefore also command a common assent. Hooker is deemed to have sought this rationally based assent not only from his opponents, but also from those within his own broadly conformist party who were currently at variance.[12] This meant that he used conformist arguments selectively, not automatically; and the logical tools which he deployed were more likely to be deliberative than forensic. While his intentions, according to Lake's formulation, can be interpreted as not willingly divisive, neither were they automatically irenic.

His argument in Book VIII demonstrates what this could mean. Hooker's conception of Church membership within a fully Christian State embraced every subject of that State regardless of their privately held religious opinions. In this sense Church and State were essentially synonymous. Thus, the supreme ruler of the Christian State must logically also be supreme ruler of the Church. However, this also meant that the Church's supreme head, as representative of the social whole, attained power through media which Hooker was happier to analyse in terms of historical precedent, rather than purely through scripturally based arguments. In other words, while Hooker would concede that the kings of the Old Testament might have received their authority directly from God, he would not conclude from this that any English monarch was necessarily thus divinely appointed. Such an argument he would have considered a violation of historical context. Instead, he argued that the status and authority of the king were both granted and limited by the consent of his subjects in the persons of their parliamentary representatives.

[11] See previous note. Speed Hill argues that Hooker completed all eight books independently, and then, upon the financial interest shown by Sandys, felt he must revise the last ones to coincide more neatly with his conformist sponsors, and that he died before finishing the revisions.

[12] Peter Lake, *Anglicans and Puritans? Presbyterianism and English Conformist Thought from Whitgift to Hooker* (London, 1988), 146.

He therefore perceives monarch and subjects each to have duties towards the other which operate in something not unlike a kind of social contract, though one with very stringent limits. Once a people had consented to the monarch's rule (and consent, for Hooker, includes the 'consent' of conquest) they did not (he implied) have rights of rebellion. On the other hand, this meant that the monarch's powers were seen as granted by the consent of the whole human body of a commonwealth (and thus, in a State religion, a Church) and not simply by divine edict.[13] This Lake calls seeking 'to rescue the puritans' political attitudes from the bad name that their religious errors were acquiring for them'.[14]

When Dr John Spenser, a trustee under Hooker's Will and possessor of the draft manuscripts of these last books, wrote the Epistle to the Reader prefixed to the 1604 edition of Books I–V, he affirmed that 'some evill disposed mindes', perhaps in 'wicked blind Zeale', had 'mangled' Hooker's work in these last books. Giving evidence in Chancery about the manuscripts in 1613, he refused to explain why he had judged them 'not fitt for the presse' after having apparently intended to print them.[15] In the event, Book VI (of which some is certainly lost) and an incomplete version of Book VIII did not appear in print until 1648.[16] It may be that Archbishop Ussher was behind their printing at this time, hoping perhaps that the king might take a more moderate view of his powers from it, while the people accepted that they must maintain their allegiance to the king. If so, neither side took the point.

Book VII had not appeared in print before 1662, and there is circumstantial evidence that it came to be included after the rest of the text. It is, for instance, paginated separately, and the two different dates on title-page and frontispiece suggest a printing

[13] See Lake, *Anglicans and Puritans?*, 208–12. For the theological and ecclesiological grounding of Hooker's position (not dealt with above), see W. J. Torrance Kirby, *Richard Hooker's Doctrine of the Royal Supremacy* (Leiden, 1990).

[14] See Lake, *Anglicans and Puritans?*, 199–212.

[15] See Novarr, 208–10. P. G. Stanwood's textual introduction to the third volume of the Folger edition of Books VI, VII, and VIII, considering this question, concludes that a fair copy of Book VI may well have been lost (hence the rumours about lost fair copies of the other books), but that Books VII and VIII had never been finished.

[16] *Of the Lawes of Ecclesiasticall Politie; the Sixth and Eighth Books. A Work Long Expected, and now Published According to the most Authentique Copies* (London, 1648).

delay. Gauden's preface is dated 'January 1st, 1661' (old style). One theory is that Gilbert Sheldon (whom Gauden names as instrumental in getting fair copies of the last books to him for publication) gave Gauden the manuscript of Book VII.[17] What Sheldon may have thought he was giving, and what Gauden certainly said he was getting, is described on the 1661 title-page as a book 'touching Episcopacy, as the Primitive, Catholick and Apostolick Government of the Church'. This description somewhat resembles Gauden's summary of Book VIII as asserting the 'Supremacy of Soveraign Princes': without being untrue, it is (in a favourite contemporary formulation) 'partial'.

The arguments of Books VII and VIII would have made a particular political sense in the 1590s (had they not been censored by Spenser), and yet another for the critical year 1648. For 1662 these former meanings were the palimpsest upon which new interpretations of episcopal and royal power (and, crucially, their relations to each other) were written, erased, and rewritten as different interested parties fought over the parchment. Politically, the state of affairs was extremely fluid, at least to begin with. While it was clear that the Church of England was certainly to be re-established in some form, there were for a while definite signs, in the king's own conciliatory attitude and in the initially hopeful negotiations between moderate churchmen and Presbyterian representatives, that an uncompromisingly Laudian version of church discipline was unlikely to be reinstated. Sees were in 1660 offered to prominent Presbyterians, notably Richard Baxter (to Hereford), Edmund Calamy (to Lichfield), and Edward Reynolds (to Norwich), though only Reynolds in the end accepted. The unpopular Laudians Matthew Wren (then bishop of Ely) and Peter Heylyn were conspicuous by their absence from the lists for episcopal promotion; Gauden, a moderate, was appointed to Exeter by the express wish of the king, though possibly against the advice of Sheldon.[18] The general signs were that some form of reduced episcopacy seemed to be gaining ground through 1660, although

[17] See Novarr, 218–22. Another theory—that Gauden had 'completed' Book VII himself, is thrown out by P. G. Stanwood (see n. 15 above) on the reasonable grounds that his *Life of Hooker* was so turgid it was inconceivable he could have managed a believable imitation of Hooker's style.

[18] See Ian Green, *The Re-Establishment of the Church of England* (Oxford, 1978), 83–98.

unpopular with a large (but not overwhelmingly large) body of clergy sequestered at the Interregnum.

Prominent in the negotiations between moderate Presbyterians and churchmen in that year were Gauden and George Morley (later Walton's commissioner), each of whom was to become a bishop (Gauden of Exeter and Morley of Worcester) by the end of 1660. Both appointments may be seen as attempts to comprehend the moderates; Sanderson's was another appointment (to Lincoln) with arguably the same aim.[19] But Morley, although known to have Calvinist leanings earlier in his career, had also a regard for ceremony which proved a real sticking-point in the negotiations with Baxter *et al.* in 1660.[20] Walton was Morley's steward after he was elevated to the See of Winchester in 1662, and may have been encouraged by him to write the *Life* of Sanderson—another ceremonialist Calvinist. (Walton's own theology shows no Calvinistic trace; and the Calvinism of the ceremonialist Sanderson he was to narrate in 1678 is muffled.)

Viewed in this context, Gauden's publication, in the early years of the Restoration, of these disputed books of Hooker's is explicable. It may have seemed to him possible publicly to espouse a limited form of episcopacy without endangering his position within the establishment. By using Hooker as spokesman, Gauden would have hoped to assure churchmen that limited episcopacy had a rational and respectable conformist precedent, at the same time as indicating to Presbyterians that their views could be comprehended by the newly established Church. This was even though Spenser had made it clear that there had been a deliberate suppression of Books VI–VIII, and even though Ussher (whose view of a limited episcopacy was being put forward by moderates as a possible model for the new Church in 1660–1) had not himself been prepared to print Book VII in 1648, evidently because in it Hooker had sat on the fence concerning the apostolic grounds for episcopal authority.

There is some evidence that Sheldon's position was itself more moderate in 1660 than it was to become by 1662.[21] If so, that would

---

[19] See John Spurr, *The Restoration Church of England, 1646–1689* (New Haven, 1991), 30–5.

[20] Novarr, 449–51; Green, *Re-establishment*, 8–9.

[21] Green, *Re-establishment*, 21–3.

certainly explain why he might have chosen to hand this particular manuscript to Gauden at this point. Gauden was in this, and
in his moderation, a king's man (he probably wrote the *Eikon
Basilike*); his intention in publishing a complete *Polity* with royalist trappings one of conciliation, or at any rate of compromise.

If Sheldon had ever been tempted by moderation, his alteration
of mind by the time the 1661 *Polity* came out was bad news for
Gauden. The 1662 Act of Uniformity (which Sheldon supported
against the king) saw the establishment of church discipline
on lines which ensured that the moderate Presbyterian interest
could not be accommodated within the establishment. This meant
that not only the problematic part of Book VII, but also Gauden's
own opinions as to the Church's culpability before the Civil War
had become severe tactical mistakes; this, married to a less than
subtle style, made his biographical preface a political disaster.
He openly attributed the Church's fall not only to nonconformist excess but to 'a supine *neglect* in others of the main matters
in which the *Kingdom of God* . . . do[es] chiefly consist'. He
described the Church before 1649 as 'immoderately intent on meer
Formalities, and more zealous for an *outward conformity* to those
shadows, then for that inward or outward conformity with
Christ, in *holy hearts*, and *unblameable lives*, which most adorn true
Religion'.[22] What was almost more unfortunate, given the primacy
of paraenetic narrative over political argument in the biographical agenda, was his unfortunate tendency (following Fuller) to
make Hooker sound like a boring failure. He tended also to imply
that the *Polity*'s text was unreadable. His description of Hooker's
debates with Walter Travers at the Temple (which again follow
Fuller in their warmth for Travers) managed to combine all these
impressions with embarrassing completeness:

Though there was no compare between the *amplitude* of their *hearing*,
and *latitude* of their *real abilities*; yet Mr. *Hooker* meekly suffered himself to be *eclipsed* and *undervalued* in comparison of Mr. *Travers*: If the
paucity of vulgar *hearers* when Mr. *Hooker* preached, and the frequency
or crowd when Mr. *Travers*, were the *competent Judge* and discrimination of their worth, Mr. *Hookers* Sermons were as some rougher coyn,
good gold, and full weight, but not of so fair and smooth a stamp to
vulgar eyes and hands as Mr. *Travers*.[23]

---

[22] Gauden, *Hooker*, 4.   [23] Ibid. 29.

He also failed to notice that Hooker was married, and compounded the sin by relaying a tasteless story about Hooker being black-mailed by a prostitute. Perhaps this was one reason why Walton was to make such a point of Hooker's (if not of his wife's) passive matrimonial virtues.[24]

Gauden had hoped that his new edition would help effect his translation from the relatively poor See of Exeter to the more lucrative one of Winchester. It did not. In 1662 Morley was translated to Winchester and Gauden was offered his position at Worcester. Deeply disappointed, he died shortly afterwards.[25]

Once Gauden's edition of the *Polity* had appeared, it was clearly impossible to suppress it. Some attempts were made to discredit Gauden's manuscripts of the unpublished material, but no alternative version could be proffered. Sheldon appears, therefore, to have decided upon bringing out a new edition of the same text, but with a *Life of Hooker* prefixed to it written in a more congenial style and with the specific aim of discrediting Gauden's version. Walton, a layman known to deplore the religiously chaotic conditions of the Interregnum, to espouse a 'unity' firmly based on a uniformity of religious obedience, and a well-known author and biographer into the bargain, was an obvious choice. Sheldon approached him with his suggestion, making the prospect extra attractive by offering Walton the lease of a house in Paternoster Row at the same time. Walton accepted both house and commission.[26]

Walton as Hooker's Author

Evidence exists that Walton was thinking about a biography of Hooker before 1662. On the flyleaf of his copy of Eusebius' *Ancient Ecclesiastical Histories* (now in Salisbury Cathedral Library) are manuscript notes in Walton's hand which mention Hooker several times. 'Make his discription', he writes, '. . . that he was like the dove w^{t}h out gall'. In print Walton, in common with his sources Gauden, Spenser, and Fuller, characterizes Hooker by his 'Dove-like temper'.[27] The jottings in his Eusebius appear with

---

[24] See e.g. *Lives*, 177–80.   [25] See Novarr, 225.   [26] Ibid. 226–8.
[27] Izaak Walton, *The Life of Mr. R. Hooker* (London, 1665), 107; Gauden, *Hooker*, 16; Hooker, *Of the Laws of Ecclesiastical Polity*, ed. Spenser (London, 1604), sig. A2^v.; Thomas Fuller, *The Church History of Britain* (London, 1655), Book 9, 235.

others which refer to the revisions he made for the 1658 *Life of Donne*, and Novarr argues persuasively that all the notes were written at the same time.[28] Walton, therefore, is by these tokens also Hooker's self-chosen author, as well as a commissioned writer who had inherited his commissioners' political agenda.

How compatible were these two positions? Sheldon and Morley needed Walton to discredit Gauden's *Life* with his own, using any suitable means to gain narrative authority (including checking, correcting, or adducing straightforward factual evidence, all of which Walton was to do). He was to reiterate all available arguments (including in this definition hearsay and anecdote) that the last three books of the *Polity* might not be genuine, to make a good deal more of Hooker's contemporary reputation than Gauden had, and to claim for him an authoritarian position on issues of church government which he had never unambiguously asserted. All these requirements Walton met, though he tried as far as possible to keep the wrangling about the *Polity* confined to appendices, and in dealing with Hooker's theological politics was not, for a variety of reasons, in a position to make authoritative judgements in his own voice. He therefore fell back on the biographer's remit, and made narrative imply what argument could not declare.

Novarr finds the prominence of this agenda in Walton's *Hooker* sufficient reason to treat Walton's own assertion of his impartiality with caution.[29] Walton writes, in the Appendix affixed to the *Life*, that, concerning these three doubtful books of Mr. *Hookers*, my purpose was to enquire, then set down what I observ'd and know, which I have done, not as an ingaged person, but indifferently; and now, leave my Reader, to give sentence, for their legitimation, as to himself' (p. 236). The important word in this passage is 'ingaged'. As Novarr reads it, Walton's obligations to Sheldon were an 'ingagement' which compromised his statement here. Had Walton concealed that *Hooker* was commissioned, we might assume a rhetoric of expediency; but he did not. In his general preface 'To the Reader' which appears in the collected editions of 1670 and 1675 he writes

having writ these two lives [*of Donne and Wotton*] I lay quiet twenty years, without a thought of troubling my self or others, by a new ingagement

---

[28] See Novarr, 230–1.   [29] Ibid. 227–35.

in this kind, for I thought I knew my unfitness. But, about that time, Dr. *Gauden* (then Lord Bishop of Exeter) publisht the *Life of Mr. Richard Hooker*, (so he called it) with so many dangerous mistakes, both of him and his *Books*, that discoursing of them with his *Grace, Gilbert* that is now Lord Archbishop of *Canterbury*; he, injoined me to examine some Circumstances, and then rectifie the Bishops mistakes, by giving the World a fuller and truer account of Mr. *Hooker* and his *Books*, then that Bishop had done, and, I know I have done so. And, let me tell the Reader, that till his *Grace* had laid this injunction upon me, I could not admit a thought of any fitness in me to undertake it: but, when he had twice injoin'd me to it, I then declin'd my own, and trusted his judgment, and submitted to his Commands: concluding, that if I did not, I could not forbear accusing my self of disobedience: And indeed of Ingratitude for his many favours. *Thus I became ingaged into the third Life.* (pp. 5–6)

Walton uses the word 'ingage' twice more in this passage to describe his own internal relationship to a new literary obligation. To be 'ingag'd' in this sense is to be committed to an undertaking. As far as his biographical duties are concerned, his tone is confident: asked to present a 'fuller and truer account' of Hooker's life he can state, in his own person, 'I know I have done so'. What, then, does it mean when he claims *not* to be an 'ingag'd' person in his Appendix, clearly this time meaning that he had no hidden agenda, no *external* obligation beyond and above the demands of truth? The passage above demonstrates that he actually forgoes his right to judge in his own person on this matter at all: he has 'declin'd' his private judgement in favour of Sheldon's. At no point, therefore, will he be prepared to admit any disparity between the demands of truth and that judgement. These are, in part, clear professional demarcations: bishops determine theological questions; biographers write Lives. While Walton might be the right person to discover, for instance, that Hooker was married, and not the bachelor Gauden claimed he was, it was Sheldon's job to decide on the authenticity of the *Polity*'s last three books. Walton would not usurp Sheldon's function.

Walton's position in these accompanying writings is consistent with that expressed in the main narrative. 'Laws', asserts Walton's *Hooker*, 'are not made for private men to dispute, but to obey' (p. 207). The theme of the *Life* is obedience to authority, which Walton represents as the only sure safeguard against the primary evil of civil disorder. His reference in the passage above to 'disobedience' is not made lightly. Walton himself is a 'private man': his political and religious opinions are therefore most virtuous where they are most obedient to the episcopal authority Sheldon represents.

Walton characteristically combines these civil obligations with an expression of a personal debt to Sheldon, in a dual tie of obedience with friendship. Without Sheldon's insistence, and Sheldon's faith in his biographical abilities, he explains, he would never have attempted *Hooker*. This is, of course, also a form of the standard biographer's modesty topos, deployed to arrogate Sheldon's public authority to Walton's biography. Walton actually accentuates Sheldon's responsibility for its existence in exaggerating the time during which he 'lay quiet' from five years (i.e. from 1658) to 'twenty'. And we know that when he was revising *Donne* he was thinking about writing *Hooker*.

From this initial point, where Walton claims an authority transferred to him via a private friendship with a powerful man, we find throughout *Hooker* some remarkably deft uses of transferred authority through personal ties. This most Waltonian manoeuvre discovers more than a regard for holy amity. The claims of friendship always underwrite Walton's biographical method; but in *Hooker* they are deployed in their most complex variety. This happens partly because Walton had not known Hooker himself, and this was his first attempt at a biography of that kind. (He was not to write *Herbert* for another five years; and even then he was to point out that, though they were not acquaintances, he knew a lot of his close friends and had 'seen' him.) It also happens because Walton's lay status, in a biography about obedience to clerical authority, causes him problems of authorial voice which he solves by becoming a mediator of other people's authoritative opinions. One sort of mediation he achieves by relying heavily on oral information derived from mutual contacts, and the other kind by the description of some skilful pairings, within the biography, of Hooker with key contemporary figures whose politics might colour Hooker's through propinquity. This last strategy relieves Walton largely of responsibility for discussing Hooker's own position directly, though his summaries of Hooker's sermons are an honourable (and, for different reasons, a suggestive) exception to this general rule. Both methods have implications for his presentation of evidence.

Walton uses his own propinquity to the dead straightforwardly. He lends to them a living authority marked by biographical evidence of the 'horse's mouth' variety (what Novarr calls
'doubtful oral information from people he trusted');[30] and they
transfer to him their authority of function. This manoeuvre
appears in the first words of his Introduction, where he first
expresses, and then solves, his unease at the idea of writing a Life
of a man he did not know:

I have been perswaded, by a Friend whom I reverence, and ought to obey,
to write *The Life of* RICHARD HOOKER . . . And though I have undertaken
it, yet it hath been with some unwillingness . . . For I knew him not in
his Life, and must therefore not only look back to his Death, now 64 years
past; but almost 50 years beyond that, even to his Childhood, and Youth
. . .

This trouble I foresee; and foresee also, that it is impossible to escape
Censures; against which, I cannot hope my well-meaning and diligence
will protect me, (for I consider the Age in which I live) and shall therefore but intreat of my Reader a suspension of his Censures, until I have
made known to him some Reasons, which I my self would now gladly
believe do make me in some measure fit for this undertaking. (pp. 159–60)

Walton here uses Sheldon in the way described above to provide
his initial justification. But he must also explain how he had
satisfied his own misgivings. Since those are all about not knowing Hooker, it comes as no surprise that the 'Reasons' he proceeds
to give are a list of relatives and acquaintances of Walton's who
had known him.

The list includes William Cranmer, his brother George
Cranmer, and two of his sisters. Walton was related through his
first marriage to the Cranmer family, and claims a friendship of
forty years with William and an intimacy with the others which
included some years of 'happy Cohabitation'. He represents the
Cranmers (with the exception of George) as having had 'a most
familiar friendship with Mr. *Hooker*', and adds that his own
independent interest in Hooker had made him to them a 'diligent
Inquisitor into . . . his Person, his Nature, the management of his
Time, his Wife, his Family, and the Fortune of him and his'. In
addition to this he reveals that one of the Cranmer sisters had been

[30] See Navarr, 266.

married to Dr Spenser, the executor under Hooker's Will who had
been so hard put to it to explain why the last three books of the
Polity had been suppressed.

For good measure Walton adds his friendship with Archbishop
Ussher, with Dr Morton the late bishop of Durham, and 'the
learned *John Hales* of *Eaton-Colledge*', all of whom had known
Hooker, and all of whom had 'had many discourses concerning
him' with Walton. Walton deplores the fact that he had not preserved the information on Hooker he had received, or solicited
more, before his informants had 'put off Mortality', but 'yet my
Memory hath preserved some gleanings, and my Diligence made
such additions to them, as I hope will prove useful to the com-
pleating of what I intend' (pp. 160–1). In fact, Walton spends more
than half of his Introduction justifying having written the *Life*
on his own terms, the biographer's terms of personal knowledge,
having disposed of Sheldon's claims in less than a sentence.

The passage I have quoted contains Walton's apprehension
that his work will receive 'Censures'. That the 'Censures' Walton
expects are politically motivated is clear from his parenthetical reference to 'the Age in which I live'; but Walton is careful to defend
himself solely via the authenticity of his contacts and information. He may have been 'ingaged into the third Life' by Sheldon,
but he chooses to make his primary justification for the *Life of
Hooker* a biographer's one. Sheldon's motives, like his integrity,
stay Sheldon's business. Walton does not therefore claim to be
politically disinterested, for Hooker's friends will have been
no less 'ingaged' than Sheldon, as the presence of Spenser in
Walton's list indicates. But it does shift the burden of responsibility for that 'ingagement' firmly onto the shoulders of Walton's
informants.

I have stated that part of Walton's brief was to discredit
Gauden in factual details. He uses his own acquaintanceship with,
in particular, the Cranmers to gain the necessary authority for
this process. Of all Walton's *Lives*, the *Life of Hooker* is probably
the most carefully researched and annotated (although it is
not, therefore, accurate), and where Walton does not provide
documentary proof for his facts, he indicates, though not always
directly, that he has received them verbally from reliable sources.
In his 1666 'Epistle to the Reader' he calls this kind of information 'tradition', and says of his narrative's handling of it:

And now for my self, I can say, I hope, or rather know, there are no Material Mistakes in what I here present to you, that shall become my Reader. Little things that I have received by Tradition (to which there may be too much and too little Faith given) I will not at this distance of time undertake to justifie; for, though I have used great Diligence, and compared Relations and Circumstances, and probable Results and Expressions: yet, I shall not impose my Belief upon my Reader; I shall rather leave him at liberty.[31]

Walton here shows a regard for ascertainable evidence, but is making quite a spirited claim for the weight of oral testimony—the anecdotes, or 'Relations' of 'tradition'. (The comparable weight he gives to 'Expressions'—that is, to matters of style—is also worth noticing in passing.) He avoids the problem of tradition's unverifiability, acknowledged in his fence-sitting parenthesis 'to which there may be too much and too little Faith given', by releasing his reader from the burden of having to share his conviction. He goes on, after the passage quoted, to ask readers to write in with evidence he might have missed, for later editions.

The main blunder Walton corrects is over Hooker's marriage, and he marks it with memorable detail. Reluctant, as always, to assign passions to his subjects, he describes Hooker as having been persuaded to it by the landlady of the lodgings he took in London, when he travelled there in order to preach at St Paul's Cross. The landlady had proposed her daughter, Joan Churchman, as a suitable wife, and so Hooker (as Walton tells it), feeling 'bound in conscience to believe all that she said', married a wife 'who brought him neither Beauty nor Portion', and became engaged 'into those corroding cares that attend a married Priest' (pp. 177–8).

Walton offers no source for this story, but follows it with another illustrating what Hooker's married life was like, in which George Cranmer, with Edwin Sandys (who was also known to Walton), figures prominently. Walton describes Sandys and Cranmer as having gone to see Hooker, at that time their tutor. On arriving, they famously

found him with a Book in his hand (it was the *Odes* of *Horace*) he . . . tending his small allotment of sheep in a common field, which he told

---

[31] Izaak Walton, 'To the Reader', in Richard Hooker, *Of the Lawes of Ecclesiastical Polity* (London, 1666), sig. A4[r].

his Pupils he was forced to do then, for that his servant was gone home to Dine, and assist his Wife to do some necessary household business. But when his servant returned and released him, then his two Pupils attended him unto his house, where their best entertainment was his quiet company, which was presently denied them: for, *Richard was call'd to rock the Cradle*; and the rest of their welcome was so like this, that they staid but till next morning, which was time enough to discover and pity their Tutors condition. (p. 179)

Walton lets a combination of insinuation and assumption do much of his work for him here. Mrs Hooker's actions look to a modern eye as much like wifely desperation as wifely hostility. Even given contemporary expectations of her duty, a different treatment of the anecdote could make it equally illustrative of the miseries of clerical poverty. In Anthony á Wood's version of 1661 Mrs Hooker's evil intentions are made much more explicit: she makes her husband rock the cradle 'purposely to hinder his study', and 'would not allow him paper to write upon'; after his death she turns his children into the street to starve.[32]

As a principle, Walton's stress on the oral evidence of surviving contemporaries or their near relatives was unexceptionable. In the event, though, his narrative—in particular his unflattering portrait of Joan Hooker—got caught on the wrong end of family litigation. Novarr plausibly conjectures Walton's informant to have been Mrs Dorothy Spenser, wife of John Spenser and sister to George Cranmer, who was reporting a piece of spiteful gossip which Walton took to be reliable because of his faith in his personal contacts. There was bad feeling after Hooker's death among his friends and family, resulting in a number of lawsuits between Sandys and Hooker's heirs. John Spenser had had to give evidence in these cases, which might easily have prejudiced Mrs Spenser.[33]

Walton's version of the story is not itself spiteful in its details, but disapproving; and some of the reasons for Walton's disapproval may well lie with another story about Joan Hooker supplied to him by Mrs Spenser. This second story appears in the Appendix, where it is claimed that after Hooker's death a

[32] See Andrew Clark, *The Life and Times of Anthony Wood, Antiquary, of Oxford, 1632–1695, Described by Himself*, 2 vols. (Oxford, 1891), i. 425.

[33] See Novarr, 269–71.

chaplain was sent from Whitgift to Mrs Hooker, asking for the manuscripts of the remaining three books of the *Polity*, 'of which she would not, or could not give any account'. Upon being questioned at Lambeth, however, she confessed

That one Mr. *Charke*, and another Minister that dwelt near *Canterbury*, came to her, and desired that they might go into her Husbands Study, and look upon some of his Writings: and that there they two burnt and tore many of them, assuring her, that they were writings not fit to be seen, & that she knew nothing more concerning them. (p. 231)

This story, presenting Mrs Hooker as being at best negligent, was naturally being offered as evidence discrediting the last three books of the *Polity*. Walton gives his oral sources as 'one that very well knew Mr. Hooker, and the affairs of his family', and says that he had been told the story 'almost 40 Years past' (p. 230). Later he adds the supporting evidence that Mrs Spenser, 'who was my Aunt and Sister to *George Cranmer*', had told him that her husband had been forced to finish the last three books of the *Polity* himself, because the drafts he had received at Hooker's death had been incomplete. This information too Walton states that he had received 'forty Years since' (p. 233). It seems reasonable to assume that Mrs Spenser had been the source for both.

Mrs Spenser's is not the only evidence Walton uses to discredit the last three books. He provides a passage from Nicholas Bernard's *Clavi Trabales* (1661), purporting to be one of the missing passages from Book VII of the *Polity*, which argues that only God may judge the actions of kings (p. 234). Actually the passage, which is genuine, is from Book VIII, and is indeed to be found in the manuscript possessed by Archbishop Ussher and donated from his manuscript collection in Trinity College, Dublin, in 1661.[34] Walton also provides the sworn statement of one Fabian

---

[34] See *Polity*, Book VIII, ch. 9.2: *Folger Edition*, iii. 437; Nicholas Bernard, *Clavi Trabales* (London, 1661), 94. Walton misquotes his source. See also Novarr, 245–7. There is circumstantial evidence in favour of Walton's story. On Hooker's death Lancelot Andrewes wrote to Henry Parry, a contemporary at Corpus, suggesting he thought it a good idea for someone to preserve Hooker's books and papers as quickly as possible. It was also deposed by one Edmund Parbo that the supposed defacers of the MSS included Roger Raven, headmaster of the King's School, Canterbury. C. J. Sisson dismisses Parbo's testimony because Whitgift wrote a reference for Raven, but on the other hand we do know Raven was given to defacing books. John Manningham of the Middle Temple, in his

Philips (an extreme royalist barrister), that Dr Sanderson had told him he had seen a manuscript of the *Polity* in Hooker's handwriting, 'in which there was no mention made of the King or Supreme Governours being accomptable to the People' (p. 235). The entire Appendix, with the single exception of the manuscript-burning anecdote, is hedged about with documentary evidence, admittedly of a circumstantial kind. Most of it does not relate directly to the *Polity*, but to the state of Hooker's affairs and family after his death, but the effect created is that Walton had taken great care to authenticate what he said. The passage I have already quoted, in which Walton leaves it to the reader to make a final judgement on the 'legitimation' of Hooker's 'three doubtful books' while describing his own position as 'not . . . engaged', appears at the end of this flurry of supporting evidence (p. 236). Walton here disclaims final responsibility for his own interpretation of the *Polity*'s printing history, and places it firmly with his informants.

Novarr's patience with Walton's biographical method finally breaks when he is discussing his use of evidence in *Hooker*. He writes:

Walton's usual tendency was to follow his own predisposition, to bend facts to support his predisposition, to abide by his thesis despite the facts, to make insufficient concession to the facts, to temper the facts to comply with doubtful oral information from people he trusted, and this tendency [he concludes exasperatedly] is a great detriment to biographical writing. (p. 266)

diary for 1602–3, mentions Raven's tendencies this way in an entry for December 1602: according to him, his cousin 'told me what dissembling hypocrites these Puritans be, and how slightly they regard an oath: Rauens having a booke brought unto him by a puritane to have his opinion of it, the booke being written by B. Bilson, Rauens as he had reade it would needes be shewing his foolishe witt in the margent, in scoffing at the booke. When the fellowe that had but borrowed it was to carry it home again, he swore it neuer went out of his hands. After, when it was shewed him what had bin written in it when himselfe could not write, he confessed that Rauens had it; then Rauens forswore his owne hand.' This reference was generously drawn to my attention by Professor George Edelen, one of the editors of the Folger Hooker. See also C. J. Sisson, *The Judicious Marriage of Mr Hooker and the Birth of the 'Laws of Ecclesiastical Polity'* (Cambridge, 1940), 79–91; P. Collinson, 'Hooker and the Elizabethan Establishment', in A. S. McGrade (ed.), *Hooker and the Construction of Christian Community* (Tempe, Ariz., 1997), 154; *Diary of John Manningham of the Middle Temple, 1602–3*, edited from the original MS by John Bruce (Westminster, 1868), fol. 84.

But Walton's biographical authority is a derived authority. As far as Walton's faith in his 'doubtful oral information' goes, it is important to bear in mind that his personal knowledge of Hooker's friends is his justification for writing *Hooker* at all. He was not likely to dismiss or even to mistrust the information they gave him within it. While Novarr's own ethics of research are clearly based on a fundamental regard for the *written* record, and are predicated on a relationship with it which assumes his right to an independent judgement, Walton read with obedient eyes, and eschewed interpretation. His most open scorn is reserved for the lay interpreter who fosters schism though an ignorant meddling with affairs she was not trained to understand. His anecdote of the 'ingenious *Italian*' who marvels 'scoffingly' that in England 'the very *Women* and *Shopkeepers*, were able to judge of Predestination, and determine what Laws were fit to be made concerning Church-government' is typical of his stance; and the same relationship with lay dispute is reflected in the method of his only (anonymous) political pamphlet, *Love and Truth*—right down to the insistence on the particular instability of the female and retailing members of the population.[35]

How then could Walton (who had kept a shop himself) speak directly on Hooker's theological politics? He may have been obedient, but he was not politically naive. This is where he finds a use for a kind of Plutarchan pairing, narrating bonds between Hooker and individuals whose public politics had a particular Restoration meaning in order to avoid making direct assertions. In this way he lets his reader infer a political consensus he never discusses.

Walton describes Hooker's friendships in highly exalted terms. Partly this reflects Walton's clear regard for that kind of relationship, which for him (*pace* the Song of Songs) works as a far closer terrestrial template of divine love than anything which could happen between husbands and wives. Partly he uses it here to counter the effect of Gauden's single comment on the subject ('his Friends or Confidents were few, but choise') with some emphatic detail.[36] But part of Walton's motive is, of course, political. Hooker's strongly stressed spiritual friendship with the obdurately *iure divino* Hadrian Saravia, which Walton confirms

---

[35] *Lives*, 186–7; *Love and Truth*, 21.   [36] Gauden, *Hooker*, 9.

with a description of Saravia's deathbed attendance on Hooker, is such a pairing.

This is how he describes their friendship:

In this year of 1595, and in this place of *Borne*, these two excellent persons began a holy friendship, increasing daily to so high and mutual affections, that their two wills seemed to be but one and the same: and their designs both for the glory of God, and peace of the Church, still assisting and improving each others vertues, and the desired comforts of a peaceable piety. (p. 215)

Hooker and Saravia here are assigned a common will. Saravia's absolutist position on the divine right of the monarch, and on the similarly divine authority conferred on the episcopate by apostolic succession, are being rubbed off on Richard Hooker by propinquity. Walton has recognized that the idea of legitimate and internal dissensions is now of all others the most problematic: instead, the rhetoric must be that there was absolute ecclesiastical agreement about what the Church's foundations could have been 'anciently settled' on; threatened, not by its own divines, but from the midst of an ungrateful, ignorant, and above all disobedient lay body.

Walton's insertion of a thumbnail biography of Archbishop Whitgift into the text has a comparable function. Gauden had not known what to make of the fact that Hooker had not climbed very far up the preferment ladder, and had made this plain, writing that Whitgift added 'much quickning edge' to Hooker's 'otherwise slow, and *hesitant* temper'.[37] Walton follows suit, with less obviousness: he chooses to narrate Whitgift as Hooker's statesmanlike—almost, one might say, his Erastian—alter ego, his powerful political self. The post-Plutarchan method is virtually explicit.

Walton represents his Hooker as having absolutely no taste for controversy. This is part of a strategy thoughout his book in which the language of passivity is deployed to signify virtue, and I discuss it in its own right below.[38] The *Polity* itself he makes grow out of Hooker's desire for secluded study in some rural hamlet. In a significant speech made (supposedly) to Whitgift himself, Walton has his Hooker claim

---

[37] Ibid. 15.   [38] See pp. 264–72.

... I am weary of the noise and oppositions of this place; and indeed, God and nature did not intend me for Contentions, but for Study and quietness ... I have ... begun a treatise, in which I intend a Justification of the laws of our *Ecclesiasticall Polity*; in which design God and his holy Angels shall ... bear me ... witness ... that my meaning is not to provoke any, but to satisfy all tender Consciences, and I shall never be able to do this, but where I may Study, and pray for Gods blessing upon my indeavours, and keep my self in Peace and Privacy, and behold Gods blessing spring out of my Mother Earth, and eat my own bread without oppositions ... (p. 209)

Given that Hooker is thus characterized as retiring and peaceable, Walton needs another figure to head his inevitably controversial analysis of the 'character of the Times' (p. 182) in the first half of the *Life*. He chooses Whitgift. 'He found', explains Novarr, 'in Whitgift's life that singularity of purpose, expressed in deeds, which was at most implied in the words of Richard Hooker.'[39] It is notable that Walton will only represent 'action' as virtuous in relation to Whitgift: he is the exception that proves the rule, the proponent of a statesmanlike 'active Wisdom'. In his function as archbishop of Canterbury, he must be the authority to which the Church's body owes obedience. It is fascinating that Walton represents even the monarch as subject to archepiscopal rebuke, in his introduction of a (fictional) speech reprimanding Elizabeth I for the sale of Church property:

I beseech Your Majesty to hear me with patience ... and therefore give me leave to do my Duty, and tell You, That Princes are deputed Nursing Fathers of the Church, and owe it a protection; *and therefore God forbid that You should be so much as passive in her Ruines, when You may prevent it; or that I should behold it without horror and detestation, or should forbear to tell Your Majesty of the sin and danger of* Sacriledge. (p. 191)

Walton used a number of pamphlets and other writings in defence of Church property to invent this speech.[40] The phrase which refers to 'Princes' as the 'Nursing Fathers of the Church' is taken from Isaiah 49: 23, 'And kings shall be thy nursing fathers',

---

[39] Novarr, 242–3.

[40] Ibid. 263–5. For the relevance of the issue Walton chooses for the 1590s, see W. B. Richardson, 'The Religious Policy of the Cecils, 1588–1598', 232–5; Felicity Heal, *Of Prelates and Princes: A Study of the Economic and Social Position of the Tudor Episcopate* (Cambridge, 1980), 202–36, 265–311.

which is a Coronation text.[41] It seems likely that Walton was recalling the use Hooker had made of the Isaiah text in Book VII: 'For as those ancient Nursing Fathers thought they never did bestow enough [upon the Church] even so in the eye of this present age, as long as anything remaineth, it seemeth to be too much.'[42]

Walton's Whitgift is careful to clothe his strictures in a deferential rhetoric of duty. Yet his monarch is genuinely not characterized as subject to the speaker. 'God forbid that You should be so much as passive in her Ruines', says Whitgift of Elizabeth's responsibility to the Church: in thus reversing the moral significance of passivity, he identifies the monarch also as active, because authoritative, requiring rather than performing obedience. Whitgift merely reminds authority of its responsibilities; he does not usurp its place. Walton relies again here on a consensual understanding of clear demarcations of function to keep the speech within the limits of proper secular deference.

Walton is helped by his monarch's sex. Walton's Elizabeth calls her archbishop her 'little black Husband' (p. 190), and yields to him in spiritual advice what the archbishop repays her in respect. Here the Song of Songs comes into its own: Whitgift speaks for Christ, and the Church's Head is his bride. It is a better marriage than Hooker's; and Walton celebrates the union in a language of mutuality he reserves for those rare amities between the sexes of which he approves. Whitgift and Elizabeth feel 'so mutual a joy and confidence, that they seemed born to believe and do good to each other' (p. 195). This foreshadows the 'mutual and equal affections, and compliance' with which Walton was to characterize Herbert's marriage with Jane Danvers, as well as the 'chain of sutable inclinations and vertues' binding Magdalen Herbert and John Donne (pp. 286 and 265).

Novarr exhibits some disapproval of Walton's inclusion of a fictional speech on Church property into a work which he presented as fact. 'How detrimental to the writing of biography is this sort of misrepresentation and what does it show of Walton as a biographer?' he asks.[43] But the judgement is anachronistic. It is routine for the early modern historian to invent speeches for

---

[41] I am indebted to my father, the Revd Prof. David Martin, for drawing my attention to this.

[42] *Folger Edition*, iii. 306.   [43] Novarr, 265.

his characters. Nor do they necessarily assign plausible political positions to their speakers: Foxe has *Henry VIII* defend Church property in a speech very like Walton's:

There are a sort of you, to whom I have liberally geven of the posses-sions and revenewes of the suppressed Monasteries, which lyke as you have lightely gotten, so have you more unthriftily spent, some at Dice, other some in gay apparell, and other wayes worse, I feare me: and now as all is gone, you would fayne have me make an other chevaunce with the Bishops landes to accomplish your greedy appetites.[44]

The unlikelihood of this from the mouth of the Church's first and greediest Head locates Walton's anxiety to ventriloquize a con-demnation of further confiscations in 1665 well within the limits of generic convention.

Walton's presentation of himself as submissive layman means that even in his sketch of Whitgift he is not specifically required to defend either his actions or his policies. If Walton's Whitgift is compared with one of his sources, the *Life of Whitgift* written by his secretary Sir George Paule, some significant differences of treatment emerge.

The Epistle to the Reader prefixed to Paule's *Life* bears at first sight a similarity, in its use of the modesty topos, to Walton's Introduction to the *Life of Donne*:

It was farre from my thoughts that these first draughts of mine, which I onely intended as minutes and directions for a more skilfull penne-man, should ever haue shewed themselves to the world, had not the back-wardness of some, and the importunitie of others, driuen me to the Orators resolution; who saith, I had rather any man should doe it, then my selfe; yet my selfe, rather then none at all.[45]

As the Epistle continues, the difference of social perspective between the two men becomes more obvious. Both claim that their personal knowledge of their subject justifies their writing; but whereas Walton describes that knowledge as 'love' to Donne's 'memory', Paule, significantly, replaces love with 'obligation'. Paule exhibits a much greater confidence in his authorial status; while Walton explicitly looks up to Donne, Paule's view of

[44] Foxe, *Actes and Monuments* (1570), ii. 2039.
[45] George Paule, *The Life of the Most Reverend and Religious Prelate John Whitgift, Lord Archbishop of Canterbury* (London, 1612), sig. A4.

Whitgift is that of a near equal. To be sure, he calls him his 'Maister' and states an intention to 'imitate' him in his 'mild and moderate carriage', but he evidently means it only in the sense of an immediate superior:

> But as no man can rightly commend a Commander, or skilfull Pilot, without relating their passed exploits, or dangerous stormes: so neither could I, without wronging my Reader, and the principall Subiect, commend him for so worthie and prudent a Governour, vnlesse I had withall giuen a taste of his aduentures, and the stormy time wherein he liued. (sig. A4ᵛ)

Paule here is preparing his reader for a work which will justify Whitgift's political actions via a narration of his times. His model is Tacitus, which limits his concern with exemplarity. Nor will he have scruples about narrating precise details of contemporary controversy in his own voice. In justifying Whitgift he to some extent also justifies himself, for Whitgift is his 'Commander', and he assisted him in his exercise of power. This is a very different kind of personal knowledge from Walton's of Donne. Paule is in a position to 'commend' his subject, and this implies that he could decide not to commend him. Walton does not have this option.

Paule, however, does run into considerable difficulties in his portrayal of Whitgift, because he attempts to privilege, in an otherwise statesmanlike history, a quasi-scriptural theme of Whitgift as suffering and persecuted. He makes a good deal of Whitgift's (in the circumstances handy) motto VINCIT QUI PATITUR, which Walton also quotes.[46] Whitgift the dignitary and Whitgift the sacrificial lamb are yoked uneasily together by an attempt to describe his policy as winningly moderate. If Paule's treatment of the Admonition Controversy is compared with Walton's summary dismissal of its issues, the wisdom of Walton's refusal to go into much detail on public events in a work mainly commending private piety is evident, and his skill in vindicating a largely undescribed public stance implicitly through the narration of private details is notable.

---

[46] *Lives*, 197 and 237; Paule, *Whitgift*, 33. See also Whitgift's portrait facing the title-page of the 1612 edition. Its original hangs in the Council Room of the Old Schools in the University of Cambridge. Whitgift's hand rests upon a psalter open at Psalm 42, 'Like as the hart'. His identification with hunted, rather than hunter, was evidently a commonplace.

Paule devotes about 400 words to the events leading to the expulsion of Thomas Cartwright from the University of Cambridge. First he presents Whitgift's attitude to Cartwright and his supporters in the following terms:

Notwithstanding, so farre was he from entering into any rigorous course of proceeding against them (as iustly he might have done by the Statutes of the Colledge, and publique laws of the state) as that with great sufferance, he winked at and passed by many of these wrongs, and enormities, and instead of reuenge, he by gentleness and goodnesse heaped coales on the aduersaries, as also for rough and unseemly speeches, hee breathed nothing but sweet breath of loue, and peace, often exhorting them to call to God for grace, that they might have more sober consideration and better iudgment of orders established, which then they mistooke to be amisse.[47]

Paule is making spiritual capital out of a vision of a passive Whitgift beleaguered by aggressors. Whitgift's Christlike demeanour as he is victimized demonstrates that he must be in the right better than any argument. Paule shows his hand by adding a quotation from the *Polity* to the effect that the confidence of 'bolde spirited men' opposing 'things established by publique authority' arises for the most part from the fact that 'too much credit' is given to 'their own wits'. Whitgift is not going to give them that kind of credit. Rather than stooping to dispute, he will ignore them and call it patience, or even (as the coals of fire image implies) forgiveness. 'If thine enemy hunger, feed him; if he thirst, give him drink: for in so doing thou shalt heap coals of fire on his head.' It seems only fair to point out that feeding your enemy and delaying punitive legal action against him are not really comparable actions. What all the contexts share, however, is that forgiveness is being recommended as the best form of *retaliation*.[48]

Paule's hopeful picture of Whitgift as sufferer, and thus of passivity as the best kind of aggression, is shattered by what happens next. The archbishop, finding Cartwright 'alwaies wilfully bent, and finally obstinate', eventually marshals his powers, and 'called him in question, and hauing sufficient matter of expulsion against him, for vttering some errors in his Lectures . . . hee expelled him the house; and being Vize-Chancellor, caused him

---

[47] Paule, *Whitgift*, 10–11.
[48] Romans, 12: 20, quoting Proverbs 25: 21–2.

likewise to be depriued of the Lady Margarets Lecture, which then he reade' (pp. 11–12). Walton is faced by no such difficulties of justification, and is able to dismiss Whitgift's action in a single sentence:

> Many of [Whitgift's] . . . many Trials were occasioned by . . . especially one Thomas Cartwright, a man of noted Learning, sometime Contemporary with the Bishop in Cambridge, and of the same Colledge, of which the Bishop had been Master; in which place there began some . . . open and high Oppositions betwixt them; and in which you may believe Mr. Cartwright was most faulty, if his Expulsion out of the University can incline you to it. (p. 197)

Here the fact of 'Expulsion' justifies itself, and there is no need to plead particular circumstances.

Walton's deft use of the life of Whitgift to narrate the relevant religious politics via (on the whole) the Admonition Controversy, eases his problems in narrating Hooker's Temple disputes with the Presbyterian divine Walter Travers in the 1590s, 'a Friend and Favorite of Mr. *Cartwrights*' (p. 198). Given that Walton wished to establish Hooker's irenic disposition, and to suggest a consensus of religious opinion among divines, the Travers disputes needed careful handling. Travers, an imperfectly disguised Genevan cuckoo in the Temple nest, had opposed Hooker persistently and publicly from the same Temple pulpit, and Whitgift, dismayed by the unfortunate impression the warring divines were creating in front of England's trainee lawyers, had attempted to suppress him. The minor political storm this created reflected on Hooker, and more widely on Walton's attempt to present the divines, at any rate, as broadly in (conformist) agreement.

Walton, therefore, softens the opposition between the two by describing Travers as 'a man of Competent Learning, of a winning Behaviour, and of a blameless Life' (p. 199), and adding that there was 'little of bitterness' between the two opponents (p. 200).[49] It is fair to say that Travers is described outside Walton as very well liked, and himself points out that Hooker and he felt no

---

[49] He paraphrases Travers, 'the matter was not bitterly and immodestly handled between us'. See Walter Travers, 'A Supplication to the Councel', in Hooker, *Works* (1666), 494. See also Fuller's downright fulsome account of Travers in *Church History* (London, 1655), Bk. 9, pp. 213–19.

personal antagonism, and indeed were related by marriage.[50] Like
Cartwright, Travers in fact falls into the category of acceptable
adversaries; the arguments of each are, as Peter Lake puts it for
Cartwright, those of 'university educated divines who accepted the
standards and argument and proof used in the universities for academic disputation'.[51] They played by the rules. On the other hand,
it was a game of immense seriousness, and the stakes were high.

Walton summarizes two main points of disputation between
them. Travers had accused Hooker of asserting, first, 'that the
assurance of what we believe by the Word of God, is not to us
so certain as that which we perceive by sense', and then, 'that he
doubted not but that God was merciful to many of our fore-fathers
living in Popish superstition, for as much as they sinned ignorantly'. The first of these is Travers's own description, taken
from his 'Supplication to the Councel' which argued against his
suppression by Whitgift.[52] The second Walton paraphrases from
Travers, for reasons which will be discussed below.

Walton then makes careful use of the two sermons by Hooker
rebutting Travers's accusations, first printed by Spenser's assistant Henry Jackson in 1612.[53] The first, drawing on the sermon *Of
the Certainty and Perpetuitie of Faith in the Elect*, is an extremely
scrupulous cameo of Hooker's argument, both in method and
substance, and it is worth discussing in detail to give some sense
of Walton's competence.

In his sermon Hooker must deal (as its title makes very clear)
with the central problem of whether the elect can experience doubt
inherent in Travers's summary. Recalling Hebrews 11: 1, where
faith is defined as 'the ground of things hoped for, the evidence of
things not seene',[54] the centrality of faith to salvation in reformed
doctrine makes the question crucial. If the elect cannot doubt,
it becomes possible to identify the unregenerate soul at the first
whisper of unease. It is also a question which, as Travers formu-

    [50] See Speed Hill, 'The Evolution of Hooker's *Laws of Ecclesiastical Polity*',
123; Travers, 'A Supplication to the Councel', 491.
    [51] Lake, *Anglicans and Puritans?*, 14.
    [52] See Richard Hooker, *Works* (London, 1666), 487–96.
    [53] *A Learned and Comfortable Sermon of the Certaintie and Perpetuitie of Faith
in the Elect* . . . (Oxford, 1612); *A Learned Discourse of Justification, Workes, and
How the Foundation of Faith is Overthrown* (Oxford, 1612).
    [54] From Tyndale's translation of 1535.

lates it, sets a kind of empirical assurance explicitly in competi-
tion with (even, implicitly, in opposition to) the divine promise.
Hooker argues the point with charity. He rejects Travers's
formulation of the Hookerian position, of course (never having
been a likely empiricist), but is urgently concerned that it should
not be possible for human creatures to identify the unregenerate
from outward signs, with all that might follow from that. Judgement is God's prerogative. He therefore takes as his starting-point
that 'they in whose hearts the light of grace doth shine' may
nevertheless feel doubt, and asks why this should be. In answer-
ing his question, he draws a fundamental distinction, which
Walton swiftly and deftly cites, between 'Certainty of Evidence'
and 'Certainty of Adherence'.[55] Certainty of evidence covers what
Hooker calls 'manifest' truths—matters the truth of which can be
perceived sensually or reasoned. These, argues Hooker, are not
truths 'in themselves' but matters proceeding from observation.
For the angels, 'things spiritual' are matters of observation, are
part of the certainties of evidence, but for men and women they
are things unseen, and therefore truths in themselves. The certainty the human spirit can feel on matters not observable or
deducible is a certainty of adherence, and is a greater certainty than
the other, but cannot be by its nature 'so evidently certain'. He is
properly rejecting reason as an ultimate ground for faith: 'proofs
are vain and frivolous except they be more certain than is the thing
proved'.[56] Walton puts it that 'we must be surer of the Proof than
of the thing Proved; otherwise it is no Proof' (p. 201).

Hooker attributes the fact that the saved do not *feel* such certainty of adherence all the time to 'the foggy damp of original
corruption' (p. 528). In the rest of his sermon he is concerned to
demonstrate that the faith of a self can be inherent, and indeed
can govern and limit its sinful actions, yet still remain dark to that
self: 'men . . . are through the extremity of Grief many times in
judgment so confounded, that they find not themselves in themselves.' It will, therefore, not be possible to identify unregeneracy from outward signs, for 'God will have them that shall walk
in light to feel now and then what it is to sit in the shadow of Death.
A grieved spirit therefore is no arugment [*sic*] for a faithless mind'

[55] Hooker, *Works* (London, 1666), 550–1; *Lives*, 201–2.
[56] Hooker, *Works*, 551.

(p. 529). He concludes by considering the case of those who feel such sorrow at their unbelief that they become themselves convinced of their unregeneracy—the fundamental dilemma of the adherent to a faith-centred theological system. Hooker deals with it briskly:

> are they not grieved for their unbelief? They are. Do they not wish it might . . . be otherwise? . . . Whence cometh this, but from a secret love and liking which they have of those things that are believed? No man can love things which in his own opinion are not. . . . then it must needs be, that by desiring to believe they prove themselves true Believers. For without Faith, no man thinketh that things believed are. Which argument all the subtilty of infernal powers will never be able to dissolve.

Walton quotes this last section more or less word for word (there are small differences in his text), with some abridgements which he acknowledges, summarizing the argument which precedes it accurately and with clarity. His approval of Hooker's position finds expression in his summary of the second argument, that 'he doubted not but that God was merciful to many of our fore-fathers living in Popish superstition, forasmuch as they sinned ignorantly', which he describes as a 'Charitable opinion' (p. 203). As Travers had put it, Hooker's position had been 'That he doubted not, but that thousands of the Fathers, which lived and dyed in the Superstitions of that Church, were saved, because of their ignorance, which excuseth them'.[57] Travers exacerbated the political implications of Hooker's position (with some justice, since Hooker did take this view of the salvation of Roman Catholics)[58] by referring explicitly in his accusations not only to the 'Fathers' but to contemporary Roman Catholics dying inside the faith:'Such as dye, or have dyed at any time.' Walton, understandably, keeps strictly to the implications of the former statement, and his paraphrase reflects its clear emphasis on the pre-Reformation dead.

Hooker's sermon *Of Justification, Works, and How the Foundation of Faith is Overthrown* deals with the question deftly, by using justification by faith to dismiss Roman errors as works, and so as irrelevant compared to the faith in which the doer might have lived.[59] Very much as with the previous argument, Hooker assumes

---

[57]   Travers, 'Supplication to the Councel', 492.
[58]   See Lake, *Anglicans and Puritans?*, 155–60.
[59]   Hooker, *Works* (London, 1666), 511–36.

human judgements of salvation and damnation made on visible grounds to be improper and presumptuous, and Walton hammers the point home: only those who embrace 'the boldness of . . . becoming Gods' make such judgements (p. 198). As with the previous question, Walton summarizes intelligently and with some political skill, and quotes Hooker himself, also accurately, with visible approbation and clear exemplary intention: 'I was willing to take notice of these two points, as supposing them to be very material; and that, as they are thus contracted, they may prove useful to my Reader; as also for that the Answers be arguments of Mr. *Hookers* great and clear Reason, and equal Charity' (p .206).

Given his accuracy in these cases where we possess a text to check against, Walton's summary of Hooker's Paul's Cross sermon of 1581 (the text for which is lost) is interesting. According to Walton, Hooker taught: 'That in God there were two Wills; an Antecedent, and a Consequent Will: his first Will, that all Mankind should be saved; but his second Will was, that only those should be saved, that did live answerable to that degree of Grace which he had offered, or afforded them' (p. 177). The implications of 'live answerable' in a reformed climate—if that was indeed what Hooker preached—are worth pondering. Walton's Hooker here argues that the 'degree of Grace' granted to men and women is observable through their actions. Not only does this imply a theology of works; it crosses Hooker's later insistence that salvation could not be computed through visible signs. While Walton is not known, in this biography or elsewhere, for his accuracy in general, his particular theological summaries of Hooker, where they can be checked, are fine. Hooker declines to summarize his sermon in his answer to Travers ('for', he explains frustratingly, 'I have it written'), and instead defends it only by saying that the bishop of London, John Aylmer, had been present when he gave it and had taken no exception to it. Walton follows him in this.[60] It is a defensive rejoinder; perhaps Hooker felt more vulnerable on this than on other points.[61]

---

[60] 'Mr. Hookers Answer to Mr. Travers Supplication', in ibid. 500; *Lives*, 177.

[61] I am indebted to Sean Hughes for pointing out to me the implications of Walton's accuracy in the Travers debate for his reporting of the 1581 Pauls Cross Sermon.

Walton is spared Paule's problems in describing the outcome of the Travers–Hooker disputes, for although he describes Travers 'Oppositions' as having been suppressed, it is not Hooker that does the suppressing but Whitgift.[62] It seems reasonable to concur, with Novarr, that Walton deals with the Travers controversy in such detail in order to counteract Gauden's version of the same event, which implied that Hooker had retired, routed, from the field.[63] It is at this point that Walton's Hooker instead discovers his preference for 'Study and quietness' over 'Contentions', and disappears off to Borne to write the *Polity* (p. 209).

With these exceptions, Walton is concerned to avoid the particulars of religious dispute. But, since the 1580s and 1590s raged with dissensions, this creates for him a problem of method. His intention is to recommend private duty, and throughout *Hooker*, therefore, he deploys a rhetoric which assumes passivity to be a property of rectitude. As he narrates it, national and religious stability are threatened by action: 'there appeared', he explains outrageously in his 'Character of the Times':

three several Interests, each of them fearless and restless in the prosecution of their designs; they may for distinction be called, the active *Romanists*, the restless *Nonconformists* (of which there were many sorts) and the passive *peaceable Protestant*. The Counsels of the first considered, and resolved on in *Rome*: the second both in *Scotland*, in *Geneva*, and in divers selected, secret, dangerous Conventicles, both there, and within the bosom of our own nation: the third pleaded and defended their Cause by establisht Laws, both Ecclesiastical and Civil; and, if they were active, it was to prevent the other two from destroying what was by those known Laws happily establisht to them and their Posterity. (pp. 182–3)

Walton's adjectives are polarized; indeed moralized. To be 'active' where what is 'establisht' is already complete and satisfactory, is to be destructive. To be 'restless' is to be violent, potentially if not actually. These drives for 'action' come from abroad to threaten our peace at home. The governing faction—or 'passive *peaceable Protestant*'—has law, and indeed a word Walton finds very powerful, 'reason', on its side. These are words which grab the *via media* for obedient stasis. Its staid defenders both protect and make up

---

[62] Again following Fuller, *Church History* (London, 1655), Book 9, pp. 216–17.
[63] Novarr, 252.

the 'lively stones'[64] of that threatened edifice, the Church; for this commonplace of the righteous as edifice surely underlies, at least in part, Walton's identification of the passive with the good. Certainly, contemporary engravings using this commonplace in the service of a comparable highly conformist rhetoric at the same time cast their active human figures as the villains. Three of these may serve to illustrate the point: two are reproduced (Figs. 5.3, 5.4).[65]

All are the work of William Marshall, who had also produced the portrait of Donne prefixed to the 1635 edition of his *Poems*, which appears accompanied by a verse by Walton himself. Each appeared in the 1640s, and thus have a particular relevance for a party determined to circumvent a repetition of the events of those troubled years. The first, a frontispiece to Fuller's *Holy State*, and the earliest of the three, is the only one to present the Church as irrefragable edifice. The second, prefixed to Francis Quarles's *The Shepheards Oracles* (the anonymous Preface of which is usually attributed to Walton[66]) shows the tree of religion as hacked away at the roots, and the third, the famous frontispiece to *Eikon Basilike* (not reproduced), has the Church's Supreme Head as unmistakable victim (albeit a highly successful martyr) with his hand upon the crown of thorns. In all three the emblem representing the Church is a still and solid central figure: an archway, a tree, the king—a figurehead—kneeling motionless in prayer. The adversaries absent from the Fuller image but portrayed in the Quarles and the *Eikon* are, by contrast, both marginalized and active. They hack at the root (from the outside) or the branch (from the inside), or riot in the darkness somewhere off to the left. Physically they are curiously small. Indeed, their very positioning removes from

[64] See 1 Peter 2: 5: 'Ye also, as lively stones, are built up a spiritual house, an holy priesthood, acceptable to God by Jesus Christ' (AV).

[65] Reproduced from Thomas Fuller, *The Holy State* (London, 1642), frontispiece; Francis Quarles, *Shepheards Oracles* (London, 1644), frontispiece; *Eikon Basilike* (London, 1649), frontispiece (not reproduced). I am grateful to Cambridge University Library for allowing the reproduction of the images from Fuller and Quarles.

[66] Included as Walton's work in Geoffrey Keynes's *The Compleat Walton* (London, 1929), and in *Waltoniana: Inedited Remains in Verse and Prose of Izaak Walton*, ed. Richard Herne Shepherd (London, 1878). But Gordon S. Haight, in 'The Author of "The Address" in Quarles' *Shepheards Oracles*', *Modern Language Notes*, 59 (1944), 118–20, suggests Phineas Fletcher to be the author.

FIG 5.3. Marshall engraved title-page of Fuller's *Holy State* (1641)

FIG 5.4. Marshall engraved title-page of Quarles's *Shepheards Oracles*
(1644)

them the right to dispute on equal terms, for the whole idea of any action whatsoever has acquired a moral illegitimacy. Within Walton's own narrative form, the assumption of rectitude in passivity is exploited in several ways. A simple initial manoeuvre is that, in describing Hooker as reluctant to engage in dispute, Walton strongly implies his position to be highly conformist without 'ingaging' himself by saying so. Nor need he go into detail about the content of Hooker's arguments; again, his position is implied by his reluctance to act. As well as this, Walton of course uses his story of Hooker's private demeanour as he narrates it to imply his political rectitude without having to talk about it. Like Naylor's Morton, Hooker is a 'living argument'. Walton was always to stress the greater efficacy of private actions over public utterances: even in his only pamphleteering venture, the anonymously printed *Love and Truth* of 1680, Walton quotes one of his (fictional) nonconformist addressees as having regretted, on his deathbed, the hours 'spent in disputes, and opposition to Government', describing them as 'a Corrosive, or (as *Solomon* says of ill-gotten riches) *like gravel in his teeth*'[67] while at the same time finding 'comfort' in 'those hours spent in devotion, and acts of Charity'.[68]

Walton adorns this with a pervasive vocabulary of significant oppositions. As the 'passive' is set against the 'active', so is 'serenity' against 'passion', 'quiet' against 'noise', and the 'moderate' against the 'extream'. (Hooker's sermons, in Walton, are 'neither long nor earnest', p. 218.) Here too, the public significance of private demeanour is very helpful to him. Although 'moderate' and 'modest' were not quite synonymous terms, they were strongly linked: John Barwick juxtaposes the two qualities in his *Life of Morton* because he perceives 'so much affinity' between them.[69] (In fact, of course, it is their difference which makes their juxtaposition effective.) Walton reverses the significance of these loaded terms occasionally when narrating public decisions, as with his description of Elizabeth I's advisors' 'active Wisdom' (p. 195). But the terms are never used in this way for individuals whose primary function is to obey. When Walton

---

[67] Walton here conflates Proverbs 20: 17 (hence his reference to Solomon) with Lamentations 3: 16, which resembles his paraphrase much more closely.
[68] *Love and Truth*, 21.   [69] Barwick, *Life*, 155.

describes the 'Romanists' as 'active' he means something very different (pp. 182–3).

It should be said that Walton shares this vocabulary of potent passivity with his adversaries. 'Moderation', in particular, is a quality claimed by a wide spectrum of opposed factions, and is as frequently proved by a 'modesty' of private demeanour in Clarke's biographical narratives as it is in Walton's. In the case of *Hooker*, it is striking how much Walton's phraseology resembles Gauden's. Although Novarr finds Walton's debt to Gauden largely to be defined by what he did not imitate, there is in terms of verbal similarity a debt to be paid there.[70] To take just one obvious derivation, Walton and Gauden both state their difficulties in writing the *Life* in virtually the same words. Walton writes, 'I knew him not in his Life, and must therefore not only look back to his Death, now 64 years past; but almost 50 years beyond that, even to his Childhood, and Youth' (p. 159). Gauden's version is, 'I well know, that a Picture taken at so great a distance from the life and death of Mr. Hooker (now sixty years past) can hardly hit the life exactly'.[71] Elsewhere Gauden describes Hooker's soul at one point as 'spacious', at another as 'capacious':[72] Walton refers to Hooker's 'quiet and capacious Soul' (p. 173). Gauden calls Hooker a 'Learned, Grave, Humble, Devout and diligent Divine';[73] Walton describes him as increasing in 'Learning and Prudence . . . Humility and Piety' (p. 166), and his 'diligence' as 'constant and unwearied' (p. 169). Gauden describes the nonconformists as full of 'passion' and 'prejudice';[74] Walton says of Hooker that he was 'never known to be angry, or passionate, or extream in any of his Desires' (p. 170). Gauden also describes the nonconformists as 'railing or clamouring', implies that they are full of the 'insolent passions and presumptions of their own hearts', and adds that they are guilty of 'Faction and Confusion';[75] Walton quotes Hooker as saying 'God abhors confusion as contrary to his nature' (p. 174), and as remarking to an adversary, 'Your next argument consists of railing and of reasons; to your Railing, I say nothing, to your Reasons, I say what follows' (p. 206).

But Gauden's and Walton's Hooker are different men. Walton deploys his (highly succesful) rhetoric of private—usually

---

[70] Novarr, 252–3.   [71] Gauden, *Hooker*, 6.   [72] Ibid. 8 and 16.

[73] Ibid. 17.   [74] Ibid. 3.   [75] Ibid. 20–1.

rural—clerical piety to celebrate Hooker's retiring disposition and relative obscurity, where Gauden was dismayed by it. There is, for instance, a striking contrast between Walton's (erroneous) assumption that Hooker was resident at every benefice presented to him,[76] and the unease which Gauden displays about the fact that Hooker 'contented himself as with one living at a time'.[77] Since Gauden feels the need to add that 'from this something rising, but not very high ground, did this excellent Person take his ascent and rise to Heaven, the only preferment worthy of him', the reader is constrained to believe that he had little time for the spiritual advantages of the humble life. On the other hand, Walton's story of the meeting between Jewel and the young Hooker goes to some lengths to suggest that even on the 'high ground' these advantages are deeply felt. Jewel, in handing Hooker his 'Walking-staff', and calling it a 'Horse, which hath carried me many a Mile, and I thank God with much ease', is giving his protégé a lesson in the importance of humility (p. 167).

Both Walton and Gauden follow Restoration biographical precedent in writing the reason-led *via media* straight onto the body and demeanour of Hooker. Gauden's Hooker, we learn, had a habit of body 'neither *gross* nor *meager*, sparing indeed, but not *withered*; he was neither large nor little. It is in mens *statures*, as in *trees*, if very tall, they are commonly *barren*; if shrubs and dwarfs, they bear but *little fruit*, though good.'[78] This is standard language. John Fell performs the same service for the Laudian divine Henry Hammond, when he describes his body as being 'such as suited with the noble use to which it designed . . . His stature was of just height and all proportionate dimensions, avoiding the extremes of gross and meagre advantaged by a graceful carriage, at once most grave, and yet as much obliging.'[79] The anonymous author of *Reason and Judgement*, the 1663 Life of Robert Sanderson, makes the same manoeuvre:

It pleased God he had a body suited to that pains he was designed for; a faithful Assistant rather than an impediment to his great Soul; symbolizing with it an exact temper, neither failing it through the weakness

[76] See Novarr, 267–8.   [77] Gauden, *Hooker*, 34.   [78] Ibid. 8.
[79] John Fell, *Life of . . . Henry Hammond*, in Henry Hammond, *A Practical Catechism*, ed. Nicholas Pocock (Oxford, 1847), p. lx. Pocock reprints the 1684 revision; Fell's *Life* was first published in 1661.

of organs, nor bothering it with the redundancy of humours, nor clog-
ging it with sad melancholy, nor disturbing it with an active unsetlednes,
nor ruffling it with angry choler; neither too large for it, nor too narrow,
but every way proportionable.[80]

This is skilful—the body that 'symbolizes' the moderate soul
and never disturbs it with 'active unsetlednes' is streets ahead of
Gauden's portrayal of Hooker as 'rather comely than courtly . . .
His whole garb and presence . . . rather plain then polished, and
not very promising beyond a studious simplicity'.[81] But Walton's
version takes the palm for deftness, poetic power, precision of
detail, scriptural opportunism, and suggestive force. Hooker, he
writes, had not been at his country parsonage of Borne a year
before people started going to visit him out of sheer admiration:

and . . . as our Saviour said of St. *John Baptist, What went they out to
see? a man clothed in purple and fine linnen?* no indeed, but an *obscure, harmless man, a man in poor Cloaths, his loins usually girt in a course Gown, or
Canonical Coat; of a mean stature, and stooping, and yet more lowly in the
thoughts of his Soul; his Body worn out, not with Age, but Study, and Holy
Mortifications; his Face full of Heat-pimples, begot by his unactivity and
sedentary life . . . of so mild and humble a nature, that his poor Parish Clerk
and he did never talk but with both their Hats on, or both off, at the same
time.* (p. 216)

This man is messenger for a better future[82]—the 'Posterity'
Hooker himself invokes in the preface to the *Polity*. It is a good
future for the lay person, because its great men are great in humility. As Hooker's body stoops, so his soul bends in adoration
before his God. Where Gauden talks of a 'speculative gravity, as
becomes a great Scholar, and solemn Divine',[83] Walton inserts
an anecdote that shows Hooker talking, as if to a social equal, to
his 'poor Parish Clerk'. (It is worth remembering that Walton
had himself been Donne's 'poor Parish Clerk'). His perspective
(like his implied readership) is a lay one: and extraordinarily influential. As Peter Lake has pointed out, Walton was crucial to the

---

[80] D. F., *Reason and Judgement: or, Special Remarques on the Life of the
Renowned Dr. Sanderson* (Oxford and London, 1663), 12–13.

[81] Gauden, *Hooker*, 8.

[82] In 1666 Walton, to make the point crystal clear, added that Hooker seemed
'like *St. John Baptist*, to be sanctified' from his mother's womb. See *The Life of
Mr. Richard Hooker*, in Hooker, *Works* (London, 1666), 4.

[83] Gauden, *Hooker*, 8.

construction of an 'Anglicanism' which Hooker never saw and Walton only imagined, but which we know intimately.[84] Walton's Hooker, with his pre-emptively Christlike humility, bearing on his body not only the signatures of that humility but the marks of an atoning suffering, brings about the restored future by calling it the past.

THE *LIFE OF DR. ROBERT SANDERSON*

Hooker, Hooker, *Inheritances, and Reinventions*

Walton wrote *The Life of Sanderson* in his early eighties. The finished *Life*, published in 1678, came out when he was 85. Even for Walton, whose talent flowered late, this was old to be embarking on a new project. It is not really surprising that his Preface, while gallant, also sounds tired: 'my Age, might have procur'd me a Writ of Ease,' he writes '. . . yet I met with such perswasions to begin, and so many willing Informers since . . . that when I found my self faint, and weary of the burthen with which I had loaden myself, and ready to lay it down; yet time and new strength hath at last brought it to be what it now is' (pp. 345–6). *Sanderson* does, in some ways, show signs of its author's age. Walton, an extensive employer of scriptural typology, seems always to have drawn on a capacious memory rather than looking things up; the same is true, in other *Lives*, of both the scripture and the poetry he quotes.[85] In *Sanderson* his memory seems sometimes to have let him down: perhaps you do not need to be eighty-something to mix up Jeremiah (or Solomon) and Job, as he does in assigning the phrase 'like gravel in his teeth' to the latter, or at another point to get the two (remarkably similar, and one either

---

[84] Lake, *Anglicans and Puritans?*, 229–30.

[85] See e.g. *Life of Donne*, quoting Hezekiah's words in Isaiah 38: 20 in a unique form: 'The Lord was ready to save, therefore will I sing my songs to the stringed instruments all the days of my life in the temple of my God' (*Lives*, 67). Of the main translations available to Walton (Geneva, Coverdale, Bishops' Bible, King James of 1611) this version is closest to the King James: 'The LORD *was ready* to save me: therefore we will sing my songs to the stringed instruments; all the dayes of our life, in the house of the LORD.' See also *Life of Donne*, version of 'Hymn to God my God, in my Sickness', where the last line is rendered in an order not found anywhere else (*Lives*, 66).

ironical or incomprehensible) 'unjust steward' parables melded
together; but it is mildly surprising.[86] Nothing, however, had either
impaired his political *nous* or blunted the subtlety of the ways
in which he attempted to reconcile the contingent with both exemplary and (in the more modern sense) biographical ethics. If
Sanderson is the political successor to *Hooker*, then the techniques
tried in *Hooker* find refinement in *Sanderson*.

It seems plausible that *Sanderson*, like *Hooker*, was a kind of
episcopal commission. Novarr reads this into Walton's reference
to 'persuasions', and argues well for Morley as commissioner
(Sheldon was by that time dead).[87] The political motive which,
he suggests, may plausibly originate from Morley, is evidently
compatible with Walton's own position. *Sanderson* updates
Hooker's agenda, providing a Civil War parable which preached
on disunity in the unsettled years which led up to the Exclusion
Crisis, as *Hooker* had been a lesson from the 1580s and 1590s
on civil dissension intended for the fearful aftermath of war.
The *Life of Sanderson* would take a 'moderate' but obdurately
anti-nonconformist figure, and use him to argue the necessity of
obedience in questions of ceremony and church-government, in
part to reinforce an argument, particularly common to the 1670s
and 1680s, that toleration for nonconformists opened the door to
the far greater Roman Catholic threat. Walton's usual preference
for the dramatic over the abstract decided him to make that point
by borrowing a version of Laud's words at the scaffold: 'the several Sects and divisions then in *England* . . . were like to bring the
Pope a far greater harvest, than he could ever have expected without them . . . we have lost the substance of Religion by changing
it into Opinion.'[88] He immediately reinforced the lesson by citing
works by Sanderson, which he claimed expressed the same fear.

[86] See *The Selected Writings of Izaak Walton*, ed. Martin, 133 and 134; see also
Proverbs 20: 17.
[87] See Novarr, 365–70.
[88] See *Lives*, 388; cf. *The Archbishop of Canterbury's Speech: or, his Funerall
Sermon, Preacht by Himself on the Scaffold on Tower-Hill, on Friday the 10. of
January, 1644* . . . (London, 1644), 12: 'Men that introduce prophanesse are
cloaked with a name of imaginary religion; for we have in a manner almost lost
the substance, and dwell much, nay too much a great deal in Opinion; and that
Church which all the Iesuites machinations in these parts of Christendome could
not ruine, is now fallen into a great deale of danger by her own.'

Certainly Sanderson, like Hooker, and for like reasons, was simultaneously a useful and a distinctly problematic figure to pick as Restoration exemplar. This was not surprising. The real Sanderson seems to have perceived himself as inheriting, against the odds, a Hookerian vision of Church polity.[89] Walton was to imply the same relationship; but given the nature of the 'Hooker' he had constructed in 1666, this was to differ sharply in its implications from what Sanderson actually meant. In choosing Sanderson, Walton (or Walton *et al.*) had certainly picked a self-consciously direct successor to a Whitgiftian take on church-government.[90] This, combined (at least before 1657) with an uncompromisingly grim predestinarianism, condemned him to a complex relationship with the growing Arminian-led ceremonialism of the conformist parties of the 1620s and 1630s. (Born in 1587, Sanderson was at this time at the prime of his life). Put crudely, in Sanderson Walton picked a rare hybrid beast, a Calvinist Laudian.[91] Preacher, in 1627, of the last sermon on predestination ever to be delivered at St Pauls Cross before Laud put his foot down,[92] Sanderson held for much of his life to a theology in most respects identical with the nonconformist adversaries he detested. The irony was not lost on him, though he drew from

[89] See H. Hammond, quoting a letter written to him by Sanderson in 'A Letter to Dr. Sanderson Concerning God's Grace and Decrees', in Sanderson, *Works*, ed. W. Jacobson, 6 vols. (Oxford, 1854), v. 297. This first appeared in print in H. Hammond, Χάρισ καί εἰρήνη, *A Pacifick Discourse* . . . (London, 1660). Sanderson here cites Hooker's *Polity* as a primary influence on his thinking.

[90] How far Hooker and Whitgift were in full agreement on the nature of church-government is a question on its own: it, and the related question of whether Hooker's *Polity* was written under Whitgift's aegis, are both helpfully and wittily discussed in P. Collinson, 'Hooker and the Elizabethan Establishment', in McGrade (ed.), *Richard Hooker and the Construction of Christian Community*, 149–81. It seems reasonable, however, to argue that Hooker and Whitgift were broadly in agreement, as (say) Hooker and Cartwright were not—an alignment Sanderson himself was quick to invoke. They also had more in common with each other than either of them had with Laud.

[91] For a discussion of Sanderson's problems with this cocktail see Peter Lake, 'Serving God and the Times: The Calvinist Conformity of Robert Sanderson', *Journal of British Studies*, 27 (1988), 81–116; for his connections with Laud, see esp. 102–3.

[92] Published a year later as R. Sanderson, *Two Sermons Preached at Paules-Crosse* (London, 1628). See N. Tyacke, *Anti-Calvinists: The Rise of English Arminianism c.1590–1640* (Oxford, 1987), 261.

it different conclusions. In his vauntedly irenic (though visibly anti-Arminian) tract *Pax Ecclesiae* (which reached the public eye first in 1678, trailing obscurely after Walton's pro-Arminian *Life*) he wrote:

I find more written against the Puritans, and their Opinions, and with more real satisfaction, and upon no less solid grounds, by those that have, and do dissent from the *Arminian* tenets than by those who have or do maintain them. Could that blessed Archbishop *Whitgift*, or the modest and learned *Hooker* have ever thought, so much as by dream, that men concurring with them in Opinion, should for some of those very Opinions be called *Puritans?*[93]

His flicking reference to Hooker's Preface manages to imply that even in his bleakest night-vision of the future Hooker could not have envisaged so unrecognizable a 'Reformed' Church. From Sanderson's point of view, it was not 'Puritan' theology that was the problem, but the famous 'tender conscience' on *adiaphora*. Conscience, he felt, could have nothing to do with it; he recognized no divine (that is, no scriptural) command concerning ceremonies or church-government; therefore Puritans were bound by a *civil* imperative to obedience; they were required to render unto Caesar his own. In the same spirit he rebuked the iconoclasm of John Cotton's Boston congregation in 1621, not on the grounds that iconoclasm was wrong (though he would not exactly say it was right either), but because the iconoclasts had not first gained the consent of the magistrate.[94] (His listeners were, by all accounts, unimpressed.) It is obvious, therefore, that arguments made on *iure divino* grounds in these questions could hold no weight with him, because they would play immediately into his adversaries' hands. On the contrary, Sanderson urgently needed to claim that, say, the perpetuation of episcopacy was a human *administrative* decision, rather than a question with which God was involved one way or the other. Only then could he argue that the question involved no one's religious conscience in itself. Thus, opposing episcopacy became a violation of God's command to obey the

[93] R. Sanderson, *Pax Ecclesiae*, in I. Walton, *The Life of Dr. Robert Sanderson late Bishop of Lincoln . . . to which is Added, some Short Tracts . . .* (London, 1678), 63–4.

[94] See Sanderson's sermon *Ad Clerum* at Boston, Lincs., 24 April 1621, in R. Sanderson, *Twelve Sermons . . .* (London, 1632), 99.

secular ruler in all things indifferent. In this Sanderson followed a Hooker whom Walton (*et al.*) had chosen to ignore.

All the same, however much Sanderson cited Hooker as the ultimate precedent for the homogeneity of his position, he knew he was whistling in the dark. It was futile to claim that there was no religious dimension to debates on episcopal or royal power when scriptural arguments concerning both had been current since the Reformation—and gathering speed, to say the least, in his life-time. You might as well argue that the question had no political dimension either. And his claims for the conformist centrality of Calvinist theology were unexceptionable in a way, but had to ignore the fact that the nature of what 'the elect' meant was altering.

The alteration was as much social as theological. Sanderson took the old-fashioned view that, while some were elect and some reprobate, only God could know which were which; no visible sign intelligible to human understanding, neither good works, nor virtuous living, nor any other thing, could make it possible to presume on God's sole prerogative to know the secrets of the human heart. This was very pure, of course, but in practice it led to an unendurable ambiguity about the state of one's soul. Nothing could deliver the Calvinist from the fear that she might be reprobate—not acts, nor even an inward conviction which might, after all, be delusory. In such circumstances despair was too likely to attend devotion.[95]

In response to the desperate need for 'assurance' (that is, assurance of election) among the communities of the would-be faithful, systems by which to establish assurance which combined the will, the understanding, and the desires of the anxious individual evolved.[96] While these were necessarily systems of self-examination, they stemmed from, and then fed back into, wider

---

[95] Sanderson did know this, and allowed for it while maintaining his stress on the unknowability of the divine decree by arguing that assurance was possible, but not a prerequisite for salvation.

[96] This is to make a most cursory allusion to a very large area, but some idea of the variety of possible systems can be gleaned from e.g. R. T. Kendall, *Calvin and English Calvinism to 1649* (Oxford, 1979) esp. 79–125 on experimental predestinarianism and the 'practical syllogism', which necessarily discusses at some length what, for different individuals under different pastors, could constitute assurance.

issues. Theologically, the question of the extent and nature of human agency in questions of salvation had over and over again to be evaluated and re-evaluated; Arminianism, after all, was one of many responses to the urgent need to believe that you could make a moral difference to your future—even if, strictly speaking, the choices you then made had been foreordained before the beginning of the world.[97] Socially, anxiety of this order led to the creation of tighter and tighter social units inside which the methods of self-examination and training would take place. These were governed, arbitrated, and upheld by figures who could effectively grant authority for each individual's assurance of salvation at the appropriate point in the process. The social cohesiveness of these groups formed a mutual-support network for those inside it, defining them in reassuring opposition to the reprobate outside the group.[98]

Sanderson detested the godly. Since his belief in the elect took as axiomatic that only God knew their names, the tight communities of self-styled elect (inside and outside the Church) he found both dangerous and unattractive; they were smug, they arrogated to themselves judgements only in God's ordinance, and in practical, pastoral terms, they were bad for the cohesiveness of whole parishes. Worst of all, they tended to separation.[99] But perhaps his detestation was given an extra edge by the fact that the alignment this set up between 'election' and separation set up at the same time the unpleasant possibility that he might one day be forced to choose between his conformity and his theology.

It is not surprising, then, that Sanderson spent the 1620s preaching a predestinarian viewpoint which, in affirming the validity of the visible Church (of which the whole nation were members incorporate), pleaded for a wider charity in human dealings. 'The fan is not in our hand to winnow the chaff from the wheat', he

---

[97] See ibid. 142–3.

[98] Discussed by Lake in 'Serving God and the Times', 99. The exclusive nature of these networks is in part what has made for modern historians' difficulties with who 'the godly' could be said to be. See Margaret Spufford, 'Can we Count the "Godly" and the "Conformable" in the Seventeenth Century?', *Journal of Ecclesiastical History*, 36 (July 1985), 428–38.

[99] See C. Holmes, *Seventeenth Century Lincolnshire* (Lincoln, 1980), 42–4, where Sanderson's opinions on Puritans are discussed in the context of his Lincolnshire parish.

wrote.[100] This tended to reinforce the sense that he was in part years out of date[101]—a quality which might go some way to explain his attractiveness for Walton, whose viewpoint, formed before the war, was similarly uncharmed by 'partiality'. Walton's obvious affection for the Puritan divine Richard Sibbes (dead by 1635) is instructive here; like Sanderson, Sibbes in the end chose to subordinate a strictly predestinarian theology he certainly held, to concentrate on what he felt to be more practical issues. What the issues were differed between Sanderson and Sibbes, but looked at in one way, the effect was the same. To balance a concern for the troubled souls of a flock desperate for assurance against the dangers of partiality, Sibbes located assurance at the point of desire. To cleave to Christ was to have faith; to have faith was to be saved. 'Reason not', he commanded, 'whether God hath elected or Christ hath died for thee. This is the secret will of God. But, the commandment is, to believe in Christ. This binds.' Conversion, he preached, was an act for which 'the grace is from the Spirit, but when the grace is received, the act is from ourselves, not only from ourselves, but immediately from ourselves . . . we do not actually believe, but by an act of the Spirit; but yet the act of believing is our own'.[102] In this way, without leaving hold of a grace-centred theology, and without trespassing on the divine pre-rogative solely to distinguish between the elect and the reprobate, Sibbes was able to clear a little room for something suspiciously like free will, and even to argue for works as a visible sign of assur-ance. He managed to exist comfortably under Laud (he was Master of Catherine Hall, Cambridge, from 1626) by maintaining an exact conformity in all indifferent questions.[103] Sibbes is linked to Sanderson through John Cotton, whom Sibbes converted,[104] and who was Sanderson's Lincolnshire neighbour. Sanderson held the living of Boothby Pagnell and Cotton that of Boston before his

[100] Sanderson, *Works*, ed. Jacobson, iii. 7.

[101] The time-lag of his concerns is discussed in Lake's article 'Serving God and the Times', 91–2.

[102] R. Sibbes, *Complete Works*, ed. A. Grosart, 7 vols. (Edinburgh, 1862–4), v. 391; iv. 449.

[103] See Kendall, *Calvin and English Calvinism*, 103.

[104] According to Cotton Mather, John Cotton kept a picture of Sibbes 'in that part of his house where he might oftenest look upon it'. See Cotton Mather, *Magnalia Christi Americana*, 2 vols. (Hartford, Conn., 1853), i. 280.

emigration to America. Sanderson, of course, deplored the tendency to separatism he felt Cotton invited in making the godly so
discrete a group; yet both Sanderson and Cotton can still be seen
as (rather different) models of pastoral concern. Clive Holmes, in
his study of seventeenth-century Lincolnshire, compares the two
in discussing ministerial responsibility; while he reinforces their
theological differences, he does so by stressing to what extent they
share common ground.[105] We know Sanderson preached twice at
Boston (presumably at Cotton's invitation), though it cannot be
said he made a hit with the godly either time.[106] Finally, there was
Walton himself, whose famous verse on Sibbes,

> Of this blest man, let this just praise be given
> Heaven was in him, before he was in heaven

Walton wrote in the flyleaf of his own copy of Sibbes's *Returning
Backslider* (1650).[107] He represents, arguably, the most convin-
cing link between the two men.

What, for Sanderson, was the practical concern which took
precedence over his Calvinism? We know (partly, but not exclusively, through Walton) that his opposition to Arminianism
waned through the 1650s, and we are invited (by Walton, Henry
Hammond, and the unpopular Master of Magdalen College,
Oxford, Dr Thomas Pierce[108]) to infer that he formally abjured
Calvinism at the Restoration. And he does seem to have changed
some part of his mind. It seems reasonable to assume that a kind
of ethical *realpolitik*, as much as conviction, lay behind this. The
Puritan beast was, evidently, more beastly than the Arminian
in so far as it threatened the unity of the visible Church. When,

[105] See Holmes, *Seventeenth Century Lincolnshire*, 42–63.
[106] See Sanderson, a sermon *Ad Clerum*, 78. Sanderson refers to the unfriend-
liness with which his last sermon—during which he made some direct criticisms
of members of the congregation—was met, but this one (in which he argues that
no visible sign can distinguish the elect from the reprobate, and that 'if the very
Divel of hell should preach the truth, he must be heard, and beleeved, and obeyed',
seems hardly more calculated to please its auditors.
[107] Now preserved in Salisbury Cathedral Library. See also *Selected Writings
of Izaak Walton*, ed. Martin, 161.
[108] See *The Life and Times of Anthony Wood*, i. 420: 'For 10 yeares that he
[Pierce] *raigned* (for he use to stile himself "prince") the College was continually
in faction . . . High, proud, and somtimes little better than mad. But at last they
got him out for the deanery of Salisbury.'

therefore, he found his own anti-Arminian convictions aligning him with potential or actual schismatics, he found himself prepared to modify—perhaps even to sacrifice—those convictions for the sake of that unity.

Walton's sympathy with a point of view which put unity before differences of religious opinion is easy to imagine. Throughout the *Life of Sanderson* he refuses to comment in his own person on the rightness or wrongness of either side of the debate on election (rather desperately, at one point, calling the terms of both sides 'truths, or untruths, or both, be they which they will', p. 386). Instead (as with *Hooker*), he refers the reader to appendices written by senior clergymen to determine the matter. But although his main text is so characterized by a visible desire not to have to take sides, he is still careful to chronicle (and to praise) Sanderson's gradual alterations of position.[109]

For it was all done with a visible reluctance on Sanderson's part. As Walton himself records, by 1657 (when his sermons of 1632 were reprinted) Sanderson had altered his marginal notes to exclude the word 'Arminian' from his armoury of insult.[110] Before that he seems to have regarded Arminianism as a branch of Pelagianism—evidently feeling that the element of human agency it allowed for implied a denial of Original Sin, and thus a claim for the autonomous perfectibility of human nature.

Sometime before 1660 Sanderson wrote Dr Hammond, the Arminian monarchist who had, with Sanderson himself, been chaplain to Charles I during the 1640s, a letter in which he thrashed the whole business out. Hammond found the letter too ambivalent to print as written (which was what Sanderson wanted him to do), and instead extracted its acceptable parts in a treatise-cum-letter of his own, published in 1660, *A Pacifick Discourse*.[111] Evidently it went hard with Sanderson to be spoken for in this way. A letter Dr Pierce wrote to Gilbert Sheldon on the subject in October 1659 makes this sufficiently clear. 'He is now resolved', he wrote, '. . . that I shall either print his whole

[109] See e.g. *Lives*, 387, finishing: 'And let me here tell the Reader also, that if the rest of mankind would, as Dr. *Sanderson*, not conceal their alteration of Judgment, but confess it to the honour of God and themselves, then our Nation would become freer of pertinacious Disputes, and fuller of Recantations.'
[110] Ibid. p. 387; Lake, 'Serving God and the Times', 84–5.
[111] Hammond, *A Pacifick Discourse*.

Letter, (which will not be to my advantage, much less to his, whilst he condemns or doubts in some places the very things he allows and affirms in others,) or lose the advantage which I expected in printing any part of it.' Five weeks later Sanderson bowed to the inevitable. 'Dr Sanderson', wrote Pierce to Sheldon, 'hath at last consented.'[112] Pierce was also to link Hammond's views on prescience with Sanderson's in his treatise (against John Hickman), *An Impartial Inquiry into the Nature of Sin*, published the same year.

Walton's treatment of Sanderson's 'change of heart' is discussed in very helpful detail by David Novarr.[113] One of the letters he appends to *Sanderson* is from Dr Pierce himself, a statesmanlike missive which places the change of heart as early as can feasibly be asserted (1625), given the doctrine he preaches in other published works. Walton, in keeping the letter as an appendix, leaves Pierce to assert his own authority without further endorsement of the letter's contents. The other letter he appends, from Thomas Barlow, avoids discussing Sanderson's doctrinal position almost entirely. Walton had asked Barlow because he was an eminent casuist, because he had known Sanderson, and because like Sanderson he had been bishop of Lincoln. Barlow avoided discussing the question because he had no sympathy with Sanderson's move (however ambiguous) away from strict Calvinism. He stuck instead to reminiscences.

One of the more apparently puzzling features of Walton's treatment of Sanderson's doctrinal shift is his printing of Sanderson's *Pax Ecclesiae* for the first time with the *Life* in 1678. *Pax Ecclesiae* pre-dates Hammond's Sanderson letter by about thirty years—though it probably post-dates 1625. It begins pacifically, but deftly uses its very reasonable tone to put the followers of Arminius firmly beyond the pale of orthodoxy. 'Let us keep our understandings within some competent bounds of sobriety and truth,' it concludes, 'that we neither lose our selves in curious Enquiries to little purpose nor suffer our judgments to be envenomed with the Poison either of rank *Pelagian* heresie, or *Semi-Pelagian* popery, or quarter-*Pelagian* and *Arminian* novelty.'[114]

[112] Sanderson, *Works*, vi. 355 n.   [113] See Novarr, 411–34.
[114] R. Sanderson, *Pax Ecclesiae*, in I. Walton, *The Life of Dr. Robert Sanderson . . . to which is Added, some Short Tracts . . .* (London, 1678), 83–4.

Perhaps, as Novarr argues, the reprinting of the *Pax Ecclesiae* was a mistake issuing from a combination of causes: Walton's readiness to trust the political judgement of his advisors, and his own sense of the piece as winningly moderate. Certainly it sets out to walk a middle way, in terms Walton might easily have found grateful: its first tenet (in discussing predestination, grace, faith, and free will) wishes

That particular Churchs [*sic*] would be as tender as may be in giving their definitions and derminations [*sic*] in such Points as these; not astricting those that live therein determinately either to the affirmative or negative, especially where there may be admitted a latitude of dissenting without any prejudice done to the Substance of the Catholick Faith, or to the Tranquillity of the Church, or to the Salvation of the Dissenter. In which respect the moderation of the Church of *England* is much to be commended, and to be preferred, not only before the *Roman* Church, which with insufferable tyranny bindeth all her Children, upon pain of Damnation, to all her Determinarions [*sic*] even in those Points, which are no way necessary to Salvation; but also before sundry other Reformed Churches, who have proceeded further this way than our Church hath done.[115]

It is worth pointing out that Sanderson's 'moderation' in these matters cuts both ways. If Sanderson continued to think like this, he had a latitude of private belief of his own which, so long as he did not make it public, would allow him a continued (though tacit) dissent from the new Arminian 'orthodoxy' after the Restoration with a clear conscience.

That is speculation. As far as Walton's motives went, he may indeed have been naive or credulous. He fiddled with his statements about the treatise when he came to revise *Sanderson* in 1681 in a way which suggests he was not quite sure of himself. While stating that the *Pax Ecclesiae* 'still remains to be of great estimation', this was no longer, apparently, a view held 'among the most learned', because that last phrase vanished. And he added a sentence at the end of that paragraph sending us to Sanderson's letters to Pierce, and to his Will, as evidence that he had 'alter'd his Judgment in some Points' since writing it.[116] On the other hand,

---

[115] *Pax Ecclesiae*, 51–2.
[116] Compare *Life of Sanderson*, 1678, sigs. d7^v–8^r with *Life of Sanderson* in Sanderson, *XXXV Sermons . . .* (London, 1681), 16.

it is reminiscent of his technique with Hooker's *Polity*. Here again, Walton was publishing hitherto unpublished material which had politically problematic elements; here again, arguably, Walton was attempting to control readings of his subject's works by means of an—increasingly important—biographical preface.

For by the time *Sanderson* was published, the relative status of 'life' and 'works' had shifted yet further. The title tells us that alone: *the Life of Dr. Sanderson, late Bishop of Lincoln . . . to Which is Added, Some Short Tracts or Cases of Conscience, Written by the said Bishop*. Walton's narrative was clearly ascendant over the other material with which it was published.

What the 'tracts' actually were is also instructive. Three were apparently by Sanderson, but one of these, *Bishop Sanderson's Judgement in One View for the Settlement of the Church*, was actually a collage of scattered statements, taken from his prefaces and sermons and unified by an anonymous editor.[117] With these tracts 'by' Sanderson was printed the *Reasons of the Present Judgment of the University of Oxford, Concerning the Solemn League and Covenant, Negative Oath, Ordinances Concerning Discipline and Worship*, dated 'June 1, 1647', and a sermon by Hooker purporting to have been 'Found in the Study of the Late Learned Bishop Andrews.[118]

Both *Hooker* and *Herbert* had been the selling-attractions of the volumes in which they had appeared. Both had been published separately before appearing as prefaces; and *Herbert* was first

[117] Anthony á Wood thought the editor was also the publisher. See Anthony á Wood, *Athenae Oxonienses*, ed. Philip Bliss, 4 vols. (London, 1813–20), iii., col. 630.

[118] A brief survey of copies of this 1678 edition owned by institutions in Cambridge reveals the majority to conform to this pattern. Nine copies were found (one incomplete), two in Cambridge University Library, two in the Library at St John's College, three in the Wren Library at Trinity College (of which one is a fragment only containing three of the tracts usually found published with the *Life*), one in Selwyn College Library, one in the Butler Library at Corpus Christi College (not seen), and one in the Founders' Library of the Fitzwilliam Museum. Of the books seen, only one of the Wren Library copies was found to contain anything unusual: John Cosin's *History of Popish Transubstantiation . . .* (London, 1676). Nevertheless, the linkage of Walton with Cosin does indicate that someone perceived Walton's sympathies to be comparable: perhaps with regard to Cosin's 'Laudian' stance and his concern with the value of private piety in the laity (see Spurr, *Restoration Church*, 371).

issued as a flyer for Walton's collected *Lives* of 1670, only appearing as a preface to Herbert's own work in 1674.[119] Walton's biographies, then, were seen to contain information *at least* as important as anything else the book might contain. Not that this was a new idea for biographers: John Harris had made the same claim for his account of Lake. But Harris's subject was also his 'Avthovr', and he had made it very plain that the whole aim of his account (which he did not define as a 'Life') was to facilitate a just reading of Lake's *Sermons*, with which it was bound. In the *Life of Sanderson* the balance has altered radically; neither publisher nor biographer even claim the ascendance of Sanderson's words, which are instead pressed into service for Walton's ends.

The *Judgment in One View* had followed Hammond's lead in censoring and fragmenting its author. More interesting still, it had first appeared (in 1663, three years after *A Pacifick Discourse*) bound in with a pamphlet called *Reason and Judgement: or, Special Remarques of the Life of the Renowned Dr. Sanderson*. This presented itself as a biography in epistolary form: a letter from someone signing himself 'D.F.' which enumerated Sanderson's living virtues on hearing the news of his death, and which was addressed to 'the Reverend J.W.D.D.P.L.'.[120] But the 'biography', as we shall see, combined a relentless exemplarity with generalities so vague as to make the work something closer to a Character.

The thrust of D.F.'s narrative was the virtues of moderation, here being used as a term implying limited toleration. Sanderson was, of course, a good choice: he had been nominated for the Westminster Assembly (though he turned it down),[121] and had been elevated by the king arguably because he appeared likely to welcome conciliatory measures. The composite tract sang the same tune; while its 'judgments' were all found in favour of conformity, its language was carefully tempered 'for *tender* [consciences] . . . must be *tenderly* dealt withal' (p. 90).

---

[119] Novarr, 365 and 511–12.

[120] Professor Diarmaid MacCulloch suggests a possible identification of the dedicatee's initials 'J.W.D.D.P.L.' with 'Johannes Wilkins, DD, Pastor Londiniensis'. In 1663 Wilkins was rector of St Lawrence Jewry: his career spanned the Interregnum and Restoration and he would have thus have been receptive to messages about moderation.

[121] See Lake 'Serving God and the Times', 108.

By the time Walton reprinted the *Judgment in One View*, its political meaning had changed emphasis, inviting a Protestant accord maintained against a Catholic threat. Walton would never have considered any other route to accord than an unconditional obedience by the nonconformist interest: this is clear enough from his own *Love and Truth*, which appeared two years later in 1680. Framed as a letter which spoke the truth in love to a nonconformist cousin, the pamphlet was bald:

> And you ought to consider, that if this Church were overthrown, the *Church* of *Rome* would make it their great advantage, and therefore many of them do encourage and assist you in this present disturbance . . . look about you in time; and do not say, when it is too late, *You meant not to bring in Popery* . . . if ever *Popery* or a *standing Army* be set up in this Nation . . . it is the indiscreet zeal, and restless activity of you and your Party that will bring both in, though you mean it not.[122]

Walton never acknowledged *Reason and Judgment* as a source for his *Life of Sanderson*. Perhaps that was because his political intentions for its accompanying tract (the *Judgment in One View*) were so different; but it is more persuasive that he simply did not regard *Reason and Judgment* as a real biography of Sanderson. In his Preface to *Sanderson* he exhibits 'wonder' that 'indeavours to preserve his Memory' had been 'already fifteen years neglected' (p. 345). We know that no one researched *Reason and Judgment* for him, because he says that he 'met with these little Tracts annex'd' when researching *Sanderson* himself (p. 346).

But *Reason and Judgment* has an odd provenance. It is anonymous, and it lies about where it was printed.[123] And, fascinatingly, those parts of it not lifted from Bishop Fell's *Life of Hammond* seem to have been filched from Gauden's *Life of Hooker*. Walton, of course, knew Gauden's *Life* exceedingly well, and it is inconceivable that he should not have read Fell's *Hammond*, given his profession and after having met the living Hammond through his intimate patron Bishop Morley. And the borrowings are barefaced, even for a genre which thrived on narrating exemplary types. To take just one example, Fell says of Hammond that, 'in his sicknesses, if they were not so violent to make the recollection

---

[122] *Love and Truth*, 21–2.
[123] The following is helpfully discussed in greater detail in Novarr, 458–67.

of thoughts impossible, he never intermitted study, but rather
re-enforced it then as the most appropriate revulsive and diversion of pain.[124] And D.F. writes this of Sanderson: 'In sicknesses, if they were not so violent as to make the recollection of
his thoughts impossible, he never intermitted study, but rather
re-inforced, as the best ease of his distemper, and diversion of
his pain.'[125] D.F. also borrows phrases and details from Gauden.
While it comes as no surprise that both authors should stress the
commonplaces of comeliness, gravity, simplicity of dress, and
modesty of demeanour, their identical phraseology is striking.
Gauden describes Hooker as having a '*garb* and *presence* . . . rather
plain then *polished* . . .', and refers to his '*speculative gravity*, as
becomes a great Scholar, and *solemn Divine*'.[126] D.F. writes of
Sanderson that, 'His Carriage [was] grave, comely and modest;
his Garb plain and studious, such as became a great Scholar and
a solemne Divine'.[127] Even Gauden's odd remark that Hooker's
friends were 'few, but choise'[128] is perpetuated: Sanderson,
apparently, was 'choice in his friends'.[129] And the paragraph in
praise of friendship that follows is lifted straight from the *Life of
Hammond*. 'The union of minds thereby produced he judged the
utmost point of human happiness, the very best production that
nature has in store, or grows on earth', wrote Fell of Hammond.
'Friendship . . . was the greatest happiness and relief among the
cares and troubles of the world . . . an union of mind is next the
union of soul and body', agreed D.F.[130] More fundamentally than
these details of similarly expressed commonplaces can convey,
the 'moderate' Sanderson is a rewrite of the Hooker Gauden
attempted to invent; an inheritor on terms observably different
from those Sanderson might have acknowledged, and certainly
from those Walton would identify. Sanderson would have disliked
the nature of its stress on limited toleration because it was based
on an acknowledgement that 'conscience' had a place at all in the
debate on *adiaphora*, and Walton's brief for obedience and his lean-
ing towards the numinous importance of ceremonies per se put

---

[124] John Fell, *Life of Dr. Henry Hammond*, in Henry Hammond, *A Practical
Catechism*, 16th edn., ed. Nicholas Pocock (Oxford, 1847), lxx.
[125] *Reason and Judgement*, 12.   [126] Gauden, *Hooker*, 8.
[127] *Reason and Judgement*, 14.   [128] Gauden, *Hooker*, 9.
[129] *Reason and Judgement*, 15.
[130] Fell, *Hammond*, p. lxxii; *Reason and Judgement*, 15.

limited toleration out of consideration. Indeed, he had disliked Gauden's *Life* partly on those very grounds.

Walton's *Sanderson*, perhaps, suppressed the 'Sanderson' of 1663: a figure made up of a tract the real Sanderson did not organize and can barely be said to have written, whose characteristics combined the narrated qualities of another Arminian monarchist with a Hooker constructed by a different author (Gauden) for comparable political purposes. These purposes the real Sanderson would not have approved. Walton was to replace D.F.'s figure with another kind of Hookerian inheritor, who followed his *Hooker* in structure and substance as D.F. had followed Gauden's. Yet Walton's Sanderson had developed politically not only out of, but from, Walton's Hooker, and had had thirteen years (between 1665 and 1678) to do it in. (*Reason and Judgment*, on the other hand, had come out only two years after Gauden's *Hooker*, and only three after the Restoration: what room for 'development' there?) Not only that, but Walton's *Life of Sanderson* (if any more nudging were needed) appeared in company with a tract by Hooker himself, fortuitously 'discovered' in Andrewes's study in a way which balanced the heinousness of Charke's 'destruction' of the last books of the *Polity* in Hooker's own study after his death. While Sanderson might not wholly have recognized either the 'Hooker' he grew from or the 'Sanderson' he became in Walton's version, he was, paradoxically, slightly more likely to have approved of the political intentions underwriting Walton's portraits.

Walton's Sanderson and Walton's Sanderson

Thus far, Walton's motives for his *Life* have had a rather two-dimensional look. I have concentrated on political intention as if it were separable from ethics or virtue, when it is sufficiently obvious that, as far as Walton was concerned, it was not; and I have discussed religious questions as if they were straightforwardly synonymous with political intention. Finally, I have taken no account of what may have been a prime reason for Walton's biography: love. Walton was a fine and effective exemplary writer, but paradoxically, his very skill that way led him to seek ways of individualizing his portraits with their originals' signature—a tendency which was to mark the beginning of the end for the exemplary type in biography, and to open a route for Boswellian detail.

Sanderson demonstrates a new step in that direction. It is true that its political imperatives make it more of a 'life and times' work than any other biography but *Hooker*; but in it Walton, for the first time, allows his own direct observing, speaking presence. 'This malice and madness was scarce credible; but I saw it', he writes of the mass reaction to the news that Laud's sentence had been suspended, when 'many of the malicious Citizens fearing his pardon, shut up their Shops, professing not to open them till Justice was executed'.[131] (The deft double meaning that hinges on 'Justice' is typical: the manipulation of the fourth verse of Psalm 99, less so.) He even tells us that at times he had 'been so bold as to paraphrase what he (whom I had the happiness to know well) would have said' (p. 345). His 'Sanderson' says how much more important 'meekness and charity' are than debate on 'hard Questions' (p. 394)—but then that was, in a way, a theoretical position of the real Sanderson, as it had been of Sibbes, that he could and did defend with erudition. Sanderson, after all, preached charity for the 'whole society of Christian men, the system and body of the whole visible church', because the decrees of God were secret.[132] Sanderson had been Walton's good friend, and he receives a friend's commemoration; the *Life*'s strong exemplary strand is reinforced subtly with detail. Walton even found ways of converting Sanderson's words into deeds—something of a feat, given the deliberative nature of his material. *Reason and Judgment*'s main defect, from a Waltonian perspective, was its living subject's absence. *Sanderson* attempts to resurrect the loved dust of a real man.

Commissioned or not by Morley, Walton had expressed an interest in a Sanderson biography before ever he was likely to have been approached, in 1670. He writes in his Epistle to the Reader which prefaces the collected *Lives* that:

when the next age shall (*as this do's*) admire the Learning and clear Reason which that excellent Casuist *Doctor Sanderson* (*the late Bishop of Lincoln*) hath demonstrated in his Sermons and other writings, who, if they love vertue, would not rejoyce to know that this good man was as remarkable for the *meekness and innocence of his life,* as for his great learning; . . . And though I cannot hope, that my example or reason can

[131] *Lives*, 379.   [132] See Holmes, *Seventeenth Century Lincolnshire*, 42.

perswade to this: yet, I please my self, that I shall conclude my Preface, *with wishing that it were so.*[133]

This is another 'Example versus Precepts' argument; as if Walton were anxious to remove Sanderson's name from debate and put it where it belonged, with private integrity. He saw the 'meekness and innocence' Sanderson's conduct exemplified as having been at least as important, and as worthy of a permanent record, as the 'great learning' displayed in his writings. In 1670, though, he was clearly hoping that someone else would record Sanderson's virtues for him.

When this did not come about, and Walton yielded to his 'persuasions' internal or external or (as Walton would say) 'both', he characteristically took up a position of witness rather than polemicist. He warns the present with the lessons of the past almost purely through anecdote. Demonstrable private sanctity is set in relief against public chaos, and the reader is invited to make the inference. Walton sharpens this with personal reminiscence, as in the famous story in which he meets Sanderson 'accidentally in *London* in sad-coloured clothes' during the years of the Commonwealth on a wet and windy day.[134] They take shelter in an inn, and Sanderson takes this opportunity to furnish Walton with a number of his opinions (p. 393). He laments the abolition of the liturgy and praises the use of the psalter, condemns 'irregular and indiscreet preaching', recommends the regular use of homilies, and finishes on a personal note, deprecating his own 'unmanly bashfulness' (pp. 393–6). Walton thus defines their joint stand on the prayer–preaching debate, deftly ensuring that only preaching is characterized as a medium for dispute, while the liturgy retains the passive virtues of a static form—virtues which, he adds, may much more readily be translated into real acts of *caritas*. It is at this point that he 'quotes' Sanderson as having 'seem'd to lament' that the practice of devotion using the liturgy and psalms 'should in common Pulpits be turn'd into needless debates about *Free-will, Election,* and *Reprobation,* of which, and many like

---

[133] *Lives* (1670), sig. A7.

[134] *Lives*, 393. This description of Sanderson's dress combines both meanings of 'sad'—both drab-coloured and spiritually saddened. There is some suggestion, too, of mourning garments, appropriate to the 'sombre, penitential mood' among Anglicans in those years. See Spurr, *Restoration Church*, 20–3.

Questions, we may be safely ignorant, because Almighty God intends not to lead us to Heaven by hard Questions, but by meekness and charity, and a frequent practice of Devotion' (p. 394). For Walton, the learning and casuistry which are Sanderson's gifts are informed and tempered by a sanctified simplicity of life. A saint shares a pint of beer in a war-zone; it is no accident that Walton's 'Character' of Sanderson's 'person and temper' follows this scene. The quotation from the apocryphal book Ecclesiasticus which appears on the title-page, 'Mysteries are revealed to the meek', draws together Sanderson's two essential aspects (subtlety and humility) by means of a fundamental Christian paradox (p. 341). The quotation from the Psalms with which the *Life* ends is less equivocal (and a lot less suitable): 'Blessed is the man in whose Spirit there is no guile' (p. 415).

Walton's authorial presence as witness, then, serves to lend authenticity to his observations. This is extended to his characterization of the warring sides as representing a particularized, contemplative, and obedient private virtue against a general, thoughtless, and rebellious mass feeling. It is clear that Walton assumes that his personal attestation will be enough: he does not always bother with sources for his anecdotes. The reader is presumably expected to assume first-hand knowledge.

What complicates our assessment of how individual a portrait Walton's Sanderson is, is that many of the anecdotes, though memorable, are also identifiably either generic or borrowed. This does not actually dispose of the matter of their authenticity, but it does put it into question. For instance, he narrates an incident at Boothby Pagnol [Pagnell], the benefice Sanderson held during the Interregnum, where Sanderson is disturbed as he reads the service by soldiers who 'forc'd his Book from him and tore it, expecting extemporary Prayers' (p. 382). No need here for the device he employs in the *Life of Hooker*, where he reports Hooker's 'Parish-Clerk' as saying that there had been so many sequestrations of 'good men' from their livings during the Commonwealth that 'he doubted if his good Master Mr. Hooker had lived till now, they would have Sequestred him too' (p. 217).[135] This anecdote from *Hooker* prefigures the incident in *Sanderson*;

---

[135] Sanderson, though, was not sequestered; Walton's anecdote substitutes a smaller martyrdom for the greater.

but Clarke tells an identical story of Samuel Crook—with the royalist soldiers, this time, as the agents of destruction.[136] But then the anecdote is a shared property because it actually happened on both sides, which complicates the issue.

Walton gives Sanderson personal idiosyncracies (such as his embarrassment about his '*unmanly bashfulness*') to particularize him; but every one of his idiosyncracies has an exemplary function. His 'unmanly bashfulness' recalls Hooker's 'blessed . . . bashfulness' (p. 216): in both cases, it demonstrates humility. And Sanderson's bad memory for his sermons (which looks very like particularized detail) is also a quality ascribed to Hammond by Fell. Walton tells a story in which Hammond persuades Sanderson to preach a short sermon without his text. Sanderson agrees, gives the text to Hammond to look after during the service, and becomes hopelessly confused so that Hammond '(looking on his Sermon as written) observed him to be out, and so lost to the matter, that he also became afraid for him; for 'twas discernable to many of the plain Auditory' (p. 385). On the way home after the service Sanderson tells Hammond that no man will ever again persuade him to preach 'without Book' (p. 385). Fell writes that Hammond's memory was 'serviceable, but not officious', and that he found it 'harder with him to get one sermon by heart than to pen twenty'.[137]

Here the presence of Hammond in Walton's anecdote is at least circumstantial evidence that Walton had borrowed from Fell's *Hammond*; but he uses his detail differently. The whole anecdote is really an additional point about 'bashfulness', because Walton also claims that Sanderson had a really remarkable memory, even by the high early modern standards which would ordinarily expect a divine to deliver a lengthy sermon by heart. 'His memory', claims Walton, 'was so matchless and firm, as 'twas only overcome by his bashfulness; for he alone, or to a friend, could repeat all the *Odes of Horace*, all *Tully's Offices*, and much of *Juvenal* and *Persius* without Book' (p. 398). This is a good example of the deft way Walton would mix the generic and the specific, or would borrow from other *Lives* to a particular end. We cannot know whether in doing so he narrates a quality Sanderson had fortuitously, or one Sanderson himself may have cultivated or developed in response

---

[136] Clarke, *Lives*, 211.   [137] Fell, *Hammond*, lxiii.

to an exemplary expectation which bore at least as heavily on real lives as on narratives of lives, or whether it was simply a quality Walton thought Sanderson ought to have possessed—one, perhaps, which demonstrated a truth about him even if it was not itself a true detail.

We find another, somewhat different example of this mix of generic and individual in Walton's version of another incident at Boothby Pagnell. He describes Sanderson as having persuaded a landlord to forgive his tenant his rent when 'a sudden Flood' had carried away the tenant's hay and rendered him unable to pay it (pp. 365–7). Fell tells a remarkably similar story to illustrate Hammond's humanity in collecting his tithes. Fell writes that Hammond,

having set the tithe of a large meadow, and upon agreement received part of the money at the begining of the year; it happening that the profits were afterwards spoiled and carried away by a flood, he, when the tenant came to make the last payment, not only refused it, but returned the former sum, saying to the poor man, 'God forbid I should take the tenth where you have not the nine parts'.[138]

Perhaps Walton borrowed the story from Fell; he will certainly have met with it there. But it is also true that Sanderson accompanied his fierce support of the doctrine of callings with an equally fierce interpretation of the duties of those set over the poor. In (amongst other places) a sermon preached in Grantham in 1623, Sanderson makes it exceedingly clear what he thinks of grasping landlords. Preaching on Job 29: 14–17, he argues that landlords are the men

wherein *Iob* alludeth to rauenous and saluadge beasts; *beasts of prey*, that lye in wait for the smaller Cattell, and when they once catch them in their *pawes*, fasten their *teeth* vpon them, and teare them in pieces and deuoure them. Such *Lyons*, and *Wolfes*, and *Beares*, and *Tygers*, are the greedy great ones of this world, who are euer rauening after the estates and the liuelihoods of their meaner neighbours, *snatching*, and *biting*, and *deuouring*, and at length eating them vp and consuming them . . .
   . . . there are *Grinders* too; men whose teeth are *Lapides Molares*, as the ouer and the nether mill-stone: *Depopulators*, and *racking Landlords*, and such great ones, as by heauy pressures and burdens and sore bargains breake the backes of those they deal withall. These first by little

---

[138] Fell, *Hammond*, xxiii.

and little *grinde the faces of the poore*, as small as dust and powder; and when they haue done, at length *eate them vp* one after another, *as it were bread*: as the Holy Ghost hath painted them out vnder those very phrases.[139]

I have quoted Sanderson at some length because it seems possible to me that a version of this passage underwrites Walton's anecdote. Walton's Sanderson is enough like the real Sanderson that he becomes 'a law to himself, practising what his Conscience told him was his duty, in reconciling differences, and preventing Lawsuits, both in his Parish and in the Neighbourhood' (p. 365).[140] In the case of the poor tenant, we see Sanderson employing exactly this kind of arbitration. He goes to the landlord, and preaches to him about the importance of mercy as an adjunct to judgement. (It is at this point that 'Sanderson' gets his unjust stewards mixed up, with a dash of the Sermon on the Mount mixed in with it.[141]) 'Sanderson' 's other quotation, though, is (or so Walton says) from Job: Walton has him say to the landlord that 'riches so gotten, and added to his great Estate, would, as *Job* says, *prove like gravel in his teeth*: would in time so corrode his Conscience, or become so nauseous when he lay on his Death-bed, that he would then labour to vomit it up, and not be able' (p. 366). Actually the quotation is a mixture of Lamentations 3: 16 and Proverbs 20: 17 (the source he attributes for it in 1680, in *Love and Truth*), not Job at all. But the imagery is a kind of reverse echo of Sanderson's Grantham sermon, the text of which *was* from Job. Walton imagines this landlord racking and grinding, has imagined the tenant's bones in his mouth as 'dust and powder' and has pointed out that this would be a bitter meal, and bad for, as it were, his conscience's teeth. Later, after the landlord has seen sense and given the tenant a full rebate, Walton quotes Job again: 'That he had seen none perish for want of clothing: and that he had often made the heart of the widow to rejoyce.' This is, as Walton says, a paraphrase of two verses of Job 31; and Walton applies them to Sanderson himself. They quote Job's assertion of his own righteousness, of

---

[139] R. Sanderson, from a sermon preached *Ad Magistratum* at Grantham, 11th June 1623, in *Twelve Sermons* . . . , 148–9.

[140] That Sanderson did indeed take it upon himself to arbitrate local disputes in an attempt to avert lawsuits is attested in Holmes, *Seventeenth Century Lincolnshire*, 61–3. Though he quotes Walton, he cites other supporting evidence.

[141] See Matthew 18: 26–35; Luke 16: 1–13; Matthew 5: 26.

which Job 29: 14–17 (Sanderson's Grantham text) is a part. The last verses of this text (in the AV) run:

16: I was a father to the poor: and the cause which I knew not I searched out.

17: And I brake the jaws of the wicked, and plucked the spoil out of his teeth.

Here Walton has effectively used Sanderson's own sermon to name him a 'father to the poor' and successful arbiter of disputes. He becomes, like Job, a blameless doer of good works in the face of great and undeserved tribulation, plucking spoil out of the jaws of the wicked (where they are, in any case, guaranteed to taste unpleasantly like 'gravel' to the spoiler). It is a typical strategy, and again combines quotation (or at any rate paraphrase), allusion, and generic anecdote to illustrate something we know was true about Sanderson. This is a very problematic mixture; but that is because Walton does it so well.

Walton's 'Character'of Sanderson gives us yet another problem of this kind. Here we might reasonably expect an individualized portrait, but Walton in fact offers us a familiar type: grave in countenance, seemly in demeanour, modest in habit. 'His behaviour', writes Walton, 'had in it much of a plain comliness, and very little (yet enough) of ceremony or courtship' (p. 397). This is extraordinarily reminiscent of Gauden's Hooker, whose '*outward* aspect and carriage was rather *comely* then *courtly* . . . His whole *garb* and *presence* . . . rather *plain* then *polished*'.[142] In fact, this was the very description of Hooker which Walton had so transformed in his own *Life of Hooker* (see pp. 270–2), here applied with very little modification to Sanderson—whom Walton had *actually known*.

Perhaps we again see an appropriation here; Gauden's overtolerant Hooker transformed into Walton's fully conformist Sanderson. Walton may have expected his readership—one he was, after all, likely to share with Gauden—to take the point. Or he may, much more simply, have decided the conventional description suited Sanderson as he actually was. It helps not at all that his description matches the engraving of Sanderson—neat, presentable, well-dressed, with an expression of some reserve—which was the frontispiece of the 1678 *Sanderson*. Perhaps the portrait is slightly anxious-looking about the mouth; perhaps this is a chance effect happened on by the engraver. Perhaps Sanderson

---

[142] Gauden, *Hooker*, 8.

looked like that, and perhaps he did not. Sanderson himself, after
all, had a multitude of texts around him, descriptive and prescriptive, in which he was invited to imitate just such a demeanour as an integral part of his priestly function.
Who was imitating whom? It is not possible at this distance to
separate the exemplary intentions of subjects from those of biographers; many worked together (Thomas Morton's chroniclers
are a case in point). The frontispiece to Barnard's *Life of Heylyn*
(reproduced as Fig. 5.5) shows the subject firmly governing his
biographer: we see the subject speaking—literally dictating—his
life to the writer who sits across from him, taking down every
word.[143] And while we know that Sanderson, in common with
many other strict Calvinist subjects, resisted and disapproved of
the making of any exemplary *record* of his conduct, he will nevertheless have observed exemplary imperatives in requiring of *himself* the actions of charity.

Nor was Walton the only writer who, in observing a friend's
caritas, felt himself justified in making a narrative record of it
—knowingly, and against his subject's explicit wishes. This too
militates against regarding the sheer repetitiveness of exemplary
anecdote as evidence that the anecdotes were therefore untrue.
Subjects, as well as biographers, read exemplary literature: subjects, most urgently, were concerned to write their lives directly
onto their bodies—whether or not they might then expect it to be
perpetuated in print or manuscript. We know that the urge to *read*
exemplary life-narrative spans the entire range of belief, from
separatist to highly conformist, although how texts were presented
and interpreted would vary widely within that span. In the case
of this broadly conformist group of literature which surrounds
Walton's *Lives*, it is clear that words are deemed to have the power
to engender acts; and it seems reasonable to assume that they did
so, and that a number of those acts were converted back into words.
If the great Dr Donne could die so, then why not I? If a visible
gravitas is so important, I should cultivate it. The interaction
between life and word was both cyclical (in that the same stories,
the same requirements, came around over and over again) and
developmental (as each generation refined on the stories of the last).

[143] From John Barnard, *Theologo-Historicus, or the True Life of . . . Peter Heylyn
. . .* (London, 1683). It should be added that the 'horse's mouth' element of the
iconography is the more urgent in that this biography rebuts an earlier account
by Vernon.

FIG 5.5. Frontispiece of John Barnard, . . . *The True Life* . . . *of* . . . *Peter Heylyn* (1683)

Perhaps this is what we see in William Hawkins's *Life of Thomas Ken*, published in 1713.[144] Hawkins was related by marriage to both Walton and Ken, and his *Life* (or possibly Ken's) shows a strong Waltonian influence. Hawkins is careful (on the whole, more careful than Walton) of his ascertainable facts. The dates he gives of Ken's attainment of the degrees of Bachelor of Arts and later Master of Arts are precise enough to suggest that he searched the university records, for he gives not just the year but the month and the day as well in each case.[145] Where Hawkins does not know a precise date (for instance, the date that Ken was sent to Winchester School, and the date he was elected to New College, Oxford) a gap is left in the text.[146]

But Hawkins also says that it was Ken's habit to 'sing his Morning-Hymn . . . to his Lute before he put on his Cloaths' (p. 5), which recalls Herbert singing devotional verses to his own accompaniment on his deathbed (pp. 316–17). He stresses Ken's love for devotional music in Waltonian terms, describing him as performing 'some of his Devotional Part of Praise with his own Compositions, which were Grave and Solemn' (p. 24). He says that Ken was remarkably unafraid of death, and adduces as evidence for this the fact that he 'had for many Years travelled with his Shrowd in his *Portmantua*, as what he often said, *might be as soon wanted as any other of his Habilments*' (p. 44). He adds that Ken's shroud 'was by himself put on, as soon as he came to *Long-Leate*, giving notice of it the Day before his Death, by way of Prevention, that his Body might not be stripp'd' (pp. 44–5). This is Donneian behaviour; and whether Ken, or Hawkins, had the lion's share of the imitation, it seems sufficiently clear that Walton was the model.

Conclusion

Like all Walton's biographies, the *Life of Sanderson* is partly written in praise of friendship, to the memory of a friend. As

---

[144] William Hawkins, *A Short Account of the Life of Reverend Father in God, Thomas Ken, D.D., sometime Bishop of Bath and Wells* (London, 1713).

[145] Hawkins's dates tally exactly with the dates given by Anthony á Wood in the *Fasti Oxonienses*, ed. Philip Bliss, 3rd edn., 1 volume (2 parts) (London, 1815–20). Cf. Hawkins, *Thomas Ken*, 2–3 with Wood, *Fasti*, part 2, cols. 248, 278, 368, and 370.

[146] Hawkins, *Thomas Ken*, 2–3.

such it is, as it were, *inevitably* particular, however exemplary its intentions. But Walton uses friendships in *Sanderson*, as in other *Lives*, to justify his writing presence (and thus his opinions, which differed from Sanderson's in certain respects), and to align his subjects politically as he paired them off with significant figures. Walton's charming story of Sanderson's first meeting, during his Oxford Proctorship, with the young Sheldon is a case in point: its function is comparable to the passages which link Hooker and Saravia in the *Life of Hooker*. His own affectionate speaking presence in *Sanderson* renders his subject a kind of ceremonialist.

It may even be that his abstract praises of friendship were theologically aligned. Hooker's relationship with Saravia charts 'the beginning of as spiritual a friendship as human nature is capable of' (pp. 361–2), Walton explains; friendship is a '*sympathy of souls*', he writes in *Donne* (p. 41). It is intriguing to find this kind of language amongst the Great Tew circle. Walton himself had good friends associated with Great Tew, including Sheldon, Morley, and Hammond; and Fell's *Life of Hammond* praises friendship in positively Waltonian terms as 'the next sacred thing unto religion'.[147] Hugh Trevor-Roper, writing on Great Tew, praises Falkland's 'wonderful capacity for friendship'[148] (one is reminded of Geoffrey Keynes's remark about Walton's 'genius for friendship'[149]). J. C. Hayward, in his study of the mores of Great Tew, takes friendship to be the group's important unifying feature, the ground upon which men of very diverse opinions could meet without discord. 'Integrity and sweetness of temper', he claims, 'were valued more highly than intellectual brilliance, although both were respected.'[150]

Where Walton considers friendship to guarantee a correlation of political and religious views, Hayward seems at first to represent the Great Tew group as assuming only that friendship will transcend religious and political differences. 'Piety', on the other hand, 'was best expressed in a manner of living'.[151] This,

[147] Fell, *Hammond*, lxxii.
[148] Hugh Trevor-Roper, *Catholics, Anglicans and Puritans* (London, 1987), 171.
[149] *Compleat Walton*, 614.
[150] J. C. Hayward, 'The Mores of Great Tew: Literary, Philosophical and Political Idealism in Falkland's Circle', unpublished dissertation, University of Cambridge (1982), 53.
[151] Ibid. 140.

in Hayward's view, enabled its members to regard theological differences as subordinate to personal integrity, which in its turn affected their attitude to dispute. He writes that, 'although Falkland included in his circle some able disputants, he believed that above all "truth, in likelihood, is where her author God was, in the still voice, and not in the loud wind" '.[152] He points out Walton's reluctance to engage directly in dispute; and although the examples he gives from the *Life of Sanderson* all refer specifically to issues related to Calvinism, his reason for citing them (*pace* Sanderson) is that he is arguing that the members of the circle essentially embraced a theology of works.[153]

Whether one accepts Hayward's view or not (and it has its problems), it seems to be a necessary irony that Walton's direct personal involvement with the real Sanderson led him to a far bigger misrepresentation of his position than any inaccuracy of detail (or even of doctrine) could be. In offering a narrative of his private virtue as demonstrative of his public rectitude, Walton used Sanderson to an end Sanderson himself would surely have found abhorrent (rather as Walton's *Life of Sanderson* directly contradicted the wishes of his Will that 'nothing at all' be spoken 'concerning my person, either good or ill' (p. 410). Sanderson, in his preaching life, had no time for arguments which inferred rectitude from conduct: belief, he argued, was absolutely separable from behaviour. Every day the unregenerate preached Christ to the regenerate: and it might do the preachers no good, because their hearts were sinful. Never could someone's private morals put them on the right side of any divide: if not with regard to fundamental questions of salvation, then surely not with regard to doctrinal or political divisions. 'Whether', he wrote,

we *Preach Christ of envie*, and *strife*, or of *goodwill*; whether *sincerely*, or *of contention*; whether in *pretence*, or in *truth*; it is our owne good, or hurt: we must answer for that. But what is that to you? *Notwithstanding every way*, so long as it is *Christ*, and his truth which *are preached*, it is your part *therein to rejoyce*.[154]

---

[152] Lucius Cary, Viscount Lord Falkland, *Of the Infallibilitie of the Church of Rome* (Oxford, 1645), sec. 49. Quoted by Hayward, 'Mores of Great Tew', 134.

[153] Hayward, 'Mores of Great Tew', 143.

[154] Sanderson, from a Sermon preached *Ad Clerum*, 78.

6

Walton's Legacy

In Walton's own century his *Lives* were popular. By the time the *Life of Sanderson* was published his reputation was obviously high, since the biography was marketed as the selling-point for the rest of the volume. Thomas Fuller praises the *Life of Donne* in 1655 in *The Church-History of Britain*: it is 'no lesse truly than elegantly written', and Walton is 'worthily respected'.[1] Fuller's praise is worth noticing, because it explicitly aligns Walton's artistry with his truthfulness: the work's elegance contributed to its worth as a biographical record. Walton is also praised by Elias Ashmole, who writes in 1672 that his 'ingenious pen' will ensure that he will be remembered by 'posterity' for the four *Lives* appearing in the collected edition of 1670.[2] He calls Walton himself a man 'well known and as well beloved of all good men'. Anthony á Wood is meaner, writing of the five *Lives* that they were 'well done, considering the education of the author'[3]—the first of many class-governed judgements to be passed on Walton masquerading as critical assessment. Wood was not an easy man (his quarrels with Aubrey are famous), and may have clashed with Walton; at another point he describes him coolly as 'my sometime friendly acquaintance'.[4]

At the end of the century Walton receives high praise from an early biographer of Milton, Edward Phillips. Phillips, in an assessment of ancient and modern life-writing, identifies three modern writers for special commendation: Fulke Greville and Thomas Stanly for their respective *Lives* of Sidney, and Walton for his *Lives* of Donne, Wotton, and Herbert. Phillips places

[1] Thomas Fuller, *The Church History of Britain* (London, 1655), Book 10, 112.

[2] Elias Ashmole, *The Institution, Laws and Ceremonies of the Most Noble Order of the Garter* (London, 1672), 228.

[3] *Athenae Oxonienses*, i., col. 698.   [4] Ibid., iii., col. 957.

Walton's achievement in company with the other writers he discusses—Plutarch, for instance, and Machiavelli. He was not a friend, like Fuller or Ashmole; nor was he a royalist. His praise can only have been animated by genuine admiration for Walton's artistry.[5]

By the mid-eighteenth century a view of Walton had developed which was as much informed by his own supposed piety as by his literary achievement. This was partly because he had become identified with the pious 'Piscator' of the *Angler* by its editor of 1760, Sir John Hawkins. Hawkins sounds like Walton on Walton as he expatiates on his 'piety, prudence, humility, peace and chearfulness'.[6] He adds:

if it should be objected, that what is here said may be equally true of an indolent man, or of a mind insensible to all outward accidents . . . to this it may be answered, that the person here spoken of was not such a man: on the contrary, in sundry views of his character, he appears to have been endowed both with activity and industry; an industrious tradesman, industrious in collecting biographical memoirs and historical facts, and in rescuing from oblivion the memory and writings of many of his learned friends; and surely against the suspicion of insensibility he must stand acquitted, who appears to have had the strongest attachments that could consist with christian charity, both to opinions and men.[7]

Hawkins means, of course, that Walton was a royalist and supported episcopacy. He points out that Walton had seen the Church of England destroyed, and had had to submit 'to those evils which he could not prevent'. 'We must', he finishes, 'pronounce him to have been an illustrious exemplar of the private and social virtues, and upon the whole a wise and good man' (p. xxii).

Hawkins's unease about the passivity of Walton's virtues is fascinating. He cites the 'industry' of his biographical work, and the strength of his opinions, to ensure that no reader confuses gentleness with apathy. He also assumes that without Walton's *Lives* his subjects would be quite forgotten; a Walton outflanked in obscurity by John Donne is quite a concept for the post-1920s

---

[5] Edward Phillips, 'The Life of Mr. John Milton', in *The Early Lives of Milton*, ed. Helen Darbishire (London, 1932), 49.

[6] Izaak Walton, *The Complete Angler*, ed. Sir John Hawkins, 4th edn. (London, 1791), p. xxi. The first Hawkins edition appeared in 1760.

[7] Ibid., pp. xxi–xxii.

reader to grasp. By linking the strength of Walton's opinions to his personal loyalty in his reference to 'opinions and men', Hawkins perceives even Walton's political loyalties as being informed by his personal attachments. Finally, he constructs a sixth 'Walton's Life', in making Walton himself an 'illustrious exemplar of the private and social virtues'.

Hawkins assumes Walton's personal loyalties and private virtues to be more important than his public opinions. Later in his account he remarks that 'the religious opinions of good men are of little importance to others, any farther than they necessarily conduce to virtuous practice' (p. l), which implies that he extended this view to the *Lives* themselves. Hawkins is writing of Walton's life in these Waltonian terms (although with the important difference that he considers opinions irrelevant to virtue, rather than believing that virtue demonstrates a rectitude of opinion), because he believes the narration of an author's life to be of very great importance in reading his work. Walton's practice in his *Lives*, not to mention the remarkable rise of the biographical preface as a genre since 1640, had evidently influenced public perceptions of the importance of biography. For Hawkins, to praise Walton's virtue was integral to commending his work.

Hawkins had been aided by Boswell, and Dr Johnson had approved of the result. According to Moses Browne, who produced the 1760 edition of the *Compleat Angler*, he had planned to write Life of Walton.[8] Boswell quotes Johnson's assessment of Walton as a 'great panegyrist',[9] and Johnson, in April 1774, wrote to Dr Horne of Magdalen College, Oxford, where he talks about his interest in Walton:

Somebody has observed that there seem to be times when writers of value emerge from oblivion by general consent. Walton's time is at last come. You are reviving him at Oxford. Lord Hail one of the Judges of Scotland appears to have the same design. I once had it too.

---

[8] See *The Compleat Angler*, ed. Moses Browne (London, 1750), sigs. a2ᵛ–3. Browne writes that he had embarked on the edition at 'the instigation of an ingenious and learned friend, whose judgement of men and books is sufficiently established by his own writings'. The footnote identifies the 'friend' as 'Mr. Samuel Johnson, who may probably on another occasion, oblige the Public with the Life of Mr. Walton'. Cited in Novarr, 7.

[9] Boswell, *Life of Johnson*, ii. 364.

. . . The life of Walton has happily fallen into good hands. Sir John Hawkins has prefixed it to the late edition of the Angler, very diligently collected and elegantly composed. You will ask his leave to reprint it, and not wish for a better.[10]

The 'design' Johnson mentions here is his plan to produce a new edition of the *Lives* with annotations. Johnson discouraged Horne from this project, being under the misapprehension that Lord Hailes already had it in hand.[11] Boswell records a later conversation between himself, Johnson, and Horne, in which Johnson explains what he had in mind for this new edition:

We drank tea with Dr. Horne, late President of Magdalen College, and Bishop of Norwich . . . He had talked of publishing an edition of Walton's Lives, but had laid aside that design, upon Dr. Johnson's telling him, from mistake, that Lord Hailes intended to do it. I had wished to negociate between Lord Hailes and him, that one or other should perform so good a work.

JOHNSON. 'In order to do it well, it will be necessary to collect all the editions of Walton's Lives. By way of adapting the book to the taste of the present age, they have in a later edition left out a vision which he relates Dr. Donne had, but it should be restored; and there should be a critical catalogue given of the works of the different persons whose lives were written by Walton, and therefore their works should be carefully read by the editor.'[12]

Johnson's remarks, like Hawkins's, again assume that Walton's subjects would chiefly be remembered for his accounts of their lives, and not for their own works, which would have to be unearthed, read, and then listed in the new edition. Boswell records his suspicion that, between Dr Horne and Lord Hailes, 'the republication . . . with Notes will fall upon me', and read all the *Lives*, but never got round to it.[13]

Johnson's intention to write an accompanying Life of Walton never came to anything either, probably because he felt Hawkins had already done it well. His praise of Hawkins' Life of Walton, like Fuller's of the *Life of Donne*, invokes the biographical imperatives of diligence and elegance. Like Walton, Hawkins was

[10] *The R. B. Adam Library Relating to Samuel Johnson 1709–84*, 3 vols. (London and Buffalo, NY, 1929), i. 48. See Novarr, 8.
[11] See *Life of Johnson*, ii. 279.   [12] Ibid. 445–6.
[13] *Letters of James Boswell*, collected and edited by Chauncey Brewster Tinker, 2 vols. (Oxford, 1924), i. 260; *Life of Johnson*, iii. 107.

being praised for achieving both, but Johnson does not even imply that the one guarantees the other; and his ambition to issue Walton's *Lives* 'benoted a little' implies that he knew Walton's artistry outstripped his accuracy.[14]

Although Boswell by his own showing had embarked upon his reading of the *Lives* in order to be ready to aid Dr Horne, they evidently made a great impression on him in themselves. Interestingly, given his complexities of intention in his own biographical practice, this manifests itself very largely as a reverence for their spiritual influence. The projected edition he describes in a letter to Johnson as 'what I think a pious work', adding that, for himself, he had been 'most pleasingly edified' by Walton's biographies.[15] Certainly Boswell's references to the *Lives* show him to have regarded them as reading-matter so pious as to function in the place of more orthodox (and more laborious) methods of worship. His entry in his Journal for Sunday 17 July 1774 narrates his first encounter with Walton's biographical style:

Was in a calm, reflecting frame . . . I thought of lying in bed all forenoon and indulging the humour in which I then was. I had a slight conflict between what I really thought would do me most good and the desire of being externally decent and going to church. I rose and breakfasted, but being too late for church, I read a part of my Bible and began the Life of Bishop Sanderson by Walton which I have heard Mr. Samuel Johnson commend much . . . The simplicity and pious spirit of Walton was, as it were, transfused into my soul. I resolved that amidst business and every other worry I should still keep in mind religious duty.[16]

In Boswell's view, it seems, he was virtually sanctified by the activity of reading, the 'pious spirit' breathing from the pages 'transfused' into his own. Not that Walton was the only tranquil influence; Boswell adds that his sense of well-being was heightened by having 'stripped and gone to bed again in my night-gown after breakfast'. However, the other *Lives*, read on the 31 July in slightly less easy circumstances (Boswell was convalescent), also had the effect of putting him into 'a most placid and pious frame' (p. 248). And when Boswell came to make an audit of his state of

---

[14] *Letters of James Boswell*, i. 205; *Life of Johnson*, ii. 283–4.
[15] Novarr, 10.
[16] *Boswell for the Defence*, Yale Edition of the Private Papers of James Boswell, ed. William K. Wimsatt and Frederick A. Pottle (London, 1960), 238–9.

mind at the end of the summer, Walton was the focus of a spiritual credit: 'Old Izaak Walton had done me good; and frequently
in the course of the day I had meditated on death and a future state.
Let me endeavour every session and every year to improve'
(p. 281).

It is worth noting that Boswell in all these entries assumes the
pious qualities of the work to be a true expression of the piety
embodied by Walton himself. Walton does not merely record
virtue, he exhorts to it, and (by implication) practises it too.
Boswell made his admiration for Walton plain; he quotes the *Life
of Hooker* from memory in an essay on hospitality written for
the July 1782 issue of the *London Magazine* (in the context of a
light-hearted allusion to the episcopal duty of hospitality laid down
in 1 Timothy 3), as well as highly commending the *Life of Donne*
for its edifying properties in the issue of December 1781.[17] But
Boswell was not to be the man responsible for disseminating
Walton's edifying properties in the form of a new edition; the
nearest he got to it was to restore the volume of the *Life of
Sanderson* which he had borrowed from the Advocates' Library
to read in bed, six years after he had borrowed it, with the
following note on the flyleaf:

Having borrowed this excellent life out of the Advocates' Library, I
found that it wanted seven leaves. Having purchased the same edition at
the Reverend Patrick Cummings' auction, with the head of the Bishop
which has been taken away from this copy, I had the seven leaves supplied by my clerk; and I now return it, hoping that it may edify many
readers.

James Boswell. 1780.[18]

In the event, Walton's *Lives* were not reissued until 1796,
when they appeared in an edition prepared by Thomas Zouch
(with encouragement from Boswell, as Zouch acknowledges in his
Preface) which was reprinted a number of times early in the next

---

[17] Essay LVIII, 'On Hospitality', in *The Hypochondriack, Being the Seventy
Essays by . . . James Boswell, Appearing in the* LONDON MAGAZINE *from November,
1777, to August, 1783,* ed. Margery Bailey, 2 vols. (Stanford, Calif., 1928), ii. 192;
Essay LI, 'On Suicide', in ibid. ii. 134.

[18] *Boswell for the Defence,* 239 n. The volume is still in the Advocates'
Library, now part of the National Library of Scotland.

century.[19] Zouch too venerated Walton personally; and he was
not above making a Waltonian link between private virtue and
conformity—now a concept being deployed in rather different
battles. Raoul Granqvist, in an article studying reactions to the
Lives in the nineteenth and early twentieth centuries, writes of
Zouch that his 'ardent wish' was 'to raise a monument for his
church, the High Church or Anglican Church [*sic*], by restitut-
ing and securing Walton's divines for her interests'.[20] He finds
Zouch's project opportunistic, and his declared objective of
giving the reader simple information about Walton's subjects
disingenuous (p. 248). Walton's views on obedience, his serene
acceptance of the doctrine of callings, and his belief, apparently
based on experience, that social unrest was purely wicked and
chaotic, were powerful arguments for social stasis in a culture
shaken (but also stirred) by the recent Revolution in France.
Existing somehow alongside this was a perception that, in
Granqvist's words, 'Walton and his divines and the time in
which they lived formed a single cultural entity, an emblem of an
ideal church . . . Believing that the church was threatened by the
rise of the Evangelical movement on the one hand, and Chartism
on the other, conservative Anglicans took Walton to their hearts'
(p. 249). Somehow Walton had successfully managed to represent
a century which boasted Britain's only civil war (and that one
largely animated by religious strife) as a kind of golden age for
conformity. The Tractarians were certainly to treat the Caroline
divines as in improbably full agreement with Laud—and each
other—on points of ceremonial and selected theological issues,
though Erastianism gave them (and especially Newman) more
trouble.

   In 1822 Wordsworth included a sonnet commending 'Walton's
Book of Lives' as part of his *Ecclesiastical Sonnets*.[21] The sonnet
received the dubious privilege of being frequently and reverently

---

[19] In 1807, 1817, 1823, 1825, and 1830. See Georges Bas, 'Thomas Zouch's
Life of Walton and the Alleged Friendship Between James Shirley and Izaak
Walton', in *Notes & Queries*, 24 (1977), 125–6.

[20] Raoul Granqvist, 'Izaak Walton's Lives in the Nineteenth and the Early
Twentieth Centuries: A Study of a Cult Object', in *Studia Neophilologica*, 54: 2
(1982), 248.

[21] William Wordsworth, *Ecclesiastical Sonnets*, ed. A. F. Potts (New Haven,
1922), 164.

quoted by editors of nineteenth-century editions of Walton's *Lives*, many of whom shared Zouch's political motives. However, the poem is of real interest in that it spectacularly outdoes Walton in his own mode:

> There are no colours in the fairest sky
> So fair as these. The feather, whence the pen
> Was shaped that traced the lives of these good men
> Dropped from an angel's wing. With moistened eye
> We read of faith and purest charity
> In Statesman, Priest, and humble Citizen:
> O could we copy their mild virtues, then
> What joy to live, what blessedness to die!
> Methinks their very names shine still and bright;
> Apart—like glow-worms on a summer night;
> Or lonely tapers when from far they fling
> A guiding ray; or seen like stars on high,
> Satellites burning in a lucid ring
> Around meek Walton's heavenly memory.

Wordsworth's image of the ring of stars recalls Walton's own reference to the collected *Donne, Wotton, Hooker,* and *Herbert,* where he hopes that his reader may find 'this Conjunction of them after their deaths' acceptable.[22] Wordsworth includes Walton (the 'humble Citizen') in his list, and this also recalls Walton's own deliberate connection of himself with his subjects in the same passage. He might, however, have been startled to find Wordsworth assuming that Walton himself formed the centre of the 'lucid ring'. In doing so Wordsworth faithfully reflects a hundred years celebrating Walton's personal virtues on the rather shaky basis that only a pious man could write so well about piety.

Walton and Wordsworth share an assumption that the main strength of the *Lives* lies in their artistry—both writers for different reasons finding it easy to assume a straightforward correlation between artistry and truth. In his celebration of Walton's achievement, Wordsworth finds the *Lives'* historicity important chiefly in locating perfection in one of its two possible elsewheres—the past. 'There are', the sonnet begins, 'no colours in the fairest sky | So fair as these.' It is not just that Walton's world is neither now, nor here, because that is true of all history. Wordsworth's

---

[22] *Lives* (1670), 7–8.

words acknowledge that Walton's world was *never* now nor here. It (like the primitive Church for Walton's own generation) is ideal history.

Yet Walton, like Wordsworth, would not have claimed that ideal history was in any way *invented*. Walton's appeals to primitive piety involve an identification of a sanctity authoritative because historically fixed. In the same way, Wordsworth describes the 'feather' of 'Walton's pen' as having 'dropped from an Angel's wing'; but the pen so described is supposed to have 'traced' its subjects' lives. For Wordsworth, Walton was evidently guided by the hand of Truth.

Ideal histories which claim real historicity are powerful foci for nostalgia. Francisque Costa, thinking about Walton's nineteenth-century reader, agrees:

> Pour çeux qui s'avèrent moins sensibles que Zouch ou Hawkins, au implications politico-religieuses de l'oeuvre, notre auteur propose malgré tout la vision convainçante d'un monde 'prélapsaire', dont l'Angleterre, déjà alterée et enlaidie par la Revolution industrielle, éprouve de plus en plus la nostalgie.[23]

The anonymous editor of an edition of the *Lives* published in 1827, as well as reproducing Wordsworth's poem, celebrates Walton's own sanctified nature. He writes opposite the title-page that Walton's work

> tends to illustrate the character of the author, which is almost as much developed as that of the person of whom he speaks; and the mind must be formed of the most unenviable elements which can refrain from reverencing the goodness of heart, unaffected piety, and tranquillity of soul, which it proves him to have possessed.

John Keble, in his edition of Hooker's *Ecclesiastical Polity*, is moved to make a more temperate version of the same observation in his discussion of Walton's *Hooker*. Having remarked upon the evidence of his own research that the *Life* is 'favourable to Walton's veracity, industry, and judgement', he adds:

> the Editor has no wish to deny, that which is apparent of itself to every reader—the peculiar fascination, if one may call it so, by which Walton was led unconsciously to communicate more or less of his own tone and

---

[23] Francisque Costa, 'L'Oeuvre d'Izaak Walton 1593–1683', *Études Anglaises*, 48 (Paris, 1973), 11.

character to all whom he undertook to represent. But this is like his custom of putting long speeches into their mouths: we see at once that it is his way, and it deceives no one.[24]

But even Keble, whose own religious sympathies chime with Walton's version of Hooker, notices the devices with which Walton controls that Hooker's utterances. Keble comments that Walton 'seems to judge rather from anecdotes which had come to his knowledge, than from the indications of temperament which Hooker's own writings afford'.

An early-nineteenth-century evangelical editor of Hooker's *Polity*, Benjamin Hanbury, reprints Walton's *Life of Hooker* but hates its assumptions.[25] It will come as no surprise that he uses Gauden's *Life* (which figures extensively in his copious footnotes) as a stick with which to beat Walton. On the other hand, he must still have regarded Walton's as the 'best' Life of Hooker around—by criteria which did not place factual accuracy or political religious sympathies at the top of the list. Perhaps readability won hands down in spite of everything. Hanbury expresses some very reasonable doubts concerning Walton's account of the *Polity*'s last three books, and laments that Walton lived in an age 'when rational liberty, civil and ecclesiastical, was neither so well understood nor enjoyed as in the times our happier eyes behold' (p. lvi). He adds: 'The näiveté and garrulity of Walton impart a fascination to his narrative which will not bear the touch of the disenchanter's rod; for when the veil is withdrawn, and the smoke of the incense is dissipated, we see nothing left but the dregs of incredulity and intolerance' (p. lvi). By the 1830s, then, Walton had become identified—at least in evangelical eyes—with the interests of thurible-swinging Anglo-Catholics. But his was not a sectarian appeal, in so far as Anglo-Catholicism in the mid-nineteenth century can be described as a sectarian interest. The whole conformist ground was Walton's territory. Granqvist describes the Revd William Teale at about the same time attacking the mechanics' institutes, 'waving in his right hand Walton's

[24] Richard Hooker, *Works*, ed. John Keble, revised by R. W. Church and F. Paget, 7th edn., 3 vols. (Oxford, 1888), i., x.
[25] Richard Hooker, *The Laws of Ecclesiastical Polity and Other Works*, ed. Benjamin Hanbury (London, 1830), pp. lvi–lvii.

Lives',[26] and describes the SPCK editions of the *Lives* of 1819
and 1833 as including 'hardcore' Anglican tracts.

The Waltonian version of peculiarly English piety, as it was
seen to be represented by the *Angler* as well as by the *Lives*, was
influential outside politics, in personal perception and devotion.
The young Charles Kingsley, during his difficult and overworked
early years at Cambridge, appears from his letters to have had
fishing as his only recreation, and sandwiched between worries
about the attractions and dangers of Christianity in general
and Tractarianism in particular are references to Walton and
angling.[27] In 1844 Kingsley, now in holy orders—who twenty
years later was to make deft and graceful use of Plinian natural
history in a manner very reminiscent of the *Angler* in *The Water
Babies*—wrote to his wife from Salisbury after a day's fishing:

> I spent a delightful day yesterday. Conceive my pleasure at finding myself
> at Bemerton, George Herbert's parish, and seeing his house and church,
> and fishing in the very meadows where he, and Dr. Donne, and Izaak
> Walton may have fished before me. I killed . . . a brace of grayling . . .
> —a fish quite new to me, smelling just like cucumbers. The dazzling
> chalk-wolds sleeping in the sun, the clear river rushing and boiling down
> in one ever-sliding sheet of transparent silver, the birds bursting into song
> . . . everything stirred with the gleam of God's eye when 'he reneweth
> the face of the earth'![28]

Kingsley is having a 'Walton experience' here, and it is equally
self-consciously a religious experience. He records a perception
of nature as a manifestation of the glory of God, and at the
same time he treats the *Angler* and the *Lives* both as virtually
interchangeable, and as reliably factual.

However, the assumption amongst Walton's supporters that
his work reflected both true perceptions and accurate facts was
beginning to change. An 1857 edition of the *Lives*, published with
a memoir by William Dowling (and the inevitable sonnet by
Wordsworth), shows the beginnings of a critical spirit among
his admirers.[29] Dowling commends Walton's elevated notions of
friendship which, he asserts, 'belong only to men of refined and

---

[26] Granqvist, 'Izaak Walton's Lives', 249.
[27] See e.g. Frances Eliza Kingsley, *Charles Kingsley: His Letters and Memories
of his Life*, 2 vols. (London, 1877), i. 52.
[28] Ibid. 118.
[29] Izaak Walton, *Lives*, with a memoir by William Dowling (London, 1857).

poetical minds' (p. xiii), but he also remarks a little later that perhaps the 'depth of feeling' which he states Walton to exhibit led to 'some of Walton's faults as a biographer'. He continues: ' "Love is blind", the proverb tells us; and friendship cannot expect to be very keen-eyed. All Walton's friends are described as living on the very border-land of perfection; and some of them are made to appear angelic' (p. xiv). In 1876 Alexander Grosart, in a study of Herbert's life very largely informed by Walton and initially conducted in the spirit of utmost credulity, was finally forced to acknowledge Walton's inaccuracies in his account of the Melville controversy. His reaction is violent:

Dear as are 'meek' Walton's name and memory, the truth must at long-last be told, and this mingle-mangle of unhistoric statement and mendacious zeal exposed. There are nearly as many blunders as sentences in the narrative, and the *animus* is as base as the supercilious ignorance is discreditable. Alas that I must say these 'hard things' of anything from the pen of one I so revere (substantially!) Alas that they should be true![30]

But Grosart was a prominent Presbyterian, and notoriously cantankerous.[31]

Edmund Gosse, writing of the *Life of Donne* at the end of the century in his *Life and Letters of John Donne*, is kinder. He identifies Walton's inaccuracies as being informed by the 'truth of love', writing that, 'it is said that the late George Richmond, R. A., on being accused of not telling the truth in his delicate portraiture, replied with heat: "I do tell the truth, but I tell it in love". The ideal of the seventeenth century biography was to tell the truth in love.'[32] Leslie Stephen, reviewing Gosse's book, had no time for this, complaining that if Walton's *Life* was to be regarded as a fine work, it must be one of fiction. He writes: 'if the book is to be read as we read the Vicar of Wakefield—as a prose idyl—a charming narrative in which we have as little to do with the reality of Donne as with the reality of Dr. Primrose, I can only submit to the judgement

---

[30] *The Works of George Herbert*, ed. A. B. Grosart, 3 vols. (London, 1876), i., p. xv.

[31] See *DNB*, [1st] *Supplement*, ed. Sidney Lee, 3 vols. (London, 1901), ii. 364–6. Reference is also made in the biography to the 'querulousness, dogmatism and ill-temper' of some of Grosart's notes and prefaces, although those of the 'later reprints' are specified (p. 366).

[32] Edmund Gosse, *The Life and Letters of John Donne*, 2 vols. (London, 1899), i., p. viii. Telling the 'truth in love' is a reference to Ephesians 4: 15.

of my betters.[33] Both Gosse and Stephen refer disparagingly to Walton's station as part of their criticism of his practice, Gosse calling him that 'immortal piscatory linen-draper'[34] and Stephen a 'worthy tradesman'. H. C. Beeching, defending Walton in 1902, lets the silliness of this speak for itself: 'undoubtedly', he writes, 'Walton is often spoken of as "worthy" by his friends, and undoubtedly he was a "tradesman", but his capability of appreciating Donne is not adequately summed up by the compound phrase.'[35]

In his chapter 'The Spirit of the English Church, as Exhibited in the Literature of the Seventeenth Century', Beeching places Donne and Herbert next to Andrewes and Hooker as having exerted 'the influences which helped to shape the peculiar temper of the English Church' (p. 60). But he acknowledges that it is Walton's *Lives*, as much as Donne's and Herbert's own writings, which have exerted these influences: that Walton's 'religious genius' is responsible. He adds that Walton 'may himself be said to have first exhibited the type of the Anglican layman as we know him to-day—devout, reasonable, modest'. Again, Walton has become his own subject.

Beeching is the last of Walton's critics to find his religious persuasions an unequivocal recommendation. Harold Nicolson, whose book *The Development of English Biography* announces the existence of an entity called 'pure biography', regarding it as a science rather than as an art, is, not surprisingly, critical of Walton's methods. He describes him as 'too confident of his own ethical values', and states baldly that 'where Walton fails is in truth' (an 'ethical value' being, apparently, something unlike truth). This failure he identifies as the 'intrusion of his own feelings and predilections', whereas (for instance) Keble had seen this intrusion as so obvious as to be a (different) kind of truth of its own.[36]

Most of the mid-twentieth-century academic critics of Walton's *Lives* since 1930—John Butt, Donald Stauffer, and R. E. Bennett—are essentially in agreement in assessing his work.[37]

[33] Leslie Stephen, 'John Donne', *National Review*, 34 (1899), 595–6.
[34] Gosse, *John Donne*, ii. 253.
[35] H. C. Beeching, *Religio Laici* (London, 1902), 60.
[36] Harold Nicolson, *The Development of English Biography* (London, 1927), 65.
[37] John Butt, 'Izaak Walton's Methods in Biography', *Essays and Studies*, 29, (1933); Donald Stauffer, *English Biography Before 1700* (Cambridge, Mass., 1930); R. E. Bennett, 'Walton's Use of Donne's Letters', *Philological Quarterly*, 16

It is seen as containing a truth of impression countered by inaccuracies. As a general point, critics this century seem to find their
own methodology more manageable if they concentrate either
on fact-checking or on style. Those who take on both, without
considering context or genre, have real problems of tone.

R. C. Bald and Helen Gardner both decide to address specific
factual details in the *Life of Donne*, with predictably mixed
results and some signs of exasperation. Judith Anderson, in her
book *Biographical Truth*, also discusses *Donne*; but she formally
recognizes that the ethics of modern scholarship are not Walton's
ethics. As a result her criticism is less afflicted by internal contradictions than that of almost every other critic who considers
it. Richard Wendorf is another who reads Walton's *Donne* more
on its own terms: he devotes some time to Walton's strategies in
his book, *The Elements of Life: Biography and Portrait Painting
in Stuart and Georgian England*, offering some of the most
perceptive (and incidentally the most generous) conclusions on
Walton's artistry as it relates to his use of portraits.[38] Meanwhile
Walton scholars await the new scholarly edition of the *Lives* begun
by John Butt, and now continued by Jonquil Bevan (who has
already produced the modern definitive edition of the *Angler*)
and Glenn Black.

Walton's most scrupulous and thorough critic this century has
been, of course, David Novarr. He is also the most sceptical,
even about what Bennett called Walton's 'essential' truthfulness:
he thinks that Walton is essentially manipulative. His own text
betrays increasing irritation, even straightforward disapproval,
as his book develops. But there are real difficulties about his
approach. Its most fundamental problem is that he does not
recognize the claims of any imperative outside those which
govern mid-twentieth-century historical scholarship.

(1937). Of all Walton's modern critics, only John Carey attacks on literary grounds,
and he does so with a vehemence (and at a length) which actually detract from
his thesis that Walton's flaccid style puts him beneath notice. In any case, it is
something to be pilloried in company with Thomas Browne. See John Carey,
'Sixteenth and Seventeenth Century Prose', in Christopher Ricks (ed.), *English
Poetry and Prose, 1540–1674* (London, 1970), 339–431.

[38] Judith Anderson, *Biographical Truth*; R. C. Bald, 'Historical Doubts
Respecting Walton's Life of Donne', 69–84; Helen Gardner, 'Dean Donne's
Monument in St. Paul's', 29–44; Richard Wendorf, *The Elements of Life*.

This hurts his judgement of Walton in two ways. First, a primarily evidence-based assessment, even of modern biography, does not consider the mixed nature of the genre: it is no accident that the first novels masqueraded as true life histories. Narrative is not amenable to deliberative techniques; and while a good biography must be a kind of story, it is also true that evidence itself varies in reliability, and the methods of evidence-assessment available to the historian do not sit at all well with narrative. Walton actually provided very few absolutely unsupported assertions, but his methods for using evidence were either idiosyncratic, or followed different ethics. They were, however, almost never unconsidered, or careless. From a purely 'literary' point of view, Walton will sometimes decide to betray his narrative with indigestible facts, as with his handling of the Melville controversy. From a historical one, he will (in modern terms) misrepresent shockingly, to achieve narrative coherence or to make a point he feels to contain a more important kind of truth than evidence will provide.

Secondly, Novarr is sufficiently confident of his own 'ethical values' not to consider other imperatives besides evidence. His criteria for judgement do not include Walton's problematical inheritance of at least two exemplary traditions, though he does dislike his 'hagiographical' urge. Novarr also distrusts the bits of celebratory convention Walton culls from his form (the biographical preface), identifying them, rightly, as not objective. In effect this means that he discounts every rhetorically governed judgement, when Walton necessarily wrote within traditions saturated by rhetoric. Walton was not, himself, a trained rhetorician: his modern assessor does not have the difficulties vividly conveyed by Timothy Wengert in his consideration of Camerarius' *Melanchthon*—itself written as a textbook example of 'elocutio splendida, copiosa atque ornata singularis'. (Camerarius, Wengert points out, has misled a number of historians as to Melanchthon's achievements and qualities.)[39] But the biographical preface, within the conventions of which Walton wrote with some considerable skill, owed a good deal to the funeral sermon, with its

[39] Timothy J. Wengert, '"With Friends Like This . . .": The Biography of Philip Melanchthon by Joachim Camerarius', in Thomas F. Mayer and D. R. Woolf (eds.), *The Rhetorics of Life-Writing in Early Modern Europe* (Ann Arbor, Mich., 1995), 115–31.

own mixed bag of rhetorical hand-me-downs. Johnson's judgement of Walton as a 'great panegyrist' seems a more just and a fitting description of that part of his achievement.

Walton has done something else as well. As I have argued elsewhere in this long book, Walton's lay status, and the implications this had for the authority of his textual voice, forced him to alter the way he used the traditions he inherited. In doing so, he transformed the genre into something new: into an intimate record of a particularized individual. Today, that is our ordinary expectation of biography: we expect a reading experience which allows us to 'know' an individual via an underlying chronological and narrative structure. In this we are not Walton's judges, but his inheritors.

BIBLIOGRAPHY

The manner of citation adopted generally follows Modern Humanities Research Association (MHRA) practice; however, some STC or Wing titles are suitably abbreviated. Surnames follow the normalizations in STC or Wing. Biographical works appearing as prefaces are cited under the biographer's name, though I have also been generous in double referencing them under their main authors.

I. REFERENCE WORKS

ALLISON, A. F. and GOLDSMITH, V. F., *Titles of English Books . . . an Alphabetical Finding List by Title of Books published under Author's Name, Pseudonym or Initials*, 2 vols. (London, 1977).

ALLISON, A. F. and ROGERS, D. M., *A Catalogue of Catholic Books in English Printed Abroad or Secretly in England, 1558–1640* (London, 1968).

DEVEREUX, E. J., *Checklist of English Translations of Erasmus to 1700*, Oxford Bibliographical Society (Oxford, 1968).

English Historical Documents, ed. David C. Douglas, 12 vols. (London, 1967).

FORTESCUE, G. K., *Catalogue of the Pamphlets, Books, Newspapers and Manuscripts Relating to the Civil War, the Commonwealth, and Restoration*, collected by George Thomason, 1640–61, 2 vols. (London, 1908).

Liturgy and Worship, A Companion to the Prayer Books of the Anglican Communion, ed. W. K. Lowther Clarke and assisted by Charles Harris (London, 1932).

LONDON, WILLIAM, *A Catalogue of the Most Vendible Books in England (London, 1657), with a supplement to 1660*. Facsimile reprint from English Bibliographical Sources, ed. D. E. Foxon (London and Holland, 1965).

MAUNSELL, ANDREW, *The First Part of the Catalogue of English Printed Bookes: which Concerneth such Matters of Divinitie as have Bin either Written in our own Tongue, or Translated out of other Languages. And Have Bin Published, to the Glory of God, and Edification of the Church of Christ in England* (London, 1595). Facsimile reprint from English Bibliographical Sources, ed. D. E. Foxon (London and Holland, 1965).

New Testament Octapla: Eight English Versions of the New Testament, edited by Luther S. Weigle (New York, 1962).

A Short-Title Catalogue of Books Printed in England, Scotland and Ireland, and of English Books Printed Abroad, 1475–1640, first compiled by A. W. Pollard and G. R. Redgrave, revised and edited by Katharine F. Pantzer, 3 vols. (London, 1986–91).

Short-Title Catalogue of Books Printed in England, Scotland, Ireland, Wales, and British America, and of English Books Printed in Other Countries, 1641–1700, compiled by Donald Wing, 3 vols., revised edn. (New York, 1972).

YOUNG, JOHN and AITKEN, HENDERSON, *A Catalogue of the Manuscripts in the Library of the Hunterian Museum in the University of Glasgow* (Glasgow, 1908).

2. PRIMARY WORKS

A. M. [Anthony Munday], *Discoverie of Edmund Campion, and his Confederates, their Most Horrible and Traiterous Practices, against Her Majesties Most Royall Person and the Realme* (London, 1582). STC 18270.

ADAMUS, MELCHIOR, *Vitae Germanorum Theologorum qvi Superiori Seculo Ecclesiam Christi Voces Scriptisqve Propagarunt et Propugnarunt* (Heidelberg, 1620).

—— *Life of Dr. Martin Luther*, freely translated by Thomas Hayne (London, 1641). Wing A505.

[Thomas Alfield], *True Reporte of the Death and Martyrdome of M. Campion Jesuite and Preiste, and M. Sherwin and M. Bryan Preistes, at Tiborne the First of December 1581* (London, 1581). STC 4537.

ALLESTREE, RICHARD, *Works* (1684): see under John Fell.

AMYOT, JACQUES: see under Plutarch.

ANDREWES, LANCELOT: see under J. Buckeridge and H. Isaacson.

ASHMOLE, ELIAS, *The Institution, Laws, and Ceremonies of the most Noble Order of the Garter* (London, 1672). Wing A3983.

AUBREY, JOHN, *Brief Lives, Chiefly of Contemporaries, Set Down by John Aubrey, Between the Years 1669 and 1696*, edited by A. Clark, 2 vols. (Oxford, 1898).

—— *Three Prose Works*, ed. John Buchanan-Brown (London, 1972).

BABINGTON, GERVASE: see under Miles Smith.

BACON, FRANCIS, *Of the Proficience and Advancement of Learning, Divine and Humane* (London, 1605). STC 1164.

—— *The Essayes or Covnsels, Civill and Morall . . . Newly Enlarged* (London, 1625). STC 1147.

B[addeley], R[ichard], *The Life of Dr. Thomas Morton, Late Bishop of Duresme. Begun by R.B. Secretary to His Lordship. And Finished by J.N., D.D. his Lordship's Chaplain* (York, 1669). Wing B387.

BAILLIE, R., *The Life of William* [Laud], *now Lord Arch-Bishop of Canterbury, Examined* . . . (London, 1643). Wing B463.

BALE, JOHN: see under Justus Jonas.

BANKS, JONATHAN, *Life of the Right Reverend Father in God, Edward Rainbow* . . . *to which is Added a Sermon Preached at his Funeral by Thomas Tully at Dalston April the 1st 1684* (London, 1688). Wing B669.

BARNARD, JOHN, *Theologo-Historicus, or the True Life of* . . . *Peter Heylyn* (London, 1683). Wing B854.

BARROW, ISAAC, *Works*: see under Abraham Hill.

BARWICK, JOHN, Ἱερονίκης *or the Fight, Victory and Triumph of St. Paul. Accommodated to the Right Reverend Father in God, Thomas* [Morton] *Late Lord Bishop of Duresme, in a Sermon Preached at his Funeral* . . . *on Michaelmas Day, 1659. Together, with a Life of the said Bishop* (London, 1660). Wing B1008.

BASIRE, ISAAC, *The Dead Mans Real Speech: A Funeral Sermon* . . . *Together with a Brief of the Life* . . . *and* . . . *Death of* [John Cosin] *Lord Bishop of Durham* (London, 1673). Wing B1031.

BEDELL, WILLIAM, *Life of Bishop Bedell, by his Son*, ed. J. E. B. Mayor (Cambridge, 1871).

Two Biographies of William Bedell, Bishop of Kilmore, ed. E. S. Shuckburgh (Cambridge, 1902).

BENNET, HENRY, *A Famous and Godly History, Contaynyng the Lives of Three Reformers. M. Luther, J. Ecolampadius, and H. Zvinglius. All set forth in Latin by P. Melancthon* [sic] . . . *Newly Englished by H. Bennet Callesian* (London, 1561). STC 1881.

BERNARD, NICHOLAS, *The Life and Death of the Most Reverend and Learned Father of our Church, Dr. James Usher, Late Arch-Bishop of Armagh, and Primate of all Ireland* (London, 1656). Wing B2012.

—— *Clavi Trabales* (London, 1661). Wing B2007.

BERNARD, RICHARD, *The Faithfull Shepheard: or the Shepheards Faithfulnesse: Wherein is for the Matter Largely* . . . *Set Forth the Excellencie of the Ministerie; a Ministers Propertie and Dutie* . . . (London, 1607). STC 1939.

—— *Thesaurus Biblicus*: see under John Conant.

BEZA, THEODORE, *A Discourse* . . . *Conteyning in Briefe the Historie of the Life and Death of Maister John Calvin, translated by I.S.* (London, 1564). STC 2017.

—— *Icones. Les Vrais Pourtraits des Hommes Illustrées en Pieté et Doctrine* . . . *Traduicts du Latin*, trans. Simon Goulard, 2nd edn. (Geneva, 1581).

BOSWELL, JAMES, *Boswell's Life of Johnson*, ed. George Birkbeck Hill and revised by L. F. Powell, 6 vols. (Oxford, 1934–50).

—— *Letters of James Boswell*, collected and edited by Chauncey Brewster Tinker, 2 vols. (Oxford, 1924).

—— *Boswell for the Defence*, Yale Edition of the Private Papers of James Boswell, ed. William K. Wimsatt and Frederick A. Pottle (London, 1960).

—— *The Hypochondriack, Being the Seventy Essays by . . . James Boswell, Appearing in the* LONDON MAGAZINE *from November, 1777, to August, 1783*, ed. Margery Bailey, 2 vols. (Stanford, Calif., 1928).

BRETON, NICHOLAS, *The Good and the Badde, or, Descriptions of the Worthies and Unworthies of this Age* (London, 1616). STC 3656.

BROWNE, HUMPHREY, *A Map of the Microcosme, or, a Morall Description of Man, Newly Compiled into Essayes* (London, 1642). Wing B5115.

BUCKERIDGE, JOHN, *A Sermon Preached at the Funeral of Lancelot [Andrewes] . . .*, in Lancelot Andrewes, *XCVI Sermons*, ed. Archbishop William Laud and John Buckeridge (London, 1629), 1–22 (3rd pag.). STC 606 and 4004.

BUNYAN, JOHN, *Grace Abounding to the Chief of Sinners, or, A Brief and Faithful Relation of the Exceeding Mercy of God in Christ to his Poor Servant, John Bunyan* (London, 1666). Wing B5523.

BURKITT, WILLIAM, *The Peoples Zeal Provok't by the Pious and Instructive Example of their Dead Minister . . . Mr. William Gurnall* (London, 1680).

BURNET, GILBERT, *Life of William Bedell, D.D., Bishop of Kilmore in Ireland* (London, 1685). Wing B5830.

BYAM, HENRY, *XIII Sermons . . . Preached Before His Majesty King Charles the II, in His Exile . . .* (London, 1675). Wing B6375.

CARY, LUCIUS: see under Falkland.

CHARRON, PIERRE, *Of Wisedome: Three Bookes Written in French*, translated by Samson Lennard (London, 1606). STC 5051.

CHETWINDE, JOHN, *The Dead Speaking, or the Living Names of Two Deceased Ministers of Christ . . . Sam. Oliver and Samuel Crook. Containing the Sermons at the Funeralls of the One Preached by J. Chetwind and Two Severall Speeches Delivered at the Funeralls of Them Both by W. Thomas* (London, 1653). Wing C3795.

CLARKE, SAMUEL, *A Mirrour or Looking Glasse both for Saints and Sinners, Held Forth in some Thousands of Examples . . .*, 3rd edn. (London, 1657). Wing C4551.

—— *An Antidote Against Immoderate Mourning for the Dead* (London, 1659). Wing C4501.

—— *The Lives of Ten Eminent Divines* (London, 1661–2). Wing C4506.

—— *The Lives of Twenty-Two English Divines* (London, 1661–2). Wing C4540.

CLARKE, SAMUEL, *The Blessed Life and Meritorious Death of our Lord and Saviour Jesus Christ* . . . (London, 1664). Wing C4502.

—— *The Marrow of Ecclesiastical History, Divided into Two Parts: the First, containing the Life of our Blessed Lord and Saviour Jesus Christ, with the Lives of the Ancient Fathers, School-Men, First Reformers, and Modern Divines. The Second, Containing the Lives of Christian Emperors, Kings, and Sovereign Princes . . . Together with the Most Lively Effigies of the most Eminent of them Cut in Copper*, 3rd edn. (London, 1675). Wing C4545.

—— *A General Martyrologie, Containing a Collection of all the Greatest Persecutions which have Befallen the Church of Christ, from the Creation, unto our Present Times . . . whereunto is Added the Lives of Thirty Two English Divines . . .*, 3rd edn. (London, 1677). Wing C4515.

CLOGIE, ALEXANDER, *Memoir of the Life and Episcopate of William Bedell. Printed for the First Time . . . from the Original Manuscript in the Harleian Collection, British Museum*, ed. W. W. Wilkins (London, 1862).

COLET, JOHN, *Daily Devotions*: see under Thomas Fuller.

COSIN, JOHN, *The History of Popish Transubstantiation* (London, 1676). Wing C6359.

CROOK, SAMUEL, Tὰ Διαφέροντα, *or Divine Characters in Two Parts, Acutely Distinguishing the More Secret and Undiscerned Differences between . . . the Hypocrite in his Best Dress of Seeming Virtues . . . and the True Christian in his Real Graces . . .* (London, 1658). Wing 7227.

Descrypcyon of a Verye Chrysten Bysshop, and of a Couunterfaye Bysshop (n.p., 1536?). STC 16983.5.

D.F., *Reason and Judgement: or, Special Remarques on the Life of the Renowned Dr. Sanderson* (Oxford or London, 1663). Wing F9.

DONNE, JOHN, *Pseudo-Martyr. Wherein out of Certaine Propositions this Conclusion is Evicted. That those of the Romane Religion Ought to Take the Oath of Allegeance* (London, 1610). STC 7048.

—— *Devotions upon Emergent Occasions, and Severall Steps in my Sicknes* (London, 1624). STC 7033.

—— *Sermon of Commemoration of the Lady Danvers* (London, 1627). STC 7049.

—— *Deaths Dvell, or, a Consolation to the Soule, against the Dying Life, and Living Death of the Body. In a Sermon . . .* (London, 1632). STC 7031.

—— *Deaths Dvell, or, a Consolation to the Soule, against the Dying Life, and Living Death of the Body. In a Sermon . . .*, 2nd edn. (London, 1633). STC 7032.

—— *Poems, by J.D., with Elegies on the Authors Death* (London, 1633). STC 7045.

—— *Poems, by J.D.*, 2nd edn. (London, 1635). STC 7046.

—— *LXXX Sermons* (London, 1640). STC 7038.

—— *Letters to Severall Persons of Honour* (London, 1651). Wing D1864.

—— *Paradoxes, Problems, Essayes, Characters* . . . (London, 1652). Wing D1866.

—— *XXVI Sermons* . . . (London, 1660). Wing D1872.

—— *Complete Poetry and Selected Prose*, ed. John Hayward (London, 1929).

—— *The Sermons of John Donne*, ed. Evelyn M. Simpson and George R. Potter, 10 vols. (Berkeley, Los Angeles, and London, 1953–62).

—— *Divine Poems of John Donne*, ed. Helen Gardner, 2nd edn. (Oxford, 1978).

DRYDEN, JOHN, 'The Life of Plutarch', in *The Works of John Dryden*, ed. E. N. Hooker and H. T. Swedenborg, Jr., 20 vols. (Berkeley, 1958–74), xvii. 227–88.

EARL of CLARENDON, EDWARD HYDE, *The History of the Rebellion and Civil Wars in England*, ed. W. D. Macray, 6 vols. (Oxford, 1888).

EARLE, JOHN, *Microcosmographie, or, a Piece of the World Discovered*; in *Essayes and Characters*, 6th edn., augmented (London, 1633). STC 7444.

Ἐικὼν Βασιλική. *The Povrtraictvre of His Sacred Maiestie* (London, 1648). Wing E268.

ELLYOT, GEORGE, *A Very True Reporte of the Apprehension and Taking of that Arch-Priest EDMUND CAMPION, the Pope his Right Hand, with Three other Lewd Jesuit Priests*, in *Tudor Tracts* (London, 1903).

ERASMUS, DESIDERIUS, *Ad Illustrissimum Principem Philippum: Archiducem Austriae* . . . *Panegyricus* . . . (Antwerp, 1504).

—— *Institutio Principis Christiani* (Basle, 1516).

—— *Ecclesiastae, sive de Ratione Concionandi* . . . (Basle, 1535).

—— *Preparation to Deathe* (London, 1538). STC 10505.

—— *Desiderii Erasmi Opervm Omnivm*, 10 vols. (Leiden, 1703–6).

—— 'Letter to Jodocus Jonas', in *Christian Humanism and the Reformation: Selected Writings*, ed. John C. Olin (New York, 1965), 164–91.

—— *De Civilitate Morum Puerilium*, trans. and annotated by Brian McGregor, in *The Collected Works of Erasmus*, 66 vols., vol. 25, ed. J. M. Sowards (Toronto, 1985), 269–89.

—— *Oratio Funebris*, trans. Brad Inwood, in *The Collected Works of Erasmus*, 66 vols., vol. 29, ed. Elaine Fantham and Erika Rummel (Toronto, 1989), 15–30.

[Eusebius], *The Auncient Ecclesiasticall Histories of the First Six Hundred Years after Christ, Wrytten in the Greeke Tongue by Three Learned Historiographers, Eusebius, Socrates, and Evagrius* . . .

*4th edition, corrected and revised. Hereunto is added Eusebius his Life
of Constantine. Translated by W. Saltonstall* (London, 1636). STC
10576.

FEATLEY, DANIEL, letters to Thomas Morton and George Paule,
Bodleian Library, Oxford, MS Rawlinson D 47.

—— *Life of the Worthie Prelate and Faithfull Servant of God Iohn Iewel
sometimes Bishop of Sarisburie*, in John Jewel, *Works* (London, 1609).
STC 14579.

—— *Clavis Mystica: A Key Opening Divers Difficult and Mysterious Texts
of Holy Scripture* (London, 1636). STC 10730.

FELL, JOHN, *The Life and Death of that Reverend Divine . . . Thomas
Fuller* (Oxford, 1662). Wing F616.

—— *Life of Richard Allestree*, in Richard Allestree, *Sermons* (Oxford and
London, 1684). Wing A1082.

—— *Life of Dr. Henry Hammond*, in Henry Hammond, *A Practical
Catechism*, ed. Nicholas Pocock (Oxford, 1847).

Life of Nicholas Ferrar, in *The Ferrar Papers*, ed. B. Blackstone
(Cambridge, 1938).

FITZ-GEFFRY, CHARLES, *Deaths Sermon Vnto the Liuing. Delivered at
the Funerals of the Religious Lady Philippe, Late Wife vnto . . .
Sr. Anthonie Rovs . . .* (London, 1620). STC 10940.

FOXE, JOHN, *Actes and Monuments of these Latter and Perillous Dayes,
Touching Matters of the Church, wherein are Comprehended and
Described the Great Persecutions and Horrible Troubles . . . from the
Yeare of our Lorde One Thousand, unto the Tyme now Present*
(London, 1563). STC 11222.

—— *The Ecclesiasticall History, Contayning the Actes and Monuments
of Things Passed in Every Kinges Tyme in this Realme Especially in
the Church of England Principally to be Noted . . . from the Primitive
Tyme till the Reigne of K. Henry VIII*, 2nd edn., 2 vols. (London, 1570).
STC 11223.

[Simeon Foxe], *The Life of Mr. John Fox, Translated out of the Latine*,
in John Foxe, *Acts and Monuments of Matters Most Special and
Memorable, Happening in the Church: with an Universal History of the
Same. Wherein is Set Forth, at Large, the Whole Race and Course
of the Church, from the Primitive Age to these Times of Ours . . .
Especially in this realme of England and Scotland*, 8th edn., 3 vols.
(London, 1641), ii., sigs. A3–B6ᵛ. Wing F2035.

FULLER, THOMAS, *The Holy State* (Cambridge, 1642). Wing F2443.

—— *Abel Redevivus, or the Dead yet Speaking* (London, 1651). Wing
F2400.

—— *The Church History of Britain* (London, 1655). Wing F2416.

—— 'The Life of . . . Henry Smith', in Henry Smith, *Sermons* (London,
1657). Wing S4045.

—— *History of the Worthies of England* (London, 1662). Wing F2440.

—— *Life of that Reverend Dean Dr. Colet, sometime Dean of St. Paul's*, in John Colet, *Daily Devotions, or, the Christian's Morning and Evening Sacrifice* (London, 1674). Wing C5092.

FULLER, WILLIAM, *The Mourning of Mount Libanon, or the Temples Teares* . . . (London, 1628). STC 11468.

GAUDEN, JOHN, *Richard Hooker* . . . *An Account of his Holy Life and Happy Death*, in *The Works of Richard Hooker* (London, 1662). Wing H2630.

HALL, JOSEPH, *Characters of Vertues and Vices, in Two Bookes* (London, 1608). STC 12648.

HAMMOND, HENRY, Χάρις καί Εἰρήνη, *or A Pacifick Discourse of God's Grace and Decrees* . . . *in a Letter, of Full Accordance, written to* . . . *Dr. Robert Sanderson* (London, 1660). Wing H519.

HAMMOND, HENRY, *A Practical Catechism*: see under John Fell.

HARRIS, JOHN, 'A Short View of the Life and Vertves of the Avthovr', in Arthur Lake, *Sermons with some Religious and Divine Meditations* (London, 1629). STC 15134.

HARRISON, WILLIAM and LEYGH, W., *Deaths Advantage Little Regarded, and the Soules Solace against Sorow. Preached in Two Funerall Sermons, at the Buriall of K. Brettergh* . . . *whereunto is annexed the Life of the Said Gentlewoman* . . . (London, 1602). STC 12866.

HARRISON, W., *The Life and Death, of Mistris K. Brettergh* (London, 1612). STC 12864.

HARVEY, CHRISTOPHER, *The Synagogue*, 4th edn. (London, 1661). Contains Walton's dedicatory verses to Harvey; bound in with George Herbert, *The Temple*. Wing H1047.

HAWKINS, WILLIAM, *A Short Account of the Life of the Reverend Father in God, Thomas Ken, D.D., sometime Bishop of Bath and Wells* (London, 1713).

HAYNE, THOMAS: see under Melchior Adamus.

HEALEY, JOHN: see under Theophrastus.

HERBERT, GEORGE, *Remaines*, ed. Barnabas Oley (London, 1652). Wing H1515.

—— *The Complete Works in Verse and Prose of George Herbert*, ed. A. B. Grosart, 3 vols. (London, 1874).

—— *The Works of George Herbert*, ed. F. E. Hutchinson (Oxford, 1941).

HEYLYN, PETER, *Briefe Relation of the Death and Sufferings of* . . . [William Laud], *L. Archbishop of Canterbury* (Oxford, 1644). Wing H1685.

—— *Cyprianus Anglicus, or, the History of the Life and Death of the most Reverend and Renowned Prelate, William* [Laud] . . . *Lord Archbishop of Canterbury* . . . (London, 1668). Wing H1699.

HILL, ABRAHAM, 'Some Account of the Life of Dr. Isaac Barrow', in Isaac Barrow, *Works*, 4 vols. (London, 1683), vol. 1. Wing B925.

H[olland], H[enry], *Herωologia Anglicana Hoc est Clarissimorum et Doctissimorum aliquot Anglorum . . . Vivae Effigies* (London, 1620). STC 13582.

HOLLAND, HENRY, *History of the Moderne Protestant Divines*: see under Jacobus Verheiden.

HOOKER, RICHARD, *Of the Laws of Ecclesiastical Polity*, ed. John Spenser (London, 1604). STC 13713.

—— *A Learned and Comfortable Sermon of the Certaintie and Perpetuitie of Faith in the Elect* . . . (Oxford [London], 1612). STC 13707.

—— *A Learned Discourse of Justification, Workes, and How the Foundation of Faith is Overthrown* (Oxford [London], 1612). STC 13708.

—— *Of the Lawes of Ecclesiasticall Politie; the Sixth and Eighth Books. A Work Long Expected, and now Published According to the most Authentique Copies* (London, 1648). Wing H2635.

—— *Works* (1662): see under John Gauden.

—— *Works* (1666): see under Izaak Walton.

—— *Of the Laws of Ecclesiastical Polity and other Works*, ed. Benjamin Hanbury (London, 1830).

—— *Works*, ed. John Keble, revised by R. W. Church and F. Paget, 3 vols., 7th edn. (Oxford, 1888).

—— *The Folger Library Edition of the Works of Richard Hooker*, 6 vols. (Cambridge, Mass., 1972–93).

HUMPHREY, LAURENCE, *Joannis Juelli, Episcopi Sarisburiensis Vita et Mors eiusque; Verae Doctrinae Defensio* (London, 1573). STC 13963.

HYPERIUS, ANDREAS, *De Formandis Concionibus Sacris; seu de Interpretatione Scripturam Populi* (Marburg, 1553).

—— *Enseignement a Bien Former les Sainctes Predications et Sermons* (Geneva, 1563).

—— *The Practise of Preaching, otherwise Called the Pathway to the Pulpet; Conteyning an Excellent Method how to Frame Divine Sermons . . . Englished by Iohn Ludham* . . . (London, 1577). STC 11758.5

ISAACSON, HENRY, *An Exact Narration of the Life and Death of . . . Lancelot Andrewes* (London, 1650). Wing I1058.

JACKSON, THOMAS: see under E. Vaghan.

JEWEL, JOHN, *Works* (1609): see under Daniel Featley.

—— *Works of John Jewel*, ed. John Ayre, 4 vols. (Cambridge, 1845–50).

(JOHNSON, SAMUEL), *The R.B. Adam Library Relating to Dr. Johnson and his Era*, with an Introduction by C. G. Osgood and a Preface by A. E. Newton, 3 vols. (Buffalo, NY, 1929).

JONAS, JUSTUS and others, *The True Hystorye of the Christen Departynge of D. Martyne Luther*, trans. John Bale (Marburg, 1546). STC 14717.

KING, HENRY, *A Sermon Preached at Pauls Crosse, Touching the Supposed Apostacie of J King, late Bishop of London* . . . (London, 1621). STC 14969.

KINGSLEY, FRANCES ELIZA, *Charles Kingsley: His Letters and Memories of his Life* (London, 1877).

LAKE, ARTHUR: see under John Harris.

LEYGH, W.: see under William Harrison.

LAUD, WILLIAM, *The Archbishop of Canterbury's Speech or his Funerall Sermon, Preacht by Himself on the Scaffold at Tower-Hill, on Friday the 10. of January, 1644* (London, 1644). Wing L599.

—— 'Diary': see under William Prynne.

—— *A History of the Troubles and Tryal of the Most Reverend Father in God, and Blessed Martyr, William Laud, Lord Archbishop of Canterbury, Wrote by Himself during his Imprisonment in the Tower. To which is Prefixed the Diary of his own Life*, ed. Henry Wharton (London, 1693–4). Wing L586.

LEIGH, EDWARD: see under Henry Scudder.

Life off [sic] *the 70. Archbishopp of Canterbury Presentlye Sittinge Englished/and to be Added to the 69. Lately Sett Forth in Latin* ([Zurich], 1574). STC 19292a.

LIPSIUS, JUSTUS, *Two Bookes of Constancie* . . . *Containing, Principallie, a Comfortable Conference, in Common Calamities* . . . *Englished by Iohn Stradling* . . . (London, 1595). STC 15695.

LORD HERBERT of CHERBURY, EDWARD, *The Life and Raigne of King Henry the Eighth* (London, 1649). Wing H1504.

—— *Autobiography*, ed. Sidney Lee (London, 1888).

LUPSET, THOMAS, *A Compendiovs and a Very Frvtefvl Treatyse, Teachynge the Waye of Dyenge Well* . . . (n.p., 1534). STC 16934.

LUTHER, MARTIN, *Commentarie upon the Epistle to the Galathians* (London, 1575). STC 16965.

MARBECKE, JOHN, *The Lyves of Holy Saincts, Prophetes, Patriarches, and others, Contayned in Holy Scripture* . . . *Collected and Gathered into an Alphabeticall Order* . . . (London, 1574). STC 17303.

MARTYR, PETER, *Martyrs Divine Epistles*, bound in with *The Common Places of Peter Martyr* . . . , translated by Anthony Marten (London, 1583). STC 24669.

MATHER, COTTON, *Magnalia Christi Americana*, 2 vols. (Hartford, Conn., 1853).

MELANCHTHON, PHILIP, *Historia de Vita et Actis Reverendissimi Viri D. M. Lutheri, Verae Theologiae Doctoris* . . . (Wittemberg, 1549).

—— *A Famous and Godly History*: see under Henry Bennet.

MONTAIGNE, M., *Essaies*, trans. John Florio, with an Introduction by D. MacCarthy, 3 vols. (London, 1928).

MORLEY, GEORGE, *The Bishop of Worcester's Letter to a Friend for Vindication of Himself from Mr. Baxter's Calumny* (London, 1662). Wing M2790.

MOSSOM, R[obert], *Narrative Panegyrical of the Life, Sickness and Death of George* [Wilde], *Lord Bishop of Derry in Ireland* (London, 1665/6). Wing M2684.

MUSCHET, GEORGE, *The Bishop of London his Legacy. Or Certain Motives of D King, late Bishop of London, for his Change of Religion* (St Omer, 1623). STC 18305.

N[aylor], J[oseph]: see under R[ichard] B[addeley].

NICHOL SMITH, DAVID (ed.), *Characters from the Histories and Memoirs of the Seventeenth Century* (Oxford, 1918).

[Nixon, Anthony], *Londons Dove: or, a Memorial of the Life and Death of Master Robert Dove* (London, 1612). STC 18588.

OVERBURY, Sir THOMAS, *His Wife, with Additions of New Characters, and Many other Written Conceits Never Before Printed*, 11th edn. (London, 1622). STC 18913.

PARKER, MATTHEW, 'The Testimony of the Guiftes of Matthue Archb of Cant.' Parker Library, Corpus Christi College, Cambridge, MS 582. Recorded in Richard Vaughan and John Fines, 'A Handlist of MSS in the Library of Corpus Christi Cambridge, Not Described by M. R. James', *Transactions of the Cambridge Bibliographical Society*, 3, ed. Bruce Dickins and A. N. L. Munby (London, 1963).

—— *How We Ought to Take the Death of the Godly. A Sermon Made in Cambridge at the Buriall of the Noble Clerck, D. M. [artin] Bucer*, trans. T. Newton (London, 1551). STC 19293.

—— *De Antiquitate Britannicae Ecclesiae et Privilegiis Ecclesiae Cantuariensis cum Archiepiscopus eiusdem 70.* (London, 1572). STC 19292.

PAULE, GEORGE, *The Life of the Most Reverend and Religious Prelate John Whitgift, Lord Archbishop of Canterbury* (London, 1612). STC 19484.

PECKARD, PETER, *Memoirs of the Life of Mr. Nicholas Ferrar* (Cambridge, 1790).

PHILLIPS, EDWARD, *The Life of Mr. John Milton*, in *The Early Lives of Milton*, ed. Helen Darbishire (London, 1932).

PIERCE, THOMAS, *An Impartial Inquiry into the Nature of Sin* (London, 1660). Wing P2184.

PLUTARCH, *Les Hommes Illustres Grecs et Romains*, trans. Jacques Amyot (Paris, 1559).

—— *Plutarch's Lives, translated from the Greek by Several Hands . . .* (London, 1683). Wing P2633–41.

—— *Lives of the Noble Grecians and Romans. Englished by Sir T. North anno 1579*, ed. W. E. Henley, 'The Tudor Translations' VII–XII, 6 vols. (London, 1895–6).

—— *The Educacion or Bringing vp of Children* . . . (anon., attrib. Plutarch), trans. Sir Thomas Elyot (London, before June 1530). STC 20056.7.

—— *A President for Parentes, Teaching the Vertuous Training vp of Children* . . . (anon., attrib. Plutarch), trans. and augmented by E. Grant (London, 1571). STC 20057.5.

—— *Plutarchi Chaeronei Opusculum de Liberorum Institutione. Item Isocratis Orationes Tres* . . . (anon., attrib. Plutarch) (London, 1581). STC 20054.

—— *The Preceptes of the Excellent Clerke and Grave Philosopher Plutarche for the Preservacion of Good Healthe* (anon., attrib. Plutarch), trans. J. Hales (London, 1543). STC 20060.

—— *The Governaunce of Good Helthe, Erasmus Beynge Interpretoure* (anon., attrib. Plutarch) (London, 1549?). STC 20060.5.

PRICKE, ROBERT, *The Doctrine of Superioritie, and of Subiection, Contained in the Fift Commandment* . . . (London, 1609). STC 20337.

PRIOR, T., *A Sermon Preached at the Funeralls of* . . . *Miles Smith*, in Miles Smith, *Sermons* (London, 1632). STC 22808.

PRYNNE, WILLIAM, *Breviate of the Life of W. Laud* . . . *Extracted* . . . *out of his Owne Diary and other Writings, under his Owne Hand* (London, 1644). Wing P3904.

QUARLES, FRANCIS, *The Shepheards Oracles* (London, 1646). Wing Q114A.

SANDERSON, ROBERT, *Twelve Sermons* (London, 1632). STC 21706.

—— *Two Sermons Preached at Paules-Crosse London* (London, 1628). STC 21708.5.

—— *XXXV Sermons* . . . (1681): see under Izaak Walton.

—— *Works*, ed. W. Jacobson, 6 vols. (Oxford, 1854).

—— *Pax Ecclesiae*, in Izaak Walton, *Life of* . . . *Sanderson* (1678).

SAVILE, HENRY: see under Tacitus.

SCUDDER, HENRY, *Life and Death of Mr. William Whateley* . . . , in William Whateley, *Prototypes, or the Primary President Precedents ovt of the Booke of Genesis* . . . (London, 1640). STC 25317.3.

SIBBES, RICHARD, *Complete Works*, ed. A. Grosart, 7 vols. (Edinburgh, 1862–4).

SMITH, G. G. (ed.), *Elizabethan Critical Essays*, 2 vols. (Oxford, 1904).

SMITH, HENRY: see under Thomas Fuller.

SMITH, MILES, *Sermons*: see under Thomas Prior.

—— 'Preface to the Reader', in Gervase Babington, *Works*, 3rd edn. (London, 1637). STC 1080.

SMITH, THOMAS, *Life of* . . . *Colet*, in John Colet, *A Sermon of Conforming and Reforming made to the Convocation at St. Paul's Church in London* . . . (Cambridge, 1661). Wing C5096.

DE SOLA PINTO, VIVIAN (ed.), *English Biography in the Seventeenth Century: Selected Short Lives* (London, 1951).

SPINGARN, J. E. (ed.), *Critical Essays of the Seventeenth Century*, 3 vols. (London, 1908).

SPRAT, THOMAS, 'An Account of the Life and Writings of Abraham Cowley, Written to Mr. M. Clifford', in *The Works of Mr. Abraham Cowley*, 2 vols. (London, 1721), i., pp. i–xxxvi (misnumbered xxxv).

STRYPE, JOHN, *The Life and Acts of Matthew Parker, in Four Books, to which is Added, An Appendix* (London, 1711).

—— *Annals of the Reformation and Establishment of Religion, and other Various Occurrences in the Church of England, during Queen Elizabeth's Happy Reign: Together with an Appendix of Original Papers of State, Records, and Letters*, 4 vols. (Oxford, 1824).

—— *The Life and Acts of John Whitgift, D.D., the Third and Last Lord Archbishop of Canterbury in the Reign of Queen Elizabeth. The Whole Digested, Compiled and Attested from Records, Registers, Original Letters and other Authentic MSS . . . Together with a Large Appendix of the Said Papers*, 3 vols. (Oxford, 1848–54).

STUBBES, PHILIP, *A Christall Glasse for Christian Women* (London, 1591). STC 23381.

SUETONIUS, *Historie of Twelve Caesars Emperors of Rome*, trans. Philemon Holland (London, 1606). STC 23422.

TACITUS, *The End of Nero & Beginning of Galba* and *The Life of Iulius Agricola*, trans. Henry Savile (Oxford [London], 1591). STC 23642.

—— *Annales* and *The End of Nero . . .* , trans. Richard Greenwey and Henry Savile, 5th edn., 2 Pts. (London, 1622). STC 23647.

TAYLOR, JEREMY, *The Great Exemplar of Sanctity and Holy Life . . . Described in the History of the Life and Death of the ever Blessed Jesus Christ . . . with Considerations and Discourses upon the Several Parts of the Story, and Prayers Fitted to the Several Mysteries* (London, 1649). Wing T342.

—— *Holy Dying . . .* (London, 1652). Wing T361.

THEOPHRASTUS, *Theophrasti, Characteres Ethici . . .* , trans. Isaac Casaubon (1592). Not in STC.

—— *Epictetus Manuall, Cebes Table, Theophrastus his Morall Characters*, trans. John Healey (London, 1616). STC 10426.

Θρενοικός. *The House of Mourning . . . Delivered in XLVII Sermons, Preached at Funeralls of Divers Faithfull Servants of Christ. By Daniel Featly Richard Sibbs Martin Day Thomas Taylor and other Reverend Divines* (London, 1640). STC 24049.

THOMAS, W.: see John Chetwinde.

TULLY, THOMAS: see under Jonathan Banks.

VAGHAN, E., *Life and Death of the Reverend, Learned, and Pious Dr. Jackson, Dean of Peterborough, and President of Corpus-Christi College in Oxford*, in *The Works of the Reverend and Learned Divine, Thomas Jackson, D.D.*, ed. Barnabas Oley, 3 vol., vol. 1 (London, 1673), sigs. *–**4. Wing J90.

VENNING, RALPH, *Orthodox Paradoxes, or, a Beleiver* [sic] *Clearing Truth by Seeming Contradictions, with an Appendix, called the Triumph of Assurance* (London, 1647). Wing V217.

VERHEIDEN, JACOBUS, *Praestantium aliquot Theologorum, qui Rom. Antichristum Praecipue Oppugnarent, Effigies: quibus Addita Elogia, Librorumque Catalogi, opera J. Verheiden* (The Hague, 1602).

—— and H[olland], H[enry], *History of the Moderne Protestant Divines* (London, 1637). STC 24660.

VERMIGLI: see under Peter Martyr.

VERNON, G., 'The Life of the Reverend D. Peter Heylyn, Chaplain to Charles I and Charles II', in Κειμήλια Ἐκκλεσιάστικα. *The Historical and Miscellaneous Tracts of . . . Peter Heylyn . . . And an Account of the Life of the Author never before Published* (London, 1681), pp. i–xxviii. Wing H1684.

VISCOUNT LORD FALKLAND, LUCIUS CARY, *Of the Infallibilitie of the Church of Rome* (Oxford, 1645). Wing F322.

WALKER, WILLIAM, *A Sermon Preached at the Funeralls of the Right Honourable William Lord Russell, Baron of Thornhaugh . . . the 16 of September, 1613* (London, 1614). STC 24964.

WALTON, IZAAK, *The Life of Dr. John Donne*, in John Donne, *LXXX Sermons*, ed. John Donne the younger (London, 1640). STC 7038.

—— *The Compleat Angler, or, the Contemplative Man's Recreation* (London, 1653). Wing W661.

—— *Life of Sir Henry Wotton*, in Henry Wotton, *Reliquiae Wottonianae*, 2nd edn. (London, 1654). Wing W3649.

—— *Life of John Donne, Dr. in Divinity &c.*, 2nd edn., corrected and enlarged (London, 1658). Wing W668.

—— *Life of Mr. R. Hooker* (London, 1665). Wing W670.

—— *Life of Mr. R. Hooker*, in *The Works of Mr. Richard Hooker* (London, 1666). Wing H2631.

—— *Life of Mr. George Herbert* (London, 1670). Wing W669.

—— *Lives of Dr. John Donne, Sir Henry Wotton, Mr. Richard Hooker, Mr. George Herbert* (London, 1670). Wing W671.

—— *Lives of Dr. John Donne, Sir Henry Wotton, Mr. Richard Hooker, Mr. George Herbert* (London, 1675). Wing W672.

—— *Life of Dr. Sanderson, Late Bishop of Lincoln . . . to which is Added, Some Short Tracts . . .* (London, 1678). Wing W667.

WALTON, IZAAK, *Love and Truth, in Two Modest and Peaceable Letters. Written from a Quiet and Conformable Citizen of London, to Two Busie and Factious Shop-Keepers in Coventry* (London, 1680). Wing W673.

—— *Life of Dr. Robert Sanderson,* in *Robert Sanderson, XXXV Sermons . . . with a Large Preface . . .* , 8th edn. (London, 1681). Wing S637.

—— *The Complete Angler,* ed. Moses Browne (London, 1750).

—— *The Complete Angler,* ed. Sir John Hawkins (London, 1760).

—— *Lives,* ed. Thomas Zouch (York, 1796).

—— *The Lives of Richard Hooker, George Herbert and Robert Sanderson,* SPCK (London, 1819).

—— *Lives,* ed. J[ohn] M[ajor] (London, 1825).

—— *Lives* (London, 1827).

—— *Lives,* with a memoir by William Dowling (London, 1857).

—— *Waltoniana: Inedited Remains in Verse and Prose of Izaak Walton,* ed. with notes by Richard Herne Shepherd (London, 1878).

—— *The Compleat Angler,* ed. James Russell Lowell (Boston, 1889).

—— *Lives,* with an Introduction by Vernon Blackburn (London, 1895).

—— *The Compleat Angler,* ed. Richard Le Gallienne (London and New York, 1897).

—— *Lives,* ed. George Saintsbury (Oxford, 1927).

—— *The Compleat Walton,* ed. Geoffrey Keynes (London, 1929).

—— *The Compleat Angler 1653–1676,* ed. Jonquil Bevan (Oxford, 1983).

—— *Izaak Walton: Selected Writings,* ed. Jessica Martin (Manchester, 1997).

WHATELEY, WILLIAM: see under Henry Scudder.

WHITEFOOTE, JOHN, Ἰσραὴλ Ἀνγχιθανῆς. *Death's Alarum, or the Presage of Approaching Death: Given in a Sermon . . . for . . . Joseph Hall, Late Lord Bishop of Norwich . . .* (London, 1656). Wing W1863.

WHITGIFT, JOHN, *The Works of John Whitgift,* ed. J. Ayre, 3 vols., Parker Soc. (Cambridge, 1851).

W[ilson], J[ohn], *The English Martyrologe, Conteyning a Summary of the Lives of the Saints of England, Scotland and Ireland. Collected and Distributed into Monethes* (St. Omer, 1608). STC 25771.

WOOD, ANTHONY á, *Athenae Oxonienses,* ed. Philip Bliss, 3rd edn., 4 vols. (London, 1813).

—— *Fasti Oxonienses,* ed. Philip Bliss, 3rd edn., 1 vol. (2 parts) (London, 1815 and 1820).

—— *The Life and Times of Anthony Wood, Antiquary, of Oxford, 1632–1695, Described by Himself,* 2 vols. (Oxford, 1891).

WORDSWORTH, WILLIAM, 'Walton's Book of Lives', in *Ecclesiastical Sonnets,* ed. A. F. Potts (New Haven, 1922), 164.

WORTHINGTON, THOMAS, *A Relation of Sixteene Martyrs Glorified in England in Twelve Monethes* (Douay, 1601). Not in STC. Allison and Rogers, no. 917.

—— *A Catalogue of Martyrs in England; for Profession of the Catholique Faith, since the Year of our Lord, 1535 . . . unto this Year 1608* ([Douay], 1608). Not in STC. Allison and Rogers, no. 916.

WOTTON, SIR HENRY, *A Parallel Betweene Robert Late Earle of Essex, and George Late Duke of Buckingham* (London, 1641). Wing W3647.

—— *Reliquiae Wottonianae*, see under Izaak Walton.

3. OTHER BOOKS, ARTICLES, AND DISSERTATIONS

ADDLESHAW, G. W. O., *The High Church Tradition: A Study in the Liturgical Thought of the Seventeenth Century* (London, 1941).

ANDERSON, JUDITH, *Biographical Truth: The Representation of Historical Persons in Tudor-Stuart Writing* (New Haven, 1984).

AULOTTE, R., *Amyot et Plutarque* (Geneva, 1965).

BALD, R. C., 'Historical Doubts Respecting Walton's Life of Donne', in Millar MacLure and F. W. Watt (eds.), *Essays in English Literature from the Renaissance to the Victorian Age* (Toronto, 1964), 69–84.

BAS, GEORGES, 'Thomas Zouch's Life of Walton and the Alleged Friendship between James Shirley and Izaak Walton', *Notes & Queries*, NS (Continuous Series no. 222), 24 (1977), 125–6.

BAYLEY, PETER, *French Pulpit Oratory 1598–1650: A Study in Themes and Styles* (Cambridge, 1980).

BEDDARD, R. A., 'The Restoration Church', in J. R. Jones (ed.), *The Restored Monarchy* (London, 1979), 155–75.

BEECHING, H. C., *Religio Laici* (London, 1902).

BENNETT, H. S., *English Books and Readers 1603–40* (Cambridge, 1970).

BENNETT, R. E., 'Walton's Use of Donne's Letters', *Philological Quarterly*, 16 (1937), 30–4.

BEVAN, JONQUIL, 'Izaak Walton and his Publisher', *The Library*, 5th series, 32 (1977), 344–59.

—— 'Some Books from Walton's Library', *The Library*, 6th series, 2: 3 (1980).

—— *Izaak Walton's The Compleat Angler: the Art of Recreation* (Brighton, 1988).

—— 'Henry Valentine, John Donne, and Izaak Walton', *Review of English Studies*, 40: 158 (May 1989), 179–201.

BOLGAR, R. R., *The Classical Heritage and its Beneficiaries* (Cambridge, 1954).

BOSHER, R. S., *The Making of the Restoration Settlement* (London, 1951).
BOSSY, JOHN, *The English Catholic Community, 1570–1850* (London, 1975).
BOYCE, B., *The Theophrastan Character in England to 1642* (London, 1967).
BROOK, V. J. K., *A Life of Archbishop Parker* (Oxford, 1962).
BRYSON, ANNA, 'The Rhetoric of Status', in Lucy Gent and Nigel Llewellyn (eds.), *Renaissance Bodies* (London, 1990), 136–53.
BURKE, PETER, 'A Survey of the Popularity of Ancient Historians 1450–1700', *History and Theory*, 5 (1966), 150–5.
BUTT, JOHN, 'Izaak Walton's Methods in Biography', *Essays and Studies*, 19 (1933), 67–84.
—— *Biography in the Hands of Walton, Johnson and Boswell* (Los Angeles, 1966).
—— 'Izaak Walton's Collections for Fulman's Life of John Hales', *Modern Language Review*, 29 (1934), 269–73.
CAREY, JOHN, 'Sixteenth and Seventeenth Century Prose', in Christopher Ricks (ed.), *English Poetry and Prose 1540–1674* (London, 1970), 339–431.
—— *John Donne: Life, Mind and Art* (London, 1981).
CARLTON, CHARLES, *Archbishop William Laud* (London, 1987).
CHRISTIANSON, PAUL, *Reformers and Babylon: English Apocalyptic Visions from the Reformation to the Eve of the Civil War* (Toronto, 1978).
CLEBSCH, W. A., 'The Elizabethans on Luther', in Jaroslav Pelikan (ed.), *Interpreters of Luther: Essays in Honor of Wilhelm Pauck* (Philadelphia, 1968), 97–120.
CLIFFORD, JAMES L. (ed.), *Biography as an Art: Selected Criticism 1560–1960* (London, 1962).
COLERIDGE, S. T., 'A Prefatory Observation on Modern Biography', *The Friend*, 21 (25 Jan. 1810).
COLLINSON, PATRICK, *The Religion of Protestants* (Oxford, 1982).
—— *Godly People: Essays on English Protestantism and Puritanism* (London, 1983).
—— *The Puritan Character: Polemics and Polarities in Early Seventeenth Century English Culture* (Los Angeles, 1989).
—— 'Shepherds, Sheepdogs and Hirelings: The Pastoral Ministry in Post-Reformation England', *Studies in Church History*, 26 (1989), 185–220.
—— 'Hooker and the Elizabethan Establishment', in A. S. McGrade (ed.), *Richard Hooker and the Construction of Christian Community* (Tempe, Ariz., 1997), 149–181.
COSTA, FRANCISQUE, 'L'Oeuvre d'Izaak Walton 1593–1683', *Études Anglaises*, 48 (Paris, 1973).

—— 'Walton: Bibliographie Selective et Critique', *Bulletin de la Société d'Études Anglo-Americains du 17ème et 18ème Siècles*, 1 (1975), 5–14.

COSTELLO, W. T., *The Scholastic Curriculum at Early Seventeenth Century Cambridge* (Cambridge, Mass., 1958).

DISLEY, E., 'Degrees of Glory, Protestant Doctrine and the Concept of Rewards Hereafter', *Journal of Theological Studies*, 42 (1991), 77–105.

DOERKSEN, D. W., 'The Laudian Interpretation of George Herbert', *Literature and History*, 3 (1984), 36–54.

DONNO, E. S., 'Old Mouse-Eaten Records: History in Sidney's Apology', *Studies in Philology*, 72 (1975), 275–98.

DONOVAN, DENNIS G., 'Recent Studies in Burton and Walton', *English Literary Renaissance*, 1 (1971), 294–303.

ELIOT, T. S., 'Shakespeare and the Stoicism of Seneca', in *Selected Essays* (London, 1932), 126–40.

FAIRFIELD, LESLIE P., 'John Bale and Protestant Hagiography in England', *Journal of Ecclesiastical History*, 24 (1973), 145–60.

FINCHAM, KENNETH, *Prelate as Pastor: The Episcopate of James I* (Oxford, 1990).

FOXALL, NIGEL, *A Sermon in Stone: John Donne and his Monument in St. Paul's* (London, 1978).

FUDGE, THOMAS A., 'Myth, Heresy and Propaganda in the Radical Hussite Movement, 1409–1437', unpublished Ph.D dissertation, University of Cambridge (1992).

GARDNER, HELEN, 'Dean Donne's Monument in St. Paul's', in René Wellek and Alvaro Ribeiro (eds.), *Evidence in Literary Scholarship: Essays in Memory of James Marshall Osborne* (Oxford, 1979), 29–44.

GARRISON, JAMES D., *Dryden and the Tradition of Panegyric* (Berkeley, 1975).

GOLDIE, MARK (ed.), *The Politics of Religion in Restoration England*, with Tim Harris and Paul Seaward (Oxford, 1990).

GOSSE, EDMUND, *The Life and Letters of John Donne*, 2 vols. (London, 1899).

GRANQVIST, RAOUL, *The Reputation of John Donne 1779–1873* (Uppsala, 1975).

—— 'Izaak Walton's Lives in the Nineteenth and the Early Twentieth Centuries: A Study of a Cult Object', *Studia Neophilologica*, 54: 2 (1982), 247–61.

GREEN, IAN, *The Re-Establishment of the Church of England 1660–1663* (Oxford, 1978).

GREENBLATT, STEPHEN, *Renaissance Self-Fashioning: From More to Shakespeare* (Chicago, 1980).

HAIGHT, GORDON S., 'The Author of "The Address" in Quarles' Shepheards Oracles', *Modern Language Notes*, 59 (1944), 118–20.

HALLER, WILLIAM, *The Rise of Puritanism; Or, the Way to the New Jerusalem as Set Forth in Pulpit and Press from Thomas Cartwright to John Lilburne and John Milton* (New York, 1938).
—— *Foxe's Book of Martyrs and the Elect Nation* (London, 1963).
HAMILTON, IAN, *Keepers of the Flame: Literary Estates and the Rise of Biography* (London, 1992).
HAMPTON, TIMOTHY, *Writing from History: The Rhetoric of Exemplarity in Renaissance Literature* (New York, 1990).
HAUGAARD, W., *Elizabeth and the English Reformation: The Struggle for a Stable Settlement of Religion* (Cambridge, 1968).
HAYWARD, J. C., 'The Mores of Great Tew: Literary, Philosophical and Political Idealism in Falkland's Circle', unpublished Ph.D dissertation, University of Cambridge (1982).
HAZLITT, W., 'On John Buncle', in *The Round Table: A Collection of Essays on Literature, Men and Manners*, vol. 1 (Edinburgh, 1817), 161–2.
HEAL, FELICITY, *Of Prelates and Princes: A Study of the Economic and Social Position of the Tudor Episcopate* (Cambridge, 1980).
—— *Hospitality in Early Modern England* (Oxford, 1990).
HEMBRY, P., *The Bishops of Bath and Wells 1540–1640* (London, 1967).
HILL, GEOFFREY, *The Enemy's Country: Words, Contexture, and other Circumstances of Language* (Oxford, 1991).
HOLMES, CLIVE, *Seventeenth Century Lincolnshire* (Lincoln, 1980).
HOWARD, MARTHA WALLING, *The Influence of Plutarch in the Major European Literatures of the Eighteenth Centuries* (N. Carolina, 1970).
JORDAN, RICHARD DOUGLAS, 'Herbert's First Sermon', *Review of English Studies*, 27 (1976), 178–9.
JORDAN, W. K., *Philanthropy in England 1480–1660* (London, 1959).
KAY, DENNIS, *Melodious Tears: The English Funeral Elegy from Spenser to Milton* (Oxford, 1990).
KENDALL, R. T., *Calvin and English Calvinism to 1649* (Oxford, 1979).
KOLB, ROBERT, 'Burying the Brethren: Lutheran Funeral Sermons as Life Writing', in Thomas R. Mayer and D. R. Woolf (eds.), *The Rhetorics of Life-Writing in Early Modern Europe* (Ann Arbor, Mich., 1995), 97–113.
LAKE, PETER, *Anglicans and Puritans? Presbyterianism and English Conformist Thought from Whitgift to Hooker* (London, 1988).
—— 'Feminine Piety and Personal Potency: The "Emancipation" of Mrs. Jane Ratcliffe', *The Seventeenth Century*, 2 (1987), 143–65.
—— 'Serving God and the Times: The Calvinist Conformity of Robert Sanderson', *Journal of British Studies*, 27 (1988), 81–116.
LEIN, C. D., 'Art and Structure in Walton's Life of Mr. George Herbert', *University of Toronto Quarterly*, 46 (1976–7), 162–76.

LEWALSKI, BARBARA, *Protestant Poetics and the Seventeenth Century Religious Lyric* (Princeton, 1979).

—— *Donne's 'Anniversaries' and the Poetry of Praise: The Creation of a Symbolic Mode* (Princeton, 1973).

McCONICA, J. K., *English Humanists and Reformation Politics under Henry VIII and Edward VI* (Oxford, 1965).

MacCULLOCH, DIARMAID, 'The Myth of the Reformation', *History Today*, 41 (July 1991), 28–35.

—— *Thomas Cranmer: A Life* (New Haven, 1996).

McGEE, JAMES SEARS, *The Godly Man in Stuart England: Anglicans, Puritans, and the Two Tables, 1620–70* (New Haven, 1976).

MAUROIS, ANDRÉ, *Aspects of Biography*, trans. Sydney Castle Roberts (New York, 1929).

MAYCOCK, A. L., *Nicholas Ferrar of Little Gidding* (London, 1938).

MORGAN, JOHN, *Godly Learning: Puritan Attitudes Towards Reason, Learning and Education, 1560–1640* (Cambridge, 1986).

MOZLEY, J. F., *John Foxe and his Book* (London, 1940).

NEALE, J. E., *Elizabeth I and her Parliaments 1584–1601* (London, 1958).

NICOLSON, HAROLD, *The Development of English Biography* (London, 1927).

NORTH, J. A., 'These He Cannot Take', *Journal of Roman Studies* (1983), 169–74.

NOVARR, DAVID, *The Making of Walton's Lives* (Ithaca, 1958).

—— 'The Anglican Quietude of Izaak Walton', *Études Anglaises*, 28 (1975), 314–24.

OLSEN, V. NORSKOV, *John Foxe and the Elizabethan Church* (Berkeley, 1973).

PACKER, J. W., *The Transformation of Anglicanism, 1643–1660: With Special Reference to Henry Hammond* (Manchester, 1969).

PEARSON, DAVID, 'The Libraries of English Bishops, 1600–40', *The Library*, 6th series, 14 (1992), 221–57.

PINEAS, RAINER, 'Robert Barnes' Polemical Use of History', *Bibliothèque d'Humanisme et Renaissance*, 26 (1964), 55–69.

POWELL, ANTHONY, *John Aubrey and his Friends*, 2nd revised edn. (London, 1988).

READ, J. W., *English Biography in the Early Nineteenth Century, 1801–38* (New Haven, 1966).

RENAULT, MARY, 'History in Fiction', *Times Literary Supplement*, 23 March 1973.

RICHARDSON, W. B., 'The Religious Policy of the Cecils 1589–1598', unpublished D.Phil. dissertation, University of Oxford (1994).

ROTHSCHILD, HERBERT, Jr., 'The "Higher Hand" in Walton's Life of John Donne', *Notes & Queries*, 25, NS (Continuous Series no. 223) (1978), 506–8.

RUSSELL, D. A., *Plutarch* (London, 1973).

SHIRLEY, F. J., *Richard Hooker and Contemporary Political Ideas* (London, 1949).

SIMPSON, EVELYN M., 'The Biographical Value of Donne's Sermons', *Review of English Studies*, 2 (1951), 339–57.

SISSON, C. J., *The Judicious Marriage of Mr. Hooker and the Birth of the Laws of Ecclesiastical Polity'* (Cambridge, 1940).

SMEED, J. W., *The Theophrastan 'Character': The History of a Literary Genre* (Oxford, 1985).

SMITH, PRESERVED, *Life and Letters of Martin Luther* (Cambridge, 1911).

SPEED HILL, W., 'The Evolution of Hookers *Laws of Ecclesiastical Polity'*, in *Studies in Richard Hooker* (Cleveland and London, 1972), 117–58.

SPUFFORD, MARGARET, 'Can we Count the "Godly" and the "Conformable" in the Seventeenth Century?', *Journal of Ecclesiastical History*, 36 (July 1985), 428–38.

SPURR, JOHN, *The Restoration Church of England, 1646–1689* (New Haven, 1991).

STAUFFER, DONALD, *English Biography before 1700* (Cambridge, Mass., 1930).

—— *The Art of Biography in Eighteenth Century England* (Princeton, 1941).

STEPHEN, LESLIE, 'John Donne', *National Review*, 34 (1899), 595–6.

STEVENS, JOHN, *Music and Poetry in the Early Tudor Court* (London, 1961).

TATHAM, G. B., *The Puritans in Power* (Cambridge, 1913).

TAYLOR, A. J. P., 'Fiction in History', *Times Literary Supplement*, 23 March 1973.

TEMPERLEY, NICHOLAS, *The Music of the English Parish Church*, 2 vols. (Cambridge, 1983).

TREVOR-ROPER, HUGH, *Archbishop Laud*, 2nd edn. (London, 1962).

—— *Catholics, Anglicans and Puritans* (London, 1987).

TORRANCE KIRBY, W. J., *Richard Hooker's Doctrine of the Royal Supremacy* (Leiden, 1990).

TYACKE, NICHOLAS, 'Puritanism, Arminianism and Counter-Revolution', in Conrad Russell (ed.), *The Origins of the English Civil War* (London, 1973), 119–43.

—— *Anti-Calvinists: The Rise of English Arminianism c.1590–1640* (Oxford, 1987).

WARDMAN, ALAN, *Plutarch's Lives* (London, 1974).

WENDORF, RICHARD, 'Ut Pictura Biographia: Biography and Portrait Painting as Sister Arts' in Richard Wendorf (ed.), *Articulate Images: The Sister Arts from Hogarth to Tennyson* (Minneapolis, 1983), 98–124.

—— *The Elements of Life: Biography and Portrait Painting in Stuart and Georgian England* (Oxford, 1990).

WENGERT, TIMOTHY J., ' "With Friends Like This . . .": The Biography of Philip Melanchthon by Joachim Camerarius', in Thomas F. Mayer and D. R. Woolf (eds.), *The Rhetorics of Life-Writing in Early Modern Europe* (Ann Arbor, Mich., 1995), 115–31.

WHITE, HELEN C., *Tudor Books of Saints and Martyrs* (Madison, Wisc., 1963).

INDEX

All numbers in **bold** refer to illustrations.

ἀπάθεια 8, 38, 44
αὐξησις 4

Abel 91–2
Abiram 17
Abraham 11
Acciaiuoli, Donato 36 n. 15
Act of Uniformity 241
Adam 133, 155
Adams, Thomas 121 n. 93
Adamus, Melchior 61 n. 56, 69, 134, 140–1
adiaphora 230, 237, 275, 286
Admonition Controversy 21, 257
Agricola 54
Aitken, Henderson 36 n. 15
Alcman 43–4
Alexander the Great 5, 52, 53, 156
Alfield, Thomas 46
Alfonsus of Aragon 93
Ambrose 6 n. 8, 11, 22
  on his brother Satyrus 21
Amyot, Jacques 32 n., 36–8
Anderson, Judith 173, 175, 178, 184, 185, 188, 313
Andrewes, Lancelot **23**, 69, 93, 108, 120, 159, 177 n. 20, 217, 250 n., 283, 287, 312
Anglicans xv, xvi, 90 n. 40, 101, 108, 129, 158 n. 148, 220, 272, 289 n. 134, 306, 310, 312
Aristotle 40, 155
Arminianism xv, 274–5, 277, 279–82, 287
ars moriendi 132, 192, 197
artes concionandi 14
Arundel, Thomas 56
Ash, Simeon 65, 86

Ashmole, Elias 300–1
assurance 129–30, 183, 202, 276–8
Athanasius 19, 79
Aubrey, John 300
Augustine 6 n. 8, 11, 17, 19, 26, 50, 61, 127, 177
Augustinians 61
Aulotte, R. 32 n.
Aurifaber, Johannes 134
autobiography xi, 172, 180, 189, 191, 204, 206, 209, 213, 222, 226
Aylmer, John, Bishop of London 263
Ayre, John 88 n. 36

Baddeley, Richard 70, 79, 81, 82 n. 16, 102 n., 113–14, 127 n. 100, 149, 157 n. 146, 231 n. 6
Bacon, Sir Francis 6 n. 9, 217
Bailey, Margery 305 n. 17
Bald, R. C. 203 n., 313
Bale, John 68, 134
Banks, Jonathan 71, 85, 100, 110, 160
Barlow, Thomas 281
Barnard, John 295, **296**
Barrow, Dr Isaac xxii
Barrow, Henry 22
Barwick, John 70, 78–9, 81, 85 n. 26, 92, 120, 126, 149, 159 n. 150, 160, 268
Bas, Georges 306 n. 19
Basil 160 n.
Basire, Isaac 70, 92 n. 44
Baxter, Richard 239, 240
Bayley, Peter 21 n. 33
Bede 78

Bedell, William Bishop of Kilmore
xvii, 69, 70, 71, 82 n. 17,
88 n. 33, 157 n. 146,
220 n. 113
death 142–4
Bedell, William (fils) 142–4, 158
Beeching, H. C. 312
Bellarmine, Cardinal 184
Bennet, Henry 13 n., 16 n. 25, 62–3,
68, 134, 138 n. 116
Bennett, R. E. 187–8, 312–13
Berengarius 58–9
Bernard 94
Bernard, Nicholas 69, 93–4, 250
Bernard, Richard 75
The Faithfull Shepheard 88–9,
103–4, 118–20
Bevan, Jonquil 38 n. 22, 39 n. 23, 313
Bewley, Thomas 109, 145
Beza, Theodore 102 n.
Icones 15 n. 22, 57–9, 63
Life of Calvin 59, 63, 68, 88, 139
Bible, *see* Scripture
Bilney, Thomas 215 n. 102
biography ix, x, 7, 11, 12, 13, 14, 16,
22, 25, 28, 29, 30, 32, 36, 40,
49, 52, 56, 66, 81, 85, 92, 97,
99, 100, 108, 111, 112, 120,
129, 144, 149, 152–3, 156,
160, 167, 172, 173, 176, 180,
193, 196, 202, 203, 204, 210,
214, 219, 227, 229, 232, 243,
244, 246, 247, 252, 253, 255,
263, 269, 270, 273, 283, 284,
285, 288, 295, 300–4, 311–15
ecclesiastical 38, 148
parallel with portraiture 54–5
Black, Glenn 313
Blackstone, B. 212 n. 96
Bliss, Philip 283 n. 117, 297 n. 145
Bolgar, R. R. 32 n.
Book of Common Prayer 139, 220,
221
Boswell, James xii–xiii, 287, 302–5
Life of Samuel Johnson xii, xiii n. 2
Bourne, Gilbert Bishop of Bath and
Wells 45–6
Boyce, B. 82 n. 18

Bradford, John 33, 45–6, 58
Breton, Nicholas
The Good and the Badde 58, 71,
104
Brettergh, Katharine 129
Browne, Humphrey 71, 83–4
Browne, Moses 302
Browne, Thomas 313 n. 37
Bruce, John 251 n.
Bucer, Martin 16, 17–21, 22, 26
in Cambridge 20
Scripta Anglicana 18
Buckeridge, John 23, 69, 93, 108,
120
Bunyan, John 88
Burkitt, William Bishop of Durham
71, 92 n. 44
Burnet, Gilbert 71, 143–4
Butt, John 312, 313
Byam, Henry 28, 70, 110

Calamy, Edmund 76, 239
Callicratides 54
Calvin, John 59, 63, 68, 88, 129,
139
Calvinism 129, 210, 240, 274, 276,
279, 281, 295, 299
Camerarius 314
Campion, Edmund 46
Capel, Richard 33, 49–50
Carey, John 193 n. 63, 313 n. 37
caricature 118
caritas, *see* charity
Carter, John 22 n. 37, 30
Cartwright, Thomas 22, 274 n. 90
debate with Whitgift 21, 258–9
Casaubon, Isaac 83 n. 22
casuistry 281, 288, 290
Characters 32, 58, 71, 79, 82–5, 99,
102–5, 110, 118, 121, 123–4,
174, 190, 196, 197 n. 71, 207,
211, 254, 264, 284, 290, 294
charity 90 n. 40, 93, 107, 109, 112,
123, 145, 155–6, 186, 194,
220, 263, 268, 277, 288–90,
292–4, 295, 301
Charke, John 287
Charles I 265, 280

Charles II 28 n. 48, 229 n., 232, 239, 284
Charles V 123, 124
Charron, Pierre 48–9
  Of Wisedome 39, 46–7
Chartism 306
Cherbury, Edward Herbert Lord 225–6
  Autobiography 213, 226
  Life and Raigne of King Henry the Eighth 47–8
Chetwinde, John 69, 92 n. 44
Chrysostom, John 11, 161
Church, R. W. 309 n. 24
Church of England 230, 232, 235, 239, 282, 301, 306, 312
Cicero 4 n. 4, 5
  Pro M. Marcello 5
  exile to Brundisium 38
Cimon 54, 62
Civil War 5 n. 5, 113–14, 126, 202, 204, 207, 227, 241, 273, 306
Clarendon, Edward Hyde Earl
  History of the Rebellion 81, 231
Clark, Andrew 249 n. 32
Clarke, Jo. 94–5
Clarke, Samuel 32–3, 40, 269
  Antidote against Immoderate Mourning 70, 109, 145
  General Martyrologie 71
  Life and Death of Master Ignatius Jurdaine 33
  Life and Death of Master Richard Capel 33, 49–50
  Life of Doctor Collet 64–5
  Life of Gregory Nazianzen 104–6
  Life of Master Richard Greenham 65 n. 67
  Life of Samuel Crook 86–7, 94, 291
  Lives 22 n. 37, 25, 49, 57, 64, 95, 97
  Marrow of Ecclesiastical History 33, 65, 70, 76, 86, 87 n. 32, 94–5, 104–6
Clarke, W. K. Lowther 139 n. 118
Clebsch, W. A. 88 n. 34
Clifton, Gervase 24

Clifton, Lady Frances 24
Clogie, Alexander 70, 88 n. 33, 143
clothing, *see* deportment
Coelius, Michael 134–8, 140
Colet, John 61–5
Collinson, Patrick 18 n. 29, 22 n. 35 and 37, 24, 33 n. 2, 75, 97 n. 53, 119 n. 85, 149 n. 136, 220, 227 n., 236 n. 9, 251 n., 274 n. 90
commemoration 3–4, 7, 21, **23**, 28, 41, 81–2, 99, 108, 190, 194, 202, 288
commonplaces x, 41, 81, 86, 101, 124, 129, 196–7, 224, 265, 286
  dead yet speaking 94
  deathbed decorum 71, 183 n. 33
  fittest death in the pulpit 149
  inadequacy 18
  life as sermon or living sermon 67, 74, 87, 97
  living 19
  needing examples not precepts 76
  subject as book, text, or engraving 67, 71, 79, 81, 87–9, 92–3
  subject as scriptural precept 71, 81–2
  textual immortality 95, 97, 98
  world as book 84–5
Commonwealth, *see* Interregnum
Compline liturgy 140
confessional tradition 130
conformists x, xv, 108, 129–30, 221, 230, 236, 237, 240, 265, 268, 274, 276, 284, 294, 295, 306, 309
consolation 8, 139
constancy 154
conversation 174, 278
conversion 49–50, 52, 115
Corah 17
Cornelia 44
Cosin, John 70, 92 n. 44, 283 n. 118
Costa, Francisque 308
Cotton, Charles 100, 175–6, 179
Cotton, John 275, 278–9
Cranmer, George 246, 248–50

Cranmer, Thomas 68, 76–8,
        157 n. 146, 220
    Bishops' Bible 77
    Book of Common Prayer 139, 220
Cranmer, William 246
Crashaw, Elizabeth 24 n. 38
Crassus 42, 50
Crisp, Rebecca 24 n. 38
Cromwell, Thomas 77
Crook, Samuel 40, 69, 71, 86–7,
        92 n. 44, 94, 121–3, 124, 291
Cruserius 32 n.
Cummings, Revd Patrick 305
Cuthbert 78
Cyprian 127

Danvers, Lady 98, 195 n. 67
Darbishire, Helen 301 n. 5
Dathan 17
David 33, 77, 192
Day, Martin 24 n. 40
    Θρενοίκος. The House of Mourning
        24, 28, 64, 69, 106–7
death 25–6, 71, 91–4, 98, 102,
        129–52, 176, 179, 181–4, 187,
        190–202, 216, 261, 262, 268,
        269, 284, 287, 295, 297, 305,
        307
    dead as exemplary 26 n. 43
    deportment 73–4, 79–82, 102, 107,
        116, 122, 131, 139, 159,
        270–1, 286, 294
    carriage 102, 120, 286, 294
    clothing 73, 102, 124–8, 153, 155,
        174, 286, 294
    in death 102, 129–141, 150,
        196–7, 216
    face and facial expression 102–5,
        115
    gesture 102, 115–19
    sumptuary laws 106
Dering, Sir Edward 101
Descrypcyon of the Images of a Verye
    Chrysten Bysshop and of a
    Counterfayte Bysshop 71, 72
Devereux, E. J. 61 n. 58
didacticism 37, 61, 68, 83, 148, 207,
        217, 220, 226

Diet of Worms 16
Disley, E. 138 n. 116
dissimulation 125–6
Dix, Gregory 220 n. 114
Donne, Anne 179, 189
Donne, John xi, 3–4, 41, 50–1, 70,
        97–8, 101, 111–15, 148, 161,
        168–203, 215, 225, 290, 300,
        301–2, 310–13
    youth 48, 114, 184, 190, 193, 200
    engraved portrait and motto 200–1
    marriage 51–2, 187
    in Mitcham 187–8
    conversion and ordination 50, 115,
        177–9, 184–6, 201
    religious life and piety 49, 177,
        190, 206
    first sermon at Paddington 177
    friendships 190, 193–4, 197, 202,
        213
        friendship with Lady Magdalen
            Herbert 64, 161, 155
        friendship with George Herbert
            64, 190–1, 198, 204, 206–7
        friendship with Walton 100,
            167–9, 256–7, 271
        friendship with Wotton 169,
            206–7
    death of his wife 179, 189
    death 114–15, 139, 146, 148, 181,
        183, 190–6, 204, 216, 295, 297
    funeral and burial 98, 183, 190–1
    funerary monument 98–9, 176,
        199–200, 202
    writings 176, 193
        Anniversaries 3–4, 7
        Holy Sonnet XIX 50–1
        Letters to Severall Persons of
            Honour 3 n. 2, 187–8, 196–7
        Biathanatos 193
        Pseudo-Martyr 184–7
        LXXX Sermons 3 n. 1, 69, 168,
            169 n., 176, 188, 205, 228
        Sermon of Commemoration of
            the Lady Danvers 98,
            183–4
        Sermon for Easter Day 1626
            182–3

Deaths Duell 98, 146, 180–3, 197

Devotions on Emergent Occasions 192

Poems 177–9, 188–92, 265

'To Mr. Tilman after he had taken orders' 177–9

'A Valediction forbidding mourning' 179, 188

'Hymn to God the Father' 190, 213

'Hymn to God, my God, in my sicknesse' 191–2, 216, 272 n. 85

'Holy Sonnets' 190

'The Holy Ghost' 101 n. 61

Donne, John, the younger 41 n. 26, 169 n.

Donno, E. S. 37 n. 17

Douay 130

Dowling, William 310–11

Dowsing, William 33 n. 3

Drury, Elizabeth 3–4

Dryden, John 34, 36 n. 16, 37 n. 19

Duport, James 33

Earle, John:
Character of a Grave Divine 196
Microcosmographie 71, 101, 197 n. 71

edification 4, 8, 14, 142

Edward VI 36 n. 15, 77

effigy 58, 79

elegy 3, 100, 175

Eliot, T. S. 9

Elizabeth I 218, 236 n. 9, 254–5, 268

Ellyot, George 46

Elyot, Sir Thomas 35 n. 14

emblems 84, 98, 114

encomium 4, 16, 25–30

Epaminondas 32 n.

epideictic 21, 28–9, 37

epigram 3

Epiphanius 19

episcopacy 72, 79, 82, 155 n. 143, 229, 231, 235, 236, 239–40, 245, 253, 275–6, 201

epitaph 29, 98, 99, 101, 161

Erasmus 5–10, 12, 14, 17, 35, 36–7, 61–2, 64, 90, 119 n. 85

accounts of Bucer 20

Adagia 43

De Civilitate Morum Puerilium 105, 124

Ecclesiastae 61

Institutio Principis Christiani 7

Oratio Funebris 7–10, 14

Panegyricus ad Philippum Austriae Ducem 5–7, 37

Paraclesis 89, 106, 133

Preparation to Deathe 132–4, 146

Erastianism 253, 306

eulogy 10, 66

Eusebius, Jeremy 130, 179, 242

Eustochium 8

Evangelism 306

Exclusion Crisis 227, 273

exemplarity ix, x, xii, xvi, 3, 7, 10, 11, 20, 22, 25, 26, 27, 28, 30, 34, 36–8, 48, 50, 52, 55, 56, 61, 64, 65, 66–7, 69, 71, 76, 80, 82–3, 86, 87, 90–1, 94, 97, 100, 102, 108, 111, 130, 137–8, 140, 149, 153–4, 158, 162–3, 172, 176, 204, 209, 211, 212, 217, 221, 229, 257, 263, 273, 274, 284, 285, 287, 288, 289, 291, 292, 295, 298, 301, 314

exemplary death 26 n., 129–42, 196–7, 199

exemplary parallels 11 n. 16

exemplary portraiture 109, 179

priests as exemplars 148

exhortation xi, 7, 13, 16, 17, 18–19, 21, 22, 28, 29, 30, 39, 41, 75, 77, 86, 89, 94, 143, 193, 200, 212, 305

extreme unction 136, 140

Falkland, Lucius Cary Viscount 298–9

Featley, Daniel xvii, 120–1
Life of John Jewel 69, 139, 149–52, 157 n. 146, 159 n. 150, 167, 194–9

Featley, Daniel (*cont.*):
  Θρενοίκος. *The House of Mourning*
    24, 28, 64, 69, 106–7
Fell, John Bishop of Oxford 270,
    285–6, 291–2, 298
Felton, Nicholas Bishop of Ely 161
Ferrar community 123–4, 212, 218
  Nicholas Ferrar 123–4, 204–5,
    208, 212, 217–18, 224
  John Ferrar 125
  Mary Collett (the 'Chief') 123
  Ann Collett (the 'Patient') 123
  Susanna Collett Mapletoft (the
    'Goodwife') 123
  Hester Collett Kestian (the
    'Cheerfull') 123
  Margaret Collett Ramsay (the
    'Affectionate') 123
  Joyce Collett Wallis (the
    'Submisse') 123–6
  Judith Collett Mapletoft (the
    'Obedient') 123
Fincham, Kenneth 72 n. 1, 149,
    153 n. 141, 196 n. 68
Fitz-Geffry, Charles 92–3
flattery 5, 35 n. 11, 222–3
Fletcher, Phineas 265 n. 66
Florio, John 37 n. 19
fortitude 8, 17
Foxall, Nigel 99 n. 57
Foxe, John 32–3, 58, 68, 69, 112,
    119 n. 85, 120, 130
  Acts and Monuments 32, 45, 56–7,
    69, 76, 134, 215 n. 102, 256
  death 142
  Life, State and Story of Cranmer
    68, 76–8, 157 n. 146
Foxe, Simeon 69, 99, 112, 120,
    141–2, 198
Francis 61
Franciscans 61
Freeborn, Caron xiii n. 2
French Revolution 306
friendship 63–4, 161, 167–9, 175,
    190–1, 193, 204–7, 217–18,
    245–7, 252–3, 286, 288,
    297–8, 310–11
Fudge, Thomas 59 n. 54

Fuller, Thomas 70, 241, 242, 259 n.,
    264 n. 62, 300–1, 302
  Abel Redevivus 57 n. 45, 59, 68,
    69, 95, 96, 97, 100, 134, 140,
    141, 150
  'Character of the Faithfull
    Minister' 211–12
  Holy State 71, 76, 124, 211, 265,
    266
Fuller, William 24
funerals 22, 24, 25 n., 27, 28, 30, 41,
    92, 98–100, 110, 139, 160

Galloway, Patrick 218 n. 109
Gardiner 78
Gardner, Helen 179 n. 23, 199 n. 74,
    203 n., 313
Gauden, John Bishop of Exeter 240,
    286
  Eikon Basilike 241, 265
  Life of Richard Hooker 242–4, 247,
    252–3, 264, 269, 285–7, 294,
    309
  Preface to *Ecclesiastical Politie* 229,
    232–5, 239, 241, 242–3
Gerrard, George 3
gesture, *see* deportment
Glorious Revolution xv
Gospels, *see* Scripture
Gosse, Edmund 188, 311–12
Goulard, Simon 15 n. 22
Gracchi 44
Granqvist, Raoul 306, 309–10
Grant, E. 36 n. 14
gratiarum actio 5
Great Fire of London 175
Great Tew Circle 298–9
Green, Ian 239 n. 18, 240 n. 20
Greenham, Richard 64
Greenwey, Richard 54 n. 42
Greville, Fulke 300
grief, *see* mourning
Grosart, Alexander 58 n. 50,
    278 n. 102, 311
Gurnall, William 71, 92 n. 44

Haight, Gordon S. 265
Hailes, Lord 302–3

Hales, John 35, 247
Hall, C. P. 200 n. 75
Hall, Joseph Bishop of Norwich **23**,
    29, 59–60, 85, 95–7, 101 n. 61,
    110, 120, 160
  Characters of Vertues and Vices 70,
    71, 83, 102–3, 128
Haller, William 33 n. 3
Hamilton, Ian xiii n. 3
Hammond, Henry 270, 274 n. 89,
    279–81, 284–6, 291–2, 298
Hampton, Timothy 7 n. 11
Hampton Court Conference 218
Hanbury, Benjamin 309
Harris, Charles 139 n. 118
Harris, John 69, 71, 152–63, 284
Harrison, W. 129 n.
Harsnett, Samuel 159
Hawkins, Sir John 301–3, 308
Hawkins, William 297
Hayne, Thomas 69, 134, 140–1
Hayward, J. C. 146 n. 132, 179 n. 23,
    298–9
Heal, Felicity 90 n. 40, 155 n. 143,
    157 n. 145, 220 n. 113,
    254 n. 40
Healey, John 83 n. 22
Hembry, P. 162 n.
Henley, W. E. 36 n. 16
Henry VIII 36 n. 15, 78, 256
Herbert, George 40, 70, 76, 97, 125,
    161, 300, 310, 311–12
  at Bemerton 211, 217, 219–22
  death 216, 222, 225, 297
  dispute with Andrew Melville
    218–19, 311, 314
  education 208
  family and nobility 208–9, 217,
    222–3
  friendship with John Donne 64,
    190–1, 198, 206–7
  friendships 217
  love of music 214–16, 297
  marriage 51–2, 125–6, 255
  ordination 125, 204, 209, 223–5
  piety 204, 208, 213, 215–8,
    226
  rebuilds churches 211

  writing 211, 216, 284
  Country Parson 85 n. 25, 207–9,
    212, 219, 220
  poetry 221, 225, 226
  Remains 207–8, 214 n. 100
  'Affliction (I)' 221
  'Affliction (IV)' 221
  'Content' 222, 224–5
  'Jordan (I)' 210
  Priest to the Temple 98
  'Sunday' 222
  'The Forerunners' 210
  'The Odour' 222, 224–5
  'The Pearl' 222–4
  'The Posie' 198 n., 204
  'The Quip' 222
  The Temple 198, 204–5, 217
  'The Thanksgiving' 216, 222
Herbert, Jane Danvers 51, 125–6,
    255
Herbert, Lady Magdalen 64, 161,
    155
Hercules 62
Herman, Archbishop of Cologne
    139
Hervey, Christopher 205
Heyen, Berta 7–10, 14
Heylyn, Peter 69, 101, 131–2, 295,
    296
Hezekiah 192, 272 n. 85
Hickman, John 281
Hill, Abraham xxii
  *An Account of the Life of Dr Isaac
    Barrow* xxii
Hill, W. Speed 236 n. 10, 237 n. 11,
    260 n. 50
Hinde, John 131
Holland, Henry 15 n. 22, 58 n. 49
Holland, Philemon 35 n. 11
Holmes, Clive 277 n. 99, 279,
    288 n. 132, 293 n. 140
Holt, Sir Robert 110 n. 76, 205 n. 85
Hooker, Joan Churchman 244,
    248–50
Hooker, Richard 64, 70, 161, 202,
    203, 205, 227–75, 285, 287,
    294, 312
  death 249, 251, 287

Hooker, Richard (*cont.*):
deportment and appearance
270–1, 286, 294
desire for retirement 253–4, 264,
269–70
dispute with Travers 241–2,
259–64
friendship with Cranmers 246–7,
252
friendship with Hadrian Saravia
252–3, 298
irenic disposition 259, 264, 268
lack of advancement 253, 269–70
marriage 171, 242, 244, 248–50,
255
*Of Justification, Works, and How
the Foundation of Faith is
Overthrown* 262–3
Of the Lawes of Ecclesiastical Politie
70, 81, 177, 215, 228–35, **234**,
243, 248 n. 31, 249–51, 253,
258, 271, 274 n. 89, 275, 283,
287, 308–9
Books I-IV 235–6, 238
Book V 235
Book VI 229, 236, 238, 240,
247
Book VII 229, 236, 238–9,
240–1, 247, 250, 255
Book VIII 229, 236–7, 239,
240, 247, 250
preaching and sermons 235, 245,
260–4, 268
theological politics 252, 274
Works 228, **233**, 235 n. 7
Hooper, John 33 n. 2
Horace 248, 291
Horne, Dr xii, 302–4
hospitality 154–7, 305
Hubberdyne, William 119 n. 85
Hughes, Sean 263 n. 61
Huldrick, Hans 135, 138
humility 9, 30, 126, 154, 174–5, 269,
270–1, 288–91
Humphry, Laurence 139, 149,
150 n. 137
Hunt, Dr Arnold 24 n. 38
Huss, John 58–9

Hutchinson, F. E. 198 n., 210 n., 212
n. 95, 213 n., 216 n., 217 n.,
219 n., 221 n. 115, 222 n.
Hyperius, Andreas (Gerardus)
11–16, 17, 21, 27, 37
De Formandis Concionibus Sacris
11–12
funeral 14, 75
The Practise of Preaching 12, 74,
115–19

imitation xiii, 7, 14, 20, 29, 41, 64,
74, 83, 86, 88, 89–90, 94, 97,
99–100, 109, 117–19, 122,
128, 205, 207, 217, 223, 257,
269, 295, 297
Interregnum 207–8, 240, 242,
289–90
intimacy, author-subject xii–xiii
Irish Rebellion 142
Isaacson, Henry 69, 177 n. 20
Isaiah 17, 107
Isocrates 36 n. 14

Jackson, Henry 260
Jackson, Thomas 70, 80, 81 n., 112,
160, 208
Jacob 60, 85, 146, 198
Jacobson, W. 278 n. 100
James VI and I 57, 91, 153, 181, 186,
217, 218 n. 109, 232
Jerome 6 n. 88, 19, 22, 126, 132, 145,
161
Jerome of Prague 56, 58
Jesuits 101, 184
Jesus Christ 69, 70, 74, 89–91, 97,
121, 128, 133, 140–1, 146,
160, 178, 208, 225, 258,
265 n. 64, 271–2, 278, 299
Jewel, John Bishop of Sarisbury
(Salisbury) 69, 88 n. 36, 139,
157 n. 146, 167, 194, 215, 270
death 149–52, 195–8
Works 149
Job 11, 85, 272, 292–4
John the Baptist 17, 228, 271
Johnson, Dr Samuel xii, 302–3,
315

Jonas, Jodocus 61–2, 64 n. 63 & 66, 68, 119 n. 85, 134–8, 140, 202
Josephus 171
Josselin, John 199 n. 74
Julian the Apostate 104–5
Juvenal 291
Juxon, Elizabeth 24 n. 38

Keble, John 308–9
Ken, Thomas 297
Kendall, R. T. 276 n. 96, 278 n. 103
Keynes, Geoffrey 265 n. 66, 298
King, Henry Bishop of Chichester 159 n. 149, 173, 202
King, John Bishop of London 159
Kingsley, Charles 310
Kingsley, Frances Eliza 310 n. 27
Kirby, W. J. Torrance 238 n. 13

Lake, Arthur Bishop of Bath and Wells 69, 71–2, 152–63, 284
death 158–62
diocesan administration 158
education and preferments 153
founding of libraries 156
Protestant faith 159–60
Sermons 162–3
Vice-chancellor 156
virtues 154–7
Lake, Peter 25 n., 237–8, 260, 262 n. 58, 271–2, 274 n. 91, 277 n. 98, 278 n. 101, 280 n. 110, 284 n. 121
lamentation, *see* mourning
Lanfrancus, Archbishop of Canterbury 145
Languet, Hubert 37 n. 17
Latimer, Hugh 119 n. 85
Laud, William Archbishop of Canterbury 69, 101, 131–2, 143, 155 n. 142, 273, 274 n. 91, 278, 288, 306
Laudians 239, 270, 274, 283 n. 118
laudatio funebris 4
Leigh, Edward 69, 80, 87, 95
Lein, Clayton 210–11
Lennard, Samson 39

Lewalski, Barbara 4 n. 3, 11 n. 17, 22 n. 36, 27 n. 45, 205 n.
Leygh, W. 129 n.
Lilburne, John 40
Lipsius, Justus 45
  Two Bookes of Constancie 44
Little Gidding 123, 212, 218
  Conversations recorded at xvii, 123
Lives ix, xii, 18, 30, 32, 37, 43–4, 47–8, 52, 53, 55–6, 62–5, 68, 76, 81–2, 86, 90, 97, 100, 101, 112, 120, 129–30, 136, 150, 153, 172, 244, 291, 292, 295, 300
descriptive 115
ecclesiastical Lives 38, 67–8, 157
physical description in 105–6
Luckett, Dr Richard 124 n.
Ludham, John:
  translation of *The Practise of Preaching* 12 n. 19, 14, 115–16
Lupset, Thomas:
  The Waye of Dyenge Well 132–3
Lupton, Donald 15 n. 22
Luther, Martin xi, 13 n. 21, 16, 19, 21, 62, 68, 69, 72
  Commentarie upon the Epistle to the Galatians 88
death 129, 134–41, 202
libel of his death 141
Lutheranism 134 n. 113
Lysander 54

MacCarthy, D. 37 n. 19
McCauley, R. P. 21 n. 34
McConica, J. K. 36 n. 15
MacCulloch, Diarmaid 76 n. 8, 78, 90 n. 40, 284 n. 120
McCullough, Dr Peter 218 n. 109
McGee, J. Sears 90 n. 40
McGrade, A. S. 236 n. 9, 251 n., 274 n. 90
Machiavelli, Niccolo 301
MacLure, Millar 203 n.
Maister, Wylliam 36 n. 15
Manningham, John 250–1 n.
Marcellus 5
Marian persecutions 33

Marriot, Richard 168
Marshall, William 200, 265
Marten, Anthony 18 n. 30
Martin, Revd Prof. David 255 n. 41
Martyr, Peter 16, 215
    on Martin Bucer 18
martyrs and martyrologies 27,
    33 n. 2, 45–6, 58, 76, 129–33,
    141, 151, 290 n.
Marvell, Andrew 132
Mary I 77
Mather, Cotton 278 n. 104
Maule, Jeremy 150 n. 136
Maycock, A. L. 212 n. 93
Mayer, Thomas R. 134 n. 113
Mayor, J. E. B. 143 n. 123
Melanchthon, Philipp 16, 58, 68, 314
    on Luther 13 n. 21, 16–17, 19, 62,
    134, 138
Melville, Andrew 218–19, 311, 314
memento mori 26, 98, 199, 200
memory 172, 272, 285, 291, 311
Menander 43
Merchant Taylors School 108
Millenary petition 219
Milton, John 120, 300
moderation 5 n. 5
modesty 126, 153, 171, 173, 269,
    286
modesty topos 97, 209, 256
monarchists 231–2, 235, 237–8, 253,
    280, 287
Montaigne, Michel de 37 n. 19,
    48–9, 50, 52
Montford, Dr 202
Montgomery Castle 211
monuments 41, 67, 98–101, 108,
    161–3, 175–6, 176, 199–200,
    306
Morgan, John 15 n. 24
Morley, George Bishop of
    Winchester 228, 230, 240,
    242–3, 273, 285, 288, 298
Morton, Thomas Bishop of Durham
    70, 78–9, 81–2, 85, 92, 102 n.,
    113–14, 120, 126–7, 149,
    157 n. 146, 160, 167 n., 231,
    247, 268, 268, 295

Mossom, Robert 29, 70, 99–100,
    196 n. 68
Moulson, John 25, 120
mourning 15, 20, 21, 26, 70, 176,
    179, 180, 289 n. 134
Moxley, J. R. 112 n. 78
Mulcaster, Peter 108 n. 72
Mulcaster, Richard 108
Musculus, Wolfgang 16
music 190, 192, 210, 213–16, 297

narrative ix, x, xiii, xvi, 7, 10, 11, 14,
    18, 21, 27, 29–30, 40, 47, 48,
    49, 50, 52, 57, 60, 66–7, 76,
    81–2, 90, 94, 97, 98, 102, 108,
    110, 111, 113, 115, 129, 139,
    145, 153, 158, 170, 172, 173,
    183, 185, 187, 189, 194, 196 n.
    68, 204, 209, 213, 217, 218,
    219, 228, 230, 231, 241, 244,
    252, 257, 264, 268, 269, 283,
    284, 285, 292, 295, 299, 302,
    314–15
    of death 129–30, 143–4, 148, 149,
    151, 216
narrative authority 243
Naylor, Joseph 70, 79, 81, 102 n.,
    114, 127–8, 149, 157 n. 146,
    231–2, 268
Nazianzen, Gregory 11, 14, 21, 22,
    104–6, 160 n.
    on his sister Gorgonia 21
    Oration for St Athanasius 79
Neale, J. E. 236 n. 9
Nicias 42, 50
Nicolson, Harold 312
nonconformists 33, 129–30, 207,
    218, 221, 241, 264, 268, 269,
    273, 274, 285
North, J. A. 4 n. 4
North, Sir Thomas 32, 36, 38, 42,
    53, 55
Novarr, David ix, 38 n. 22, 168 n.,
    170, 171, 173, 176, 179 n. 24,
    180, 184, 185, 186, 188, 189,
    193–4, 196 n. 68, 199, 200–1,
    212 n. 93, 214, 219 n. 110,
    220 n. 112, 222 n., 235,

238 n. 15, 240 n. 20, 242 n. 25,
243, 246, 251–2, 254, 255,
264, 269, 270 n. 76, 273, 281,
282, 284 n. 119, 285 n. 123,
303 n. 10, 304 n. 15, 313–14
novel x, xiii, 314
Nunc Dimittis 136, 201
Nyxon, Anthony 22 n. 36

occupatio 27
Oecolampadius, Johann 59, 63, 68
Oley, Revd Barnabas 207–9, 211,
214, 217
Olimpias 161
Olin, John C. 61 n. 58, 89 n. 38
Oliver, Samuel 69, 92 n. 44
oratory 37, 122
    Christian 11, 162
    civic 22
    demonstrative 10, 17
    forensic 12
    funeral x, 4, 10, 12, 13 n., 14, 16,
    75, 99
    laudatory 11–13
Orthius, Wigandus 13 n., 14–16, 75
Overbury, Sir Thomas 71, 83–5, 118

Paget, F. 309 n. 24
painting, *see* portraiture
panegyric 3, 5–7, 13, 29, 35, 302
paraenesis 7, 35, 38, 241
parallel 60–2, 79, 140
paraphrases 67, 78, 81
Parker, Matthew xvii, 22, 58–9,
199 n. 75
    on Martin Bucer 17–21
Parbo, Edmund 250 n.
Parry, Henry 250 n.
particularity xiii
passion 42, 50–1, 155, 268, 269
pattern, *see* exemplarity
Paul 5, 9, 15, 17, 18, 46, 67, 72–6,
79, 80, 85, 99, 101, 102, 132,
156–7
Paula 8, 161
Paule, Sir George 68, 153 n. 140,
159 n. 150, 160, 256–9, 264
Pearson, David 156 n., 159

Peckard, Peter 124
Pelagianism 280–1
Pelikan, Jaroslav 88 n. 34
Pericles 55
Perkins, William 82 n. 17
Persius 291
Peter 74, 120, 132
Peters, Hugh 40
Philip of Macedon 32 n.
Philip, Archduke 5, 37
Philips, Fabian 250–1
Phillips, Edward 300
Philopoemon 61
Pierce, Dr Thomas 279–82
Plato 5
Pliny 35, 310
Plutarch ix, x, 32–8, 40–4, 49, 50,
52–6, 60, 62, 63, 64, 66,
154–5, 252, 253, 301
    Lives x, 35, 37, 38, 61 n. 56, 156
    Life of Alexander 52, 53, 156
    Life of Cimon 54
    Life of Lysander 54
    Life of Pericles 55
    Life of Pompey 41, 52–3, 60
    Life of Sulla 42–3, 47, 50, 53–4, 56
    Moralia 35–6, 38, 162
    use of physical characteristics 103
Pocock, Nicholas 270 n. 79,
286 n. 124
Pollard, A. F. 46 n. 34
Pompey 5, 41, 52–3, 60
portraiture 52–60, 63, 67, 79, 83–4,
95, 106–14, 139, 162, 170,
173, 176, 188, 199–201, 231,
265, 269, 287, 290, 294, 311,
313
Potter, George R. 183 n. 32
preaching 11, 37, 67, 74–5, 80–1, 86,
87, 92–3, 97, 116–19, 177–8,
192, 195–6, 198, 212, 232,
235, 274, 277, 299
Presbyterians 230, 236, 239–41, 259,
311
    Scottish Presbyterians 218
Pricke, Robert 119 n. 86
Prior, Thomas 69, 145–6, 151 n.,
159 n. 149

Protestantism 18 n. 29, 119 n. 85,
 138 n. 115, 205 n. 84, 264, 285
Prudentius 192
Prynne, William 155 n. 142
Puritans xv, xvi, 25, 40, 90 n. 40,
 108, 129, 220, 238, 251 n.,
 275, 277 n. 99, 278–9

Quarles, Francis:
 The Shepheards Oracles 265, **267**
Quintilian 12, 115

Rainbow, Edward 71, 85–6, 100,
 110, 159 n. 150, 160
Rainbow, Thomas 160
Ratcliffe, Jane 25 n.
Raven, Roger 250–1 n.
Rawlinson, John 121 n. 93
reason 42, 45, 51, 118–19, 155, 261,
 263, 270
Reason and Judgment 231, 270–1,
 284–5, 286–8
recreation xiii
Reformation x, xv, 72, 90 n. 40, 132,
 136–7, 155 n. 143, 215, 220,
 227, 260, 262, 276
res publica 9
Restoration xi, 35 n. 11, 68, 228–9,
 232, 240, 252, 270, 274, 279,
 282, 284 n. 134, 287
resurrection 182–3, 193
Reynolds, Edward 239
rhetoric 10, 60, 82, 115–16, 122,
 134 n. 113, 162, 178, 210, 235,
 243, 253, 255, 264, 265, 269,
 314–15
Ribeiro, Alvaro 199 n. 74
Richardson, W. B. 236 n. 9,
 254 n. 40
Richmond, George 311
Ricks, Christopher 313 n. 37
Ridley, Nicholas 33 n. 2
Roman Catholicism 130, 136, 159,
 184–6, 236, 262, 264, 269,
 273, 282, 285, 309
Rous, Lady Philippa 24 n. 38, 92–3
Russell, D. A. 32 n., 35 n. 11,
 44 n. 32

Saintsbury, George 175 n. 16, 188
salvation 136–7, 202, 260, 262, 282,
 299
Sanderson, Robert xi, 30, 40, 71, 72,
 152, 158, 203, 227, 228, 231,
 232, 240, 251, 270, 272–99
 charity 292–4
 death 284
 deportment 286, 294
 during the Interregnum 289–90
 humility 288–91
 *An Impartial Inquiry into the
  Nature of Sin* 281
 Pax Ecclesiae 275, 281 n. 114, 282
 preaching 274, 277, 279, 283, 288,
  292–3, 299
 religious beliefs 274, 276–82
 theological politics 275–6
Sandys, Edwin 235–6, 237 n. 11,
 248–50
Sandys, Miles 236 n. 9
Saravia, Hadrian 252–3, 298
Savile, Henry 54 n. 42
Scipio Africanus 36 n. 15
Scripture 61 n. 56, 74, 76, 77 n.,
 79, 81–2, 86, 88, 89, 90–2,
 130 n. 105, 134, 135–8, 149,
 151, 237, 272 n. 85
 Genesis 1 102
 Genesis 32.10 85 n. 26, 198
 Genesis 32.11 60
 Genesis 47.29 29, 59
 Numbers 6.23–6 158
 Numbers 16.1–32 17 n. 28
 Deuteronomy 32.48–52 17 n. 28
 Joshua 88
 2 Kings 4.32–5 94 n. 49
 Job 179, 272
 Job 29.14–17 292, 294
 Job 31 293
 Psalms 180, 204, 289, 290
 Psalm 31 140
 Psalm 51 33
 Psalm 68 140, 182
 Psalm 71 151
 Psalm 99 288
 Proverbs 20.17 268 n. 67, 293
 Proverbs 25.21–2 258 n. 48

Ecclesiastes 7.1 160
Ecclesiastes 12 151
Song of Songs 252, 255
Isaiah 17, 107
Isaiah 38.20 272 n. 85
Isaiah 49.23 254–5
Lamentations 180, 272
Lamentations 3.16 268 n. 67, 293
Ezekiel 181–3, 197
Matthew 5.26 293 n. 141
Matthew 18.26–35 293 n. 141
Matthew 25.36–40 10
Matthew 26.7–12 160
Mark 14.8 160
Luke 18.13 28
Luke 16.1–13 293 n. 141
John 131
John 3.16–17 139
John 8 135–7
Romans 13.14 128
Romans 12.20 258 n. 28
1 Corinthians 3.16 101
1 Corinthians 15.20 182
Galatians 5 195
Ephesians 4.15 311 n. 32
Ephesians 5.22 9
Colossians 2.14 133
1 Timothy 3 15, 18, 72, 74–5,
    78–9, 81, 85, 154, 156–7,
    305
1 Timothy 5 156
Titus 1 72, 74–8, 80–1
Hebrews 6.4 92 n. 44
Hebrews 11.4 91
Hebrews 11.1 260
1 Peter 2.5 265 n. 64
1 Peter 5.3 72
Ecclesiasticus 3.19 30, 290
Scudder, Henry:
    Life of Whateley 69, 100
Seneca 9 n. 14, 45
separatists xv
sermons x, 6, 13, 21, 30, 45, 67, 82,
    87, 92, 95, 97, 107, 120–1,
    131, 150, 153, 162, 176–7,
    180, 195–8, 212, 221, 241,
    245, 260–3, 268, 274, 283,
    284, 288, 291, 292–3

funeral x, 4, 10, 14, 21, 22–6,
    28–31, 59–60, 64, 67, 78, 81,
    85, 91–4, 98, 106, 108, 110,
    120, 144, 146, 147–8, 160,
    180–3, 195, 197–8, 314–15
  laudatory 13
  living 28, 67
Sheldon, Gilbert Archbishop of
    Canterbury 228, 230, 239–47,
    280, 281, 298
Shepherd, Richard Herne 265 n. 66
Shirley, James 306 n. 19
Shuckburgh, E. S. 82 n. 17,
    143 n. 125, 157 n. 146
Sibbes, Richard 27 n. 45, 106,
    278–9, 288
Θρενοίκος. *The House of Mourning*
    24, 28, 64, 69, 106–7
Sidney, Sir Philip 37 n. 17, 218, 300
Simeon 135–6
Simpson, Evelyn M. 183 n. 32
sincerity 209, 210, 213, 225
Sisson, C. J. 250–1 n.
Six Articles 78
Smeed, J. W. 82 n. 18, 121 n. 93
Smith, Henry 70
Smith, Miles Bishop of Gloucester
    69, 122–3, 145–6, 151 n.,
    159 n. 149, 160 n.
Smith, Thomas 62 n. 58
Solomon 77, 268, 272
SPCK 310
Spenser, Dorothy 249–50
Spenser, Dr John 238, 240, 242, 247,
    249, 260
Spufford, Margaret 277 n. 98
Spurr, John 240 n. 19, 289 n. 134
Stanly, Thomas 300
Stanwood, P. G. 238 n. 15, 239 n. 17
Stauffer, Donald xiii n. 4, 312
Stephen, Leslie 311–12
Stevens, John 215 n. 101
Stoicism 8, 9, 38–9, 44–5, 155
Strassburg Mass 139
Stubbes, Philip 24 n. 38, 144
Stubbes, Katharine 24 n. 38, 144
Suetonius 34–5
    Lives of the Caesars 34–5

Sulla 42–3, 47, 50, 53–4, 56
sumptuary laws, *see* deportment
Sydenham, Humphrey 28

table talk xiii
Tacitus 34, 257
  Agricola 54
Taylor, Jeremy:
  *The Great Exemplar of Sanctity
  and Holy Life* 69, 97, 128,
  144–5
Taylor, Thomas 24 n. 40
Θρενοίκος. *The House of Mourning*
  24, 28, 64, 69, 106–7
Teale, Revd William 309
Temperley, Nicholas 215 n. 102
theatre and theatricality 120–2, 124,
  131–3, 154
Theophrastus 83
Thomas 148
Thomas, William 69, 92 n. 44
Thorpe, William 56
Thurlby, Bishop 215 n. 102
Tinctoris, Johannes 215
Tinker, Chauncey Brewster 303 n. 13
Titus Quintus Flaminius 61
Tractarians 306, 310
Trajan 36
Travers, Watler 241–2, 259–64
Tremelius, Immanuel 180 n. 26
Trevor-Roper, Hugh 298
Tridentine 21 n. 33
Tully 291
Tully, Thomas 71, 85–6
Tyacke, N. 274 n. 92
Tyndale, William 77, 92, 260 n. 54
Tyndall, Martin 61 n. 58

Ussher, James Archbishop 69, 93,
  240, 247, 250

Vaghan, E. 70, 80, 81 n., 112,
  159 n. 150, 160
Venning, R. 71
Verheiden, Jacobus 15 n. 22,
  57 n. 45, 58
  *History of the Moderne Protestant
  Divines* 15 n. 22, 58–9

Vernon 295 n. 143
virtue xi, 4, 7, 9, 10, 11, 13, 15, 16,
  17, 18, 25–6, 35, 40, 42, 44,
  46, 49–50, 52, 54, 58–60, 61,
  63, 71, 72–5, 83, 95, 97,
  102–3, 106, 107, 109, 112,
  120, 123–4, 154–5, 172, 174,
  175, 179, 206–8, 210, 213,
  254, 284, 287, 289, 290, 299,
  301–2, 305, 306, 307
  see also charity, hospitality,
  humility, modesty,
  moderation
Vitrier, Jehan 61–4, 119 n. 85
Voraginus, Jacobus de 130

Walker, William 22 n. 36
Wall, John 65, 86
Walton, Izaak ix, xvii, 4, 32–3, 35,
  38, 39–40, 52, 63, 66–8, 98,
  101, 109, 129–30, 169,
  300–2
  affection for Richard Sibbes
    278–9, 288
  autobiography and use of subjects'
    own writings 172, 189–94,
    203, 205–6, 210, 216, 222–5
  and Calvinism 240
  Compleat Angler 170, 204, 301–3,
    310, 313
  death 68
  factual reliability or accuracy ix,
    263, 290, 297, 309, 314–15
  friendship with subjects 167–8,
    206, 245–7, 256, 287–8,
    297–8, 311
    friendship with Donne 100,
      168–70, 205, 256–7, 271
    friendship with Sanderson
      288–90, 294, 295, 297–8
  influence xii, 300–15
  layman xi, 39, 167, 245, 256, 312,
    314–15
  Life of Donne xi, 41, 48–51, 63–4,
    69, 70, 85 n. 25, 97–9, 100,
    110 n. 76, 111–15, 139, 146,
    161, 168–203, 204, 205, 206,
    209, 213, 219, 226, 228, 243,

298, 300, 302, 305, 307, 311–13
Life of Herbert ix, xi, 33, 51, 70, 76, 85 n. 25, 97, 125–6, 161, 168, 203–26, 227, 245, 283, 300, 307, 311–12
Life of Hooker 64, 70, 168, 171, 202, 203, 205, 227–73, 276, 280, 283, 287, 288, 290, 298, 305, 307–9
Life of Sanderson xi, 30, 33, 34 n. 8, 71, 72, 152, 158, 202, 227–8, 240, 272–99, 304–5
Life of Wotton xi, 70, 142 n. 122, 168, 170, 203, 206, 243, 300, 307
literary confidence 171, 173, 174
literary obligations 240, 244
Lives ix, x, xi, xii, 32, 33, 48, 70, 85 n. 25, 152, 161, 171, 173, 175, 206, 272, 291, 295, 300–15
Love and Truth 39, 40 n. 24, 127, 221, 252, 268, 285, 293
old age 272
religious conformity xv, 242
research 247–51
steward to George Morley 240
use of portraiture analogies 111–12
Ward, Hamnet 110–11
Ward, Samuel 22 n. 37, 30, 70
Wardman, Alan 4 n. 3, 35, 38 n. 21, 42, 43 n. 29, 44 n. 32, 54 n. 41
Warwick, Anne Countess 24 n. 38
Watt, F. W. 203 n.
Weigle, Luther A. 77 n. 9
Wellek, René 199 n. 74
Wendorf, Richard 54, 55 n. 43, 114 n. 81, 201 n., 313
Wengert, Timothy 314

Westminster Assembly 284
Whateley, William 69, 80, 87, 95, 100
Whitefoote, John 29
 Deaths Alarum . . . for Joseph Hall **23**, 59–60, 70, 85, 95–7, 110, 120, 159 n. 150, 160
Whitgift, John Archbishop of Canterbury 64, 68, 153 n. 140, 160, 236, 250, 253, 254–5, 260, 264, 274–5
 dispute with Cartwright 21, 258–9
 passivity and suffering 257–8
Wilde, George, Bishop of Derry 29, 70, 99, 196 n. 68
Wilkins, John 284 n. 120
Wilkins, W. W. 143 n. 123
Wilson, John 130
Wilson, Thomas
 Arte of Rhetorique 12, 115
Winniff, Dr 202
Wood, Anthony à 249, 279 n. 108, 283 n. 117, 297 n. 145, 300
Woodnoth, Arthur 204
Woolf, D. R. 134 n. 113
Wordsworth, William 306–8, 310
Worthington, Thomas 130
Wotton, Sir Henry xi, 32, 70, 161, 168–9, 173, 203, 205, 206–7, 217, 300
Wren, Matthew 239
Wright, Robert 120

Xylander 32 n.

Yiannikou, Jason 129 n.
Young, John 36 n. 15

Zouch, Thomas 305–8
Zwingli, Ulrich 63, 68